THE BIOGRAPHICAL DICTIONARY OF SCIENTISTS

Astronomers

THE BIOGRAPHICAL DICTIONARY OF SCIENTISTS

Astronomers

General Editor
David Abbott PhD

BLOND EDUCATIONAL

First published in Great Britain in 1984 by
Frederick Muller Limited, 8 Alexandra Road,
Wimbledon, London SW19 7JZ.

Blond Educational is an imprint of Frederick
Muller Ltd

British Library Cataloguing in Publication Data

Biographical dictionary of scientists.
  1. Astronomers
  1. Scientific—Biography
  I. Abbott, David
  509′.2′2   Q141

  ISBN 0-584-70002-4

Made and printed in Great Britain by
Butler & Tanner Ltd, Frome and London

Contents

Acknowledgements

Many people are involved in the creation of a major new series of reference books. The general editor and the publishers are grateful to all of them and wish to thank particularly the contributing authors: Gareth Ashurst; Jim Bailey; Alan Bishop; William Cooksey; David Cowey; Michael Darton; Judy Garlick; Robert Matthews; Nigel Morrison; Valerie Neal; Lucia Osborne; Helen Rapson; Mary Sanders; Robert Smith; Robert Stewart; Zusa Vrbova and David Ward. Our thanks are also due to Mick Saunders for his artwork and to Bull Publishing Consultants Ltd, whose experience in the development of reference books has made a significant contribution to the series: John Clark; Kate Duffy; Nikki Okell; Martyn Page; Hal Robinson and Sandy Shepherd.

Historical introduction

Astronomy is the oldest of all sciences, its origins dating back at least several thousands of years. The word astronomy comes from the two Greek words *astron*, star, and *nomos*, law, and perhaps the first attempt at understanding the laws that governed the stars and their apparent movement across the night sky was prompted by the need to produce an accurate calendar.

In order to predict the flooding of the river Nile, and hence the time when the surrounding lands would be fertile enough for crops to be planted, the Egyptians made observations of the brightest star in the night sky, Sirius. It was discovered that the date when this star (called Sothis by the Egyptians) could first be seen in the dawn sky (the heliacal rising) enabled the date of the flooding to be calculated. This also enabled the length of the year to be calculated quite accurately; by 2780 BC the Egyptians knew that the time between successive heliacal risings was about 365 days. More accurate observations enabled them to show that the year was about $365\frac{1}{4}$ days long, with a slight difference of 20 minutes between the sidereal year (the time betweeen successive appearances of a star in the same position in the sky) and the tropical year (the time between successive appearances of the Sun on the vernal equinox).

Although evidence suggests that the grouping of stars into constellations was done before a fairly accurate calendar was drawn up, this latter achievement was probably the first scientific act carried out in the field of astronomy.

The prediction of phenomena, which is the fundamental activity of any science, was also being carried out by other ancient civilizations, such as the Chinese. Some historians suggest that the existence in Europe and elsewhere of megalithic sites such as Stonehenge in England and Carnac in France (some of which date back to almost 3000 BC) shows that even minor early civilizations could calculate their calendars and, possibly, predict basic astronomical events such as eclipses.

Certainly by 500 BC the prediction of eclipses had become quite accurate. Thales of Miletus (624–547 BC), a Greek philosopher, ended a war between the Medes and the Lydians by accurately predicting the occurrence of an eclipse of the Sun on 28 May 585 BC. His prediction was probably based on the Saros, a period of about 18 years, after which a particular sequence of solar (and lunar) eclipses recurs. This interval was known to Babylonian and Chaldean astronomers long before Thales' time.

The Greeks and Early Astronomy

The next 800 years of astronomy were dominated by the Greeks. Anaximander (610–546 BC), a pupil of Thales, helped bring the knowledge of the ancient Egyptians and others to Greece and introduced the sundial as a timekeeping device. He also pictured the sky as a sphere with the Earth floating in space at the centre.

Anaxagoras (500–428 BC) made great advances in astronomical thought, with his correct explanation of the cause of lunar and solar eclipses. In addition, he considered the Moon to be illuminated by reflected light and all material in the heavens to be composed of the same material; a rocky meteorite falling on the Aegean coast in 468 BC may have brought him to this conclusion. All these thoughts are now known to be broadly correct.

The Greek philosopher Plato (*c.* 420–340 BC) effectively cancelled out these advances with his insistence on the perfection of the heavens, which according to him implied that all heavenly bodies must follow the perfect curve (the circle) across the sky. This dogma cast its dark shadow over astronomical thought for the next 2,000 years. Both Eudoxus (408–355 BC) and Callippus (370–300 BC) tried to convert observations into proof for this idea: each planet was set into a sphere, so that the Universe took on an onion-ring appearance, with the Earth at the centre. More spheres had to be added to make the theory even approximate to the observations, and by the time of Callippus there were 34 such spheres. Even so, the theory did not match observations.

It was Heraklides of Pontus (388–315 BC) who noted that the apparent motion of the stars during one night might be the result of the daily rotation of the Earth, not the stars, on its axis. He also maintained that Mercury and Venus revolved around the Sun, but he held to the geocentric belief that the Earth was the centre of the Universe.

Aristarchos of Samos (*c.* 320–240 BC) took these ideas one step further. In *c.* 260 BC he put forward the heliocentric theory of the Solar System, which puts the Sun at the centre of the system of the six planets then known, with the stars infinitely distant. This latter conclusion was based on the belief that the stars were motionless, their apparent motion resulting simply from the Earth's daily rotation. Aristarchos still maintained that the planets moved in Platonically perfect circles, however.

By noting that when the Moon was exactly half-illuminated it must lie at the right angle of a triangle formed by lines joining the Earth, Sun and Moon, Aristarchos was able to make estimates of the relative sizes and distances of the Sun and Moon. Unfortunately, although his theory was correct, the instruments he needed were not available, and his results were highly inaccurate. They were good enough, however, to show that the Sun was more distant and much larger than the Moon. Although this provided indirect support for the heliocentric theory, since it seemed logical for the small Earth to orbit the vast Sun, the geocentric dogma prevailed for another 1,800 years.

Greek astronomy had its last success between 240 BC, when Eratosthenes (276–195 BC) made his calculation of the Earth's size, and *c.* AD 180, when Ptolemy died. In between those two events, Hipparchus (*c.* 146–127 BC) replaced the Eudoxian theory of concentric spheres with an even more contrived arrangement based on the ideas of Apollonius. The Sun and planets were all considered to revolve upon a small wheel, or epicycle, the centre of which revolved around the Earth, (the centre of the universe, on a larger circle (the deferent)). Using this theory, Ptolemy (or Claudius Ptolemaeus) was able to predict the position of the planets to within 1°, i.e. about two lunar diameters.

Having begun so well, Greek astronomy ended somewhat dismally, preferring dogma to observable evidence and so failing to come to terms with the heliocentric theory of Aristarchos.

It was not until some 600 years after the death of Ptolemy that astronomy started once again to move forward. The lead was taken by the Arabs. Their great mathematical skill and ingenuity with instruments enabled them to refine the observations and theories of the Greeks and produce better star maps, which were becoming increasingly useful for navigation, one of the spurs to astronomical research for many centuries to come. During the Middle Ages, nevertheless, European astronomers did little more than tinker

with Ptolemy's epicycles. The Roman Catholic church decided that the geocentric theory was the only one compatible with the Scriptures, thus making anyone who attempted to put the Sun at the centre of the Solar System guilty of heresy, which was punishable by death.

It was, however, the publication of one book that made Europe the centre of astronomical development, after the science had effectively stood still for many centuries.

European Astronomical Thought

In 1543 the Polish astronomer Nicolaus Copernicus (1473–1543) published a book entitled *De revolutionibus orbium coelestium*, in which he demonstrated that by placing the Sun at the centre of the Solar System, with the planets orbiting about it, it was possible to account for the apparent motion of the planets in the sky much more neatly than by geocentric theory. To explain the phenomenon of retrogression, for example, cosmologists had been compelled to add complication upon complication to Ptolemy's theory. With the heliocentric theory it could be explained simply as the result of a planet's distances from the Sun.

The "Copernican revolution" was far from a complete break with the past, nevertheless. Copernicus continued to believe that all celestial motion must be circular, so that his model retained the epicycles and deferents of Ptolemy. But whereas Aristarchos' heliocentric belief had been left to moulder for centuries, Copernicus' ideas were picked up by other cosmologists who, by the end of the sixteenth century, had far more accurate observations at their disposal.

The supplier of these more accurate observations was the Danish astronomer, Tycho Brahe (1546–1601), who, using only the naked eye, was able to make observations accurate to two minutes of arc, five times more precise than those of Ptolemy. The effect was enormous. Calendar reform took place, with the Gregorian calendar, now used throughout the Western world, being instituted in 1582. More important for astronomy, Brahe's observations were used by his German assistant, Johannes Kepler (1571–1630), to establish the heliocentric theory of the Solar System once and for all. Out went the complicated systems of epicycles and the dogma of the perfect circle; for Kepler's idea that the planets followed elliptical paths around the Sun, which itself sat at one focus of the ellipses, accorded nicely with the observations of Brahe.

In *Astronomia Nova*, published in 1609, Kepler enunciated the first two laws of planetary motion; the first stated that each planet moved in an elliptical orbit; the second that it did so in such a way that the line joining it to the Sun sweeps out equal areas in equal times. Kepler's third law, that the cube of the distances of a planet from the Sun is proportional to the time required for it to complete one orbit, was announced in 1618.

At the same time as Kepler was making these theoretical breakthroughs, the invention of the telescope by the Dutch optician Hans Lippershey (1587-1619), in 1608 was effecting a revolution in observation. Galileo Galilei (1564-1642) quickly put the instrument to use. In the years 1609 to 1610 he discovered the phases of Venus (showing that planet to be orbiting inside the path of the Earth) and identified four satellites of Jupiter; he also established the stellar nature of the Milky Way. As if to underline the imperfect nature of the heavens, contrary to the Platonic dogma that had crippled astronomy for so long, Galileo also discovered spots on the Sun and mountains on the "perfect" sphere of the Moon.

The next major breakthrough was again a theoretical one, the discovery by Isaac Newton (1642-1727) of the law of universal gravitation in 1665. Gravity is the single most important force in astronomy and Newton's discovery enabled him to deduce all three of Kepler's laws.

By nature a somewhat reticent man, Newton did not publish his discoveries, in the *Philosophiae Naturalis Principia Mathematica*, until 1687, after the prompting of his friend Edmund Halley (1656-1742). Newton showed that his law could account even for small effects such as the precession of the equinoxes discovered by Hipparchus and that the slight deviations of the planets from their Keplerian orbits were the result of their mutual gravitational attraction. By applying this perturbations theory to the Earth-Sun-Moon system, Newton was able to solve problems about the various motions that had baffled Kepler and his predecessors.

Newton also made a significant contribution to observational astronomy in 1668, when he built the first reflecting telescope, with optics that were free of some of the defects of the refractors then in use.

Seven years later, in 1675, Charles II founded the Royal Observatory at Greenwich, essentially to find an accurate way of determining longitude for British ships involved in overseas exploration and colonization. The line of zero longitude was set at Greenwich, and the First Astronomer Royal, John Flamsteed (1646-1719), drew up a new star catalogue with positions accurate to 20 seconds of arc. Published in 1725, it was the first map of the telescopic age.

Careful observer as Flamsteed was, he failed to notice anything strange about the star which he noted in his catalogue as 34 Tauri. Its true nature was discovered by William Herschel (1738-1822), using the best reflector then in existence, in 1781. The "star" was in fact, a previously undiscovered planet, and was named Uranus. Its discovery doubled the dimensions of the known Solar System.

Beginnings of Astrophysics

The opening of the nineteenth century marked the beginning of one of the most important branches of astronomical observation: spectroscopy. In 1802 William Wollaston (1766-1828) discovered that the Sun's spectrum was crossed by a number of dark lines, and in 1815 Joseph Fraunhofer (1787-1826) made a detailed map of these lines. Fraunhofer noticed that the spectra of stars were slightly different from that of the Sun, but the enormous significance of this observation was not grasped until half a century later by Gustav Kirchhoff (1824-1887). In the meantime, Fraunhofer's skill as a telescope-maker enabled Friedrich Bessel (1784-1846) to determine the distance to the star, 61 Cygni; he found it to lie at a distance of about 6 light-years, a term that had then became commonly used as a measure of stellar distance.

Although Kepler's laws enabled the calculation of the relative sizes of the planetary orbits to be obtained, a figure in absolute terms for the mean Earth-Sun separation was still needed. In the nineteenth century much effort was expended on this task, using the method suggested by Kepler of observing transits of Venus from widely separated places in order to take parallax observations. By the middle of the century a figure within 2 per cent of the correct value had been obtained.

The year 1846 saw another triumph for Newton's theory of gravitation, when John Adams (1819-1892) and Urbain Le Verrier (1811-1877) predicted the position of an as-yet-unseen planet. Their prediction was based on the observed discrepancies in the motion of Uranus - discrepancies which the two astronomers took to be caused by another, massive planet orbiting beyond the path of Uranus. By calculating the new planet's orbit and its position at certain times, Johann Galle (1812-1910) spotted it on 23 September 1846, less than two lunar diameters from the predicted spot. The new planet was later named Neptune.

Fraunhofer's study of the dark lines in the solar spectrum bore fruit in 1859 with Kirchoff's explanation of them. The lines were absorption lines and were the result of the presence in the Sun of certain chemical elements. Kirchoff's discovery made it possible to determine the chemical composition of the Sun from Earth-bound observations. His work was extended by William Huggins (1824–1910), who was able to show that the stars were made of similar elements to those found on the Earth, thus supporting the 2,300-year-old contention of Anaxagoras. Huggins used the new invention of photography to record the spectra. He also made the first measurement of stellar red-shift, to determine the relative motion of stars towards or away from the Earth. These developments were crucial to the future development of astronomy and astrophysics.

By the end of the nineteenth century, photography had begun to take over from naked-eye observations of the universe. Stars, comets, nebulae and the Andromeda galaxy had all been photographed by 1900. Spectroscopy had also been used on all these objects, and the composition, motion and distance of many of them determined. This latter achievement was possible because of the discovery by Ejnar Hertzsprung (1873–1967) of a relationship between the spectrum of a star and its intrinsic luminosity. The relation was also found by Henry Russell (1877–1957) in America and published nine years after Hertzsprung in 1914. As a result, the diagram plotting the luminosities of stars against their spectra is called the Hertzsprung–Russell diagram. Its importance lies in its ability to show how stars evolve and how distant a star of a given spectrum and apparent brightness is.

Hertzsprung was able, by means of his diagram, to calculate the distance of a Cepheid variable star. As Henrietta Leavitt (1868–1921) discovered in 1904, variable stars exhibit a relationship between their intrinsic luminosity and their period of variability, so that a measurement of the period above can give the Cepheid's distance. As such a measurement could be carried out even on Cepheids in other galaxies, the distances of these galaxies could now be calculated by means of Leavitt's period-luminosity law, published in 1912.

The Origins of the Universe

In 1916 Albert Einstein published his "Foundation of the General Theory of Relativity" in *Annalen der Physik*. Essentially a theory of gravitation, it marked the greatest theoretical advance in our understanding of the Universe since Newton's *Principia* and like Newton's theory it had far-reaching implications for astronomy.

Einstein's theory immediately cleared up a long-standing problem concerning the orbit of Mercury, which was slowly rotating at the rate of

about 43 seconds of arc per century. Einstein's theory showed this to be a result of effects arising from the high orbital velocity of Mercury and the intense gravitational field of the Sun. The theory also made two predictions. First, that in the presence of an intense gravitational field, light should be red-shifted to longer wavelengths as it struggled to escape the field. In 1925 this was found by Walter Adams (1876–1956) to be true of the spectrum of the white-dwarf companion of Sirius. Second, that according to General Relativity, light should be bent by the space-time curvature pictured in the theory as being the cause of gravitation. Observations of a solar eclipse in 1919 showed the light of stars close to the position of the Sun was indeed bent by the amount predicted by Einstein.

When he applied his theory to the entire Universe, in an attempt to reach a universal understanding of dynamics, Einstein was dismayed to discover that in its pure form it would only apply to a Universe that is in overall motion. Such a prediction was contrary to the contemporary belief that, apart from the individual motions of the stars within galaxies, the Universe was static.

However, by applying spectroscopy to the light of distant galaxies, Vesto Slipher (1875–1969) was able to show that the galaxies were in a state of recession. Surprisingly, it was not until 1924 that proof that the galaxies were star-systems separate from our own galaxy was given by Edwin Hubble (1889–1953). Armed with this knowledge, Hubble was then able to show that the Universe as a whole was expanding, and that the rate at which a galaxy appeared to be moving away from Earth was proportional to its distance from us (as determined by the Cepheid law). Thus, Einstein's theory was correct in predicting an expanding Universe.

By the end of the 1920s the idea that the Universe was born in a "Big Bang", as proposed by Abbé George Lemaître (1894–1966) in 1927, had become, as it still remains, the established dogma of cosmology. Estimates based on Hubble's law currently set the date of the creation at about 15,000 million years ago.

The year 1930 saw the discovery by photographic means of a ninth planet in the Solar System, Pluto. After a painstaking search involving millions of star images, Clyde Tombaugh (1906–) detected the tiny speck of light on plates taken at the Lowell observatory in Arizona. In 1938 the long-standing problem of the power-source of the Sun and stars was finally solved by Hans Albrecht Bethe (1906–) and Carl Friedrich von Weizsäcker (1912–). They found that the vast outpourings of energy were attributable to the fusing of hydrogen nuclei deep within stars, the process being so efficient that luminosity could be sustained for thousands of millions of years.

The Universe in a New Light

Experiments in America by Karl Jansky (1905–1950) and Grote Reber (1911–   ) in the 1930s heralded the start of a new era in astronomical observation, marked by the use of wavelengths other than light, in particular radio waves. Solar radio emission was detected in 1942 and following a theoretical prediction by Hendrik van de Hulst (1918–   ) in the Netherlands in 1944, interstellar hydrogen radio emission was detected and this was used to produce a map of our Galaxy which was not limited to those regions not obscured by light-absorbing dust.

A radically different theory of the Universe, which was free of the Big Bang and its attendant difficulties was proposed by Thomas Gold (1920–   ), Hermann Bondi (1919–   ) and Fred Hoyle (1915–   ) in 1948. Called the Steady State theory, it pictured the Universe as being in a constant state of expansion, with new matter being created to compensate for the dilution caused by the Hubble recession. The theory aroused much criticism, but it was not until 1965 that the theory was considered by many to have been finally disproved.

In that year, experiments by Arno Penzias (1933–   ) and Robert Wilson (1936–   ) in America resulted in the discovery that the Universe appears to contain an isotropic background of microwave radiation. On the Big-Bang picture, that can be interpreted as the red-shifted remnant of the radiation generated in the original Big Bang. Since it is difficult to reproduce the properties of this background on the Steady State theory, the theory was abandoned by most astronomers.

Radio astronomy, which had progressed far in attempts to discover the true nature of the Universe by observations of distant galaxies, had two major successes in the 1960s. The first was the discovery of quasi-stellar objects, and their identification as extremely remote yet very powerful sources by Maarten Schmidt (1929–   ) in 1963. Their power-source remains enigmatic, but the current belief is that they are galactic centres which contain massive black holes, sucking material into themselves. The second discovery was made by Jocelyn Bell Burnell (1943–   ) at Cambridge in 1967. Rapid bursts of radio energy at extremely regular intervals were picked up and interpreted as being generated by a rapidly rotating magnetized neutron star, or pulsar. Such an object may be the result of a supernova explosion.

The late 1960s and early 1970s were marked by the advent of the manned exploration of the Moon by the American Apollo mission, beginning in 1969 with the expedition of Apollo 11. Throughout the 1960s and 1970s, unmanned probes to the planets revealed more about them than had been discovered in all the previous centuries of study combined. The missions were either fly-bys, beginning with the American Mariner 2 probe of Venus in 1962, or landings, such as the descent of the Russian Venera 4 on to the surface of Venus in 1967.

Detailed maps of the four terrestrial planets, Mercury, Venus, Earth and Mars, have now been made, and American Pioneer and Voyager probes passed by Jupiter and Saturn, taking in much of their satellite systems, in the 1970s and early 1980s. Earth-bound observations, which have always been hampered by the interference of a turbulent and polluted atmosphere, are now being supplemented by orbiting observatories operating at a wide range of wavelengths. The first X-ray observatory, UHURU, was launched in 1971, and it detected many sources of X-rays both within and beyond our galaxy.

The advent of high-speed computers has enabled astronomers to link radio observatories across entire continents in interferometric arrays, a programme pioneered by Martin Ryle in the late 1950s. As a result, very detailed maps of distant objects such as quasars and the centres of galaxies have been made, revealing some clues about the extremely violent activity occurring within them.

New electronic instruments are used by astronomers to detect objects on the fringes of visibility, while new telescope-building techniques are producing bigger, more powerful, optical telescopes. It is hoped that these instruments, together with their orbiting counterparts, will enable us to see to great distances into the Universe, and hence, because of the finite speed of light, deep into the past history of the Universe.

The discovery of Peter van de Kamp (1901–   ) in 1963 of at least one planet orbiting the peculiarly-moving Barnard's Star has increased speculation about the possibility of stars other than our Sun having inhabited planets in orbit about them. Searches at radio wavelengths for signals coming from intelligent life in the Universe have been conducted from time to time, but to date there has been no success.

In the meantime, astronomers continue their theoretical and observational investigations into the Universe around us, using knowledge gained from a wide range of other scientific fields from quantum physics to biochemistry. Many problems face astronomy today. The concept of the

Big-Bang Universe still poses some major difficulties, among them the explanation of the origin of the galaxies. Understanding the power-source of active galaxies and quasars is another major goal of contemporary astrophysicists, while on our own doorstep the Sun and its power source still seem not to be completely described by current theory.

A

Abetti, Giorgio is an Italian astrophysicist who is best known for his studies of the Sun.

Abetti was born in Padua on 5 October 1882. He studied at the universities of Padua and Rome and earned a PhD in the physical sciences. In 1921 he was appointed Professor at the University of Florence, where he remained until his retirement in 1957. From 1921 until 1952 he was Director of the Arcetri Observatory in Florence. During his tenure at Florence, Abetti travelled to Cairo in 1948 to serve as Visiting Professor at the university there, and he toured the United States in 1950. He lives in Florence and maintains an association with the National Institute of Optics.

Abetti's research contribution quickly earned him a prominent and respected position among Italian scientists. He was awarded the Silver Medal of the Italian Geographical Society in 1915, the Reale Prize of the Academy of Lincei in 1926, and the Janssen Gold Medal of the Ministry of Public Instruction in 1937. He is a member of the Socio Nazionale, the Academy of Lincei in Rome, and the Royal Society of Edinburgh and the Royal Astronomical Society in Britain.

Abetti's research has been in the field of astrophysics, with particular emphasis on the Sun. He participated in numerous expeditions to observe eclipses of the Sun, and led one such expedition to Siberia to observe the total solar eclipse of 19 June 1936. He is well known for his influential popular text on the Sun, and he has also written a handbook of astrophysics, published in 1936, and a popular history of astronomy, which appeared in 1963.

The awards that Abetti has received and the positions he has held during his career testify to the enormous respect for his research within the field and his writings on the subject of astrophysics.

Adams, John Couch (*1819–1892*), was an English astronomer who was particularly skilled mathematically. His ability to deal adeptly with complex calculations helped him to discover, independently of Urbain Le Verrier, the planet Neptune.

Adams was born in Landeast, Cornwall, on 5 June 1819. His mathematical talents and interest in astronomy were apparent from an early age, and in 1839 he won a scholarship to Cambridge University. He graduated with top honours in 1843 and took up a Fellowship at St John's College. When this lapsed in 1853 he was given a life Fellowship at Pembroke College. St Andrew's University in Aberdeen appointed Adams to the chair of Mathematics in 1858, but he returned to Cambridge a year later to become Lowdean Professor of Astronomy and Geometry, a post he held until his death.

The initial public acclaim for the discovery of Neptune went to Le Verrier, but Adams nevertheless received many honours. He was awarded the Royal Society's Copley Medal (its highest honour) in 1848 and was elected Fellow of the Royal Society a year later. He was made a member of the Royal Astronomical Society and served it twice as President. He was awarded its Gold Medal for his later research into lunar theory. He succeeded James Challis as Director of the Cambridge Observatory, but he was always a modest man. He declined the offer of a knighthood from Queen Victoria, and also turned down the position of Astronomer Royal, pleading old age. He died in Cambridge on 21 January 1892.

The planet Uranus was discovered by William Herschel in 1781. Its path was carefully studied during the first orbit after discovery, and it soon became clear that early predictions of the motions of Uranus were incorrect. On the basis of Isaac Newton's gravitational theory, certain aberrations in the orbit were accounted for as the result of perturbations caused by Jupiter and Saturn, but these were insufficient to explain the magnitude of Uranus' deviation from its predicted orbital path. This suggested that either the gravitational theory was incorrect or that an as yet undetected planet lay beyond the orbit of Uranus. The mathematical calculations necessary to solve the mystery were taken up independently by Adams and Le Verrier. Adams had become interested in this problem while still an undergraduate, but it was not until he had completed his studies in 1843 that he had the time to focus his full attention on it. By 1845 he had determined the position and certain characteristics of this hypothetical planet. He attempted to convey the information to the new Astronomer Royal, George Airy, but the significance of Adams' findings was not fully appreciated. A search for the new planet was not instigated for nearly a year and was carried out by Challis at Cambridge.

Meanwhile, in France, Le Verrier had followed the same lines of thought as Adams. The Frenchman sent his figure to Johann Galle at the Berlin

Observatory. It was Le Verrier's good fortune that Galle had just received a new and improved map of the sector of the sky in which the planet could be located. As a result, Galle was able to find the planet, which was later named Neptune, within a few hours of beginning his search on 25 September 1846. It later transpired that Challis had observed the new planet on a number of occasions, but had failed to recognize that it was new because of his inferior maps. The discovery of Neptune was credited to Le Verrier, although not without much nationalistic acrimony on both sides of the Channel.

Adams' later work included research into lunar theory and terrestrial magnetism, as well as observations of the Leonid meteor shower. Later, he improved the findings of Pierre Laplace. This resulted in a reduction of 50 per cent in the then current value for the secular acceleration of the Moon's mean motion.

Adams' contributions to observational astronomy, as well as his improvements to the accuracy of many mathematical constants, made him deeply respected – not only for the value of his work, but also for his modest attitude towards his achievements.

Adams, Walter Sydney (*1876-1956*), was an American astronomer who was particularly interested in stellar motion and luminosity. He developed spectroscopy as a valuable tool in the study of stars and planets.

Adams was born on 20 December 1876 at Antioch, Syria, where his parents were serving as missionaries. His early education was provided by his parents, who taught him much about ancient history and classical languages. In 1885 his parents returned to the United States for the sake of their children's education. When Adams entered Dartmouth College in Massachusetts he had to choose between his love of classics and mathematical sciences. He graduated in 1898 and went to the University of Chicago for his postgraduate studies.

He studied celestial mechanics, publishing a paper during his first year on the polar compression of Jupiter. The next year was spent under George Hale at the Yerkes Observatory, where Adams made a number of studies including one on the measurement of radical velocity. He went to Munich the following year. Hale then invited him to return to Yerkes, which he did and Adams spent the next three years working on stellar spectroscopy.

In 1904 he assisted Hale in the establishment of the Mount Wilson Observatory above Pasadena in California. Mount Wilson gradually became a renowned research centre. Adams served

as Deputy Director, under Hale, from 1913 to 1923, when he took over as Director. Adams was a member of many scientific organizations in both the United States and Europe. He was honoured for his achievements by being elected President of the American Astronomical Society in 1931. He died on 11 May 1956.

Adams' early work on radial velocities had used the 100 cm refractor at Yerkes, at the time the largest in the world. At Mount Wilson he was able to use larger and more sophisticated equipment. The first area that Adams investigated at Mount Wilson was the spectra obtained from sunspots as compared to those obtained from the rest of the solar disc and from laboratory sources. He found that the temperature, pressure and density of a source affects the relative intensities of its spectral lines. This and other information enabled him to demonstrate that sunspots have a lower temperature than the rest of the solar disc. Adams also studied solar rotation by means of Doppler displacements.

In 1914 Adams turned to the spectroscopy of other stars. He found that luminosity and the relative intensities of particular spectral lines could distinguish giant stars from dwarf stars. Spectra could also be used to study the physical properties, motions and distances of stars. This use of the intensity of spectral lines to determine the distance of stars has been termed spectroscopic parallax.

Adams was involved in a long-term project with other astronomers to determine the absolute magnitudes of stars; they found the value for 6,000 stars. A second long-term collaborative project was the determination of the radial velocities of more than 7,000 stars. This work led to an improved understanding of the behaviour and evolution of stars.

In 1915 Adams made a spectroscopic study of the small companion star of Sirius B. He identified it as a white dwarf containing about 80 per cent of the mass of the Sun in a volume approximately the same as that of the Earth and thus having a density more than 40,000 times that of water. Adams demonstrated that the companion star was hotter than our Sun and not cold, as everyone had assumed. Arthur Eddington suggested in 1920 that if Sirius B was indeed so dense it would produce a powerful gravitational field and show a red shift (as predicted by Albert Einstein's General Theory of Relativity). In 1925 Adams reported a displacement of 21 km sec^{-1}, thus confirming Einstein's theory.

During the 1920s and 1930s Adams studied the atmosphere of Mars and Venus, reporting in 1932 the presence of carbon dioxide in the atmosphere of Venus and, in 1934, the occurrence of oxygen in concentrations of less than 0.1 per cent on Mars. He was involved in many other research projects, and he also made an important contribution in his capacity as Director of the Observatory. He was responsible for the design and installation of the 254 and 508 cm telescopes at Mount Wilson and Palomar. Adams was a fine scholar and administrator. Astronomy matured as a science during his active research years, a development to which he was an important contributor.

Airy, George Biddell (*1801–1892*), was a British astronomer who, as Astronomer Royal for 46 years, was responsible for greatly simplifying the systematization of astronomical observations and for expanding and improving the Royal Observatory at Greenwich.

Airy was born in Alnwick, Northumberland, on 27 July 1801. His father, a collector of taxes and excise duties, was periodically transferred from one part of the country to another, with the result that his son was educated in a number of places. From 1814 to 1819 he attended Colchester Grammar School, where he was noted for his incredible memory (on one occasion he recited from memory 2,394 lines of Latin verse). In 1819 he became a student at Trinity College, Cambridge, and three years later took a scholarship there. He graduated in 1823 at the top of his class in mathematics. The following year he was elected a Fellow of Trinity College and became an assistant tutor in mathematics. The physics of light and optics began to interest him and he was the first to describe the defect of vision – later termed astigmatism – from which he also suffered. In 1826 he became Professor of Mathematics at Cambridge and in the same year, having become interested in astronomy, published *Mathematical Tracts on Physical Astronomy*, which became a standard work. He was elected Professor of Astronomy and Director of the Cambridge Observatory in 1828, and was then appointed Astronomer Royal in 1835, a post which he held until 1881. During this period he sat on many commissions and supervised the cataloguing of geographical boundaries. He was awarded the Copley and Royal medals by the Royal Society and was its President from 1827 to 1873. He was five times President of the Royal Astronomical Society, twice receiving its Gold Medal, and received various honorary degrees. He died in Greenwich, London, on 2 January 1892.

While Airy was Director of the Cambridge Observatory, it flourished under his control; he introduced a much improved system of meridian observations and set the example of reducing them in scale before publishing them. As Astron-

omer Royal, Airy had the Royal Observatory at Greenwich re-equipped and many innovations were made. He supervised the gigantic task of reducing in scale all the planetary and lunar observations made at Greenwich between 1750 and 1830. In 1847 he had erected the alt-azimuth (an instrument he devised to calculate altitude and azimuth) for observing the Moon in every part of the sky. Airy also introduced new departments to the Observatory; in 1838 he created one for magnetic and meteorology data and, in 1840, a system of regular two-hourly observations was begun. Other innovations included photographic registration in 1848, transits timed by electricity in 1854, spectroscopic observations from 1868 and a daily round of sunspots using the Kew heliograph in 1873.

As an expert mathematician Airy's skills were required in the exact mapping of geographical boundaries: he was responsible for establishing the border between Canada and the United States and later of the Oregon and Maine boundaries. He also established exact determinations of the longitudes of Valencia, Cambridge, Edinburgh, Brussels and Paris. Airy's scientific expertise was also called on during the launch of the *SS Great Eastern*, the laying of the transatlantic telegraph cable, and the construction of the chimes of the clock in the tower at Westminster ("Big Ben"). During 1854 he supervised several experiments in Harton Colliery, South Shields, to measure the change in the force of gravity with distance below the Earth's surface.

Throughout all his additional duties Airy never allowed his work with the Royal Observatory to suffer and it was due to his enthusiasm and hard work that the Greenwich Observatory grew in importance both nationally and internationally.

Aitken, Robert Grant (*1864–1951*), was an American astronomer whose primary contribution to astronomy was the discovery and observation of thousands of double stars.

Aitken was born in Jackson, California, on 31 December 1864. He took his degree at Williams College, where he forsook his earlier plans to enter the ministry for his interest in astronomy. He taught at Livermore College from 1888 until 1891, when he was made Professor of Mathematics at the University of the Pacific. From 1895 onwards he worked at the Lick Observatory on Mount Hamilton, first as Assistant Astronomer and ultimately as Director of the Observatory from 1930 until his retirement in 1935.

Aitken's work on binary systems brought him widespread recognition and many honours. He was a member of numerous professional bodies, often holding positions of responsibility within them. These included the chairmanship (from 1929 to 1932) of the Astronomy section of the National Academy of Sciences. He died in Berkeley, California, on 29 October 1951.

At first Aitken's research at Lick was in many fields, but his interest soon focused on double stars. He began a mammoth survey of double stars in 1899 and this was not finished until 1915. During the early years of the project he was assisted by W.J.Hussey, and between them they discovered nearly 4,500 new binary systems. Their primary tool was the 91 cm refractor. Aitken then began a thorough statistical examination of this vast amount of information, which he published first in 1918 and then revised in 1935. His work lay not merely in the discovery of new binary stars, but also in determining their motions and orbits.

Aitken's other famous contribution was his revision of S.W. Burnham's catalogue of double stars, first published in 1906. This was completed in 1927. Aitken was also interested in, and contributed to, the popularization of astronomy, especially after his retirement.

Alpher, Ralph Asher (*1921–*   ), is an American scientist who carried out the first quantitative work on nucleosynthesis and was the first to predict the existence of primordial background radiation.

Alpher, the youngest of four children and the son of a building contractor, was born in Washington DC in 1921. His initial interest in science was stimulated by his English teacher, Matilde Eiker, who was also an amateur astronomer, and by his chemistry teacher, Sarah Branch. Due to economic circumstances and the advent of World War II, Alpher was forced to continue his education as a night school student, receiving his BSc from George Washington University in 1943 and his PhD in 1948. His PhD research topic was nucleosynthesis in a Big-Bang universe, which was carried out under the supervision of George Gamow. During World War II Alpher worked at the Naval Ordnance Laboratory and after the war he joined the Applied Physics Laboratory of Johns Hopkins University. Here he took part in a varied research programme that, besides cosmology, included cosmic ray physics and guided missile aerodynamics. In 1955 Alpher took up a post at the Central Electric Research Laboratory in the USA where besides his professional duties he continued his vocational involvement in cosmological research.

Having graduated from George Washington University, Alpher worked with George Gamow and Robert Herman, who is now at the University of Texas, on a series of papers that sought to explain physical aspects of the Big-Bang theory of the Universe. In 1948 Alpher and Gamow published the results of their work on nucleosynthesis in the early Universe. They included the name of Hans Bethe as a co-author of this paper, so that their new theory became popularly known as the alpha-beta-gamma theory – appropriate for a theory on the beginning of the Universe. Also in 1948, Alpher, together with his colleague Robert Herman, predicted the existence of the pervasive relict cosmic black-body radiation. They postulated that this radiation must exist, having originated in the early stages of the big bang with which the Universe is thought to have begun. This primordial radiation was detected by Arno A. Penzias and Robert W. Wilson in 1965 and was found to have a temperature of 3°K. Alpher and Herman had originally theorized that the radiation would have a temperature of approximately 5°K which was remarkably close to the actual value observed.

The existence of this low temperature radiation that permeates the entire Universe is now regarded as one of the major pieces of evidence for the validity of the Big-Bang model of the Universe; thus Alpher's early cosmological work has had a profound impact towards our understanding of the nature of the Universe.

al-Sufi (*903–986*) was a Persian astronomer whose importance lies in his compilation of a valuable catalogue of 1,018 stars with their approximate positions, magnitudes, and colours.

Little detail is known about the life of al-Sufi, but it has been established that he was a nobleman whose love of his country's folklore and mythology and interest in mathematics led him to the study of astronomy.

Ambatzumian, Victor Amazaspovich (*1908–*   ), is a Soviet astronomer whose chief contribution has been to the theory of stellar origins.

Few biographical details are known, but Ambatzumian was appointed Head of the Byurakan Observatory in 1944, having taught at the University of Leningrad. He proposed the manner in which enormous catastrophes might take place within stars and galaxies during their evolution.

The radio source in Cygnus had been associated with what appeared to be a closely connected pair of galaxies, and it was generally supposed that a galactic collision was taking place. If this were the case, such phenomena might account for many extra-galactic radio sources. Ambatzumian, however, presented convincing evidence in 1955 of the errors of this theory. He suggested instead that vast explosions occur within the cores of galaxies, analogous to supernovae, but on a galactic scale.

Antoniadi, Eugène Marie (*1870-1944*), was a Turkish-born French astronomer who had a particular interest in Mars and later became an expert also on the scientific achievements of ancient civilizations.

Antoniadi was born in Istanbul (then Constantinople) in 1870. He became interested in astronomy as a young man and in 1893 he went to Juvisy-sur-Orge in France, where he worked at the Observatory with Nicolas Flammarion. He later moved to Meudon where he continued his research at the observatory there. He became a French citizen in 1928, and was appointed Director of the Mars Section of the British Astronomical Association. He died in Meudon on 10 February 1944.

Antoniadi began to make astronomical observations in 1888 at home and while visiting the Greek Islands. He was interested in the nearby celestial system – the planets of our Solar System – but was frustrated by the primitive instruments available to him. When he moved to Juvisy he was able to use the 42 cm telescope there with which, in 1893, he and Flammarion observed faint spots on the surface of Saturn. This observation stimulated a vigorous debate with the American astronomer, Edward Barnard, who claimed the spots to be illusory. Antoniadi and Flammarion were vindicated when in 1902 Barnard discovered one of these spots himself.

Antoniadi's chief interest was, however, the planet Mars. When he was at Meudon Observatory, he took advantage of a favourable opposition of Mars to observe it using the 84 cm telescope. He detected an apparent spot on the planet's surface, but soon realized that it was due merely to an optical effect caused by the diffraction of light by the Earth's atmosphere. His scepticism was not easy to announce, because there was at that time great interest in Giovanni Schiaparelli's suggestion, seized upon by astronomers such as Percival Lowell, that there was an intricate pattern of canals on the surface of Mars suggestive of advanced technology. Antoniadi eventually proposed that these "canals" were also an optical illusion, produced by the eye's linking of many tiny surface details into an apparently meaningful pattern. In 1924 he was able, however, to confirm Schiaparelli's value for the rotational period of Mars.

Antoniadi's later work included research into the angle of the axis of rotation of Venus and the behaviour and properties of the planet Mercury. He published a book on the planet (*La Planète Mercure;* 1934) and then turned to a study of the

history of astronomy and, in particular, to the work of the ancient Greek and Egyptian astronomers.

Argelander, Friedrich Wilhelm August (*1799-1875*), was a Prussian astronomer whose approach to the subject was one of great resourcefulness and thoroughness. His most enduring contribution was the publication of the *Bonner Durchmusterung* (Bonn Survey, 1859-1862) of more than 300,000 stars in the northern hemisphere. Its value is such that it was reprinted as recently as 1950.

Argelander was born on 22 March 1799 in Memel, East Prussia (now Klaipeda in the Soviet Union). He studied in Elbing and Königsberg. His initial plan had been to study economics and politics, but lectures by Friedrich Bessel soon fired his interest in astronomy. He worked under Bessel and in 1922 was awarded a PhD for a thesis in which he described work he had done as part of Bessel's systematic evaluation of bright stars in part of the northern hemisphere. In the same year Argelander earned the title of Lecturer.

In 1823 he went to Åbo (Turku) in Finland. He worked as an astronomical observer there, under difficult conditions, for four years until the observatory was destroyed by a fire that swept the town in 1827. He became Professor of Astronomy at the University of Helsinki in 1828, and from 1832 until 1836 he was Director of the observatory there.

During the upheavals that followed the Napoleonic Wars, the young princes of the Prussian Kingdom had lived for a few years with the Argelander family. In 1836, when Argelander went to the University of Bonn as Professor of Astronomy, the grateful crown prince (who later became King Friedrich Wilhelm IV), promised Argelander a magnificent new observatory, which was eventually constructed under Argelander's supervision. Meanwhile, he continued his own studies under primitive conditions.

Argelander's work was of such impeccable standard that he earned an impressive international reputation. He was elected to virtually every prominent European scientific academy and was a member of scientific organizations in the United States. He was an active member of the Astronomische Gesellschaft, serving as chairman of its governing body from 1864 until 1867. He died in Bonn on 17 February 1875.

Argelander's early astronomical studies were a continuation of Bessel's work on the mapping of stellar positions, so that his systematic approach was established from the beginning. After his move to Åbo, Argelander began to concentrate on the proper motion of stars, that is the movement of stars measured in seconds of arc per year, relative to one another. Argelander considered this movement by analogy to a ship moving among a fleet: the farther vessels appear to be almost stationary relative to those nearby, although they are all moving. He studied the proper motion of more than 500 stars and was able to publish the most accurate catalogue of the day on the subject.

His next major area of study was a continuation of a preliminary investigation done by William Herschel in 1783 on the movement of the Sun through the cosmos. Herschel's study had involved the proper motion of only seven stars. Argelander realized that observations of many more stars would be necessary before a firm conclusion about the direction of movement of the Sun, if indeed there were any, could be made. Only a large quantity of data would enable the dual effects of the movement of "fixed" stars and the movement of the Sun to be distinguished. Argelander's conclusions, based on nearly 400 stars, confirmed Herschel's results. He found that the Sun is indeed moving towards the constellation of Hercules.

In 1843 Argelander published his *Uranometrica Nova*, based on studies made exclusively with the naked eye, because the Bonn Observatory was still under construction. The most important innovation in this study was the introduction of the "estimation by steps" method for determining stellar magnitudes. It relied exclusively on the sensitivity of the trained eye in comparing the brightness of neighbouring stars.

In 1850 the system was elaborated by N.G. Pogson, who found that each step along the scale meant a change in brightness 2.5 fold. Bright stars have low numbers, for example 1 or 2, and dim stars have high numbers, such as 9. Stars of magnitude 7 and above are not visible to the naked eye. Extremely bright bodies have magnitudes with negative values, such as the full Moon with a value of -11 or the Sun with a value of -26.7.

Argelander's next project was an extension of Bessel's study of stars in the northern sky. At first he neglected stars up to a certain magnitude, which limited the usefulness of his data since it made it inadequate for statistical analysis. This was remedied during the late 1850s, with the help of E. Schönfeld and A. Kruger, and resulted in the publication of the *Bonner Durchmusterung*. This catalogued the position and brightness of nearly 324,000 stars, and although it was the last major catalogue to be produced without the aid of photography, it represents the cornerstone of later astronomical work. Argelander also initiated a mammoth project that required the cooperation of many observatories and was aimed at improving the accuracy of positional data recorded in the survey.

Argelander's work was characterized by its grand scope and admirable thoroughness. His contributions were fundamental to many later astronomical studies.

Aristarchos (*c. 320–c. 250* BC), was a mathematician and astronomer of great renown in ancient Greece.

Aristarchos was born on the island of Samos in about 320 BC. He was born before Archimedes (*c.* 287–*c.* 212 BC), although Aristarchos and Archimedes certainly knew of each other. Little is known of Aristarchos' life, but it is thought most likely that he studied in Alexandria under Strato of Lampsacos (*c.* 340–270 BC), before the latter succeeded Theophrastus (372–287 BC), as head of the Athenian Lyceum (originally founded by Aristotle) in 287 BC. Aristarchos died in Alexandria, *c.*250 BC.

The only work by Aristarchos that still exists is *On the Magnitude and Distances of the Sun and Moon*. This document describes the first attempt, by means of simple trigonometry, to measure these sizes and distances. The measurements were not very accurate and they were improved upon a century later by Hipparchus. It was, nevertheless, probably as a consequence of the figures Aristarchos obtained – however inaccurate – that he first began to conceive of his revolutionary cosmological model. In the text of his essay Aristarchos described a right-angled triangle with the Earth, the half-illuminated Moon and the Sun at the corners; the Moon was positioned at the right-angle, and the hypotenuse ran between the Sun and the Earth. Aristarchos reasoned that since the angle at the Earth corner could be measured, the angle at the Sun could be deduced.

Based on six astronomical hypotheses Aristarchos obtained eighteen propositions which described, among other things, the Sun–Earth and Moon–Earth distances in terms of Earth-diameters. The circumference (and therefore the diameter) of the Earth had already been calculated with considerable accuracy; in addition, his basic mathematics was sound, but because Aristarchos was unable to make accurate measurements he arrived at incorrect results. Not only did he have difficulty in knowing exactly when the Moon was half-illuminated (when it forms a right-angle with the Sun and Earth), he also underestimated the angle formed by the Sun, the Earth and the Moon at the Earth corner as being 87° – the angle should have been 89°$_{50}$.

This miscalculation led to the erroneous conclusion that the distance between the Sun and the Earth was only 18 to 20 times the distance between the Moon and the Earth; in fact, the correct multiple is 397 times. Aristarchos also grossly miscalculated the diameter of the Sun as being only seven times that of the Earth. Even so, it still struck him as strange that a larger body should orbit a smaller one, as was assumed by the geocentric cosmological model.

Heraklides of Pontus (*c*. 388–315 BC) had earlier proposed the idea, which had been accepted by many, that Mercury and Venus orbit the Sun. Aristarchos carried the argument further and suggested that the Earth also orbits the Sun. Aristarchos' model, the first heliocentric one to be proposed, described the Sun and the fixed stars as stationary in the cosmos, and the planets – including the Earth – as travelling in circular orbits around the Sun. He further stated that the apparent daily rotation of the sphere of stars is due to the Earth's rotation on its axis as it travels along its orbit. He anticipated the most powerful argument against his theory by stating that the reason no stellar parallax (change in position of the stars) was observed from one extreme of the orbit to the other is that even the diameter of the Earth's orbit is insignificant in relation to the vast dimensions of the Universe.

Aristarchos' model is recorded in letters, in a book by Archimedes, and in the writings of Plutarch. Copernicus certainly knew of Aristarchos' heliocentric model, but he deliberately suppressed reference to it, perhaps so as not to compromise his claims to originality.

Aristarchos is said to have carried out other astronomical research, including an observation of the summer solstice in 281 BC (according to Ptolemy). He may also have designed the skaphe – an improved sundial which consisted of a hollow hemisphere with a vertical needle, protruding from the base, which cast shadows to indicate the time.

We knew today that Aristarchos was substan-

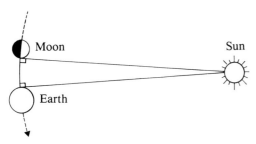

Aristarchos calculated the distance between the Earth and the Sun (in terms of the Earth–Moon distance) by measuring the angle to the Sun when it was exactly half full (and its angle to the Sun was 90°).

tially correct in his views. But his theory made little impact on his contemporaries, since the powerful philosophical, religious and astronomical ideas of the time were all based on a geocentric view of the Universe. Even Aristarchos' initial measurements of the distances and sizes of the Earth, Moon and Sun were probably based on a geocentric model. The new model, however, demanded that the Universe be considered to have dimensions which exceeded the imagination of and were unacceptable to Aristarchos' fellow cosmologists. He was accused of impiety, but perhaps even more damning was the inability of his model to account for a number of astronomical anomalies and the unequal duration of the seasons. It was never suspected that the introduction of elliptical rather than circular orbits would have gone a long way to resolving these difficulties.

Virtually alone among the Greek astronomers, Aristarchos proposed a cosmological model based not on mathematical harmony, but on observed physical "reality". This achievement is something of a paradox since he is generally credited with being a mathematician, rather than a descriptive astronomer.

Aristotle (*384* BC – *322* BC) was a Greek polymath, one of the most imaginative and systematic thinkers in history, whose writings embraced virtually every aspect of contemporary thought, including cosmology.

Aristotle was born at Stagirus, a port on the Chalcidic peninsula of Macedonia, in 384 BC. His father, Nichomachus, was court physician to Amyntas III (sometimes called Amyntas II), King of Macedonia, and it seems probable that he introduced Aristotle to the body of medical and biological knowledge at an early age. Nichomachus died in Aristotle's youth and Aristotle was placed in the care of a ward, who sent him to Athens in 367 BC to study at Plato's Academy. Plato's death in 348/347 BC coincided with a wave of anti-Macedonian fervour in Athens, a combination of events which induced Aristotle to leave the city and go on an extensive tour of Asia Minor, where for the first time he engaged in a serious study of natural history.

In 342 BC King Philip II invited Aristotle to the Macedonian court to become tutor to the crown prince, the future Alexander the Great. Shortly after Alexander came to the throne in 336 BC, Aristotle returned to Athens, where he established his own school, the Lyceum (known also as the Peripatetic School from Aristotle's habit of lecturing while walking in the garden) in 335 BC. At the Lyceum Aristotle established a zoo (stocked with animals captured during Alexander's Asian campaigns) and a library. The latter formed the basis of the great library established in Alexandria by the Ptolemies. The death of Alexander in 323 BC and another upsurge of anti-Macedonian sentiment in Athens suddenly made Aristotle's position uncomfortable. Largely because of his association with Antipater, the Macedonian regent and general, Aristotle was politically suspect. He was charged with impiety and, rather than suffer the fate of Socrates, he withdrew to Chalcis (now Khalkis), north of Athens, where he died in 322 BC.

Aristotle's writings, which have come down to us only in later, edited versions of his notes, lectures and publications, cover philosophy, logic, politics, physics, biology and cosmology. His major writings on cosmology, or astronomy, are brought together in the four-volume text, *De caelo* ("Of the Heavens"). Aristotle rejected the notion of infinity and the notion of a vacuum. A vacuum he held to be impossible because an object moving in it would meet no resistance and would therefore attain infinite velocity. Space could not be infinite, because in Aristotle's view, adopted from the work of Eudoxus (*c.* 460 BC– *c.* 370 BC) and Callippus (*c.* 370 BC–*c.* 300 BC), the Universe consisted of a series of concentric spheres which rotated around the centrally placed, stationary Earth. If the outermost sphere were an infinite distance from the Earth, it would be unable to complete its rotation within a finite period of time, in particular within the 24-hour period in which the stars, fixed, as Aristotle believed, to the sphere, rotated around the Earth.

Aristotle's cosmos – geocentric and broadly speaking mechanical, not dynamic – differed only in details from the model proposed by Eudoxus and Callippus. Callippus posited 33 spheres; Aristotle added 22 new spheres, then amalgamated some of them, to reach a total of 49. This clumsy model, which was unable to account even for eclipses, was partly replaced by the Ptolemaic system based on epicycles. In Aristotle's system the outermost sphere contained the fixed stars. Then followed the spheres of Saturn, Jupiter, Mars, the Sun, Venus, Mercury and, closest to the earth, the Moon. Each of these had several spheres in order to account for all their movements. The outermost sphere was controlled by divine influence and indirectly it determined the movement of all the inner spheres. The original motive power of the Universe was thus removed from the centre, where the Pythagoreans had placed it.

According to Aristotle's laws of motion, bodies moved upwards or downwards in straight lines. Of Empedocles' four natural elements in the Universe, earth and water fell, air and fire rose. To explain the motion of the heavenly spheres, therefore, Aristotle introduced a fifth element, ether, whose natural movement was circular. Aristotle thus posited that the laws of motions governing the celestial bodies above the Moon were different from the laws which governed bodies beneath the Moon.

Aristotle's work in astronomy also included proving that the Earth was spherical. He observed that the Earth cast a circular shadow on the Moon during an eclipse and he pointed out that as one travelled north or south, the stars changed their positions. Since it was not necessary to travel very far to observe this effect, it was clear that the Earth was a sphere, and a rather small one at that. As a result Aristotle was able to make a tolerably fair estimate of the Earth's diameter, over-estimating it by only 50 per cent.

Although Aristotle was not an experimentalist, he was, in however rudimentary fashion, an observer. It was unfortunate for the future development of astronomy that, for centuries during the Dark Ages, in Europe his ideas were eclipsed by Plato's more purely rational approach to cosmology.

Arp, Halton Christian (*1927–*   ), is an American astronomer known for his work on the identification of galaxies.

Arp was born on 21 March 1927 in New York City. He was educated at Harvard Universtiy, where he obtained his BA in 1949. Four years later he gained a PhD at the California Institute of Technology and became a Carnegie Fellow at the Mount Wilson and Palomar Observatory in 1953. He was a Research Associate at the University of Indiana from 1955 to 1957, and for the next eight years was Assistant Astronomer at the Mount Wilson and Palomar Observatory, of the Carnegie Institute in Washington and at the California Institute of Technology. From 1965 to 1969 he was Astronomer at those institutions. Since 1969, he has been Astronomer at the Hale Observatory in California and has been a Visiting Professor of the National Science Foundation since 1960. He is a member of several astronomical associations and was Chairman of the Los Angeles Chapter of the Federation of American Scientists and of Sigma XI, in 1965. He also received several awards for his achievements in the field of astronomy.

In 1956, while at Indiana University, Arp established the ratio between the absolute magnitude of novae at maximum brightness and the speed of decline of magnitude. Since then he has published several papers and in 1965 wrote the *Atlas of Peculiar Galaxies*.

During his research on globular clusters, globular cluster variable stars, novae, Cepheid variables, extragalactic nebulae and so on, Arp has attempted to relate the listings of galaxies to radio sources and has compiled a catalogue of radio sources from the galaxies shown in the Palomar sky atlas; the optical identification of these sources can now be done fairly accurately. The most interesting of the radio sources found so far are quasars, which are characterized by a strong emission in the ultraviolet part of the spectrum. Arp is working with other astronomers on the question whether the red shifts in the spectrum of quasars are due to the general expansion of the Universe. If this is proved to be true, then quasars are among the oldest and most remote objects in the Universe.

Arp has also carried out the first photometric work on the Magellanic Clouds - the nearest extragalactic system. In his research on pulsating novae, particularly those in the Andromeda Nebula, Arp has demonstrated that there is a close relationship between the maximum magnitude and the luminosity of novae so that it is now possible to obtain absolute luminosities for novae fairly easily using light curves (graphs relating apparent magnitude to time).

Arp has attempted also to obtain better data on RV Tauri stars - variables that are much brighter than other cluster stars, many of which lie well outside the clusters. In doing this research he investigated the whole series of variable stars with periods of more than one day, in a number of globular clusters, and related their magnitudes with those of cluster-type variables in the same cluster. Arp's results are referred to as the zero-point of the cluster-type variables.

In the continuing search for explanations for and identification of phenomena in the Universe, Arp has done a great deal to aid the classification of information as well as to provide a basis from which other astronomers may work to increase knowledge of these and other, yet unexplained phenomena.

Atkinson, Robert D'escourt (*1898–*), is an English astronomer and inventor.

Atkinson was born on 11 April 1898 at Rhayader in Wales. He was educated at Oxford University, where he obtained a BA in 1922, and then at the University of Göttingen in Germany, where he gained a PhD in 1928. He was a demonstrator in physics at the Clarendon Laboratory at Oxford from 1922 to 1926 and an assistant at the Technical University in Berlin from 1928 to 1929. He became Assistant Professor at Rutgers University in New Jersey (1922-1934) and then Associate Professor (1964-1973) and has since been Adjunct Professor of Astronomy there.

Atkinson was a member of the Harvard University/Massachusetts Institute of Technology eclipse expedition to the Soviet Union in 1936, and during World War II he was with the mine design department of the British Admiralty. From 1944 to 1946 he served with Ballistic Research Laboratory in Maryland.

Between 1952 and 1955 Atkinson designed the astronomical clock at York Minster in England, and he designed a standard time sundial at Indiana University in 1977. He was a member of the British National Committee for Astronomy (1960-1962) and still belongs to the American Physical Society, the American Astronomical Society, the Royal Astronomical Society, the British Astronomical Association and the Royal Institute of Navigation. He was awarded the Royal Commission Award to Inventors in 1948 and the Eddington Medal of the Royal Astronomical Society in 1960. In 1977 the International Astronomical Union named a minor planet (1,827 Atkinson) in his honour.

Atkinson's research has been in the field of atomic synthesis, stellar energy and positional astronomy. He has also been deeply involved in instrument design.

Many scientists had been concerned with the problem of discovering how the Sun has maintained a reasonably steady yet high rate of radiation for at least three million years. The problem essentially was that there was no known physical or chemical process that could generate radiation from the materials that make up the Sun at so great a rate over so long a period of time, nor was there enough energy released by the contraction of the Sun under its own gravitation. Astronomers therefore began to look elsewhere for a process that could explain the mystery. In 1924 Arthur Eddington, whose field of study was the internal make-up of stars, was computing what conditions must be like beneath the surface of stars in order that the basic laws of physics be obeyed. Eddington suggested that the only possibility was a process whereby atoms were broken down inside the central core of a star, converting matter into energy. He was supported in this view by Atkinson, who in 1932 was working at the Royal Greenwich Observatory. In that year there were new results from the physicists Ernest Rutherford, John Cockcroft and Ernest Walton, who had just succeeded in splitting the central core, or nucleus, of an atom. Atkinson was able to work out a theoretical model of the way in which matter could be annihilated. Not only did he determine the amount of energy released from atomic reactions within stars, but he was also able to suggest the kinds of reactions necessary to produce the vast quantities of radiation required.

With an enormous amount of research into

nuclear physics carried out since World War II, astronomers now have a much greater insight into how stars evolve and how long their evolution takes. There are still many questions to be answered, but it is now thought that energy is generated in the Sun by a process of nuclear fusion. The central core of an atom fuses with the nuclei of other atoms, forming a new and heavier atom and at the same time releasing a vast amount of energy. Calculations have shown that this energy is more than enough to keep a star like the Sun radiating for billions of years.

Robert Atkinson's contributions were fundamental to our basic understanding of how stars like the Sun work and how they evolve.

B

Baade, Walter (*1893-1960*), was a German-born American astronomer who is known for his discovery of stellar populations and whose research proved that the observable universe is larger than originally believed.

Baade was born in Shröttinghausen on 24 March 1893, the son of a schoolteacher. He studied at Münster and at Göttingen Universities, obtaining a PhD from the latter in 1919. For the next eleven years he worked at Hamburg University in the Bergedorf Observatory. In 1931 he emigrated to America and joined the staff of the Mount Wilson Observatory, Pasadena. He left in 1948 and went to the nearby Mount Palomar Observatory where he worked until 1958, when he returned to Germany. The following year he became Gauss Professor at Göttingen University. He died there on 25 June 1960.

The important contributions to astronomy that Baade made were numerous. In 1920 he discovered the most distant known planetoid (minor planet), Hidalgo, whose orbit goes out as far as that of Saturn. In 1948 he found the innermost planetoid, Icarus, whose orbit comes within 18 million miles of the Sun, even closer than Mercury. At Mount Wilson Baade worked with Fritz Zwicky and Edwin Hubble on supernovae and galactic distances.

During the wartime blackout of Los Angeles, in 1943, Baade made his most important discovery. He made use of the enforced darkness to study the Andromeda galaxy with a 2.5 m reflecting telescope. Until that time, Hubble had managed to view only the bright blue giant stars in the spiral arms of the galaxy, and a bright haze in its centre. Baade was able to observe, for the first time, some of the stars in the inner regions of the galaxy and he found that the most luminous stars towards the centre are not blue-white but reddish. He proposed that there exist two groups of stars with differing structures and origins. The bluish stars on the edge of the galaxy, called Population I stars, were distinguished from the reddish ones in the inner regions, Population II. Population I stars are young and formed from the dusty material of the spiral arms – hydrogen, helium and heavier elements; Population II stars are old and were created near the nucleus and contain fewer heavy elements.

After the War, the 5 m reflecting telescope was introduced and Baade continued his research using this instrument. He found that both stellar populations contain Cepheid variable stars (of which there are more than 300 in Andromeda). He also discovered that the period-luminosity curve established for Cepheid variables by Harlow Shapley and Henrietta Leavitt applied only to Population II Cepheids. This discovery meant that two types of Cepheids existed.

Baade's findings had even greater implications. In the 1920s the distances of the outer galaxies had been calculated by Hubble using light curves for Population I Cepheids. Baade decided that these calculations were incorrect and redrew a period-luminosity curve for Population I Cepheids, revealing that they are much brighter than had been previously thought. His discovery showed that the dim bluish-white Cepheids seen in the spiral arms of Andromeda were much farther away than believed and that Andromeda was not 800,000, but more than 2 million, light-years distant. Also, since Hubble had used his incorrect distance of Andromeda to gauge the size of the Universe, the new findings meant that the Universe and all the extragalactic distances in it were at least double the size previously calculated. The increased distance of the Andromeda galaxy and others meant that to appear so bright they must be larger than had been thought. Astronomers realized that our Galaxy is smaller than Andromeda and not the pre-eminent galaxy they imagined.

The enlarged scale of the Universe stimulated the construction of far-reaching radio-telescopes. Astronomers had known that a strong radio source existed in the sky but it could not be located with the 5 m telescope. With a radio-telescope, however, Baade discovered the source to be a distorted galaxy colliding with another galaxy in the constellation Cygnus. The interstellar dust created by the collision and the resulting radio waves could be detected clearly even though they were 260 million light-years away.

Baade contributed a great deal to our knowledge of the Universe. His main interests were extra-galactic nebulae as stellar systems but he also studied variable stars in our own Galaxy, in globular clusters and in the Andromeda nebula, and by doing so stimulated interest in the theory of stellar interiors as the basis of theoretical interpretations of stellar evolution.

Babcock, Harold Delos (*1882–1968*), was an American astronomer and physicist whose most important contributions were to spectroscopy and the study of solar magnetism.

Babcock was born on 24 January 1882 in Edgerton, Wisconsin. Much of his schooling was done at home, but in 1901 he enrolled at the College of Electrical Engineering of the University of California in Berkeley, and he was awarded a BA in 1907. By that time he had already taken up employment at the National Bureau of Standards. In 1908 Babcock taught a course in physics at the University of California. A year later George Hale invited him to work at the Mount Wilson Observatory.

The only breaks in Babcock's service at Mount Wilson between 1909 and 1948 came during the two World Wars. During World War I Babcock worked for the Research Information Service of the National Research Council; during World War II he served as a consultant on several programmes including the Manhattan Project. In 1933 he was elected to the National Academy of Sciences. Babcock retired formally in 1948, but he remained active in the supervision of the ruling engine for the 508 cm Hale telescope. He died on 8 April 1968.

As a child, Babcock had been interested in electricity, radio and photography. In his first job, at the National Bureau of Standards, he investigated the problems concerning electrical resistance. His early astronomical work was in stellar photography, as part of an international research programme on the structure of the Galaxy being co-ordinated by Jacobus Kapteyn. Babcock also collaborated with Walter Adams in his spectroscopic studies.

The Sun was always a subject of Babcock's particular interest. He made an investigation of the Zeeman effect (whereby a magnetic field causes a substance's spectral lines to be split) in chromium and vanadium – important elements in the solar spectrum. Babcock's next major concern was the establishment of a standard spectrum for iron. This study was part of a large programme to determine standards for astronomical spectra.

During the 1920s much of Babcock's research dealt with the production of a revised table of wavelengths for the solar spectrum. In 1928 he published a list which included 22,000 spectral lines, and this list was extended in 1947 and again in 1948.

Babcock was also the director of a project aimed at devising an engine that could reliably and accurately rule gratings for the new telescope at Mount Wilson. The superior Babcock gratings that were eventually produced were installed in all of the Observatory's spectrographs, including that of the 508 cm telescope.

There had been considerable interest among astronomers in the measurement of the Sun's magnetic field, although no reliable information had been obtained by 1938, when Babcock turned to the problem. He had little success until 1948 when, in collaboration with his son H.W. Babcock, the solar magnetic field was measured. They used an instrument of their own design which was dubbed the "solar magnometer" and which exploited the Zeeman effect to produce a continuously changing record of the Sun's local magnetic fields. These surface fields are only weak, but they could be observed satisfactorily with the new instrument. They also studied the Sun's general magnetic field and the relationship between sunspots and local magnetic fields.

Babcock was a skilled observational astronomer with a flair for the more practical side of his subject. His contributions to solar spectroscopy and magnetism were original and thorough.

Baily, Francis (*1774–1844*), was a British astronomer who is best known for his discovery of the phenomenon called "Baily's beads".

Baily was born in Newbury, Berkshire, on 28 April 1774. He began a seven-year apprenticeship in 1788 with a firm of merchant bankers in London, but as soon as his apprenticeship ended he set out to explore unsettled parts of North America. On his return to England in 1798 he became a stockbroker, and he was very successful. Astronomy, however, took up an increasingly important part of his life. He was a founder (in 1820) and first Vice-President of the Astronomical Society of London (later the Royal Astronomical Society); he was elected a Fellow of the Royal Society in 1821. He finally gave up his job as a stockbroker in 1825 and became a full-time astronomer. He was a member of numerous scientific bodies and received several distinguished awards for his contributions to astronomy, among them two gold medals from the Royal Astronomical Society. He died in London on 30 August 1844.

Baily began to publish his astronomical observations in 1811. He was the author of an accurate revised star catalogue in which he plotted the positions of nearly 3,000 stars. These positions were used for the determination of latitude, and for this work Baily was awarded the Astronomical Society's Gold Medal in 1827.

In 1836, on 15 May, Baily observed a total eclipse of the Sun from Scotland. He noticed that immediately before the Sun completely disappeared behind the Moon (and also just as it began to emerge from behind the Moon) light from the Sun appeared as a discontinuous line of brilliant spots. These "spots" have been named "Baily's beads" and are caused by sunlight showing through between the mountains on the Moon's horizon as it moves across the Sun's disc. Baily travelled to Italy in 1842 and was again able to see his "beads" during a solar eclipse.

Baily did other research, including a redetermination of the mean density of the Earth using the methods of Henry Cavendish. He also measured the Earth's elliptical shape. He earned his second gold medal from the Astronomical Society for these studies.

Baily's sighting was not the first of the "bead" phenomenon, but his description of it and of the rest of the 1836 eclipse was so exciting that it sparked greatly renewed interest in eclipses, which persists to this day.

Barnard, Edward Emerson (*1857–1923*), was an American observational astronomer whose keen vision and painstaking thoroughness made him an almost legendary figure.

Barnard was born in Nashville, Tennessee, on 16 December 1857. His family was poor and by the time he was nine years old Barnard had begun to work as an assistant in a photographic studio. The techniques he learned were to be invaluable in his later career. Barnard's fascination with astronomy led him to take a job in the observatory at Vanderbilt University. He took some courses but spent most of his time using the telescopes.

In 1877 Barnard went to California in order to work at the Lick Observatory when it opened in 1888. He was awarded a DSc from Vanderbilt in 1893, although he had never formally graduated. In 1895 he took up the chair of Practical Astronomy at the University of Chicago and became Astronomer at the Yerkes Observatory. He participated in the expedition to Sumatra to observe the solar eclipse of 1901.

Barnard's many discoveries brought him worldwide respect and many honours. He received awards from the most prestigious scientific organizations, and was elected to their membership. He died in Williams Bay, Wisconsin, on 6 February 1923.

Barnard's early astronomical studies were made with a 12.7 cm telescope which he pur-

chased in 1878. It was for the discovery of comets that Barnard first began to establish a reputation. He discovered his first comet on 5 May 1881 and by 1892 he had found 16. He also investigated the surface features of Jupiter, the *gegenschein* (a faint patch of light visible only at certain times of the year and whose nature is still not certain), nebulae and other celestial bodies.

His most dramatic discovery came on 9 September 1892 when, by blocking out the glow of the parent planet, Barnard discovered the fifth satellite of Jupiter and the first to be found since the four Galilean satellites. This was the last satellite to be discovered without the aid of photography. The fifth moon orbits inside all the others, which now number more than 20.

Barnard's later discoveries included the realization that the apparent voids in the Milky Way are in fact dark nebulae of dust and gas and the sighting in 1916 of the so-called "Barnard's Runaway Star", which has a proper motion of 10 seconds of arc per year (faster than any star known until 1968).

Although Barnard's lack of mathematical flair prevented him from making profound contributions to theoretical advances in astronomy, he was one of the most eminent observational astronomers of his time.

Beg, Ulugh (*1394–1449*), was a title meaning "great prince" and the name by which Muhammad Taragay, mathematician and astronomer, came to be known in later life.

Beg was born at Sulaniyya in Central Asia (Persia) on 22 March 1394 and was brought up at the court of his grandfather Timur (Tamarlane). At the age of 15 Ulugh Beg became ruler of the city of Samarkand and the province of Maverannakhr. Although his grandfather was interested in conquest, Ulugh Beg's leanings were towards science and, in particular, astronomy. In 1420 he founded an institution of higher learning, or "madrasa", in Samarkand. It specialized in astronomy and higher mathematics. Four years later he built a three-storey observatory and a "Fakhrī" sextant of sufficiently large dimensions to enable very accurate observations to be made. The institution and observatory were advanced for the time and consequently the work of Ulugh Beg and his hand-picked team of scientists held good for many centuries. In 1447 he succeeded his father, Shahrukh, to the Timurid throne, but he met a tragic and violent death when he was murdered at the instigation of his own son on 27 October 1449.

The observatory was reduced to ruins by the beginning of the sixteenth century and its precise location remained unknown until 1908, when the archeologist V.L. Vyatkin found its remains. The main instrument proved to be the Fakhrī sextant, the arc of which was placed in a trench about 2 m wide. The trench itself was dug into a hillside along the line of the meridian. One of the preserved artefacts is a piece of the arc consisting of two walls faced with marble and 51 cm apart. Other instruments used at the observatory included an armillary sphere, a triquet-ram and a "shamila", an instrument serving as astrolabe and quadrant.

The Fakhrī sextant was used mainly for determining the basic constants of astronomy by observing the Sun and, in particular, the Moon and planets. Since the radius of the arc was 40.4 m, the divisions of the arc were correspondingly large, allowing for very accurate measurements to be made. By observing the altitude of the Sun at noon every day, Ulugh Beg was able to deduce the Sun's meridianal height, its distance from the zenith and the inclination of the ecliptic. The value that he obtained for the inclination of the ecliptic differs by only 32 seconds from the true value for his time.

The *Zij* of Ulugh Beg and his school is a large work that was originally written in the Tadzhik language. It consists of a theoretical section and the results of observations made at the Samarkand Observatory. Included in the work are tables of calendar calculations, of trigonometry, and of the positions of planets, as well as a star catalogue.

Ulugh Beg and his collaborator Alkashi took great pains to determine accurately the sine of 1° by two independent methods. The tables give the values of sines and tangents for every minute to 45°, and for every 5 minutes between 45° and 90°. Cotangents are given for every degree. The values in the tables differ from the true values by a maximum of only one digit in the ninth decimal place.

The great accuracy to which the school worked is also evident in the values obtained for the movements of the planets Saturn, Jupiter, Mars, Venus and Mercury. The differences between Beg's data and that of modern times are amazingly small, the discrepancies being within the limits of 2 to 5 seconds for the first four and 10 seconds at the most for Mercury. The somewhat larger discrepancy for the latter is attributable to Mercury's being smaller and having a higher orbital velocity and a greater eccentricity of orbit, which makes it more difficult to observe with the naked eye.

The catalogue of stars in the *Zij* contains 1,012 stars and includes 992 fixed stars whose positions Beg re-determined with unusual precision. This was the first star catalogue to be produced since

that of al-Sufi, nearly five centuries earlier. Its great value lies in the fact that it was original, even though Beg was influenced by Ptolemy in the co-ordinates he used.

An expedition headed by T.N. Kari-Niazov discovered the tomb of Ulugh Beg in Samarkand in 1941. It was found that Ulugh Beg had been laid to rest fully clothed - a sign that, according to the Islamic religion, Ulugh Beg had been deemed a martyr, therefore a testament to his great contribution to the advancement of science, particularly astronomy.

Bell Burnell, Susan Jocelyn (*1943-*), is a British astronomer who discovered pulsating radio stars - pulsars - an important astronomical discovery of the 1960s.

Jocelyn Bell Burnell was born in Belfast on 15 July 1943. The Armagh Observatory, of which her father was architect, was sited near her home and the staff there were particularly helpful and offered encouragement when they learned of her early interest in astronomy. From 1956 to 1961 she attended the Mount School in York. She then went to the University of Glasgow, receiving her BSc degree in 1965. In the summer of 1965 she began to work for her PhD under the supervision of Anthony Hewish at the University of Cambridge. It was during the course of this work that the discovery of pulsars was made. Having completed her doctorate at Cambridge, she went on to work in gamma-ray astronomy at the University of Southampton and from 1974 to 1982 she worked at the Mullard Space Science Laboratory in X-ray astronomy, mainly with the British satellite, *Aeriel V*. In 1982 she was appointed a Senior Research Fellow at the Royal Observatory, Edinburgh, and since then she has been working on infrared astronomy, optical astronomy and millimetre wave astronomy.

Jocelyn Bell spent her first two years in Cambridge building a radio telescope that was specially designed to track quasars - her PhD research topic. The telescope that she and her team built had the ability to record rapid variations in signals. It was also nearly 2 ha (4½ acres) in area, equivalent to a dish of 150 m (500 feet) in diameter, making it an extremely sensitive instrument. The sky survey began when the telescope was finally completed in 1967 and Bell was given the task of analysing the signals received. One day, while scanning the charts of recorded signals, she noticed a rather unusual radio source that had occurred during the night and been picked up in a part of the sky that was opposite in direction to the Sun. This was curious because strong variations in the signals from quasars are caused by solar wind and are usually weak during the night. At first she thought that the signal might be due to a local interference, but after a month of further observations it became clear that the position of the peculiar signals remained fixed with respect to the stars, indicating that it was neither terrestrial nor solar in origin. A more detailed examination of the signal showed that it was in fact composed of a rapid set of pulses that occurred precisely every 1.337 seconds. The pulsed signal was as regular as the most regular clock on Earth.

One attempted explanation of this curious phenomenon was that it represented an interstellar beacon sent out by extraterrestrial life on another star and so initially it was nicknamed, LGM, for Little Green Men. Within a few months of noticing this signal, however, Bell located three other similar sources. They too pulsed at an extremely regular rate but their periods varied over a few fractions of a second and they all originated from widely spaced locations in our Galaxy. Thus it seemed that a more likely explanation of the signals was that they were being emitted by a special kind of star – a pulsar.

Since the astonishing discovery was announced, other observatories have searched the heavens for new pulsars and some 300 are now known to exist, their periods ranging from hundredths of a second to four seconds. It is thought that neutron stars are responsible for the signal. These are tiny stars, only about 7 km (10 miles) in diameter, but they are incredibly massive. The whole star and its associated magnetic field are spinning at a rapid rate and the rotation produces the pulsed signal.

Bessel, Friedrich Wilhelm (*1784-1846*), was a German astronomer who in 1838 first observed stellar parallax, and who set new standards of accuracy for positional astronomy. His measurement of the positions of about 50,000 stars enabled the first accurate calculation of interstellar distances to be made. Bessel was the first person to measure the distance of a star other than the Sun. From the parallax observation of 61 Cygni he calculated the star to be about 6 light years distant, thus setting a new lower limit for the scale of the Universe.

The son of a government employee, Bessel was born on 22 July 1784 in Minden. He began work at the age of 15 as an apprentice in an exporting company. During this period in his life, an unhappy one, he dreamed of escape and decided to travel. With this end in view, he studied languages, geography and the principles of navigation: this led to an interest in mathematics and, eventually, astronomy. In 1804 he wrote a paper on Halley's Comet in which he calculated the comet's orbit from observations made over a period of about a year. He sent the paper to Heinrich Olbers who was so impressed that he arranged for its publication and obtained a post for Bessel as an assistant at Lilienthal Observatory. There Bessel worked under the early lunar observer Johann Schröter (1745-1816). After only four years the Prussian government commissioned Bessel to construct the first large German observatory at Königsberg, where in 1810 he was appointed Professor of Astronomy. Bessel's whole life was devoted first to the completion of the observatory (1813) and then its direction until his death in 1846.

Bessel's work laid the foundations of a more accurate calculation of the scale of the Universe and the sizes of stars, galaxies and clusters of galaxies than any previous method had done. In addition, he made a fundamental contribution to positional astronomy (the exact measurement of the position of celestial bodies), to celestial mechanics (the movements of stars) and to geodesy (the study of the Earth's size and shape). Bessel enlarged the resources of pure mathematics by his introduction and investigation of what are now known as Bessel functions, which he first used in 1817 to determine the motions of three bodies moving under mutual gravitation. Seven years later he developed Bessel functions more fully for the study of planetary perturbations. Bessel played a great part in the final establishment of a scale for the Universe in terms of the Solar System and terrestrial distances. These naturally depended upon accurate measurement of the distances of the nearest stars from the Earth.

Bessel's contributions to geodesy included a correction in 1826 to the seconds pendulum, the length of which is precisely calculated so that it requires exactly one second for a swing. Between 1831 and 1832 he directed geodetical measurements of meridian arcs in East Prussia, and in 1841 he deduced a value of 1/299 for the ellipticity of the Earth, or the amount of elliptical distortion by which the Earth's shape departs from a perfect sphere. He was the first to make effective use of the heliometer, an instrument designed for measuring the apparent diameter of the Sun.

Bessel also introduced corrected observations for the so-called personal equation, a statistical bias in measurement that is characteristic of the observer himself and must be eliminated before results can be considered reliable. He concerned himself greatly with accuracy, to the point of making a systematic study of the causes of instrumental errors. His own corrected observations were far more accurate than previous ones and

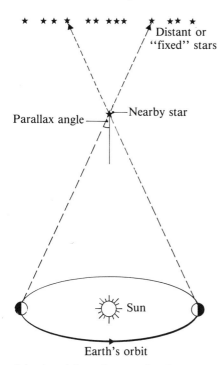

Bessel developed the technique of stellar parallax, by means of which distances to nearby stars can be calculated by observing their apparent change in position when viewed from opposite ends of a long base-line, such as a diameter of the Earth's orbit.

his methods pointed the way to a great advancement in the study of the stars.

Bessel's later achievements were possible only because he first established the real framework of the scale of the Universe through his accurate measurement of the positions and motions of the nearest stars, making corrections for errors caused by imperfections in his telescope and by disturbances in the atmosphere. Having established exact positions for about 50,000 stars, he was ready to observe exceedingly small but highly significant motions among them. Choosing 61 Cygni, a star barely visible to the naked eye, Bessel showed that the star apparently moved in an ellipse every year. He explained that this back-and-forth motion, called parallax, could only be caused by the motion of the Earth around the Sun. His calculation indicated a distance from Earth to 61 Cygni of 10.3 light-years. When Olbers received these conclusions, on his 80th birthday, he thanked Bessel who, he said, "put our ideas about the Universe on a sound basis". Bessel was honoured for this achievement by, among others, the Royal Astronomical Society.

One of Bessel's major discoveries was that two bright stars, Sirius and Procyon, execute minute motions that could be explained only by the assumption that they had invisible companions to disturb their motions. The existence of such bodies, now called Sirius B and Procyon B, was confirmed with more powerful telescopes after Bessel's death. He also contributed to the discovery of the planet Neptune. He published a paper in 1840 in which he called attention to small irregularities in the orbit of Uranus which he had observed and which were caused, he suggested, by an unknown planet beyond. Bessel's minor publications numbered more than 350 and his major ones included a multi-volume series *Astronomische Beobachtungen auf der K. Sternwarte zu Königsberg* (1815-1844).

Realizing early in his life where his potential lay, Bessel succeeded in achieving it in a profession entirely different from the one in which he had started out. Olbers said that the greatest service he himself had rendered astronomy was that he recognized and furthered Bessel's genius.

Bethe, Hans Albrecht (*1906-*   ), is a German-born American physicist and astronomer, famous for his work on the production of energy within stars. He was awarded the 1976 Nobel Prize in physics for his work on energy production on stars.

Bethe was born in Strasbourg (now in France) on 2 July 1906, the son of a university professor. He was educated at the universities of Frankfurt and Munich, and gained a PhD from the latter in 1928. From 1928 to 1929 he was an instructor in physics at the University of Frankfurt, and then at Stuttgart. He went on to lecture at the universities of Munich and Tübingen (1930-33).

With the rise to power of Adolf Hitler in Germany, Bethe moved to Britain in 1933 and spent a year at the University of Manchester. He was a Fellow of Bristol University from 1934 to 1935, becoming Assistant Professor in 1935 and Professor in 1937. He held this position until 1975, when he went to the United States to become John Wendell Anderson Professor of Physics at Cornell University. He later became a naturalized American citizen.

From 1943 to 1946 Bethe was Chief of the Theoretical Physics Division of the Los Alamos Science Laboratory in New Mexico and he has been a consultant to Los Alamos since 1947. He has been a leading voice in emphasizing the social responsibility of the scientist and since World War II he has served as part of the American delegation in Geneva during long negotiations with the Soviet Union on the control of nuclear weapons. He holds honorary doctorates from a large number of universities all over the world.

He was awarded the Morrison Prize of the New York Academy of Sciences in 1938 and 1940, the American Medal of Merit in 1946, the Draper Medal of the National Academy of Sciences in 1948, the Planck Medal in 1955 and 1961, and the Fermi Award for his part in the development and use of atomic energy. He was made a foreign member of the Royal Society in 1957. Recently he won the National Medal of Science (1976). He is a Fellow of the American Physical Society and served as its president in 1954.

When Bethe went to Great Britain in the 1930s, he worked out how high-energy particles emit radiation when they are deflected by an electromagnetic field. This work was important to cosmic ray studies. In 1938 he made his most important contribution to science when he worked out the details of how nuclear mechanisms power stars. Carl von Weizsäcker was independently reaching the same conclusions in Germany. These nuclear mechanisms were to answer the questions that had concerned Helmholtz and Kelvin 75 years earlier.

Bethe's mechanism began with the combining of a hydrogen nucleus (a proton) with a carbon nucleus. This initiates a series of reactions, at the end of which the carbon nucleus is regenerated and four hydrogen nuclei are converted into a helium nucleus. Hydrogen acts as the fuel of the star and helium is the "ash"; carbon serves as a catalyst. As stars like the Sun are mostly made up of hydrogen, there is ample fuel to last for thousands of millions of years. The amount of helium present indicates that the Sun has already existed for billions of years.

Bethe later proposed a second scheme that involves the direct combination of hydrogen nuclei to form helium in a series of steps that proceed at lower temperatures. When hydrogen is converted into helium, either directly or by means of the carbon, nearly one per cent of the mass of the hydrogen is converted into energy. Even a small amount of mass produces a great deal of energy, and the loss of mass in the Sun is enough to account for its vast and seemingly eternal radiation of energy.

With the discovery of neutron stars, Bethe turned again to astrophysical research in 1970. These stars are held by gravity at such a high density that protons fuse with electrons to produce neutrons which constitute nearly all the matter.

Although Bethe was primarily concerned with the rapidly developing subject of atomic and nuclear processes, he has also investigated the calculation of electron densities in crystals, using classical mathematical methods, and the order-disorder states in alloys. He has also concerned himself with the operational conditions in nuclear reactors and the detection of underground explosions by means of seismographic records. Apart from his contributions to atomic theory, therefore, his concern with the implications of its practical application have earned him worldwide respect within the field.

Bode, Johann Elert (*1749–1826*), was a German mathematician and astronomer who contributed greatly to the popularization of astronomy.

Bode was born in Hamburg on 19 January 1747 into a well-educated family. He taught himself astronomy and was skilled mathematically. He was publishing astronomical treatises while still in his teens, one of which remained in print for nearly a century.

In 1772 Bode joined the Berlin Academy as a mathematician, overseeing the publication of the Academy's yearbook and ensuring the accuracy of its mathematical content; he worked on all the yearbooks from 1776 to 1829. He was appointed Director of the Astronomical Observatory in 1786. He supervised the renovation of the Observatory, but he was unable to bring the standard of work there up to that of many other observatories because of the relatively simple equipment at his disposal. In 1784 he was appointed Royal Astronomer and elected to the Berlin Academy. He retired as Director of the Observatory in 1825 and died in Berlin on 23 November 1826.

Bode's early work at the Academy concerned the improvement of the accuracy of the mathematical content of the yearbook: the low standard had been depressing sales, upon which the Academy's finances largely relied. The yearbook's popularity soon increased. In addition to astronomical tables it included information about observations and scientific developments elsewhere in the world.

Bode also worked on the compilation of two atlases, the *Vorstellung der Gestirne* and the *Uranographia*, which was a massive work describing the positions of more than 17,000 stars and including for the first time some of the celestial bodies discovered by William Herschel. It was Bode who named Herschel's new planet "Uranus".

Bode is best known for the law named after him, even though he did not first state it, but merely popularized work already done by Johann Titius (1729–1796). The law, also known as the Titius-Bode rule, is a mathematical formula which approximately described the distances of all then known planets from the Sun. The series had no basis in theory, but it was accepted as an important finding at the time because of the near-mystical reverence attached to numbers and geometric progressions in descriptions of the Universe. The discovery of the planet Neptune by Urbain Le Verrier and John Couch Adams in 1846 disrupted the series and it lost its value.

Bode's main contribution to astronomy lay in the spreading of information about the subject to people from a wide range of backgrounds.

Bok, Bart (*1906-*), is a Dutch astrophysicist best known for his discovery of the small, circular dark spots in nebulae. The spots were named after him and are known as Bok's globules.

Bok was born in the Netherlands in 1906 and educated at the University of Leiden (1924-1926) and the University of Groningen (1927-1929). He went to the United States in 1929, having gained a Robert Wheeler Wilson Fellowship in Astronomy at Harvard. He gained his PhD in 1932 and remained at Harvard as Assistant Professor (1933-1939), Associate Professor (1939-1946) and Robert Wheeler Wilson Professor of Astronomy (1947-1957). In 1957 he went to Australia as Professor and Head of Department of Astronomy at the Australian National University until 1966, being also Director of the Mount Stromlo Observatory near Canberra at the same time. Bok's next appointment was as Professor of Astronomy at the University of Arizona (1966-1974). He became Professor Emeritus on his retirement.

Bok served as President of a Commission in the International Astronomical Union and President of the American Astronomical Society (1972-1974). He has been a member of a number of learned societies and has received several medals. He published *The Distribution of the Stars in Space* with Priscilla Bok in 1937 and *The Milky Way* with F.W. Wright in 1944.

Photographs had shown that the Milky Way was dotted with dark patches or nebulae. Bok also discovered small, circular dark spots, which were best observed against a bright background. Measurements of their dimensions and opacity suggested that their masses were similar to that of the Sun. Bok suggested that the globules were clouds of gas in the process of condensation and that stars might be in the early stages of formation there. His work has thus broadened our understanding of the nature of stellar birthplaces.

Boksenberg, Alexander (*1936-*), is an astronomer who devised a new kind of light-detecting system that can be attached to telescopes and so vastly improve their optical powers. His image photon counting system (IPCS) has revolutionized observational astronomy, enabling Boksenberg and others to study distant quasars, which

may help towards a deeper understanding of the early phases and nature of the Universe.

Boksenberg was born on 18 March 1936, the elder of two sons. He attended the Stationers' Company's School in London and was encouraged by his parents, who owned a shop, to study for a place at university. He gained a BSc in physics from London University and in 1957 began research at University College, London, into the physics of atomic collisions, for which he was awarded his PhD in 1961. Boksenberg then joined a research group at University College which was studying the ultraviolet spectra of stars using rocket- and satellite-borne instruments. It was during this period that he became interested in applying his knowledge of physics to astronomy. He also saw the need to improve the instrumentation being carried aboard space vehicles and began to specialize in image-detecting systems. He became a Lecturer in Physics in 1965, and in 1968 his innovative work on detectors led to his involvement in the British design team producing the instrumentation for the Anglo-Australian 4 m telescope then being constructed at Sydney Springs in New South Wales, Australia. He devised a fundamentally new approach to optical detection in astronomy with his image photon counting system.

In 1969 Boksenberg set up his own research group at University College to work on two main topics: optical astronomy, mainly using IPCSs he built for the Anglo-Australian telescope and for the 5 m Hale telescope at Mount Palomar, California; and ultraviolet astronomy, using instrumentation he designed for use on high-altitude balloon-borne platforms and on satellites, particularly the International Ultraviolet Explorer (IUE) satellite observatory. In 1975 he was promoted to Reader in Physics, a year later he was awarded the first Senior Fellowship of the United Kingdom Science Research Council, and in 1978 became Professor of Physics and a Fellow of the Royal Society. In 1981 he was appointed Director of the Royal Greenwich Observatory. In addition to holding this post, he is an associate of the California Institute of Technology and a Visiting Professor of Sussex University and University College, London. In 1982 he was awarded an Honorary Doctorate by the Paris Observatory.

During his time at University College, Boksenberg's work in ultraviolet astronomy using balloons yielded the first results for the important parameters electron density and metal abundance in the local interstellar medium. For the European observatory satellite TD-1A, launched in 1972, he conceived a simple means of using the sky-scanning action of the satellite to produce a passive spectrum-scanning of the main ultraviolet sky-survey instrument, which greatly increased the scientific value of the project. He also designed and worked on a new ultraviolet television detector system for the International Ultraviolet Explorer satellite launched in 1978, and led the pioneering work on the complex Sun-baffle systems for TD-1A and IUE to enable the telescopes to observe faint astronomical objects in full orbital sunlight. Both satellites were widely used internationally and contributed greatly to the advancement of astronomy. Boksenberg's own main contribution was to a study of galactic haloes and the nuclei of active galaxies and quasars using the IUE.

Boksenberg's development of the IPCS sprang from his considerations of the workings of the human eye, which operates not only as an optical device but also relies on the correcting effect of the processing and memory functions of the retina and the brain. Rather than recording light with a photographic emulsion, he saw the potential of literally detecting the locations of the individual photons of light collected by a telescope from the faint astronomical object being studied, and building up the required image in a computer memory. By using an image intensifier coupled to a television camera he detected and amplified photons by a factor of 10^7. He then treated the signals in a special electronic processor, which passed the photon locations to a computer with a large digital memory, both to store the accumulating image and to present the incoming results as an instantaneous picture – a great advantage to an astronomer who would otherwise have to wait for a photographic image to form and be processed. The picture on the screen appears as an accumulating series of dots, each dot representing a photon which is counted, analysed and stored by the computer.

By 1973 Boksenberg's IPCS was ready to be tested and in the autumn of that year he went to Mount Palomar and attached it to the spectrograph at the Coudé focus of the largest telescope in the world at that time – the 5 m Hale telescope. He used it in collaboration with Wallace Sargent of the California Institute of Technology to observe absorption lines in the spectra of quasars. Within 30 minutes they saw spectra that would normally take three nights or more of exposure time to reveal. Sargent, an established scientist and astronomer, immediately recognized the enormous validity and potential of Boksenberg's photon detector, and on this basis his technique was generally accepted and applied to all modern telescopes, including the 2.4 m Space Telescope.

Boksenberg, being interested in the overall nature of the Universe, continued to collaborate with Sargent, mainly using the 5 m Hale telescope and the IPCS in the study of the most distant quasars. The radiation from these has taken billions of years to reach us and so by studying their light, emitted way back in time, Boksenberg and his colleague use quasars to elucidate the early nature of the Universe. Quasars also provide clues to the story of galactic evolution because they seem to be intimately connected with the central cores of galaxies.

Since 1973 Boksenberg and Sargent have been particularly interested in studying the absorption lines in the spectra of quasars, which they discovered are not a manifestation of the quasar itself but a reflection of the state of the Universe – galaxies and intergalactic gas – that exists between the quasar and the Earth. They can thus provide direct information on the nature and evolution of the Universe. As Director of the Royal Greenwich Observatory Boksenberg is responsible for building a major new British observatory on Las Palmas in the Canary Islands. He is also taking part in plans to build the next generation of telescope. With the development of idealized light-detecting systems, such as the IPCS, using electronic devices to receive and record photons, optical astronomy has experienced a major resurgence and there is a recognized need to increase telescope aperture beyond the few metres currently available at each of the world's major observatories. The most favourable design of future ground-based optical telescopes, in terms of minimal cost and most efficient observational powers, seems to be the "multi-mirror" candidate – a telescope composed of separate mirrors that combine to produce a light-collecting area that can be equivalent to a single mirror of about 20 m in diameter.

Bond, George Phillips (*1825-1865*), was an American astronomer whose best work was on the development of astronomical photography as an important research tool. His research was carried out exclusively at the observatory founded by his father, William Cranch Bond.

Bond was born in Dorchester, Massachusetts, on 20 May 1825. He obtained a BA at Harvard and immediately began to work at the Harvard College Observatory. He served first as Assistant Astronomer to his father and then, upon the latter's death, as Director of the Observatory. In 1865, Bond became the first citizen of the United States to be awarded the Gold Medal of the Royal Astronomical Society of London, for his beautifully produced text on Donati's Comet. He died in Cambridge, Massachusetts, on 2 February 1865.

The discovery of Hyperion (Saturn's eighth satellite) and the Crêpe Ring around Saturn were

Bond's first major findings with his father. Since it was possible to see stars through the Crêpe Ring (a dim ring inside the two bright rings), Bond concluded that the rings were liquid, not solid, as most astronomers believed at the time.

During the late 1840s the Bonds worked on developing photographic techniques for astronomy. Since taking pictures even in full daylight often required long exposures in those days, photography at night was an arduous process indeed. Poor-quality daguerrotypes of the Moon had been taken in the early 1840s, but by 1850 the Bonds were able to take pictures of impressive quality. Improved techniques enabled Bond and Fred Whipple to take a picture of Vega, the first star to be photographed, in 1850. In 1857 Bond also became the first man to photograph a double star, Mizar, with the aid of wet collodion plates. Bond suggested that a star's magnitude could be quantitatively determined by measuring the size of the image it made. A bright star would affect a greater area of silver grains.

Bond also made numerous studies of comets. He discovered 11 new comets and made calculations on the factors affecting their orbits. He is, however, best remembered for his work on photography and, indeed, is often credited as the father of techniques of astronomical photography.

Bond, William Cranch (*1789–1858*), was an American astronomer who, with his son, George Phillips Bond, established the Harvard College Observatory as a centre of astronomical research.

Bond was born into a poor family in Falmouth, Maine, on 9 September 1789. He was needed in the family business and he received little formal education. He worked in the shop as a watchmaker and displayed remarkable manual dexterity and mechanical ingenuity. The solar eclipse of 1806 was the stimulus that introduced him to the study of astronomy, which became an ever more absorbing hobby. Bond was one of the independent observers who discovered the comet of 1811. He was commissioned by Harvard College to investigate the equipment at observatories in England during a trip he made there in 1815.

In the absence of an observatory in the vicinity of his home, Bond had converted one of the rooms in his house. It became the best private observatory of his day and in 1839 Harvard invited him to move it into their premises (although he was not offered any stipend for doing so). Bond thus became the first Director of the Harvard College Observatory, a post he held until his death. He was awarded the formal title of Observer, and given an honorary MA in 1842.

Public interest in astronomy was aroused by the comet of 1843 and the Observatory received

sufficient funding to equip itself with a 38 cm refracting telescope. Bond continued to make observations and to design equipment until his death in Cambridge, Massachusetts, on 29 January 1859.

In addition to his early observations of comets and other celestial bodies, Bond established an international reputation for his work on chronometers. He worked not only on their design, but also on fixing the rate of the mechanisms of chronometers used, for example, in navigation.

From the Observatory he also studied the Solar System, sunspots and the nebulae in the constellations of Orion and Andromeda. It is difficult to distinguish the contributions made by Bond from those of his son during the later years of the career of Bond senior. They collaborated on the development of photographic techniques for the purposes of astronomy, succeeding in obtaining superior photographs of the Moon (exhibited in London in 1851 to enthusiastic audiences) and took the first photographs of stars.

The two Bonds discovered Hyperion (the eighth satellite of Saturn) in 1848 and the Crêpe Ring around Saturn in 1850. This is the faint ring inside the two bright rings of Saturn. Their observation that stars could be seen through the Crêpe Ring led to their conclusion that the rings of Saturn are not solid. The Crêpe Ring had probably been observed already by other astronomers, including H. Kater in 1825 and Frederich Struve in 1826. William Lassell, who missed being credited for the discovery of Hyperion by finding it a few days after the Bonds, also observed the Crêpe Ring shortly after it was described by them.

William Cranch Bond's chief contributions to astronomy were his careful observations and innovative designs, and his founding of an eminent research centre.

Bondi, Hermann (*1919–*), is an Austrian-born scientist who was trained as a mathematician, but who went on to make important contributions to many disciplines both as a research scientist and as an enthusiastic administrator. He is best known in astronomy for his development, with Thomas Gold (1920–) and Fred Hoyle (1915–), of the Steady State theory concerning the origin of the Universe.

Bondi was born on 1 November 1919 in Vienna. At home he developed an early interest in mathematics. He taught himself the rudiments of calculus and theoretical physics and, after briefly meeting Arthur Eddington who was visiting Vienna, he decided to go to Cambridge University to study mathematics. He was recognized as a mathematician of considerable talent and was awarded an exhibition in his first year.

He earned a BA in 1940, despite being caught up in the General Order of May 1940 that required "enemy aliens" resident in the United Kingdom to be interned for security reasons. While in internment Bondi met Thomas Gold; they were to become close friends and scientific associates.

Bondi returned to Cambridge in 1941 to become a research student. He began to do naval radar work for the British Admiralty in 1942 and through this work he met Fred Hoyle. Gold soon joined them and, inspired by Hoyle, who was already an established astrophysicist, the three discussed cosmology and related subjects in their spare time. This collaboration continued after the war.

Trinity College elected Bondi to a Fellowship in 1943 on the basis of his first astrophysical research. He acquired British citizenship in 1947 and became an assistant lecturer (1945-1948) and University Lecturer (1943-1954). He was Visiting Professor to Cornell University in 1951 and he went to Harvard in 1953. After a tour of American observatories, he returned to England to take up the Chair of Applied Mathematics at King's College, London. He was elected Fellow of the Royal Society in 1959.

He has held advisory posts in the Ministry of Defence, in particular on the National Space Committee, the European Space Research Organization, the Department of Energy, and the Natural Environment Research Council. Bondi is the author of a number of books on cosmology and allied subjects. His scientific contributions have been recognized by his election to prominent scientific organizations and his public service by honours such as a knighthood (1973).

Bondi is perhaps best known for his proposal, together with Gold and Hoyle, of the Steady State theory. This is a cosmological model that explains the expansion of the Universe not as a consequence of a singularity (as proposed by the Big-Bang model), but as a feature of the Universe as it has always been and always will be. The model requires that matter be continually created – albeit at a rate of only 1 gram per cubic decimetre per 10^{36} years – in order to keep the density of matter in the Universe constant. The Steady State model was felt not only to resolve an apparent discrepancy between the age of the Universe and of our Earth, but also to be a simpler theory than the Big-Bang model. The Steady State theory was not in any way contradicted by facts then available.

The model created something of a sensation and stimulated much debate for, while its ideas were revolutionary, it was fully compatible with existing knowledge. The orthodox model of the day placed the origin of all elements in an early superhot stage of the Universe. Hoyle stated the now universally accepted theory of the origin of the elements in observed types of stars. This was the greatest triumph of the Steady State theory, but evidence against the theory in general soon began to accumulate. In 1955 came evidence that the Universe had once been denser than it is today. In 1965 came the identification of a universal "background" radiation that was readily accounted for as a remainder of an early hot state of the universe. A further severe difficulty for the Steady State theory is that the universe seems to contain more helium than the theory predicts. Thus, today few scientists regard the Steady State theory as a serious competitor to the Big-Bang theory of the origin of the Universe.

Bondi's other contributions have been to the study of stellar structure, relativity and gravitational waves. He demonstrated that gravitational waves are compatible with and are indeed a necessary consequence of the general theory of relativity. He was also able to describe the likely characteristics and physical properties of gravitational waves.

Since the 1960s, Bondi has been primarily concerned with more administrative duties. He has organized the rebuilding of King's College and the establishment of the Anglo-Australian telescope. He was also an adviser on the Thames Barrage project. Bondi is a versatile and talented scientist, whose contributions are notable for their originality, insight and scope.

Bowen, Ira S. (*1898-1973*), was an American astrophysicist who is best known for his study of the spectra of planetary nebulae. He showed that strong green lines in such spectra are due to ionized oxygen and nitrogen under extreme conditions not found on Earth.

Bowen was born in New York State in 1898 and graduated from Oberlin College in 1919. He was an assistant in the physics department at the University of Chicago from 1919 to 1921, when he joined the California Institute of Technology. He gained his doctorate in 1926 and subsequently held the posts of Instructor (1921-1926), Assistant Professor (1926-1928), Associate Professor (1928-1930) and Professor (1931-1945). From 1946 to 1964 he was Director of the Mount Wilson and Palomar observatories. Bowen was a member of a number of learned societies and was awarded several medals. He was elected to the National Academy of Sciences in 1936.

In the 1860s William Huggins noticed strong green lines in the spectra of planetary nebulae. These were attributed either to complex atomic spectra or to an element previously unknown and given the name "nebulium".

With a greater understanding of the way in which spectral lines occur, astronomers began to doubt if nebulium really existed. They suspected that the spectral lines might be produced by a gas of extremely low density.

A spectral line is produced when an electron in an atom transfers itself from one energy level to another. Spectral analysis can determine the energy levels between which the electrons are moving, since strong lines are produced where it takes place easily ("permitted" transitions) and weak lines where it takes place with difficulty ("forbidden" transitions).

Bowen suggested that the strong green lines in the spectra of planetary nebulae might be caused not by permitted transitions in the hypothetical nebulium, but by forbidden transitions in known elements under conditions not produced in the laboratory. He calculated that the wavelengths of three of the spectral lines of nebulium were the same as those that would be produced from transitions within the lowest energy levels of doubly ionized oxygen, $O(III)$. He compared his calculated wavelengths of forbidden transitions with those observed in the spectra of the nebulae and found that the strongest lines were produced by forbidden transitions of singly and doubly ionized oxygen, $O(II)$ and $O(III)$, and singly ionized nitrogen, $N(II)$.

In 1938 Bowen constructed an ingenious piece of apparatus known as the image slicer for use with the slit spectrograph. His unmasking of nebulium led to the identification of other puzzling spectral lines, particularly those associated with the corona of the Sun, previously attributed to another hypothetical element "coronium". Research into the chemical composition and physical properties of the Sun and other celestial bodies was stimulated by Bowen's work.

Bradley, James (*1693-1762*), was an English astronomer of great perception and practical skill. He was the third Astronomer Royal and the discoverer of nutation and the aberration of light, both essential steps towards modern research into positional astronomy.

Bradley was born in Sherborne, Dorset in March 1693. He entered Balliol College, Oxford, in 1711 and studied theology. He gained a BA in 1714, but he had by this time developed a fascination for astronomy through contact with his uncle, J. Pound, who was an amateur astronomer and a friend of Edmond Halley. Bradley pursued his interest in astronomy after graduating and was made Fellow of the Royal Society in 1718. In 1719 he became a vicar in Bridstow, soon after was appointed chaplain to the Bishop of Hert-

ford. He resigned his position in 1721 to become Savilian Professor of Astronomy at Oxford.

From then on Bradley devoted his whole career to astronomy. He lectured at the University until shortly before his death and pursued an active research programme. His most brilliant work was done during the 1720s, but he published material of exceptionally high standard throughout his life. In 1742, upon Halley's death, Bradley was appointed Astronomer Royal. In that position, he sought to modernize and re-equip the observatory at Greenwich, and he embarked upon an extensive programme of stellar observation. He was awarded the Copley Medal of the Royal Society in 1748 and served on the Society's Council from 1752 until 1762. He was a member of scientific academies in several European countries.

Bradley was unusually reluctant to publish his results until he had confirmed his ideas over periods of observation that sometimes exceeded 20 years. His catalogue of more than 60,000 observations made during the last years of his career was eventually published in two volumes in 1798 and 1805. He died in Chalford, Gloucestershire, on 13 July 1762.

Bradley's earliest astronomical observations were concerned with the determination of stellar parallax. Such measurement was the goal of many astronomers of his day because it would confirm Copernicus' hypothesis that the Earth moved around the Sun. Copernicus himself (echoing Aristarchus 1,800 years before him) had stated that this parallax could not be detected because even the distance from one end of the Earth's orbit to the other was negligible compared with the enormous distance of the stars themselves. Nevertheless, Bradley and his contemporaries sought to observe parallactic displacement of the nearer stars compared to those at greater distances.

Bradley worked in 1725-26 with S. Molyneux at the latter's private observatory in Kew. They chose to observe Gamma Draconis, and found that within a few days there did seem to be a displacement of the star. However, the displacement was not only too large, but was in a different direction from that which would have been expected from parallactic displacement. Bradley studied this displacement of Gamma Draconis and other stars for more than a year and observed that this was the general effect. It took him some time to realize that the displacement was simply a consequence of observing a stationary object from a moving one, namely the Earth. The telescope needed to be tilted slightly in order to compensate for the movement of the Earth on its orbit around the Sun.

Bradley called this effect the "aberration" of

light, and he measured its angle to be between 20 and 20.5 seconds (the modern value being 20.47 seconds). From the size of this angle Bradley was able to obtain an independent determination of the velocity of light (308,300 km/sec compared with the modern value of 299,792 km/sec), confirming Ole Römer's work of 1769. A conclusion of more immediate significance, however, was that the Copernican concept of a moving Earth had been confirmed. Bradley had failed to find the proof through measuring parallactic displacement, but he had proved it by means of aberration.

This discovery allowed Bradley to produce more accurate tables of stellar positions, but he found that even when he considered the effect of aberration his observations on the distances of stars were still variable. He studied the distribution of these variations and deduced that they were caused by the oscillation of the Earth's axis, which in turn was caused by the gravitational interaction between the Moon and the Earth's equatorial bulge, so that the orbit of the Moon was sometimes above the ecliptic and sometimes below it. Bradley named this oscillation "nutation", and he studied it during the entire period of the revolution of the nodes of the lunar orbit (18.6 years) from 1727 to 1748. At the end of this period the positions of the stars were the same as when he started.

Perhaps as a result of his knowledge of Römer's work on the determination of the speed of light using the Jovian satellites, Bradley then turned his attention to a study of Jupiter. He measured its diameter and studied eclipses of its satellites.

The fruits of Bradley's observations were more accurate than those of his predecessors because of his discovery of the effects of aberration and nutation. Bradley was a skilful astronomer with unusual talents in both the practical and theoretical aspects of the subject.

Brahe, Tycho (*1546–1601*), sometimes known by his first name only, was a Danish astronomer who is most noted for his remarkably accurate measurements of the positions of stars and the movements of the planets.

Tycho was born of aristocratic parents in Knudstrup in 1546. He was brought up by his paternal uncle, from whom he learnt Latin, and in early life he studied law and philosophy. A political career was planned for him, but in 1560 Tycho observed a solar eclipse and he was so fascinated by what he saw that he spent the rest of his life studying mathematics and astronomy.

Being of a noble family, Tycho did not need a university degree to establish himself in a profession, but he attended the University of Copen-

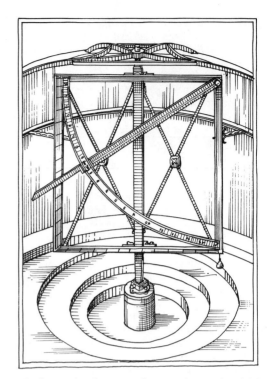

Brahe used a large quadrant with a radius of 2 metres to make accurate measurements of star positions.

hagen and studied ethics, music, natural sciences, philosophy and mathematics. From the beginning of his astronomical career he made a series of significant observations. Having seen the eclipse, he obtained a copy of Stadius' *Ephemerides*, which was based on the Copernican system. Observing a close approach of Jupiter and Saturn in 1563, Tycho noticed that it occurred a month earlier than predicted. He set about the preparation of his own tables. In 1564 he began observing with a radius, or cross-staff consisting of an arm along which could slide the centre of a crosspiece of half its length. Both arms were graduated and there was a fixed sight at the end of the larger arm which was held near the eye. To measure the angular distance between two objects, Tycho set the shorter arm at any gradation of the longer arm and moved a sight along the shorter arm until he saw the two objects through it and a sight at the centre of the transversal arm. The required angle was then obtained from the gradations and a table of tangents.

When his uncle died in 1565, Tycho travelled and studied at Wittenburg and Rostock, where he graduated from the university in 1566. After making a number of observations there, he moved to Basel before entering the intellectual life of Augsburg in 1569. Having returned home because of his father's ill-health, Tycho noticed one night in November 1572 a star in the constellation of Cassiopeia that was shining more brightly than all the others and which had not been there before. With a special sextant of his own making, Tycho observed the star until March 1574, when it ceased to be visible. His records of its variations in colour and magnitude identify it as a supernova.

In 1576 King Frederick II offered Tycho the island of Hven for the construction of an observatory. This was the first of its kind in history. Tycho's reputation grew and scholars from throughout Europe visited him.

Having observed a great comet in 1577, Tycho refuted Aristotle's theory of comets. He concluded that certain celestial bodies were supralunar, having no parallax and remaining stationary like fixed stars. Many other scientists had abandoned the Aristotelian theory in favour of the belief that something new could be created in the heavens and not necessarily out of the substances of the Earth. Tycho claimed that Aristotle's "proof" had been based on meditation, not mathematical observation or demonstration. Tycho's main objective became to determine the comet's distance from the Earth. He was also concerned with its physical appearance – colour, magnitude and the direction of the tail.

He came to the conclusion that the comet's orbit must be elongated, a controversial suggestion indeed since it meant that the comet must have passed through the various planetary spheres, and it could not do that unless the planetary spheres did not exist. This possibility went against Tycho's most cherished beliefs. He could not abandon the ideas of his Greek predecessors, although he was the last great astronomer to reject the heliocentric theory of Copernicus. He tried to compromise, suggesting that, with the exception of the Earth, all the planets revolved around the Sun.

He prepared tables of the motion of the Sun and determined the length of a year to within less than a second, making calendar reform inevitable. In 1582 ten days were dropped, the Julian year being longer than the true year. To prevent further accumulations, the Gregorian calendar was adopted thereafter.

Tycho lost his patronage on the death of the King and he left for Germany in 1597. He settled in Prague at the invitation of the Emperor and found a new assistant, Johannes Kepler. Kepler loyally accepted and propounded Tycho's tables and data and continued his work with what were to be results of great importance. Many of Tycho's great contributions to science live on and

he is remembered in particular for his correction for the better of almost every important astronomical measurement.

Brown, Ernest William (*1866–1938*), was a British mathematician with a particular interest in celestial mechanics and lunar theory.

Brown was born in Hull on 29 November 1866. He was awarded a scholarship to Christ's College, Cambridge, where he was introduced to problems in lunar theory by George Darwin (1845-1912). Brown gained a BA in 1887, and from 1889 until 1895 he held a fellowship at Christ's, although in 1891 he went to the United States to teach mathematics at Haverford College in Pennsylvania. He was Professor of Mathematics at Haverford (1893-1907) and then at Yale University until his retirement as Professor Emeritus in 1932.

Brown's work on the motions of the Moon earned him an international reputation. He received numerous honorary degrees and awards from scientific organizations such as the National Academy of Sciences and the Royal Astronomical Society. He was an active participant within the professional societies of which he was a member. Brown died in New Haven, Connecticut, on 22 September 1938.

The effect of gravity on the motions of the planets and smaller members of the Solar System was the major research interest of Brown's career. His work first focused on lunar motion, and he produced extremely accurate tables of the Moon's movements. Unable to account for the variation in the Moon's mean longitude, he proposed that the observed fluctuations arose as a consequence of a variable rate in the rotation of the Earth.

Brown was also interested in the asteroid belt. It had been proposed that asteroids might at one time have been part of one planet. Some astronomers attempted to compute the possible orbit of such a parent planet on the basis of the distribution of the asteroids, but Brown was highly critical of this approach.

One of his concerns during the later years of his career was the calculation of the gravitational effect exerted by the planet Pluto on the orbits of its nearest neighbours, Uranus and Neptune.

Brown's work on gravity did much to increase our understanding of the relationship of members of the Solar System.

Burbidge, Geoffrey (*1925–*), and **Burbidge, Eleanor Margaret** (*1922–*), are a British husband-and-wife team of astrophysicists distinguished for their work, chiefly in the United States, on nucleosynthesis – the creation of elements in space – and on quasars and galaxies.

Geoffrey Burbidge studied physics at Bristol University (graduating in 1946), then combined lecturing and research for his PhD at University College, London, before going to the United States as Agassiz Fellow at Harvard University. From 1952 to 1953 he was a Research Fellow at the University of Chicago; he then returned to England as a Research Fellow at the Cavendish Laboratories, Cambridge. In 1955 he went back to the United States as Carnegie Fellow at the Mount Wilson and Palomar Universities, Caltech and in 1957 he joined the Department of Astronomy, University of Chicago, as Assistant Professor. Appointments followed at the University of California, San Diego, as Associate Professor (1962–1963) and Professor of Physics (1963–1978). He is at present Director of the Kitt Peak National Observatory, Arizona.

Margaret Burbidge studied at University College, London, and gained her PhD for research at the University of London Observatory, where in 1948 she became Assistant Director and then Acting Director (1950–1951). Travelling to the United States, she held a Fellowship from the International Astronomical Union at the Yerkes Observatory, University of Chicago. From 1955 to 1957, she was a Research Fellow at the California Institute of Technology. Her next appointment was at the Yerkes Observatory again, firstly as Shirley Farr Fellow and later, in 1959, as Associate Professor. Three years later she moved to the University of California as Research Astronomer before coming Professor (in 1964), being granted leave of absence to be Director of the Royal Greenwich Observatory (1972–1973).

Together the Burbidges published *Quasi-Stellar Objects* in 1967. Their work in nucleosynthesis followed the discovery of the spectral lines of the unstable element technetium in red giant stars by Paul Merrill (1889–1961) in 1952. Because technetium is too unstable to have existed for as long as the stars themselves, the discovery provided the first evidence for the actual creation of elements. The paper published by the Burbidges, William Fowler (1911–   ), and Fred Hoyle (1915–   ) in 1957 began with the premise that at first stars consisted mainly of hydrogen and that most of the stars now visible are in the process of producing helium from hydrogen and releasing energy as starlight. They then suggested that as stars age some of their helium is "burned" to form other elements, such as carbon and oxygen. The carbon and oxygen may trap hydrogen nuclei (protons) to form more complex nuclei, or may trap helium nuclei (alpha-particles) to produce magnesium, silicon, sulphur, argon and calcium. The Burbidges and their colleagues distinguished five additional processes; one is the e-process, in which elements such as iron, nickel, chromium and cobalt are formed at a high temperature. Up to this point, the "iron peak", the build-up results in energy being released. Beyond the iron peak more energy is required to create heavier elements. In a supernova, a massive star exploding, this energy is available. Prior to the supernova, the star has medium weight elements.

It becomes unstable and nuclei trap neutrons so rapidly (the r-process), that newly formed nuclei do not have time to shed electrons. There is subsequent explosion and heavier elements such as selenium, bromine, krypton, tellurium, iodine, xenon, osmium, iridium, platinum, gold, uranium and a number of unfamiliar elements are formed. From theoretical considerations, the collaborators calculated the proportions of the different heavy elements which would be most likely to be formed in a supernova. Observations indicate that the distribution of heavy elements could be explained by their production in supernovae. They believe a slow process (s-process) in red giants also builds up heavy elements.

The Burbidges, also researched into quasars, objects originally detected by their strong radio emissions and believed to be travelling away from the Earth at immense speed.

Quasars give off ultraviolet radiation, and the Doppler effect, caused by their receding at great speed, results in the spectrum's being shifted towards the red (red shift), so that only faint points of blue light from the quasar reach Earth.

Determining the spectra of suspected quasars is a laborious task. Margaret Burbidge, together with Kinman, measured the red shifts of a number of objects found by means of the screening process devised by Martin Ryle (1918–   ) and Allan Sandage (1926–   ), and in the process she detected objects without radio radiation, but with large red shifts; they were called quasi-stellar objects and are now placed in the general group of quasars.

In 1963, the Burbidges and Sandage reviewed the evidence for intense activity in the nuclei of radio galaxies, quasi-stellar objects and Seyfert galaxies (those with a small bright nucleus, fainter arms and abroad spectral emission lines). In 1970, using evidence gained from observations, Geoffrey Burbidge and Wolfe calculated that the stars emitting light in elliptical galaxies could not account for more than 25 per cent of the mass.

They produced arguments to indicate that black holes, from which light cannot escape, are the most likely source of the missing mass.

Another important paper, published by the Burbidges jointly with Solomon and Stritmatter, described the discovery that four quasars (listed in the third Cambridge catalogue) lie within a few arc minutes of bright galaxies. They suggested that the quasars and galaxies were linked in some way. Evidence found since then – examples of quasars located on opposite sides of a galaxy – tends to support this belief, which is accepted by several notable astronomers.

The Burbidges remain at the forefront of research into nucleosynthesis and the nature of quasars and the work they have completed provides the basis for considerable future interdisciplinary investigation.

C

Cameron, Alastair Graham Walter (*1925-   *), is a Canadian-born American astrophysicist responsible for theories regarding the formation of the unstable element technetium within the core of red giant stars and of the disappearance of Earth's original atmosphere.

Born in Winnipeg, Cameron gained a BSc from the University of Manitoba in 1947 and a PhD from the University of Saskatchewan in 1952. While Research Officer for Atomic Energy Canada Ltd, he emigrated to the United States in 1959 (becoming naturalized in 1963). He then successively became Senior Research Fellow at the California Institute of Technology, Pasadena; Senior Scientist of the Goddard Institute for Space Studies in New York; and Professor of Space Physics at Yeshiva University, New York City. Since 1973 he has been Professor of Astronomy at Harvard University.

Following Paul Merrill's discovery in 1952 of the spectral lines denoting the presence in red giants of technetium – an element too unstable to have existed for as long as the giants themselves (thus indicating the actual creation and flow of technetium in the stellar core) – it was Cameron's suggestion that Tc^{97} (mean lifetime 2.6×10^6 years) might result from the decay of a nucleus of molybdenum, Mo^{97}, a usually stable nuclide that becomes unstable when it absorbs an X-ray photon at high temperatures.

Cameron also suggested that the Earth's original atmosphere was blown off into space by the early solar "gale" – as opposed to the present weak solar "breeze" – with its associated magnetic fields.

Campbell, William Wallace (*1862-1938*), was an American astronomer and mathematician, now particularly remembered for his research into the radial velocities of stars.

Born into a farming family in Hancock, Ohio,

Campbell taught for a short while after completing his schooling; he then decided to continue his education at the University of Michigan in 1882. Although he enrolled to study engineering, he became keenly interested in astronomy and studied avidly under J.M. Schaeberle, who was responsible for the Michigan University Observatory. Campbell received his degree in 1886 and became Professor of Mathematics at the University of Colorado. He returned to the University of Michigan in 1888 to take up the post of Instructor in Astronomy, then moved again in 1891, this time to the newly established Lick Observatory, California. He served first as a Staff Astronomer (1891-1901) and then as Director of the Observatory (1901-1930).

During Campbell's tenure at the Lick Observatory he was responsible for much of the spectroscopic work undertaken and was an active participant in and organizer of seven eclipse expeditions to many parts of the world. His administrative talents were also exercised during the period from 1923 to 1930, when he served as President of the University of California. He retired from both posts in 1930, and in the following year was elected to a four-term as President of the National Academy of Sciences. His most significant achievement in this office was the establishment of the influential Scientific Advisory Committee which serves to improve links between the National Academy and the US government.

Failing health and the fear of complete loss of his faculties led him to commit suicide on 14 June 1938, in Berkeley, California.

Campbell's talent for observation was apparent from early in his career: one of his earliest interests in astronomy was the computation of the orbits of comets. His spectroscopic observations of Nova Auriga in 1892 enabled him to describe the changes in its spectral pattern with time. He also made spectroscopic studies of other celestial bodies and was active in the design of the Mills spectrograph which was available for use from 1896.

It was in 1896 that Campbell initiated his lengthiest project, the compilation of a vast amount of data on radial velocities. He was aware that this would be of interest not merely for its own sake, but also for the determination of the motion of the Sun relative to other stars. He did not, however, anticipate that the programme would also lead to the discovery of many binary systems, nor that the data would later be used in the study of galactic rotation, nor that the programme itself would encourage the improvement of several techniques. Campbell published a catalogue of nearly 3,000 radial velocities in 1928.

The project has also led to the establishment of

an observatory in Chile, which contributed data for the radial velocities programme from 1910 until 1929.

Campbell was an uncompromising scientist, even when it meant attracting criticism. He went against the popular opinion of the time in reporting his observations on the absence of sufficient oxygen or water vapour in the Martian atmosphere to support life as found on Earth. Other astronomers, who had been less careful in the design of their observations and interpretation of their results disagreed but his findings were supported by later work – most spectacularly by the *Viking* Mars lander.

Another important result obtained by Campbell was a confirmation of the work done in 1919 by Sir Arthur Eddington (1882–1944) on the deflection of light during an eclipse, which supported the General Theory of Relativity. The positive result which Campbell obtained in 1922 was arrived at only after two previous attempts (in 1914 and in 1918) which had been frustrated by poor weather conditions and by the use of inadequate equipment.

Campbell's contributions to astronomy spanned several fields, but were perhaps most notable in spectroscopy.

Cannon, Annie Jump (*1863–1941*), was the most honoured American woman astronomer of her day, and is justly famous for her meticulous work in stellar spectral classification, with particular reference to variable stars.

She was born in Dover, Delaware, and attended local schools, showing aptitude for scientific study; she gained her bachelor's degree at Wellesley College in 1884. After a protracted period spent at her home in Dover, Cannon returned to Wellesley College at about the age of 30 to take postgraduate courses. A protégée of Edward Pickering (1846–1919), Director of the Harvard Observatory, Cannon became a special student in astronomy at Radcliffe College in 1895 and was made an assistant at the Harvard College Observatory in 1896 – a post she held until 1911. From then until 1938 Cannon was curator of astronomical photographs at the Harvard Observatory. In 1938 she was appointed William Cranch Bond Astronomer and Curator. She retired in 1940, but continued in active research.

Cannon was the first woman to receive an honorary DSc from Oxford University, and she received several other honorary degrees from other universities in the United States and in Europe.

Cannon's return to academic life in 1894 was to research in physics, rather than astronomy, and into the uses of X-rays, recently discovered by Wilhelm Röntgen (1845–1923). A year later, at Harvard, her interests had inclined towards stellar spectroscopy in the field of astronomy.

One of Cannon's particular interests was the phenomenon of variable stars. Hipparchus had established the concept of a continuous sequence of stellar magnitudes based on the assumption that a star's brightness was constant with time. The observation of variable stars, whose brightness sometimes changed quite dramatically, upset this scheme. (A star's brightness could change for any of several reasons; for example, a bright star might be orbited by a dim luminous star, which obscures it at regular intervals: an eclipsing variable.) Cannon studied photographs to record details of variable stars, and discovered 300 new variable stars. She also kept a detailed index card record of all her information, which has served as an invaluable tool for many succeeding research astronomers.

Edward Pickering and Williamina Fleming (1857–1911) had in 1890 established a system for classifying stellar spectra. It allowed each spectrum to be allocated to one of a series of categories labelled alphabetically "A" to "Q"; the groups are related to the stars' temperatures and their compositions. In 1901 Cannon reformed this system: she subdivided the letter categories into 10 sub-classes, based on details in the spectra. With time the system became further modified, some letters being dropped, others rearranged. The sequence which Cannon eventually settled for ran O, B, A, F, G, K, M, R, N and S. Stars in the O, B, A group are white or bluish, those in the F, G group are yellow, those in the K group are orange, and those in the M, R, N, S group are red. Our sun, for instance is yellow and its spectrum places it in the G group.

In 1901 Cannon published a catalogue of the spectra of more than 1,000 stars, using her new classification system. She went on to classify the spectra of over 300,000 stars. Most of this work was published in a 10-volume set which was completed in 1924. It described almost all stars with magnitudes greater than 9. Her later work included classification of the spectra of fainter stars.

The 10-volume catalogue of stellar spectra stands as her greatest contribution to astronomy. It enabled Cannon to demonstrate that the spectra of virtually all stars can be classified easily into few categories which follow a continuous sequence. Cannon's work was characterized by great thoroughness and accuracy. Her interest lay primarily in the description of the stars as they were observed; her legacy to astronomy was a vast body of accurate and carefully compiled information.

Carrington, Richard Christopher (*1826–1875*),

was a British astronomer who was the first to record the observation of a solar flare, and is now most remembered for his work on sunspots.

Carrington's family was in brewing, but neither the family business nor the Church (for which he had been intended) attracted him. He very early realized that his interests lay in astronomy and scientific activities. He left Cambridge in 1849 and his first post was as Observer at Durham, from where he made several reports to the Monthly Notices of the Royal Astronomical Society and to the *Astronomische Nachrichten* of Altona (mainly dealing with minor planets and comets), work which led to his election as a Fellow of the Royal Astronomical Society in 1851.

However, by 1852 he was impatient with the limited resources at Durham – he had in mind an ambitious programme of observation leading to a catalogue of circumpolar stars. In 1853 he set up his own house and observatory at Redhill, Surrey, with instruments made by W. Simms. One of these was based on a larger Greenwich instrument; its telescope had a 5-in (12.7 cm) aperture and a focal length of $5\frac{1}{2}$ ft (1.68 m).

By 1857 he had completed his *Catalogue of 3735 Circumpolar Stars*, which was so highly regarded that it was printed by the Admiralty at public expense. The *Catalogue* won him the Gold Medal of the Royal Astronomical Society (1859), and his election to a Fellowship of the Royal Society shortly afterwards was fitting recognition of his qualities as an astronomer.

The death of his father in 1858 meant that Carrington had to take over the management of the Brentford Brewery, a substantial undertaking which entailed a reduction in his research activity. Nevertheless, in 1859 he recorded the first solar flare.

It is felt by some that he was disappointed by his failure to succeed James Challis (his mentor) as Director of the Cambridge Observatory. At any rate his output declined in the 1860s and ill-health overtook him in 1865. He sold his business and his Redhill establishment and moved to Churt, near Farnham, Surrey, where he built another observatory containing some large telescopes.

Carrington is best known for his work on sunspots. He pursued the daylight project at Redhill for more than seven years (the original aim was for an eleven-year period), in tandem with the work on the Redhill Catalogue. The sunspot cycle – an eleven-year period between maxima of activity – had recently been discovered by Schwabe and the connection with magnetic disturbances had been noted. A study of sunspot activity was thus highly topical and Carrington was keen to tidy up the mass of observations on the subject which had accumulated in the contemporary literature.

He required a simple yet accurate means of plotting sunspot positions and movements, and with much trial and error he arrived at a simple, elegant method. His system projected an image of the Sun of about 11 in (28 cm) diameter using his $4\frac{1}{2}$-in (11.4 cm) equatorial telescope. Crosswires at right angles were placed in the focus of the telescope inclined at 45° to the meridian; the exact angles were not important. The telescope was fixed and the Sun's image allowed to pass across the field; the times of contact of the Sun's limbs and spots were recorded. The method allowed the heliographic latitude and longitude of a sunspot to be determined without recourse to micrometers or clockwork mechanisms.

The principal results of this extended work were, first, to determine the position of the Sun's axis and, second, dramatically to show that the Sun's rotation is differential, that is, that it does not rotate as a solid body, but turns faster at the equator than at the poles. This conclusion was the result of observing the great systematic drift of the photosphere as seen in the drift of individual sunspots during the cycle. Carrington also derived a useful expression for the rotation of a spot in terms of heliographical latitude. An extensive account of all the observations was published, with the help of the Royal Society, in 1863. The complete cycle of work was, however, never accomplished by him.

An immensely practical and meticulous man, interested in international co-operation and the mutual contribution of ideas, Carrington in his work and his publications represents the true Victorian ideal of the investigative scientist.

Cassegrain (*c. 1650–1700*), was the inventor of the system of mirrors within many modern reflecting telescopes – a system by transference also sometimes used in large refraction telescopes.

Nothing is known for certain about the details of Cassegrain's life – not even his first name. Believed to have been a professor at the College of Chartres, in France, he is variously credited with having been an astronomer, a physician and a sculptor at the court of Louis XIV.

In the same year as he submitted a scientific paper concerning the megaphone to the Academy of Sciences in Paris, Cassegrain presented another paper in which he claimed to have improved on Newton's telescope design. Newton himself, however, suggested that the "improvement" had been strongly influenced by the work of James Gregory (whose telescope had been described in *Optica Promota* in 1663).

Newton's own design employed a second, plane mirror to bring the reflected, magnified

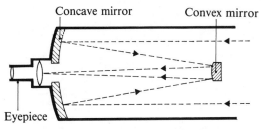

Concave mirror   Convex mirror

Eyepiece

In a Cassegrain reflecting telescope, a hole in the centre of the concave main mirror allows light reflected by the convex secondary mirror to reach the eyepiece (or a camera).

image out to the eyepiece through the side of the telescope. Cassegrain's telescope used an auxiliary convex mirror to reflect the image through a hole in the objective – that is, through the end of the telescope itself. One intention behind this innovation was further to increase the angular magnification.

An even more advantageous facet of this design was not realized until a century later, when Jesse Ramsden noted that it also partly cancelled out the spherical aberration, the blurring of the image caused by the use of two mirrors. The first practical reflecting telescope based on Cassegrain's design was "Short's 'Dumpy'" (focal length 609 mm, aperture 152 mm), built by J. Short in the eighteenth century.

The Isaac Newton Telescope at the Royal Greenwich Observatory is a Cassegrain reflector on an equatorial mounting. (Royal Greenwich Observatory)

Cassini, Giovanni Domenico (Jean Dominique) (*1625-1712*), was an Italian-born French astronomer with a keen interest in geodesy.

Born in Perinaldo, Cassini studied in Vallebone and Genoa, displaying great talent in astronomy and mathematics. In 1644 he was invited to assist the Marquis Mavasia in his observatory at Panzano, near Bologna, and there he was introduced to the two prominent local astronomers, Giovanni Battistae Riccioli (1598-1671) and Francesco Maria Grimaldi (1618-1663). Six years later, aged only 25, Cassini was made Professor of Astronomy at the University of Bologna; he remained there for 19 years.

In addition to his teaching duties at the University, Cassini was also called upon to serve a variety of civic and diplomatic duties. These included contributing to hydraulic projects, supervising construction work and mediating in a dispute between Ferrara and Bologna over navigation rights on the River Reno. In 1669 Cassini departed for Paris at the invitation of King Louis XIV, who had nominated him as a member of the new French Academy of Sciences. Despite Pope Clement IV's insistence that his stay in France be only temporary, Cassini never returned to Italy.

The first task to confront Cassini upon his arrival in Paris was the construction of the Paris Observatory. He had been unable to convince the King or the architect (Claude Perrault) that certain aspects of the design were impractical, but he nevertheless took up the Directorship of the observatory and assumed French citizenship. Cassini was extremely active in exploiting the work of astronomers in research outposts around the world, seeking to equip the observatory with the latest instruments and making use of the skills of students of Galileo.

At the end of the century Cassini's health began to fail and his son Jacques took over an increasing share of his work. The elder Cassini lost his eyesight in 1710 and Jacques assumed the Directorship of the Observatory.

Cassini was renowned for his skills as an observational astronomer, which led him to many important discoveries. He was also extremely conservative in his approach to the more theoretical aspects of astronomy, and this conservatism led him frequently to propound the incorrect view. He refused to accept the Copernican cosmological model and rejected the concept of a finite speed of light (although its proof was demonstrated by Olaus Römer (1644-1710) using Cassini's own data; it is likely that Cassini himself considered the possibility even prior to Römer's work). He also opposed a theory of universal gravitation and insisted (despite critical disagreement by Christiaan Huygens and Isaac Newton) that the Earth was flattened at the equator rather than at the poles. Despite these errors in judgement Cassini earned a well-deserved reputation as one of the finest astronomers of his day.

The best known examples of Cassini's early work are a treatise on his observations of a comet made in 1652 and his design work for a meridian constructed at San Petrino in 1653. The meridian was used to make accurate observations of the Sun and enabled Cassini to publish improved tables in 1662.

During the period from 1664 to 1667 Cassini concentrated his efforts on determining the rotation periods of Mars, Jupiter and Venus. In 1664 he found the rotation period of Jupiter to be 9 from a study of Saturn. In 1675 he distinguished two zones within what was thought to be the single ring around Saturn. The dark central "border" has since been named Cassini's Division. Cassini correctly suggested that the rings were composed of myriads of tiny satellites, although it was not until the work of James Clerk Maxwell (1831–1879) in the 1850s that he was proved correct.

From 1671 until 1679 Cassini made many observations of details on the lunar surface which culminated in the production of a beautiful engraving of the Moon, presented to the French Academy in 1679. In 1672 Cassini took advantage of a good opposition of Mars to determine the distance between the Earth and that planet. He arranged for Jean Richer (1630–1696) to make measurements from his base in Cayenne, on the north-eastern coast of South America, while Cassini made simultaneous measurements in Paris which permitted them to make a triangulation of Mars with a baseline of nearly 10,000 kilometres. This derived a good approximation for the distance between the Earth and Mars, from which Cassini was able to deduce many other astronomical distances. These included the Astronomical Unit (AU), which Cassini found to be 138 million kilometres, only 11 million kilometres too little.

Cassini's later work included a study (with N. Fatio) on zodiacal light (1683), and a triangulation of the arcs of meridian aimed at resolving a controversy concerning the shape of the Earth.

Cassini's contributions to astronomy were original and plentiful, but his best work was of an observational rather than of a theoretical nature.

Celsius, Anders (*1701–1744*), was a Swedish astronomer, mathematician and physicist, now mostly remembered for the Celsius scale of temperature.

Celsius was born on 27 November 1701 in Uppsala, where his father was Professor of Astronomy. In 1723 he became secretary of the Uppsala Scientific Society; by the age of 30 he was himself Professor of Astronomy there. It was at this time that he began to travel extensively in Europe, visiting particularly astronomers and observatories.

On his travels he observed the Aurora Borealis; he published some of the first scientific documents on the phenomenon in 1733. While in Paris he visited Pierre-Louis Maupertuis (1698–1759), who invited him to join an expedition which centred on Torneå in Lapland (now on the Finnish-Swedish border). It confirmed the theory propounded by Newton that the Earth is flattened at the poles. With knowledge and expertise gained in this way from the leading astronomers and scientists throughout Europe, Celsius returned to the University of Uppsala, where he built a new observatory – the first installation of its kind in Sweden.

In 1742 Celsius presented a paper to the Swedish Academy of Sciences containing a proposal that all scientific measurements of temperature should be made on a fixed scale based on two invariable (generally speaking) and naturally-occurring points. His scale defined 0° as the temperature at which water boils, and 100° as that at which water freezes. This scale, in an inverted form devised eight years later by his pupil, Martin Strömer, has since been used in almost all scientific work. Generally known in most of Europe under the name of Celsius, in Britain the scale has also commonly been known as Centigrade.

Celsius left several other important scientifc works, including a paper on accurately determining the shape and size of the Earth, some of the first attempts to gauge the magnitude of the stars in the constellation Aries, and a study of the falling water level of the Baltic Sea.

Challis, James (*1803–1882*), was a British astronomer renowned in his time for unconventional views concerning the fundamental laws of the Universe, but now remembered more for an almost unbelievable lapse in scientific professionalism.

Challis was born in Braintree, Essex, on 12 December 1803. He attended a local school where he showed such promise that he won a place at a London school and later at Trinity College, Cambridge, which he entered in 1821. He graduated with top honours in 1825, and was a fellow of the College from 1826 to 1831 (and later from 1870 to 1882). Challis was ordained in 1830 and served as Rector at Papworth Everard, Cambridgeshire, from 1830 until 1852. He also succeeded George

Airy (1801-1892) to the Plumian Professorship of Astronomy at Cambridge University in 1836 – a post he held until his death – and he served as Director to the Cambridge Observatory from 1836 until 1861. A member of the Royal Astronomical Society and a Fellow of the Royal Society, the author of several scientific publications, he died in Cambridge on 3 December 1882.

In 1844, John Couch Adams (1819-1892) – a young and enthusiastic astronomer and mathematician, a recent graduate of Cambridge University – approached Challis to enlist his aid in obtaining data from Airy at the Greenwich Observatory regarding the known deviations in orbit of the planet Uranus. These were suspected of indicating the gravitational influence of a planet even farther out. With Challis's mediation, Adams received from Airy all the data the Observatory possessed on Uranus for the period 1754 to 1830.

In September 1845 Adams supplied Challis and Airy with an estimated orbital path for the unknown planet and a prediction for its likely position on 1 October 1845. But Challis did not take the calculations seriously (saying later that he could not believe so youthful and inexperienced an astronomer as Adams would arrive at anything like a correct prediction), and Airy, through a series of mishaps, did not even see them until the following year.

By that time, in France, Urbain Le Verrier (1811-1877) had performed calculations similar to those of Adams, and he was more successful than Adams in obtaining the co-operation of senior astronomers. Almost immediately after he sent his predictions to Berlin Observatory in September 1846, the new planet was discovered – by Johann Galle (1812-1910) and Heinrich d'Arrest (1822-1875) – later to be called Neptune.

All Challis could do then was lamely to report that if he had indeed conducted a search at Adam's predicted position for 1 October 1845 he would have been within 2° of the planet's actual position and would almost certainly have spotted it.

Chandrasekhar, Subrahmanyan (*1910-*), is an Indian-born American astrophysicist who is particularly concerned with the structure and evolution of stars. He is well-known for his studies of white dwarfs and the radiation of stellar energy.

Chandrasekhar was born on 19 October 1910 in Lahore, India (now in Pakistan). He grew up in India and went to Presidency College, University of Madras, from which he graduated with a BA in 1930. He continued his studies at Trinity College, Cambridge, gaining a PhD in 1933.

There he studied under the Physicist Paul Dirac. He left Trinity College in 1936 to take up a position on the staff of the University of Chicago, working in the Yerkes Laboratory. In 1938 he became Assistant Professor of Astrophysics there and in 1952 was promoted to Distinguished Service Professor. The following year he became a United States citizen.

Chandrasekhar's greatest contribution to astronomy was his explanation of the evolution of white dwarf stars, as laid out in his *Introduction to the Study of Stellar Structure* (1939). These stellar objects, which were first discovered in 1915 by Walter Sydney Adams (1876-1956), are much smaller than the Sun and are similar in size to the Earth. They have a very high density and are therefore very much more massive than the Earth. This enormous density is explained in terms of degeneracy – a consequence of the Pauli Exclusion Principle in which electrons become so tightly packed that their normal behaviour is suppressed; as stars evolve, they "burn" their hydrogen which is converted to helium and, eventually, heavier elements. During his work at Cambridge, Chandrasekhar suggested that when a star had burned nearly all its hydrogen, it would not be able to produce the pressure against its own gravitational field to sustain its size and would then contract. As its density increased during the contraction the star would build up sufficient internal energy to collapse its atomic structure into the degenerate state.

Not all stars, however, become white dwarfs. Chandrasekhar believed that – up to a certain point – the greater the mass of a star the smaller would be the radius of the eventual white dwarf. But he also stated that beyond this point a large stellar mass would not be able to equalize the pressure involved and would explode. He calculated that stellar masses below 1.44 times that of the Sun would form stable white dwarfs, but those above this limit would not evolve into white dwarfs. This limit – known as the Chandrasekhar limit – was based on calculations involving the complete degeneracy of the stellar matter; the limit is now believed to be about 1.2 solar masses.

Stars with masses above the Chandrasekhar limit are likely to become supernovae and rid themselves of their excess matter in a spectacular explosion. The remaining mass may form a white dwarf if the conditions of mass and pressure are suitable, but it is more likely to form a neutron star. Neutron stars were first identified by J. Robert Oppenheimer and his co-workers in 1938. These stars are even more dense than white dwarfs, with an average radius of approximately ·15 km.

With the Polish astrophysicist Erich Schönberg,

Chandrasekhar determined the Chandrasekhar-Schönberg limit of the mass of a star's helium core; if it is more than 10–15 per cent that of the entire star, the core rapidly contracts, often collapsing. Chandrasekhar has also investigated the transfer of energy in stellar atmospheres by radiation and convection and the polarization of light emitted from particular stars.

Christie, William Henry Maloney (*1845–1922*), was an Englishman who became Astronomer Royal. He took part in some important research, but he was most successful at acquiring new equipment and overseeing the expansion of facilities of the Royal Observatory at Greenwich.

Christie was born in Woolwich on 1 October 1845. He studied at King's College School, London, and went on to Trinity College, Cambridge. He graduated in 1868, was made a Fellow of his College in 1869, and left in 1870 to become chief assistant to George Airy (1801–1892) at the Greenwich Observatory; he succeeded Airy as Astronomer Royal in 1881. That same year he was made Fellow of the Royal Society. He was also a member of other prominent scientific bodies, including the Royal Astronomical Society and the Paris Academy of Sciences. Christie retired to Downe, Kent, in 1910, but continued to be very active. He died on a sea voyage to Mogador, in Morocco, on 22 January 1922.

One of the major interests at the Greenwich Observatory has always been the study of positional astronomy, and it was to this subject to which Christie devoted most of his energies during his early years at Greenwich. He was active in the initiation of the stellar photography programme; in particular he collaborated with Edward Maunder (1851–1928) to compile a daily record of solar activity. These photographs were used in the analysis of sunspots by area and by location. Christie was also interested in the study of the radial velocity of stars.

Christie's most enduring contribution to the Greenwich Observatory was his ability to attract funds for and to co-ordinate the expansion of the Observatory's facilities and the acquisition of new instruments.

Copernicus, Nicolaus (Mikolaj Kopernigk) (*1473–1543*), was a Polish doctor and astronomer who, against the religion-reinforced tradition of many centuries, finally declared once and for all that the planet Earth is the centre neither of the universe, nor even of the Solar System. He was never a skilled observer, and probably made fewer than one hundred observations in all, preferring to rely almost entirely on data accumulated by others. In his own time he was renowned probably more as a medical man and priest than as an astronomer.

Copernicus was born in Toruń in Ermland (under the Polish crown) on 19 February 1473, and at an early age attended St John's School there. After the death of his father in 1483, however, it was arranged, probably by his uncle (and patron) L. Watzenrode, for him to study at the Cathedral School in Wloclawek. From 1491 until 1494 Copernicus studied mathematics and classics at the University of Krakow, under Brudzewski. Encouraged by Watzenrode to continue his studies, he travelled in 1496 to the University of Bologna, Italy, where he studied law and astronomy. In the latter subject he was taught by D.M. di Novara.

Despite his nephew's absence from Poland, Watzenrode (now himself a bishop) was able to arrange for Copernicus to be made Canon of Frombork (Frauenburg), a post he retained for life. This job brought in sufficient income, combined with only light duties, to enable Copernicus to devote a great deal of time to astronomy.

When in 1500 he had completed his studies in Bologna, Copernicus moved on to Padua, where he continued his studies in law and Greek. He gained a doctorate in canon law in 1503 in Ferrara and then returned to Padua to study medicine. In 1506 he went home to Poland (where he remained for the rest of his life). From 1506 until 1512, when Watzenrode died, he not only worked for his uncle as his personal doctor and private secretary, but served in the Cathedral chapter of Frombork.

After the death of Bishop Watzenrode, Copernicus was still not able to devote himself entirely to his ecclesiastical and astronomical interests. He also served on a number of diplomatic missions and as a financial advisor and administrator. Nevertheless, he wrote a brief outline of his new ideas in astronomy in about 1513; he privately circulated a more comprehensive version in 1530. Copernicus had the good sense to realize that he risked being branded a lunatic, or a heretic, and he was therefore reluctant to publish his theory more widely. G. Joachim, known as Rhaeticus, encouraged him to present his work in book form, which he finally agreed to do. The book, *De revolutionibus orbium coelestrium*, prudently dedicated to Pope Paul III, was delayed in publication, so that Copernicus did not receive a copy of it until he was on his deathbed. Copernicus died at Frombork on 24 May 1543.

Copernicus began to make astronomical observations in March 1497, although it was not until about 1513 that he wrote the brief, anonymous text, entitled *Commentariolus*, in which he outlined the material he later discussed more fully. His main points were that the Ptolemaic system of a geocentric planetary model was complex, unwieldy and inaccurate. Copernicus proposed to replace Ptolemy's ideas with a model in which the planets (*including* the Earth) orbited a centrally situated Sun. The Earth would describe one full orbit of the Sun in a year, while the Moon orbited the Earth. The Earth rotated daily about its axis (which was inclined at 23.5° to the plane of orbit), thus accounting for the apparent daily rotation of the sphere of the fixed stars.

This model was a distinct improvement on the Ptolemaic system for a number of reasons. It explained why the planets Mercury and Venus displayed only "limited motion": their orbits were inside that of the Earth's. Similarly, it explained why the planets Mars, Jupiter and Saturn displayed such curious patterns in their movements ("retrograde motion", loops and kinks). These were all a consequence of their travelling in outer orbits at a slower pace than the Earth. The precession of the equinoxes, as discovered by Hipparchus, could be accounted for by the movement of the Earth on its axis.

Copernicus' theory was not, however, by any means perfect. He was unable to free himself entirely from the constraints of classical thinking and was able to imagine only circular planetary orbits. This forced him to retain the cumbersome system of epicycles, with the Earth revolving around a centre which revolved around another centre which in turn orbited the Sun. It was the work of Kepler, who introduced the concept of elliptical orbits, which rescued the Copernican model. Copernicus also held to the notion of spheres, in which the planets were supposed to travel. It was the Dane, Tycho Brahe (1546–1601), who rid astronomy of that archaic concept.

In his greatest work, the *De revolutionibus*, Copernicus proposed that the atmosphere (at least part of it) rotated with the Earth about the planetary axis, so that the skies did not constantly flow westwards. He obtained fairly accurate estimates for the distances of the planets from the Sun in terms of the Astronomical Unit (the distance from Earth to the Sun). He echoed Aristarchos on explaining the inability to observe stellar parallax from the extremes of the Earth's orbit around the Sun as being a consequence of the fact that the diameter of the orbit was insignificant in comparison with the distance from the Earth to the stars. (In fact, stellar parallax is detectable, but only with superior instruments; it was not observed until Friedrich Bessel (1784–1846) finally succeeded in 1838.)

A. Osiander inserted a preface to *De revolutionibus* (without Copernicus's permission), stating that the theory was intended merely as an aid to the calculation of planetary positions, not as a statement of reality. This served to compromise the value of the text in the eyes of many astronomers, but it also saved the book from instant condemnation by the Roman Catholic Church. *De revolutionibus* was not placed upon the Index of forbidden books until 1616 (it was removed from the list in 1835).

Copernicus relegated the Earth from being the centre of the Universe to being merely a planet (the centre only of its own gravity and the orbit of its solitary Moon). This in itself forced a fundamental revision of man's anthropocentric view of the Universe and came as an enormous psychological shock to the whole of European culture. Copernicus's model could not be "proved" right, because it contained several fundamental flaws, but it was the important first step to the more accurate picture built up by Brahe, Kepler, Galileo and later astronomers. It is no exaggeration to view Copernicus' work as the cornerstone of the Scientific Revolution.

Cowling, Thomas George (*1906–*   ), is a British applied mathematician and physicist who has contributed significantly to modern research into stellar energy, with special reference to the Sun.

Cowling was born on 17 June 1906 and educated at the Sir George Monoux School in Walthamstow, Essex. He attended Oxford University, where he studied mathematics, and spent many years teaching in various university posts in London, Swansea, Dundee and Manchester before becoming Professor of Mathematics at University College, Bangor, in 1945. In 1948 he was appointed Professor of Mathematics at Leeds University, where he stayed until his retirement in 1970.

The author of several books on mathematics, Cowling became a Fellow of the Royal Society in 1947, and was made President of the Royal Astronomical Society for a two-year period in 1965.

Cowling's work was of important assistance in the discovery of the carbon-nitrogen cycle by Hans Bethe (1906–   ) in 1939. Bethe showed that the most significant source of energy in stars was the process by which four hydrogen atoms are converted into one helium atom, with carbon and nitrogen as intermediate products. This process was found to account satisfactorily for the rate of generation of the Sun's energy if its central temperature was 18.5 million degrees – an estimate that corresponded well with the temperature of 19 million degrees calculated following the theory of stellar structure previously proposed by Arthur Eddington (1882–1944).

Less indirectly, Cowling was responsible for demonstrating the existence of a convective core in stars, suggesting thus that the Sun may behave like a giant dynamo whose rotation, internal circulation and convection produce the immensely powerful electric currents and magnetic fields associated with sunspots. (The electric current required to produce the field of a large sunspot may be of the order of 10^{13} amps; magnetic fields similarly may reach several thousand gauss.) With the Swedish astronomer, Hannes Alfvén 1908-), Cowling showed that such currents and fields would be difficult to initiate in the solar atmosphere and are therefore likely to have existed since the Sun was first formed.

Curtis, Heber Doust (*1872–1942*), was an American astronomer who became interested in astronomy only after he had begun a career in classics, but who went on to carry out important research into the nature of spiral nebulae.

Curtis was born in Muskegan, Michigan, on 27 June 1872. He attended Detroit High School, where he displayed a flair for languages and an interest in the classics. It was primarily in these subjects that he concentrated his efforts while a student at the University of Michigan. Curtis gained his BA in 1892 and his MA a year later. His first job was teaching Latin at his old high school, and then, aged only 22, he became Professor of Latin at Napa College, California, where he shortly became aware of the availability of a refracting telescope and small observatory.

In 1897 Curtis abruptly changed the entire direction of his career and became Professor of Mathematics and Astronomy at the University of the Pacific. He worked at the Lick Observatory, California, in 1898; in 1900 he became Vanderbilt Fellow at the Leander McCormick Observatory at the University of Virginia; and in 1902 he returned to become an assistant at the Lick Observatory. There he was promoted to Assistant Astronomer in 1904. In 1906, under the auspices of the Observatory, he took charge of work being done at an observatory in Chile. Three years later, he returned to the Lick, where he worked as an astronomer until he retired from research work in 1920. His next appointment was as Director of the Allegheny Observatory, a post which he held until 1930, when he became Director of the Observatory at the University of Michigan. He died in Ann Arbor, Michigan, on 8 January 1942.

Curtis' first astronomical studies were of total solar eclipses in Thomaston, Georgia, in 1900, and in Solok, Sumatra, in 1901. But the main value of Curtis' early work at the Lick Observatory lay in his contributions to the programme for the measurement of stellar radial velocities, undertaken under the direction of William Campbell (1862–1938). He worked on this programme

at Mount Hamilton from 1902 until 1906, and then in Chile from 1906 until 1909. For the following 11 years Curtis concentrated his efforts on the photography of spiral nebulae and on research into their nature.

Ever since Charles Messier (1730–1817) had included "nebulosities" in his Catalogue of 1771, their precise composition had been the subject of dispute. There were two main schools of thought: that they were either giant star clusters far beyond our own galaxy – as proposed by Richard Proctor (1837–1888) – or that they were merely clouds of debris. The scale of the Universe itself was central to both points of view. Through his photography of spiral nebulae, Curtis began to appreciate the actual vastnesses of space and to incline towards Proctor's view of "islands in the Universe".

He also noticed that on photographs of spiral nebulae viewed edge-on there was a dark line along the rim of each nebula. This suggested to Curtis a combination of the two theories: that spiral nebulae might indeed be complex galaxies like our own, and that such galaxies produced a cloud of debris which accumulated in the plane of the galaxy. If such a cloud of debris had also gathered outside our own Galaxy, this would explain the reported "zone of avoidance" – spiral nebulae never appeared in the Milky Way (i.e. in the plane of our own Galaxy). Spiral nebulae in that position, it now was evident, would simply be obscured by dust.

Following his appointment as Director of the Allegheny Observatory in 1920, Curtis' research output declined. His most important contributions to astronomy remain therefore improving the modern understanding of the nature and position of spiral nebulae.

D

De la Rue, Warren (*1815–1889*), was a pioneer of celestial photography. Besides inventing the first photoheliographic telescope, he took the first photograph of a solar eclipse and used it to prove that the prominences observed during an eclipse are of solar rather than lunar origin.

De la Rue was born in Guernsey on 15 January 1815, the eldest son of Thomas de la Rue, a printer. Warren attended the Collège Sainte-Barbe in Paris before joining his father in the printing business. It was then that he first came into contact with science and technology. He was one of the first printers to adopt electrotyping and in 1851 he invented the first envelope-making machine. Initially he saw himself as an amateur chemist and, before making any achievements in the field of astronomy, he invented the silver chloride battery. He became a fellow of the Royal Society, the Chemical Society and the Royal Astronomical Society. In his later life, from 1868 to 1883, he conducted a series of experiments on electric discharges through gases, but his results were inconclusive. He died in London on 19 April 1889.

De la Rue was introduced to astronomy by a friend, James Nasmyth, who, like de la Rue himself, was a successful businessman besides being an inventor and telescope-maker. De la Rue began his research career in astronomy with the intention of producing more accurate and detailed pictures of the Moon and neighbouring heavenly bodies. His early observations of the Moon, the Sun and Saturn were superbly drawn and their details were enhanced by de la Rue's innovative techniques in polishing and figuring the mirror of his own 13-inch (33 cm) reflecting telescope.

De la Rue's interest in new technologies led him to apply the art of photography that had been pioneered by Louis Daguerre to astronomy. He modified his 13-inch (33 cm) telescope to incorporate a wet collodion plate. His first photographs were of the Moon, taken with exposures of between 10 to 30 seconds. They were remarkably successful, considering that there was no drive fitted to de la Rue's telescope and that he had to guide the instrument by hand to hold the image steady on the photographic plate. The lack of a good drive made longer exposures impossible to achieve and so de la Rue postponed further research in celestial photography until he had built and equipped a new observatory.

At the new observatory de la Rue began a regular programme of astronomical photography, including a daily sequence of photographs of the Sun. He designed a photoheliographic telescope in connection with this project and took it to Spain in July 1860 to photograph a total eclipse of the Sun. This expedition was made in collaboration with Father Angelo Secchi of the Collegio Romano, in order that photographs of prominences, only seen during the total phase of a solar eclipse, could be taken from two separate stations, 400 km apart. The resulting photographic plates showed conclusively that the prominences were attached to the Sun and were not, as had been suggested, either effects of the Earth's atmosphere or the result of some unknown lunar phenomenon.

De la Rue's photoheliograph was subsequently set up at the Kew Observatory, sited about 8 km from de la Rue's private observatory and home at Cranford, Middlesex. He used it to map the surface of the Sun and study the sunspot cycle.

This work led to his being able to show that sunspots are in fact depressions in the Sun's atmosphere. De la Rue continued to use his reflecting telescope to take photographs of the Moon's surface and over a period of eight years his series of plates brought certain details to light that had never been noted before. This sequence turned out to be particularly relevant to a controversy initiated by Julius Schmidt, Director of Athens Observatory, who announced in 1866 that one of the lunar craters had disappeared.

De la Rue's particular talents were his understanding of technology and his innovative flare in designing instruments and as a result his observations were so accurate that they contributed to major advances in theoretical astronomy.

Descartes, René (*1596–1650*), was a celebrated and influential French philosopher-mathematician whose endeavour to describe and explain the Solar System without offending the susceptibilities of the Roman Catholic Church helped to hold back astronomical research in Europe for decades.

Descartes was born at La Haye in Touraine, France, on 31 March 1596, the third son of Joachim Descartes, a Councillor of the Parliament of Rennes in Brittany. When René was 8, he was sent to the Jesuit College at La Flèche, where he spent five years studying grammar and literature and then three years studying science, elementary philosophy and theology; his favourite subject was mathematics. In 1612, he went to the University of Poitiers and graduated in law four years later. Wanting to see the world, he joined the army of Prince Maurice of Nassau and used his mathematical ability in military engineering. A dream in November 1619 made him think that physics could be reduced to geometry and that all the sciences should be interconnected by mathematical links: he spent the next two years applying this tenet to algebra. Returning to France in 1622, Descartes sold his estate in Poitou in order to resume his travels, visiting scientists throughout France and western Europe. He finally settled in The Netherlands in 1629. Twenty years later he was invited to go to Sweden to instruct Queen Christina. On his arrival in Stockholm, he found that the somewhat whimsical queen intended to receive her instruction at 5 o'clock each morning. Unused to the cold of a Swedish winter, Descartes very shortly afterwards caught a severe chill and died on 11 February 1650. His remains were taken back to France and buried in the church of St Geneviève du Mont in Paris.

Descartes was born into an era in which Galileo (1564–1642) was being persecuted by the Roman Catholic Church for suggesting that the Earth was neither stationary nor the centre of the Universe, despite the evidence of his telescope. That Galileo was right was realized by very few, and even though the earlier theories of Nicolaus Copernicus (1473-1543) were accepted by some professional astronomers, even fewer were prepared to consider seriously the pioneering work of Johannes Kepler (1571-1630)

Descartes set up a General Theory of the Universe, which was accepted in France for more than 100 years. This was much longer than the theory deserved, but it was accepted because of Descartes' fame as a mathematician and philosopher. It had been Descartes' intention to write a work entitled *On the World*, founded on the Copernican system. But when he heard of the Roman Catholic Church's attack on Galileo, he gave up the idea. Some years later, he resolved his dilemma by proposing that the Earth did not move freely through space, but that it was carried round the Sun in a vortex of matter without changing its place in respect of surrounding particles. In this way, it could be said (through a slight stretch of the imagination) to be "stationary". In 1644 he published *Principia Philosophiae*, in which he assumed space to be full of matter that in the beginning had been set in motion by God, resulting in an immense number of vortices of particles of different sizes and shapes, which by friction had had their corners rubbed off. In this way, two kinds of matter were produced in each vortex: small spheres which continued to move round the centre of motion, with a tendency to recede from it, and fine dust which gradually settled at the centre and formed a star or sun. Those particles which become channelled or twisted, in passing through the vortex, formed sunspots; these, declared Descartes, might eventually dissolve, or might form a comet, or might settle permanently in a part of the vortex that has a velocity equal to its own, and form a planet. In this way he was able to account for the origin of the Moon and other satellites. His theory was of course pure speculation, unsupported by any facts, and was an attempt to explain how the planets move round the Sun, able neither to move away nor to move closer. It does not explain any of the deviations of the planetary orbits, and only with difficulty accounts for the elliptical, not circular, form of the orbits.

Although his theory now seems rather illogical, it was significant in that the considerable following it had partly explains why Newton's theories and models were not generally accepted on the Continent until the middle of the eighteenth century.

De Sitter, Willem (*1872-1934*), was a Dutch mathematician, physicist and astronomer whose wide knowledge and energetic application made him one of the most respected theoreticians of his time. He was particularly influential in English-speaking countries in bringing the relevance of the General Theory of Relativity to the attention of astronomers.

De Sitter was born in Sneek, in The Netherlands, on 6 May 1872. He attended the high school in Arnhem before going on to the University of Groningen. Although his primary interests were in mathematics and physics, he soon became interested in astronomy on learning of studies being conducted by Haga and Jacobus Kapteyn (1851-1922). De Sitter was invited to take his postgraduate courses at the Royal Observatory, Cape Town, South Africa, by David Gill (1843-1914), and, since conditions for astronomical observations were excellent in South Africa, he sailed for the Cape in 1897.

Within two years de Sitter had collected sufficient data to enable him to return to The Netherlands to write his doctoral dissertation: he was awarded his PhD in 1901. From 1899 to 1908 he served as an assistant to Kapteyn, becoming Professor of Theoretical Astronomy at the University of Leiden in 1908. In 1919 he took on the additional post of Director of the Observatory at Leiden, which was undergoing a programme of redevelopment and expansion. He died of pneumonia in Leiden on 19 November 1934.

De Sitter's early work in Cape Town consisted primarily of photometry and heliometry. Gill suggested that he study the moons of Jupiter, and his subsequent observations of the Jovian satellites were the first of many such investigations, the results of which he published during the course of his career. Taking advantage of data on Jupiter's moons dating back to 1688, in 1925 he produced a new mathematical theory on them. Four years later he published accurate tables describing the satellites. He also obtained an estimate for the mass of the parent planet itself.

Einstein's Special Theory of Relativity appeared in 1905, but few astronomers recognized its importance to their field. In 1911 de Sitter wrote a brief paper in which he outlined how the motion of the constituent bodies of our Solar System might be expected to deviate from predictions based on Newtonian dynamics if relativity theory were valid. After the publication of Einstein's General Theory of Relativity in 1915 he expanded his ideas and presented a series of three papers to the Royal Astronomical Society on the matter. In the third paper, he introduced the "de Sitter Universe" (as distinct from the "Einstein Universe"). His model later formed an element in the theoretical basis for the Steady State hypothesis regarding the creation of the Universe. De Sitter also noted that the solution Einstein presented for the Einstein field equation was not the only possible one. He therefore presented further models of a non-static Universe: he described both an expanding Universe and an oscillating Universe (i.e., one which alternately increases and decreases in diameter). One of several theoretical astronomers to develop this field, de Sitter thus contributed to the birth of modern cosmology.

There were two other areas of astronomical research to which he made important contributions. The first of these was the bringing up to date of many of the astronomical constants. He published his work on this subject in two papers, one in 1915 and the other in 1927. A third, incomplete, paper on the subject was published posthumously in 1938. Using geodetic and astronomical data in his analysis, de Sitter demonstrated that there is some variation in the rotation of the Earth, and presented suggestions for its mechanism. He suggested that tidal friction might affect the rotation of not only the Earth but also the Moon, but that some factors might affect the Earth alone.

Deslandres, Henri Alexandre (*1853–1948*), was a French physicist and astronomer, now remembered mostly for his work in spectroscopy and for his solar studies.

Deslandres was born in Paris on 24 July 1853. He studied at the École Polytechnique in Paris, graduating in 1874 and then entering the Army. He retired from the Army in 1881 because of his strong interest in science, having attained the rank of Captain in the Engineers. Deslandres worked at the École Polytechnique and the Sorbonne from 1881 until 1889, when he began his astronomical career at the Paris Observatory. In 1897 he moved to the observatory at Meudon, where he became Assistant Director in 1906 and Director in 1907. The Paris and Meudon Observatories were combined in 1926 and in 1927 Deslandres became Director of the Paris Observatory. He retired officially in 1929, but he continued to publish his research until 1947. He died in Paris on 15 January 1948.

Deslandres' early scientific work in spectroscopy led to the formulation of two simple empirical laws describing the banding patterns in molecular spectra; the laws were later found to be easily explained using quantum mechanics. When Deslandres joined the Paris Observatory his task was to organize spectroscopic research. He studied both planetary and stellar spectra, but he soon began to direct his attention to the study of the Sun.

In 1891 George Ellery Hale (1868–1938) and Deslandres independently made the same discovery; both turned to the development of a photographic device for studying the solar spectrum in more detail. Hale's spectrograph was ready a full year before Deslandres' version, but the latter's spectroheliograph was a more flexible device and Deslandres used it to full advantage over the ensuing years. Deslandres found his spectroheliograph particularly well adapted to studying the solar chromosphere.

Deslandres was a member of several eclipse expeditions to observe total solar eclipses. In 1902 he predicted that the Sun would be found to be a source of radio waves, and 40 years later this was confirmed. From 1908 onwards much of Deslandres' work on the sun was done in collaboration with L. d'Azabuja. After his official retirement Deslandres returned to spectroscopy, with a special interest in the Raman effect. Much of his later work was, however, outside the mainstream of contempory research.

De Vaucouleurs, Gerard Henri (*1918–*), is a French-born American astronomer who has carried out important research into extragalactic nebulae.

Born in France on 25 April 1918, de Vaucouleurs was educated at the University of Paris and obtained his BSc in 1936. From 1945 to 1950, he was a Research Fellow at the Institute of Astrophysics, National Centre for Scientific Research, before he went to Australia, to the Australian National University from 1951 to 1954, and, as Observer, to the Yale-Columbia Southern Station in Australia from 1954 to 1957. He was awarded a DSc from the Australian National University in 1957. In 1957 de Vaucouleurs went to the United States to become Astronomer at the Lowell Observatory in Arizona. A year later, he was appointed Research Associate at the Harvard College Observatory, and in 1960 he became Associate Professor. Since 1965, he has been Professor of Astronomy at the University of Texas, at Austin.

The main object of de Vaucouleurs' research has been to find a pattern in the location of nebulae, clusters of stars formerly thought to be randomly scattered across the sky as viewed from Earth. Yet as telescopes become more powerful, there is increasing evidence that in fact nebulae themselves tend to cluster together. Extragalactic nebulae, small and faint as they appear, are more numerous and seem distinctly grouped. The nebulae that are closer to us, of up to the twelfth or thirteenth magnitude, form what are now called superclusters, and many occur in a definite band across the heavens.

In 1952, de Vaucouleurs, then at the Australian Commonwealth Observatory, Mount Stromlo, Canberra, began a thorough re-investigation of a local supercluster, using newer and more accurate data. He redetermined the magnitudes of many of the brighter southern nebulae and revised the magnitudes for most of the brighter catalogued nebulae following a modern photometric system. His aim was to obtain photometric consistency and completeness over the whole sky to approximately magnitude 12.5. In 1956, he published and discussed his material in great detail and it seemed to indicate that a "local supergalaxy" exists which includes our own Milky Way stellar system. He suggested a model in which the great Virgo cluster might be "a dominant congregation not too far from its central region". As evidence for its existence, de Vaucouleurs pointed out the similarity in position and extent of a broad maximum of cosmic radio noise, reported by other researchers both in Britain and the United States. (It may be that a local supercluster of bright nebulae including a galaxy may not be unique, since Harlow Shapley in 1934 reported among the fainter ones a distant double supergalaxy in Hercules.)

De Vaucouleurs' work in the Southern hemisphere led him to suspect that there was another supergalaxy, from a great, elongated swarm of nebulae extending through Cetus, Dorado, Fornax, Eridanus and Horologium. He estimated that its distance was only slightly greater than the Virgo cluster and he noted that the relative sizes and separations of this southern supergalaxy and the local supergalaxy appear to be comparable with Shapley's double supergalaxy in Hercules. Thus it seems that superclustering is a phenomenon that has some essential relevance to the structure of the Universe.

Dicke, Robert Henry (*1916–*   ), is an American physicist who has carried out considerable research into the rates of stellar and galactic evolution. Much of his work has been innovatory and some remains controversial.

Born in St Louis, Missouri, on 6 May 1916, Dicke completed his education at Princeton University, graduating in 1938, before obtaining a PhD from the University of Rochester in 1941. That same year, he joined the staff of the Radiation Laboratory, Massachusetts Institute of Technology, where he remained until 1946. He then returned to Princeton, where he rose from being Assistant Professor to Professor of Physics, then to Cyrus Fogg Brackett Professor (1957–1975), to Chairman of the Department of Physics and finally (since 1975) to Albert Einstein Professor of Science. Among many prizes and honours he has received, he was awarded the Medal for

Exceptional Science Achievement of the National Aeronautical and Space Administration in 1973.

In 1964 Dicke turned his attention to a version of the Big-Bang theory known as the "hot big bang"; he suggested that the present expansion of the Universe had been preceded by a collapse in which high temperatures had been generated. Realizing that he should be able to test this hypothesis by detecting residual radiation in space at a wavelength of a few centimetres, Dicke and his colleagues started to build the equipment they needed. But before they were in a position to begin their measurements, Arno Penzias (1933–   ) and Robert Wilson (1936–   ) of Bell Telephone Laboratories announced they had detected an unexpected and relatively high level of radiation at a wavelength of 7cm, with a temperature of about 3.5K. Dicke immediately proposed that this was cosmic black-body radiation from the hot big bang.

Unfortunately, this theory also required a modification in the General Theory of Relativity itself – to take account of the shortfall in quantity of residual matter in the Universe left after equal amounts of primordial matter and anti-matter have cancelled each other out as the Universe expands and cools. Dicke had no hesitation in proposing such a modification in order to alter the expansion rate of the Big-Bang models.

He found himself again in conflict with Einstein in 1966, when he carried out experiments to verify the supposition of the General Theory of Relativity that a gravitational mass is equal to its inertial mass. Einstein had demonstrated the General Theory of Relativity to be a generalization of the Newtonian equations of motion. In 1967 Dicke discovered that the Sun is not spherical and he argued that the equatorial bulge he had observed was sufficient to account in Newtonian fashion for 4 seconds of arc. This raised some problems concerned with the orbit of Mercury. Because of the gravitational interaction of the planets with one another, all the ellipses forming the orbits of the planets about the Sun turn slowly within their planes. In the last century, however, it was discovered that there was an unexplained 43 seconds of arc per century in the turning rate of Mercury's orbit which could not be explained by interplanetary perturbations. The General Theory of Relativity predicts this discrepancy as a relativistic effect. If Dicke is right and 4 seconds of arc are due to the slight flattening at the Sun's poles and a bulge at the equator, it will spoil the otherwise perfect agreement between theory and observation. (The motion of Mercury's orbit had until this time been considered an important verification of the General Theory of Relativity.) Dicke claims that the difference in the observed motion of Mercury round the Sun from the theoretical is due to the distribution of the Sun's mass rather than to the correctness of Einstein's theory. Research, using his work as basis, continues.

Dollfus, Audouin Charles (*1924–*), is a French physicist and astronomer whose preferred method of research is to use polarization of light, for which method he is prepared to put up with some disomfort.

Dollfus was born on 12 November 1924; he studied at the Lycée Janson-de-Sailly and at the Faculty of Sciences in Paris, where he gained his doctorate in mathematical sciences. Since 1946, he has been Astronomer of the Astrophysical Section of Meudon Observatory, in Paris.

Before *Viking* landed on Mars, the mineral composition of the Martian deserts was a subject of considerable dispute. Dollfus checked the polarization of light by several hundreds of different terrestrial minerals to try to find one for which the light matched that polarized by the bright Martian desert areas. He found only one, and that was pulverized limonite (Fe_2O_3), which could be oxidized cosmic iron. (Another astronomer, Gerard Kuiper (1905–) of the University of Chicago, however, did not agree with Dollfus' findings. In his work, iron oxides gave poor results and he obtained his closest match with brownish fine-grained igneous rocks.)

In pursuit of his detailed investigations into Mars, Dollfus made the first ascent in a stratospheric balloon in France.

By means of the polarization of light it is possible to detect an atmosphere round a planet or satellite. In 1950, at which time it was thought the planet Mercury, because of its small size, had probably lost its atmosphere through the escape of the molecules into space, Dollfus announced that he had detected a very faint atmosphere from polarization measurements carried out at the Pic-du-Midi Observatory in the French Pyrenees. This was also in contrast to theoretical expectations based on the kinetic theory of gases. Dollfus estimated that the atmospheric pressure at ground level was about 1 mm of mercury. (The nature of the gas making up this atmosphere is unknown, but it must be a dense, heavy gas. It is certain that the atmosphere on Mercury is not more than 1/300 that on Earth.)

Mercury shows faint shady markings, set against a dull whitish background, that were first observed by Giovanni Schiaparelli in 1889. Using the 60 cm refractor at the Pic-du-Midi Observatory, Dollfus, again in 1950, was able clearly to resolve spots about 300 km apart.

Dollfus has also looked at the possibility of an atmosphere around the Moon. The rate of thermal dissipation into space of all but the heavier gases (which are cosmically very scarce) from the Moon is so high that an atmosphere cannot be expected. The most telling evidence is the complete absence of the twilight phenomena on the Moon. Any elongation of the points (or the cusps) of the Moon beyond 90°, caused by scattered sunlight, should be detectable by polarization. But Bernard Lyot, and later Dollfus, proved that there was no detectable polarization.

In 1966 Dollfus discovered Janus, the innermost moon of Saturn, at a time when the rings – to which it is very close – were seen from Earth edgeways on (and practically invisible).

A practical astrophysicist, Dollfus has achieved remarkable results through patient and persistent research.

Donati, Giovanni Battista (*1826–1873*), was an Italian astronomer whose principal astronomic interests were the study of comets and cosmic meteorology. He made important contributions to the early development of stellar spectroscopy and to the application of spectroscopic methods to the understanding of the nature of comets.

Donati was born in Pisa on 16 December 1826. He received his university training at the University of Pisa and began his career in astronomy at the observatory in Florence in 1852. He was first employed as an assistant, but in 1864 he succeeded Amici to the Directorship of the Observatory.

One of Donati's major responsibilities after assuming the Directorship of the Observatory was the supervision of the work at Arcetri, not far from Florence, where a new observatory was being set up. It was formally established a year before Donati's death. He was struck down by the plague and died in Florence on 20 September 1873.

Donati's active research career spanned little more than 20 years, but it was very productive. During the 1850s he was an enthusiastic comet-seeker, with six discoveries to this credit – the most dramatic of these was named after him. Donati's comet, which was first sighted on 2 June 1858, was notable for its great beauty. It had, in addition to its major "tail", two narrow extra tails.

Donati then applied his talents and his time to the developing subject of stellar spectroscopy. He compared and contrasted the spectrum of the Sun with those of other stars, and then sought to use this technique to examine the properties and composition of comets. Donati found that when a comet was still distant from the Sun, its spectrum was identical to that of the Sun. When the comet approached the Sun it increased in magnitude (brightness) and its spectrum became completely different. Donati concluded that when the comet was still distant from the Sun, the light it emanated was simply a reflection of sunlight. As the comet approached the Sun the material in it became so heated that it emitted a light of its own, which reflected the comet's composition.

Shortly thereafter, William Muggins (1824–1910) reported that the tail of a comet contained carbon compounds. More definitive analyses of cometary make-up were written over the ensuing years, culminating with Whipple's report published in 1950.

Donati was also interested in the Sun. He observed the solar eclipse of 18 July 1860 from Torreblanca, Spain, and also the eclipse of 22 December 1980. For the latter occasion he designed a spectroscope which incorporated five prisms; later he made an even more complex spectroscope which used no fewer than 25 prisms. He published papers in which he gave an estimate of the distance from the Earth to the Sun and his conclusions on the structure of the Sun itself.

Other areas of interest which engaged Donati's attention were atmospheric phenomena and events in higher zones, such as the aurora borealis. His most important research was, however, his pioneering efforts in the use of spectroscopy to elucidate the nature of comets.

Draper, Henry (*1837–1882*), was one of the United States' outstanding "amateur" astronomers, noted for his work on stellar spectroscopy and commemorated by the Henry Draper Catalogue of stellar spectral types.

Draper was born in Virginia on 7 March 1837. His father, John William Draper, was a distinguished physician and chemist. He was educated at the University of the City of New York and entered the Medical School at the age of 17. By the time he was 20, he had completed the medical course, but since he had not reached the age required for graduation, he spent the following year travelling in Europe. During this period he visited, and was greatly influenced by, William Parsons and his Observatory in Parsonstown (now Birr) in Ireland. In 1860 Draper was appointed Professor of Natural Science at the University of the City of New York, but the interests that he developed during his travels (telescope-making and photography) were to be woven into his professional career. He died unexpectedly, of double pleurisy, at his home in New York on 20 November 1882.

On returning from his travels in Europe, Draper began preparing his own glass mirror and by 1861 he had installed it in his new observatory on his father's estate at Hastings-on-Hudson, New York. Draper began his research career by making preliminary studies of the spectra of the more common elements and photographing the solar spectrum. By 1873 he had devised a spectrograph that was similar to Huggins' visual spectroscope; it clarified the spectral lines by means of a slit and incorporated a reference spectra so that celestial elements could be identified more easily.

In 1874 Draper was asked to act as Director of the photographic department of the US commission to observe the transit of Venus of that year. Draper's work was stimulated by the spectroscopic studies of Huggins and Lockyer in Europe and during the last years of his life he worked towards obtaining high-quality spectra of celestial objects. He studied the Moon, Mars, Jupiter, the comet 1881 III and the Orion Nebula. He also succeeded in obtaining photographs of stars that were to faint to be seen with the same telescope by using exposure times of more than 140 minutes – exemplifying the advantages of photography in astronomy.

After Draper's sudden death, his widow established a fund to support further spectral studies. It was used by a team at Harvard College Observatory as part of a programme, begun in 1886, to establish a useful classification scheme for stars and a catalogue of spectra. The Harvard project was not completed until 1897 but the result was a comprehensive classification of stars according to their spectra, named the Henry Draper Catalogue.

Dreyer, John Louis Emil (*1852–1926*), was a Danish-born astronomer and author, whose working life was spent almost entirely in Ireland. He is best known for a biographical study of the work of the great Danish scientist, Tycho Brahe, and for the meticulous compilation of catalogues of nebulae and star clusters.

Dreyer was born in Copenhagen on 13 February 1852. Educated there, he displayed unusual talents in mathematics, physics and history, although it was not until he was aged 14 that he read a book about Tycho Brahe and became keenly interested in astronomy – an interest that was encouraged by his friendship with Schjellerup, an astronomer at the Copenhagen University. Dreyer began his studies at the university in 1869, and by 1870 he had been given a key that allowed him free access to the instruments in the University Observatory. In 1874 he was appointed assistant at Lord Rosse's Observatory at Birr Castle in Parsonstown in Ireland. Four years later he took up a similar post at Dunsink Observatory at the University of Dublin, and four years later again (1882) he became Director of the Armagh Observatory, where he remained until he retired in 1916. On his retirement he went to live in Oxford and, continuing his writing, made use of the facilities of the Bodleian Library. He died in Oxford on 14 September 1926.

Dreyer's earliest formal astronomical publication, published in 1872, was a description of the orbit of the first comet of 1870. After his move to Ireland in 1874, he became increasingly interested in making observations of nebulae and star clusters, a subject which occupied most of his time for the next 14 years. He was acutely aware of the element of error involved in astronomical observations of objects such as nebulae, and he published an important paper on the subject in 1876.

In 1877 Dreyer presented to the Royal Astronomical Society data on more than a thousand new nebulae and corrections to the original catalogue on nebulae and star clusters compiled by John Herschel (1792–1871). He extended this work at Armagh, which led to the publication in 1886 of the Second Armagh Catalogue, with information on more than 3,000 stars. The Royal Astronomical Society then invited him to compile a comprehensive new catalogue of nebulae and star clusters to incorporate all the modern data and to supersede Herschel's old catalogue. This enormous task was completed in only two years, but the rapid accumulation of more information necessitated the publication of two supplementary indexes in 1895 and 1908. Together these three catalogues described more than 13,000 nebulae and star clusters and achieved international recognition as standard reference material.

The catalogue completed, Dreyer decided to write a biography of his hero, Tycho Brahe. It was published in 1890 and preceded a 15-volume series (1913–1919) detailing all of Brahe's work. Dreyer's other writings included a history of astronomy (at that time the only authoritative and complete historical analysis), and an edition of the complete works of William Herschel (1738–1822).

On his retirement in 1916, Dreyer, a Fellow of the Royal Astronomical Society since 1875, was awarded the Society's highest honour, the Gold Medal. A patient and skilled observational astronomer, Dreyer was also an excellent mathematician, a talented scholar and an accomplished writer. He put all of these attainments to good use during his career, combining them to produce work of enduring quality.

Dyson, Frank Watson (*1868–1939*), was an astronomer especially interested in stellar motion and time determination.

Dyson was born in Ashby-de-la-Zouch, Leicestershire, on 8 January 1868. He attended Bradford Grammar School and Trinity College, Cambridge, from which he graduated in 1889. He became a Fellow of Trinity in 1891 and in 1894 he was made Chief Assistant at the Greenwich Observatory. He left in 1906 to become Astronomer Royal for Scotland, but returned to Greenwich in 1910 to serve as Astronomer Royal for England. He retired in 1933, but remained active in research and writing. In addition to his many research publications, Dyson was the author of several general books on astronomy. He died off the coast of South Africa, while on a sea voyage from Australia, on 25 May 1939.

Dyson's early research was concentrated on problems in gravity theory, but as soon as he started his work at the Greenwich Observatory he began a lengthy study of stellar proper motion in collaboration with William Thackeray. He was an active member of several expeditions to study total eclipses of the Sun, and in 1906 he published a book in which he discussed data he had obtained on these occasions on the spectrum of the solar chromosphere.

Dyson was one of a number of astronomers who confirmed the observations of Jacobus Kapteyn on the proper motions of stars, which indicated that the stars in our Galaxy seemed to be moving in two great streams. These results were later realized to be the first evidence for the rotation of our Galaxy.

The measurement of time has always been an important function of the Greenwich Observatory, and Dyson was passionately interested in this aspect of his work. It was he who initiated the public broadcasting of time-signals by the British Broadcasting Corporation over the radio, in the form of the familiar six-pip signal. (This was first broadcast in 1924 from Rugby.)

Another important research area for the Greenwich Observatory is the study of solar eclipses, and Dyson was active in the organization of expeditions to observe these. The most significant of these expeditions were the two he coordinated for the 1919 eclipse. They served as the occasion for Arthur Eddington's famous confirmation of the gravitational deflection of light by the Sun, as predicted by Einstein's General Theory of Relativity.

Other areas to which Dyson made important contributions include the study of the Sun's corona and of stellar parallaxes. He was a talented astronomer and a skilled administrator.

E

Eddington, Arthur Stanley (*1882-1944*), was a British astronomer and writer who discovered the fundamental role of radiation pressure in the maintenance of stellar equilibrium, explained the method by which the energy of a star moves from its interior to its exterior, and finally showed that the luminosity of a star depends almost exclusively on its mass - a discovery that caused a complete revision of contemporary ideas on stellar evolution. He also demonstrated that a ray of light is deflected by gravity, thus confirming one application of Albert Einstein's General Theory of Relativity.

Eddington was born on 28 December 1882 in Kendal, Cumbria, although he spent his childhood in Weston-super-Mare, Somerset, and was educated there and at Owen's College, Manchester. In 1902 he won an entrance scholarship to Trinity College, Cambridge. Graduating three years later, he taught for a short time before being appointed Chief Assistant at the Royal Observatory, Greenwich. The seven years he stayed there saw the beginning of his theoretical work.

In 1909 he was sent to Malta to determine the longitude of the geodetic station there and, in 1912, he went to Brazil as the leader of an eclipse expedition. In 1913, Eddington returned to Cambridge to become Plumian Professor of Astronomy; shortly afterwards, he became Director of the University Observatory. Eddington remained at Cambridge for the next 31 years.

During his lifetime, Eddington was considered to be one of the greatest astronomers of the age. In 1906, he was elected Fellow of the Royal Astronomical Society and he was its president from 1921 to 1923. In 1914, he was elected Fellow of the Royal Society. He was knighted in 1938.

In the autumn of 1944 Eddington underwent a major surgical operation from which he never recovered. He died in Cambridge on 22 November of that year. After his death the Eddington Memorial Scholarship was established and the Eddington Medal was struck as an annual award.

Eddington published a large number of works. His first book, *Stellar Movements and the Structure of the Universe* (1914), is considered to be a model of scientific exposition. The final chapter of the book alone, entitled "Dynamics of the Stellar System", marked the founding of an important branch of astronomical research. His book, *The Internal Construction of the Stars* (1926), became one of the classics of astronomy. His report to the Physical Society in 1918, expanded into his *Mathematical Theory of Relativity*, was the work that first gave English-speaking people the chance to learn the mathematical details of Einstein's famous theory of gravitation. Eddington's ability as a writer not only served to introduce a whole generation to the science of astronomy; it also had a stimulating effect on other astronomers.

Eddington involved himself in a great deal of practical work. He was the leader of the expedition to West Africa in 1919, where on 29 May on the island of Principe he observed the total eclipse of the Sun. The data he obtained served to verify one of the predictions contained in Einstein's General Theory of Relativity, that rays of light are affected by gravitation.

Eddington's first theoretical investigations were concerned with the systematic motion of the stars, but his great pioneering work in astrophysics began in 1916 when he started to study their composition. He established that in a star energy is transported by radiation, not by convection as had hitherto been thought. He also established that the mechanical pressure of the radiation was an important element in the maintenance of the star's mechanical equilibrium. Eddington showed that the equation of equilibrium must take into account three forces: gravitation, gas pressure and radiative pressure. One of the major questions at that time was how the gas of which stars and the Sun are composed was prevented from contracting under the tremendous force of stellar gravity. Eddington decided that the expansive force of heat and radiation pressure countered the contractive force of gravity. He also concluded that, since the pressure of the stellar matter increased rapidly with depth, the radiative pressure must also increase, and the only way in which that could happen was through a rise in temperature. Eddington showed that the more massive a star, the greater the pressure in its interior, and so the greater the countering temperature and radiation pressure, and consequently the greater its luminosity. He had found that the luminosity of a great star depends almost exclusively on its mass and, in 1924, he announced his mass-luminosity law. This work was of outstanding importance and necessitated a complete revision of contemporary notions regarding stellar evolution.

From 1930, Eddington worked on relating the theory of relativity and quantum theory. He believed that he could calculate mathematically, without recourse to observation, all the values of those constants of nature which are pure numbers, for example, the ratio of the mass of the proton to that of the electron. In his posthumously published *Fundamental Theory*, he presented his calculations of many of the constants of nature, including the recession velocity constant of the external galaxies, the number of particles in the universe, the ratio of the gravitational force to the electrical force between a proton and an electron, the fine structure constant, and the velocity of light.

In his later years, Eddington dealt with the philosophy of science and discussed the question of what sort of knowledge it was that science conveys to man. He had himself contributed considerably to that knowledge.

Edlen, Bengt (*1906–*), is a Swedish astrophysicist whose main achievement has been to resolve the identification of certain lines in spectra of the solar corona that misled scientists for the previous 70 years.

Edlen was born in Gusum in Ostergotland, south-eastern Sweden, on 2 November 1906. He was educated at Uppsala University and, in 1928, became an assistant in the physics department there. In 1936 he was appointed Assistant Professor of Physics. In 1944 he moved to southern Sweden to become Professor of Physics at Lund University. He held this post until 1973, when he became Emeritus Professor.

During the eclipse of 1869, astronomers recorded the presence of a hitherto unknown series of spectral lines in the Sun's corona. Because they failed to identify the origin of these lines, they ascribed them to the presence of a new element which they called "coronium". The origin of the lines was originally recorded as being located high above the Sun's surface, but similar lines were then discovered to originate nearer the Earth; these were accordingly attributed to another new element, which they called "geocoronium". Both the new elements were predicted to be much lighter than hydrogen, the lightest element known on Earth.

For 70 years all attempts to associate the coronal lines with known elements on Earth failed. Then, in the early 1940s, Edlen carried out a series of experiments and showed that, if iron atoms are deprived of some of their electrons, they can produce spectral lines similar to those produced by "coronium". He established that if half the normal number of 26 electrons or iron are removed, the effect produced is that of the green lines observed on the coronal line. Other lines were identified as iron atoms with different numbers of their electrons removed. Furthermore, it was found that similarly ionized atoms of nickel, calcium and argon produced even more lines.

It was determined that such high stages of ionization would require temperatures of about one million degrees Celsius and when, in the 1950s, it was verified that such high temperatures did exist in the solar corona, it became accepted that "coronium" as a separate element did not exist and that the "coronium" lines owed their existence to ordinary elements being subjected to extreme temperatures – temperatures so high that they caused the corona to expand continuously. It was also established that the lines formerly thought to be caused by the presence of "geocoronium" are produced by atomic nitrogen emitting radiation in the Earth's upper atmosphere.

Eggen, Olin Jenck (*1919–*), is an American astronomer who has spent much of his working life in senior appointments all round the world. His work has included studies of high-velocity stars, red giants (using narrow- and broad-band photometry) and subluminous stars, and he has published some research on historical aspects of astronomy.

Born in Orfordville, Wisconsin, on 9 July 1919, Eggen graduated from Wisconsin University before becoming Astronomer at the University of California in 1945. In 1956 he became the Chief Assistant at the Royal Observatory, Greenwich. Maintaining his links with the United States, he was Professor of Astronomy at the California Institute of Technology from 1960 to 1963. He returned to Greenwich for a short time before serving as Astronomer at the Mount Palomar Observatory from 1965 to 1966. In 1966 he went to Australia to take up the post of Director of Mount Stromlo and Siding Spring Observatories, combining with this Professor of Astronomy in the Institute of Advanced Study, the Australian National University. Eggen remained at Mount Stromlo until 1977, when he moved to a position at the Observatory Interamericano de Cerro Tololo, Chile.

During the mid-1970s, Eggen completed a study – based on UBV photometry and every available apparent motion – of all red giants brighter than $V = 5^m0$. As a result he was able to classify these stars, categorizing them as very young discs, young discs and old discs. A few remained unclassifiable (haloes).

He also systematically investigated the efficiency of the method of stellar parallax using visual binaries originally suggested by William Herschel in 1781, and reviewed the original correspondence of John Flamsteed (1646–1719) and Edmond Halley (1656–1742).

Encke, Johann Franz (*1791–1865*), was an influential German astronomer whose work on star charts during the 1840s contributed to the discovery of the planet Neptune in 1846. He also worked out the path of the comet which bears his name.

Born in Hamburg on 23 September 1791, Encke was the eighth child of a Lutheran preacher. As a child he was exceedingly proficient at mathematics and at the age of 20 he became a student at the University of Göttingen. His degree studies were interrupted by military service in the Wars of Liberation.

As a student Encke impressed the physicist Karl Gauss (1777–1855) who was instrumental in securing a post for him at a small astronomical observatory at Seeberg near Gotha. There the quality of his work was soon recognized and he rose in seniority from Assistant to Director. Encke then accepted the offer of a Professorship at the Academy of Sciences in Berlin and the Directorship of the Berlin Observatory in 1825. After 40 years in Berlin, Encke died there on 26 August 1865.

A fine mathematician who carried out continuous research on comets and the perturbations of the asteroids, Encke spent much of his time putting together the information with which to prepare new star charts. The compilation was from both old and new observations and many alternative sources. The charts, taking nearly 20 years to draw up, were complete in 1859 – but were soon improved upon by those prepared by Friedrich Argelander (1799–1875). Nevertheless Encke's charts were of some value in that they pointed out the existence of Neptune and several minor planets.

Encke's most successful piece of work was on what subsequently became known as Encke's Comet. This comet had been reported by Jean Pons (1761–1831), but little was known of its behaviour. Encke showed that the comet had an elliptical orbit with a period of just less than four years.

One of his tasks at Berlin was to oversee the Berlin *Astronomisches Jahrbuch* (Yearbook), of which he was the editor for the period 1830–1866. The books included large sections on minor planets, which increased their cost considerably. Encke was prepared to take the risk that high costs would diminish the market for the annual, since he considered that the data were worth publishing. He also used the books to publish many of his own mathematical determinations of orbits and perturbations, although he preferred to publish papers on planets of the Solar System in *Astronomische Nachrichten*.

During the later 1820s and the early 1830s Encke was responsible for the re-equipping and resiting of the Berlin Observatory. After raising the necessary financial support he installed a meridian circle, a large Fraunhofer refractor and a heliometer. The observatory specialized in the observation of moveable stars.

Eratosthenes (*276–c. 195* BC), was a Greek scholar and polymath, many of whose writings have been lost, although it is known that they included papers on geography, mathematics, philosophy, chronology and literature.

The son of Aglaos, Eratosthenes was born in Cyrene (now known as Shahhat, part of Libya). He underwent the equivalent of a university education in Athens before being invited, at the age of 30, by Ptolemy III Euergetes to become tutor to his son and to work in the library of the famous museum at Alexandria. On the death of Zenodotus in 240 BC he became the museum's Chief Librarian.

No single complete work of Eratosthenes, a premier scholar of his time, survives. The most important that remains is on geography – a word that he virtually coined as the title of his three-volume study of the Earth (as much as he knew of it) and its measurement. The work was concerned with the whole of the known world and divided the Earth into zones and surface features; parallels and meridian lines were used as a basis for establishing distances between places. It was accepted as the definitive work of its time (although it was criticized by Hipparchus for not making sufficient use of astronomical data). Eratosthenes greatly improved upon the inaccurate Ionian map.

The base line was a parallel running from Gibraltar through the middle of the Mediterranean and Rhodes to the Taurus Mountains in modern Turkey, onward to the Elburz range, the Hindu Kush and to the Himalayas. At right-angles to this line was a meridian passing through Heroe, Syene (now Aswan), Alexandria, Rhodes and the mouth of the River Borysthenes (now Dniepr). The data available were mostly the notes and records of travellers and their estimates of days in transit, although some data about the height and angle of the Sun at Meroe, Alexandria and Marseilles had been collected.

Eratosthenes' measurements of the height of the Sun at Alexandria used the fact that Syene was on the Tropic of Cancer (where at midday on the summer solstice a vertical post casts no shadow, for the sun is directly overhead). Alexandria and Syene were on the same meridian. Eratosthenes' measurements were made at midday, but with a thin pillar in the centre of a hemispherical bowl. He estimated that the shadow was 1/25 of the hemisphere and so was 1/50 of the whole circle. Since the rays of the Sun can be considered to be striking any point on the Earth's surface in parallel lines, by using alternate angles and incor-

49

porating the known distance between Alexandria and Syene of 5,000 stades, Eratosthenes was able to calculate that the total circumference of the Earth was just over 250,000 stades. There are several errors in his assumptions, but as the first attempt it was given much credit. The conversion of stades into modern units creates additional error, although a value of 46,500 km is usually quoted. (The modern figure is usually accepted as 40,075 km at the equator.)

Eratosthenes also divided the Earth into five zones; two frigid zones around each pole with a radius of 25,200 stades on the meridian circle; two temperate zones between the polar zones and the tropics, with a radius of 21,000 stades; and a torrid zone comprising the two areas from the equator to each tropic, having a radius of 16,800 stades. The frigid zones he described as the "Arctic" and "Antarctic" circles of an observer on the major parallel of latitude (approximately 36°N); these circles mark the limits of the circumpolar stars which never rise or set. Eratosthenes' model of the known world had a north-south length of 38,000 stades from the Cinnamon country to Thale, and an east-west length of 77,800 stades from Eastern India to the Straits of Gibraltar.

Eratosthenes was familiar with the Earth and the apparent movement of the Sun, but he did little serious astronomical study. However, he also estimated the obliquity of the ecliptic as 11/83 of a circle, equivalent to 23°51′.

In the mathematical area he was most successful in offering a solution to the famous Delian problem of doubling the cube. For his proof, Eratosthenes proposed an apparatus consisting of a framework of two parallel rulers with grooves along which could be slid three rectangular plates capable of moving independently of each other and able to overlap. In arithmetic he devised a technique called the Sieve for finding prime numbers.

Eratosthenes also spent a considerable period of his life establishing the dates of historical events. In his two major works *Chronography* and *Olympic Victors*, many of the dates he set for events have been accepted by later historians and have never been changed. (For example, the Fall of Troy was in 1184/1183 BC, and the First Olympiad took place in 777/776 BC.) He also wrote many books on literary criticism in a series entitled *On the Old Comedy*. Like much of his output it is referred to by contemporary and later scholars, but it did not survive the passage of time.

Eudoxus of Cnidus (*408–355* BC), was a Greek mathematician and astronomer who is said to have studied under Plato. Himself a great influ-

ence on contemporary scientific thought, Eudoxus was the author of several important works. Many of his theories have survived the test of centuries; work attributed to Eudoxus includes methods to calculate the area of a circle and to derive the volume of a pyramid or a cone. He also devised a system to demonstrate the motion of the known planets when viewed from the Earth.

Very little is known about Eudoxus' life, although it is recorded that he spent more than a year in Egypt, some of the time as the guest of the priests of Heliopolis. In a series of geographical books with the overall title of *A Tour of the Earth* he later described the political, historical and religious customs of the countries of the eastern Mediterranean area.

Primarily a mathematician, Eudoxus used his mathematical knowledge to construct a model of homocentric rotating spheres to explain the motion of planets as viewed from the Earth, which was at the centre of the system. The model was later extended by Aristotle (384–322 BC) and Callippus (*c.* 370–*c.* 300 BC), and although superseded by the theory of epicycles, it was still widely accepted during the Middle Ages. Eudoxus was able to give close approximations for the synodic periods of the planets Saturn, Jupiter, Mars, Venus and Mercury. The geometry of the model was impressive, but there are several weaknesses. Eudoxus assumed, for example, that each planet remains at a constant distance from the centre of its orbital circle, and in addition that each retrograde loop as seen from the Earth is identical with the last. Neither assumptions complies with observation.

The model of planetary motion was published in a book called *On Rates*. Further astronomical observations were included in two other works, *The Mirror* and *Phenomena*. Subject later to considerable criticism by Hipparchus (fl. *c.* 146–*c.* 127 BC), these books nevertheless established patterns where before none existed.

In mathematics Eudoxus's early success was in the removal of many of the limitations imposed by Pythagoras on the theory of proportion. Eudoxus showed that the theory was applicable in many more circumstances. Subsequently he established a test for the equality of two ratios, and noted that it was possible to find a good approximate value for the area of a circle by the "method of exhaustion": a polygon is drawn within the circle, the number of its sides is repeatedly doubled, and the area of each new polygon is found by using a simple formula. It was to Eudoxus that Archimedes attributed the discovery that the volume of a pyramid or a cone is equal to one-third of the area of the base times the perpendicular height.

Although none of Eudoxus' works has survived the passage of time in complete form, the mathematical skills he practised were important and influential both in his own age and for centuries afterwards.

F

Field, George Brooks (*1929-*   ), is an American theoretical astrophysicist whose main research has been into the nature and composition of intergalactic matter and the properties of residual radiation is space.

Field was born in Providence, Rhode Island, on 25 October 1929. Educated at the Massachusetts Institute of Technology, he graduated in 1951 and four years later gained a PhD in astronomy at Princeton University. In 1957 he was appointed Assistant Professor in astronomy at Princeton and he progressed to become Associate Professor. He was made Professor of the University of California at Berkeley in 1965 and was Chairman of the Department from 1970 to 1971. Since 1972 he has been Professor of Astronomy at Harvard University; from 1973 he has also been Director of the Centre of Astrophysics at the Harvard College Observatory and the Smithsonian Astrophysical Observatory.

One of Field's major areas of research has been to investigate why a cluster of galaxies remains a cluster. It seems evident that such clusters ought to be rapidly dispersing unless they are stabilized in some way, presumably gravitationally by intergalactic matter that contributes from ten to thirty times more material than the galaxies themselves. Such matter has never been detected, although considerable research has been undertaken and is still in progress. From a consideration of the composition of galaxies in clusters, it would seem probable that the most likely substance of such intergalactic matter would be in the form of hydrogen, that around 27 per cent by mass would be helium, and that a negligible fraction would be in the form of heavier elements. There is at present no means of detecting helium in intergalactic space - but intergalactic hydrogen does produce effects that are potentially detectable, and this is the work in which Field has been particularly involved.

Atomic hydrogen distributed intergalactically (in contrast to ionized hydrogen) would act both as an absorber and an emitter of radiation at a wavelength of 21 cm. Field first tried to find evidence of this absorption in 1958. He studied the spectrum of the radio source Cygnus A - the brightest extragalactic radio source in the sky - in the region of 21 cm, taking into account the known red shift associated with the expansion of the Universe. The narrow range of wavelengths over which the intergalactic hydrogen would absorb is called the "absorption trough". A wavelength of 21 cm is remarkably long for an atom to absorb or emit, and from the point of view of the two energy levels involved, the hydrogen is immersed in a heat bath at an extremely high temperature - so that there are nearly as many atoms in the upper state as in the lower, and the absorption trough cannot be very exactly observed. Field's later results have given greater precision.

Field has also carried out research into the spectral lines in the spectra of stars. In the 1930s, A. McKellar found absorption lines corresponding to interstellar cyanogen (CN) in the spectra of several stars. For the star Zeta Ophiuci, McKellar was able to obtain a measure of the relative number of molecules in the ground state and the first rotational state, which he defined in terms of an excitation temperature (the temperature at which the molecules would possess the observed degree of excitation if they were in equilibrium in a heat bath). At that time, however, excitation was assumed to occur only by collisions with other particles or by radiation with no thermal spectrum. But in 1966, microwave measurements of the cosmic background were made that suggested that this background has a black-body spectrum at all wavelengths. Field then wondered if the CN "molecules" might after all be in a heat bath. He re-observed the spectrum of Zeta Ophiuci, and obtained an excitation temperature of $3.22 \pm 0.15K$, which corresponded well with the value of 2.3K determined by McKellar. A number of other stars have since been analysed and all of them yield a temperature of about 3K. There remains much more work on this subject to be done.

Flammarion, Nicolas Camille (*1842 1925*), was a French astronomer and geophysicist whose writings were instrumental in popularizing science - particularly astronomy - although some of his books contained speculations that were wildly mistaken.

Flammarion was born in Montigny-le-Roi, in Haute Marne, on 26 February 1842. From an early age astronomy held a fascination for him, and while he was an apprentice engraver in 1858 he wrote a long essay entitled *Cosmogenie universelle*. By a sequence of lucky accidents, the text came to the attention of Urbain Le Verrier (1811-1877), Director of the Paris Observatory. Within days, the 16-year-old Flammarion was apprenticed as an astronomer at the Observatory.

After serving a period as a calculator with the Bureau de Longitudes (from 1862 to 1876), during which time he was already writing popular astronomical books and giving public lectures on astronomy and allied topics, Flammarion became an astronomer at the Paris Observatory. He left in 1882 to establish a monthly astronomical magazine, and a year later he founded and became Director of a new Observatory at Juvisy-sur-Orge – a post he retained until his death. Flammarion was active in the establishment of the French Astronomical Society in 1887, and an enthusiastic member of the Society for Psychical Research. He died in Juvisy-sur-Orge on 3 June 1925.

Flammarion's interests spanned an enormous range of subjects, taking in geophysics, astronomy, meteorology, philosophy and (especially later in life) parapsychology. In astronomy he made observations of double and multiple stars, of the Moon and of Mars. He reported changes in the colouration of the crater Pluto on the Moon which he ascribed to variations in the activity of plant life. He was active in the debate stimulated by Giovanni Schiapparelli's description of an orderly and intricate canal system on the Martian surface, and publicly and frequently promulgated the view that there was advanced intelligent life on Mars. Indeed, he was inclined to believe that there were many centres of intelligent life in the Universe and he wrote a popular book on the topic in 1861. His most famous book, *L'astronomie populaire* (1879), sold an enormous number of copies and was translated into several languages.

The author of more than a dozen other popular books, including science-oriented novels and texts on parapsychology, Flammarion gave the general public the opportunity to become familiar with the latest research and speculation in many scientific fields.

Flamsteed, John (*1646–1719*), was an English astronomer and writer who became the first Astronomer Royal based at Greenwich. His work on the stars, which formed the basis of modern star catalogues, was much admired by contemporary scientists, among whom were Isaac Newton (1643–1727) and Edmond Halley (1656–1742). Like many professional scientists of his time, he was also a clergyman.

Flamsteed was born on 19 August 1646 at Denby, near Derby, the son of a prosperous businessman. At the age of 16, ill-health forced him to leave Derby Free School and abandon, at least temporarily, his university ambitions. The next seven years he spent at home, educating himself in astronomy against the wishes of his father (who evidently saw him as his own successor in the

family business). In 1670, however, he entered his name at Jesus College, Cambridge, and took an MA degree by letters-patent. He was ordained in the following year. Through the influence of Jonas Moore, a courtier of King Charles II, Flamsteed was made "Astronomical Observator" at the newly established Greenwich Observatory in 1675. In 1684 he was presented with the living of Burstow, in Surrey, by Lord North. He died at Greenwich on 31 December 1719 and was succeeded in his post there by Edmond Halley.

Flamsteed began his astronomical studies at home by observing a solar eclipse on 12 September 1662, about which he corresponded with several other astronomers. When he decided to take his university degree in 1670, he sent his early studies to the Royal Society and they were published in *Philosophical Transactions*. This was enough to gain him general scientific recognition, but it was Jonas Moore who launched him in his career when he gave him a micrometer and promised him a good telescopic lens, thus enabling him to start serious practical work.

At the time Flamsteed's research began, 60 years had passed since Galileo (1564–1642) had made his discoveries, the star catalogue prepared by Tycho Brahe (1546–1601) was still the standard work, and the Laws of Johannes Kepler (1571–1630) were only gradually being accepted. Flamsteed resolved to end the apparent stagnation in astronomical science. In 1672 he determined the solar parallax from observations of Mars when the planet was at its closest to the Sun, using the rotation of the Earth to establish a base-line. Four years later, and only two months after his appointment to Greenwich, he began observations that were to result in a 3,000-star British catalogue. His results improved on Brahe's work by a factor of 15, but at first they were only relative measurements, with no anchor in the celestial sphere. To assist him in his work, Jonas Moore further donated two chronometers and a 2.1 m (7 ft) sextant, with which he made 20,000 observations between 1676 and 1689.

Settled in at Greenwich, Flamsteed became interested in the work on lunar theory published by Jeremiah Horrocks (or Horrox; 1619–1641) some decades earlier. He brought Horrocks's constants up to date and revised his calculations no fewer than three times. The models in Flamsteed's third set of calculations were of fundamental importance in some of Newton's theoretical work. Following his revisions of lunar theory, Flamsteed also produced three different sets of tables describing the motion of the Sun. The first was issued before Flamsteed had any original observations on which he could base his parameters. His second gave a new determination of solar eccentricity, at almost the true value of 0.01675, and was published in his book *Doctrine of the Sphere* in 1680. The third was printed in 1707 in Whiston's *Praelectiones Astronomicae*. It included more detailed observations made possible by new equipment purchased after he inherited his father's estate in 1688.

With his improved facilities, including a mural arc, Flamsteed was able to make some very precise measurements: he determined the latitude of Greenwich, the slant of the ecliptic and the position of the equinox. He also worked out an ingenious method of observing the absolute right ascension – a co-ordinate of the position of a heavenly body. His method, a great improvement on previous systems, removed all errors of parallax, refraction and latitude. Having obtained the positions of 40 reference stars, he then went back and computed positions for the rest of the 3,000 stars in his catalogue.

Flamsteed also produced tables of atmospheric refraction, tidal tables, and supervised the compilation of the first table describing the inequality of the lunar elliptic following Kepler's second Law.

A serious-minded man (possibly as a result of his constantly frail health), Flamsteed was never good at dealing with other people. Much of the last twenty years of his life was spent in controversy over the publication of his work. His results were urgently needed by Sir Isaac Newton and Sir Edmond Halley to test their theories, but Flamsteed was determined to withhold them until he was quite certain they were correct. A row with both Halley and Newton in 1704 eventually led to Flamsteed's work being unlawfully printed in 1712, but Flamsteed managed to secure and burn 300 copies of the printed production. Accordingly, the preparation of his great work, *Historia Coelestis Britannica*, was completed by his assistants six years after his death, in 1725, and his *Atlas Coelestis* was published even later, in 1729.

Fleming, Williamina Paton Stevens (*1857–1911*), was the British-born co-author (with Edward Pickering) of the first general catalogue classifying stellar spectra.

Fleming was born on 15 May 1857 in Dundee, Scotland, where she was educated. She taught for a few years there before she married and emigrated to the United States in 1878. Shortly after her arrival in Boston her marriage broke up. She was then employed, in 1879, as an assistant to Edward Pickering (1846–1919), Director of the Harvard College Observatory. Her work for him was as a "computer" and copy editor, at which she was so successful that she was soon put in charge of twelve other "computers". In 1898 she

was appointed the curator of astronomical photographs. She died in Boston on 21 May 1911.

The project initiated by Pickering was simple in concept, but required meticulous dedication and patience. Photographs were taken on the spectra obtained using prisms placed in front of the objectives of telescopes. Although the use of the technique was restricted to stars about a certain magnitude, it yielded a wealth of information. In the course of her analysis of these spectra, Fleming discovered 59 nebulae, more than 300 variable stars, and 10 novae (which is even more impressive when it is recalled that at the time of her death in 1911 only 28 novae had been found).

The spectra of the stars observed in this manner could be classified into categories. Fleming designed the system adopted in the 1890 *Draper Catalogues*, in which 10,351 stellar spectra were listed in 17 categories ("A" to "Q"). The majority of the spectra fell into one of six common categories; only 72 spectra acounted for the other eleven classes. This classification system represented a considerable advance in the study of stellar spectra, although it later was superseded by the work of Annie J. Cannon (1863–1941) at the same observatory.

Fleming's special interest was in the detailed classification of the spectra of variable stars; she proposed a system in which their spectra were subdivided into eleven sub-classes on the basis of further detailed spectral characteristics.

Fowler, William Alfred (*1911–   *), is an American physicist and astronomer who has published many papers on the measurement of nuclear reaction rates in the laboratory for application to the study of energy generation and the creation of elements heavier than hydrogen in the Sun and other stars.

Fowler was born in Pittsburgh, Pennsylvania, on 9 August 1911. Obtaining his bachelor's degree in physics at Ohio State University in 1933, he went to the California Institute of Technology, gained a PhD, and became a Research Fellow there in 1936. Since that time, he has remained at C.I.T., rising from Assistant Professor to Professor and, in 1970, Instructor Professor of Physics.

Fowler's work has, in the main, concentrated in research into the abundance of helium in the Universe. The helium abundance was first defined as the result of the "hot big bang" theory proposed by Ralph Alpher (1921–   ), Hans Bethe (1906–   ) and George Gamow (1904–1968) in 1948, and corrected through the brilliant theoretical work of Chushiro Hayashi (1920–   ) in 1950. In addition to altering the time-scale proposed in the α-β-γ theory, Hayashi also showed that the abundance of neutrons at the heart of the

Big Bang did not depend on the material density but on the temperature and the properties of the weak interreactions. Provided the density is great enough for the reaction between neutrons and protons to combine at a rate faster than the expansion rate, a fixed concentration of neutrons will be incorporated into helium nuclei, however great the material density is – producing a "plateau" in the relationship between helium abundance and material density.

In 1967, Fowler – together with Fred Hoyle (1915–   ) and R. Wagoner – made elaborate calculations of the percentage plateau abundance. His calculations took into account all the reactions that can occur between the light elements, and also considered the build-up of heavier elements; 144 different reactions were observed and the results analysed by computer. He and his collaborators claim an accuracy of helium abundance to 1 per cent and found that the percentage abundance of helium in this plateau is between 25 and 29 per cent. Their calculations for the build-up of other elements such as deuterium and lithium agree well with observations.

Fraunhofer, Joseph von (*1787–1826*), was a German glass- and lens-maker who, in his research to perfect the achromatic lens, considerably advanced scientific knowledge of stellar spectra and the development of the astronomical telescope. During his time, German optical instruments gained a reputation for high precision that they have never since relinquished.

Fraunhofer was born in Straubing, Bavaria, on 6 March 1787, the eleventh and youngest child of a poor glazier. An orphan by the age of eleven, he served a six-year apprenticeship with a master mirror-maker and glass-cutter in Munich before entering the optics department of a Munich scientific instruments company run by Josef von Utzschneider in 1802. Although Fraunhofer had undergone little formal schooling, he soon acquired a familiarity with mathematics as well as showing great skill in practical optics. In 1809, Utzschneider sent him to the workshop of one of his Swiss glass suppliers, Pierre Guinaud, to learn more about glass-making. Two years later, with a practical knowledge of this craft in addition to his understanding of optics. Fraunhofer was no longer merely an employee of Utzschneider, but his business partner. Moreover, his status was also rising in the world. From 1819, he took an active part in the affairs of the Bavarian Academy of Sciences in Munich. In 1823 he was appointed Director of the Physics Museum there and received the honorary title of Professor. Lectures on physical and geometrical optics followed this

appointment, but these had eventually to be discontinued by Fraunhofer because of his poor state of health. He contracted tuberculosis in 1825 and died in Munich on 7 June of the following year.

In striving to construct optical glass of high precision and accuracy, Fraunhofer found himself obliged to carry out tests on the dispersion of light and the refractive index of glass in order to produce achromatic lenses. In 1814, to determine as precisely as he could the optical constants of glass, Fraunhofer repeated an experiment first made by the British physicist William Hyde Wollaston (1766–1828) and examined the spectrum of solar light passing through a narrow slit. This time, however, instead of examining the phenomenon through a prism, Fraunhofer observed it with a low-power telescope. In consequence he saw not just the five lines already noted by Wollaston but a considerable number more. Some were so fine as to be barely visible, others solid and distinct. By the use of a theodolite, Fraunhofer measured the separation between the more important ones and so established the position of 324 of the 574 lines he had observed.

Later Fraunhofer extended his observations by constructing a diffraction grating with 260 parallel wires. The results showed that there was a far greater degree of dispersion by the grating than by a prism. Using the dark solar lines as reference points in the spectrum for his dispersion calculations, Fraunhofer concluded that the degree of dispersion was in inverse ratio to the distance between the slits in the grating. From this same experiment Fraunhofer was able to determine the wavelengths of specific colours.

He remained unable, however, to explain the spectral lines he had laboriously noted, and it was not until 1859 that Gustav Kirchhoff (1824–1887) showed that every element in the light source is represented by spectral lines, by the analysis of which the composition of the light-emitting substance may be determined.

Fraunhofer's most significant achievement was, perhaps, to create an achromatic objective lens for a telescope – modifications of which con-

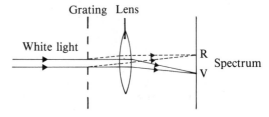

Fraunhofer made the first diffraction gratings, used instead of prisms to produce optical spectra.

tinued to be used in all observatories up to modern times. In late 1817 he finally produced an object glass of an entirely new kind. It has a diameter of 24 cm ($9\frac{1}{2}$ in) and a focal length of about 4.5 m ($14\frac{1}{2}$ ft). The unprecedented diameter of the lens was in marked contrast to the shortness of the focus, but the new lens was not only extremely accurate, it was also achromatic. Fraunhofer had finally succeeded. This lens was duly acquired by Russia for a new observatory at Dorpat (now Tartu, in Estonia) under the direction of Friedrich von Struve (1793-1864), one of the outstanding astronomers of his day.

Friedman, Aleksandr Aleksandrovich (*1888-1925*), was a skilled Russian mathematician with a keen interest in applied mathematics and physics. He made fundamental contributions to the development of theories regarding the expansion of the universe.

Friedman was born in St Petersburg (now Leningrad) on 29 June 1888. An excellent scholar, both at school and at the University of St Petersburg, where he studied mathematics from 1906 to 1910, Friedman later served as a member of the mathematics faculty staff. In 1914 he was awarded his master's degree in pure and applied mathematics, and served with the Russian air force as a technical expert during World War I. Friedman also worked in a factory (which he later managed) that produced instruments for the aviation industry. From 1918 to 1920 he was Professor of Theoretical Mechanics at Perm University, but he returned to St Petersburg in 1920 to conduct research at the Academy of Sciences. He died prematurely, after a life dogged by ill-health, on 16 September 1925 in Leningrad.

Friedman's early research was in the fields of geomagnetism, hydromechanics and, above all, theoretical meteorology. His work of the greatest relevance to astronomy was his independent and original approach to the solution of Einstein's field equation in the General Theory or Relativity. Einstein had produced a static solution, which indicated a closed Universe. Friedman derived several solutions, all of which suggested that space and time were isotropic (uniform at all points and in every direction), but that the mean density and radius of the Universe varied with time - indicating either an expanding or contracting Universe. Einstein himself applauded this significant result.

G

Galileo, Galilei (*1564-1642*), was an Italian mathematician, physicist and astronomer who discovered the laws of falling bodies and the parabolic trajectories of projectiles. With the newly invented telescope, he was among the earliest observers of sunspots and the phases of Venus; he also discovered the four major satellites of Jupiter. His most significant contribution to science was his provision of an alternative to Aristotelian dynamics, by which the motion of the Earth became a conceptual possibility.

Born at Pisa on 15 February 1564, the son of a highly educated musician, Galileo received his early schooling at a monastery before entering the University of Pisa to study medicine. During his first year there he observed a lamp swinging and noted that it always required the same amount of time to complete an oscillation however large the arc of its swing. (Later in life he verified this observation experimentally and suggested that the principle of the pendulum might therefore be applied to the regulation of clocks.) A chance overhearing of a geometry lesson aroused in him more interest than medicine ever had and he immediately took up the study of mathematics, although he had to withdraw from it before taking his degree through lack of money. In 1586 his name became known throughout Italy when he published an essay describing his invention of the hydrostatic balance.

Galileo's researches into the theory of motion began with his disproving of the Aristotelian contention that bodies of different weights fall at different speeds. In 1592 he was appointed to the Chair of Mathematics at the University of Padua, where he was to remain for 18 years, and where most of his more important work was carried out. In about 1604 Galileo proved theoretically that falling bodies obey what came to be known as the law of uniformly accelerated motion, where a body speeds up (or slows down) uniformly with time. He also defined the law of parabolic fall, stating (for example) that a ball thrown into the air follows a parabolic path.

Five years later, while visiting Venice, he heard of the invention of the telescope, and on his return to Padua he built himself one of three-fold magnifying power, which he soon improved to a power of thirty-two. Galileo's method of checking the curvature of his lenses made it possible to use the telescope for astronomical observation and, as the first person to do this, he announced in 1610 a series of astronomical discoveries. The

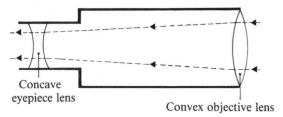

Concave
eyepiece lens

Convex objective lens

In a Galilean refracting telescope, a convex (con-
verging) objective lens and a concave (diverging)
lens in the eyepiece together produce a magnified,
upright image.

face of the Moon, he said, was not smooth, as
hitherto believed, but irregular. He defined the
Milky Way as a collection of stars, and discovered
the first satellites of Jupiter. He also observed the
phases of Venus, the rings of Saturn and spots on
the Sun's disc. The evidence he provided proved
that, like the other planets, the Earth orbited
around the Sun and was not the centre of the
Universe. His position represented such a departure from accepted thought that he was tried by
the Inquisition in Rome, ordered to recant, and
forced to spend the last eight years of his life
under house arrest. After he had become blind,
Galileo was permitted to have his two friends
Vincenzo Viviani (a geometrician) and Evange-
lista Torricelli (a physicist) to live with him until
he died on 8 January 1642.

Galileo's astronomical discoveries were a tri-
bute to both his scientific curiosity and his ability
to devise new techniques with instruments.
Within two years of first building a telescope he
had compiled fairly accurate tables of the orbits
of four of Jupiter's satellites and proposed that
their frequent eclipses could serve as a means of
determining longitude on land and at sea. His
observations on sunspots are noteworthy for
their accuracy and for the deductions he drew
from them regarding the rotation of the Sun and
the orbit of the Earth. He believed, however -
following both Greek and medieval tradition -
that orbits must be circular, not elliptical, in order
to maintain the fabric of the cosmos in a state of
perfection. This preconception prevented him
from deriving a full formulation of the law of
inertia, which he himself discovered although it is
usually attributed to the contemporary French
mathematician René Descartes. Lacking the
theory of Newtonian gravity, he hoped to explain
the paths of the planets in terms of circular inertial orbits around the Sun.

Galileo's contributions towards the establishment of mechanics as a science were a substantial
part of his work. Valuable, but isolated, facts and
theorems had previously been discovered and
proved, but it was Galileo who first clearly

grasped the idea of force as a mechanical agent.
Although he did not formulate the interdepend-
ence of motion and force into laws, his writings
on dynamics are suggestive of those laws, and his
solutions to dynamical problems involve their recognition. In this branch of science he paved the
way for the English physicist and mathematician
Isaac Newton.

Always an extremely practical man, Galileo
believed strongly in the use of experiment to confirm theoretical research. Much of his conceptual
work in the investigation of the laws of falling
bodies, the motion of a projectile, and equilibrium and motion on an inclined plane, was demonstrated by visual and public experiment
(although never, despite tradition, in the leaning
tower of Pisa). He was particularly fascinated by
motion, which led his studies in very diverse -
albeit practical - directions. In his *Discourses on*
Things that Float, published in 1612, he used the
principle of virtual velocities to demonstrate the
more elementary theorems of hydrostatics, de-
ducing the equilibrium of fluid in a syphon, and
to work out the conditions for the flotation of
solid bodies in a liquid. He also constructed a
primitive form of air thermometer.

Because of his pioneer work in gravitation and
motion, and in combining mathematical analysis
with experimentation, Galileo is often referred to
as the founder of modern mechanics and experimental physics.

Galle, Johann Gottfried (*1812-1910*), was a German astronomer who was one of the first to observe Neptune and recognize it as a new planet.

Galle was born at Pabsthaus in Prussian Sax-
ony (now in East Germany) on 9 June 1812, the
son of a turpentine-maker. He was educated at
the University of Berlin, which he entered in 1830,
and where he first met Johann Encke (1791-
1865). Graduating, he joined the staff of the Berlin Observatory, and in 1835 became Assistant
Director under Encke. In 1851 he was appointed
Professor of Astronomy and Director of the Breslau Observatory (now in Wrocław, Poland),
where he spent the rest of his working life until
his retirement at the age of 83. Galle died at the
age of 98, in Potsdam, Prussia, on 10 July 1910.

To gain his doctorate in 1845, Galle sent his
dissertation to the Director of the Paris Observatory, Urbain Le Verrier (1811-1877). By way
of reply, Le Verrier sent back his calculation of
the position of a new planet, predicted mathematically from its apparent gravitational effect
on Uranus, then the outermost known planet;
Galle received Le Verrier's final prediction in September 1846. Within one hour of beginning their
search, Galle and his colleague Heinrich d'Arrest

had located Neptune, less than 1° away from the predicted position. In fact, they located it more from its absence as a star plotted on one of Encke's new star-charts, but the discovery was acclaimed nevertheless as a triumph for scientific theory as opposed to observation.

Galle was also the first to distinguish the Crêpe Ring, a somewhat obscure inner ring around Saturn. First announced by Galle in 1838, its existence was forgotten until it was rediscovered independently by George Bond (1825-1865) at Harvard and by William Dawes (1799-1868) in England. It can be traced as a dusky band where it crosses the planet's globe. Saturn itself can be clearly seen through the Crêpe Ring.

He also suggested a method of measuring the scale of the Solar System by observing the parallax of asteroids, first applying his method to the asteroid Flora in 1873. The method was eventually carried out with great success, but not until Galle had been dead for nearly two decades.

Gamow, George (*1904-1968*), was a brilliant Soviet physicist who applied his knowledge and interests to many disciplines with remarkable success. He defected to the United States at the age of 29.

Born a Ukrainian in Odessa on 4 March 1904, Gamow attended local schools. The gift of a telescope for his thirteenth birthday proved inspirational to him. In 1922 he enrolled in the Novorossysky University, then quickly transferred to the University of Leningrad, where he studied optics and cosmology and came under the influence of Aleksandr Friedman (1888-1925). In 1928, having obtained his PhD, Gamow travelled to the University of Göttingen and stayed there briefly before going on to the Institute of Theoretical Physics, in Copenhagen, at the invitation of Niels Bohr (1885-1962), its eminent Director. He also visited the research group directed by Ernest Rutherford (1971-1937) at the Cavendish Laboratories in Cambridge in 1929, returning to Copenhagen in the following year. In 1931 he was recalled to the Soviet Union to become Master of Research at the Academy of Sciences in Leningrad. Permitted by the Soviet government to attend the Solvay Congress in Brussels two years later, Gamow seized the opportunity to defect to the West, and toured Europe and the United States for a year, visiting several establishments, before accepting the chair of physics at the George Washington University, Washington. He taught there from 1934 to 1956, when he took up the post of Professor of Physics at the University of Colorado, remaining there until he died, on 20 August 1968, in Boulder.

Gamow's early work was in nuclear physics.

His most notable achievements include his theory of alpha decay (proposed in 1928), his work on the "liquid drop model" of the nucleus (from 1928 to 1931), his calculations on the fundamental design requirements of what eventually became the first linear accelerator (constructed by John Cockcroft and Ernest Walton in 1932), and his "selection-rule for beta decay" formulated in 1936 with Edward Teller (1908-   ).

During World War II, Gamow was intimately concerned with the Manhattan Project on the development of the atomic bomb, and later contributed significantly to research at Los Alamos that led to the production of the hydrogen bomb.

His astronomical studies were concerned mainly with the origin of the Universe and the evolution of stars. He followed the model devised by Hans Bethe (1906-   ) on the mechanism by which heat and radiation are generated in the cores of stars (thermonuclear reactions), and postulated that a star heats up – rather than cools down – as its "fuel" is consumed. In 1938 he related this theory to the Hertzsprung-Russell diagram. The following year, in collaboration with M. Schoenberg, he investigated the role of neutrino emission in novae and supernovae. He then turned to the problem of energy production in red giant stars and in 1942 produced his "shell" model to describe such stars.

Gamow's most famous contribution to astronomy began with his support in 1946 for the Big-Bang theory of the origin of the Universe proposed by Abbé Georges Lemaître (1894-1966). With Ralph Alpher (1921-   ) he investigated the possibility that heavy elements could have been produced by a sequence of neutron-capture thermonuclear reactions. They published a famous paper in 1948, which became known as the Alpher-Bethe-Gamow (or α-β-γ) hypothesis, describing the "hot big bang". They suggested that the primordial state of matter – which they called *ylem*, the term Aristotle had given to the ultimate state of matter – consisted of neutrons and their decay products. This mixture of neutrons, protons, electrons and radiation was almost unimaginably hot. As this matter expanded after the hot big bang, it cooled sufficiently for hydrogen nuclei to fuse to form helium nuclei (alpha particles) – which explained the abundance of helium in the Universe (one atom in twelve is helium).

The model's inability to account for the presence – and evident creation – of elements heavier than helium was later vindicated by the work of Geoffrey and Margaret Burbidge and their collaborators, who found some evidence of what they called nucleosynthesis, or nucleogenesis.

The hot big bang model indicated that there

ought to be a universal radiation field as a remnant of the intense temperatures of the primordial big bang. In 1964 Arno Penzias (1933-) and Robert Wilson (1936-) detected isotropic microwave radiation. Research at Princeton University confirmed that this was 3K black-body radiation, as predicted by Gamow's model. Gamow had in fact postulated the temperature of this radiation as 25K, but errors were found in his method that explained why his estimate was too high. The detection of this microwave radiation led most cosmologists to support the Big-Bang model, in preference to the Steady State hypothesis proposed originally by Fred Hoyle (1915-), Hermann Bondi (1919-) and Thomas Gold (1920-).

Gamow was also a brilliant molecular biochemist, and he was instrumental in the resolution of the complex coding system of genetic information within DNA (deoxyribonucleic acid). In addition, he had time to write popular science works, in particular his series involving "Mr Tompkins", and he received the UNESCO Kalinga Prize in recognition of their value.

A true polymath, Gamow contributed enormously to the sum of contemporary scientific knowledge.

Gauss, Karl (or Carl) Friedrich (*1777-1855*), was a brilliant German mathematician, physicist and astronomer, whose innovations in mathematics proved him to be the equal of Archimedes or Newton.

Gauss was born in Braunschweig (Brunswick) (now in West.Germany) on 30 April 1777, to a very poor, uneducated family. His father was a gardener, an assistant to a merchant and the treasurer of an insurance fund. Gauss taught himself to count and read – he is said to have spotted a mistake in his father's arithmetic at the age of three. At elementary school, at the age of eight, he added the first 100 digits in his first lesson. Recognizing his precocious talent, his teacher persuaded his father that Gauss should be encouraged to train towards following a profession rather than learn a trade. At the age of eleven, he went to high school and proved to be just as proficient at classics as mathematics. When he was 14 he was present at the court of the Duke of Brunswick in order to demonstrate his skill at computing; the Duke was so impressed that he supported Gauss generously with a grant from then until his own death in 1806. In 1792, with the Duke's aid, Gauss began to study at the Collegium Carolinum in Brunswick, and then from 1795 to 1798 he was taught at the University of Göttingen. He was awarded a doctorate in 1799 from the University of Helmstedt, by which time

he had already made nearly all his fundamental mathematical discoveries. In 1801 he decided to develop his interest in astronomy; by 1807 he pursued it so enthusiastically that not only was he Professor of Mathematics, he was also Director of the Göttingen Observatory.

At about this time, he began to gain recognition from other parts of the world: he was offered a job in St Petersburg (now Leningrad), was made a Foreign Member of the Royal Society in London, and was invited to join the Russian and French Academies of Sciences. Nevertheless, Gauss remained at Göttingen for the rest of his life, and died there on 23 February 1855.

Between the ages of 14 and 17, Gauss devised many of the theories and mathematical proofs that, because of his lack of experience in publication and his diffidence, had to be rediscovered in the following decades. The extent to which this was true was revealed only after Gauss's death. There are, nevertheless, various innovations that are ascribed directly to him during his three years at the Collegium Carolinum, including the principle of least squares (by which the equation curve best fitting a set of observations can be drawn). At this time he was particularly intrigued by number theory, especially on the frequency of primes. This subject became a life's work and he is known as its modern founder. In 1795, having completed some significant work on quadratic residues, Gauss began to study at the University of Göttingen, where he had access to the works of Fermat, Euler, Lagrange and Legendre. He immediately seized the opportunity to write a book on the theory of numbers, which appeared in 1801 as *Disquisitiones arithmeticae*, generally regarded to be his greatest accomplishment. In it, he summarized all the work which had been carried out up to that time and formulated concepts and questions that are still relevant today.

The years between 1800 and 1810 were for Gauss the years in which he concentrated on astronomy. In mathematics he had had no collaborators, although he had inspired men such as Dirichlet and Riemann. In astronomy, in contrast, he corresponded with many, and his friendship with Alexander von Humboldt (1769-1859) played an important part in the development of science in Germany. The discovery of the first asteroid, Ceres – and its subsequent "loss" – by Guiseppe Piazzi (1746-1826) at the beginning of 1801 gave Gauss the chance to use his mathematical brilliance in another cause. He developed a quick method for calculating the asteroid's orbit from only three observations and published this work – a classic in astronomy – in 1809. The 1,001st planetoid to be discovered was named Gaussia in his honour. He also worked out the theories of perturbations which were eventually used by Le Verrier and Adams in their independent calculations towards the discovery of Neptune. After 1817, he did not work further in theoretical astronomy, although he continued to work in positional astronomy for the rest of his life.

Gauss was also a pioneer in topology, and he worked besides on crystallography, optics, mechanics and capillarity. At Göttingen, he devised the heliotrope, a type of heliostat that has applications in surveying. After 1831 he collaborated with Wilhelm Weber (1804-1891) on research into electricity and magnetism, and in 1833 they invented an electromagnetic telegraph. Gauss devised logical sets of units for magnetic phenomena and a unit of magnetic flux density is therefore called after him.

There is scarcely any physical, mathematical or astronomical field in which Gauss did not work. He retained an active mind well into old age and at the age of 62, already an accomplished linguist, he taught himself Russian. The full value of his work has been realized only in the twentieth century.

Giacconi, Riccardo (*1931-*), is an Italian-born American physicist, the head of a team whose work has been fundamental in the development of X-ray astronomy.

Giacconi was born in Genoa on 6 October 1931. Educated in Italy, he obtained a doctorate in 1954 at the University of Milan, where he then took up the post of Associate Professor. Two years later he emigrated to the United States and became Research Associate at the University of Indiana at Bloomington, before taking up a similar position at Princeton in 1958. He then joined American Scientific and Engineering Inc. as Senior Scientist for a year until his naturalization papers came through in 1960. Since 1963 he has been Chief of the Space Physics Division.

In June 1962 a rocket was sent up by Giacconi and his group to observe secondary spectral emission from the Moon. But to the surprise of all concerned, it detected extremely strong X-rays from a source evidently located outside the Solar System. X-ray research has since become an important branch of astronomy, leading to the discovery of the existence of many previously unsuspected types of stellar and interstellar material, whose emissions lie in the X-ray band of the electromagnetic spectrum. Because much of the high-energy radiation is filtered out by the Earth's upper atmosphere, research has had to make considerable use of equipment carried aboard balloons or rockets; but the launching of *Uhuru*, in 1970, marked the beginning of a new era in that it was the first satellite devoted entirely to X-ray

astronomy. Under the guidance of Giacconi, the team maintained a lead in the field. They devised and developed a telescope capable of producing X-ray images. Their years of experimental work in the laboratory and the more recent facility to use rocket-borne equipment employing solar power have resulted in instruments of increasing efficiency and angular resolution.

Giacconi has also worked a great deal with a Cherenkov detector, by means of which it is possible to observe the existence and velocity of high-speed particles, important in experimental nuclear physics and in the study of cosmic radiation.

Gill, David (*1843-1914*), was a Scottish astronomer whose precision and patience using old instruments brought him renown before he achieved even greater fame for his poineer work in the use of photography to catalogue stars.

Gill was born in Aberdeen on 12 June 1843, the eldest surviving son of a well-established clock- and watch-maker who intended him eventually to take over the family business and educated him accordingly. After two years at Marischal College - where he attended classes given by the physicist and astronomer James Clerk Maxwell (1831-1879) - he went to Switzerland to study clock-making. There he became expert in fine mechanisms, experienced in business methods and fluent in French, all of which later stood him in good stead. He returned to Coventry, and later Clerkenwell (London), to continue his studies and then went back to Aberdeen, where he ran his father's business for ten years, gradually developing his interests in astronomy and astronomical techniques. In 1872 he became Director of Lord Lindsay's private observatory at Dun Echt, 12 miles from Aberdeen. Seven years later he was appointed Astronomer at the observatory at the Cape of Good Hope, South Africa. He was made Knight Commander of the Order of the Bath on 24 May 1900. He retired in 1906, for health reasons, and lived in London until he died of pneumonia on 24 January 1914.

On Gill's return to Aberdeen in 1862, he was given the use of a small telescope at King's College Observatory. Through business contacts he acquired a 12-inch (30.5 cm) reflector for the College with which he began to try to determine stellar parallaxes. This work was interrupted by Lord Lindsay's invitation to become Director of his new Observatory. Gill's job was to equip and supervise the building of this new Observatory, which Lindsay was determined to make the best possible. In the course of this work, Gill met many important European astronomers and skilled instrument-makers, contacts that were to be very useful in his later position at the Cape. He also mastered the use of a heliometer, a rather old-fashioned instrument that he was to use a great deal and one which required great precision of hand and eye. The heliometer was first designed for measuring the variation of the Sun's diameter at different seasons, but it was also known to be one of the most accurate instruments for measuring angular distances between stars. Gill was perhaps the last great master of the heliometer and his measurements of the parallax of the Southern stars were unsurpassed for many years.

In 1872 Gill went on a six-year expedition to Mauritius, with Lord Lindsay and others, in order to measure the distance of the Sun and other related constants particularly during the 1874 transit of Venus. The method Gill used was first proposed by Edmond Halley and involved combining the times of the transit of Venus across the face of the Sun as observed from a number of places as widely spaced around the world as possible. While on the island of Mauritius, Gill used his heliometer to observe the near approach of the minor planet Juno, and he was able to deduce an accurate value of the solar parallax. He used the same method of determining solar parallax on a private expedition, sponsored by the Royal Astronomical Society, on Ascension Island in 1877, when he measured solar parallax by considering the near approach of Mars. On both of these expeditions he used a 4-inch (10 cm) heliometer.

In 1879 he was appointed to the Observatory at the Cape of Good Hope. This Observatory had been built in 1820 in order to observe the Southern hemisphere, but by 1879, when Gill took over, it was in poor condition. Most of the instruments were in need of repair and many of the results which had been obtained had not been published. Gill set to work at once. He was particularly unhappy about the Airy transit circle; although it was identical to the one at Greenwich, Gill designed an improved version which, when built in 1900, became the pattern for most transit circles built afterwards.

But it was the heliometer that Gill used most – at first a 4-inch (10 cm) one, then a 7-inch (18 cm) instrument which was installed in 1887. With the co-operation of many other astronomers, he made intensive investigations of several minor planets – Iris, Victoria and Sappho – and in 1901 he made the first accurate determination of the solar parallax: 8.80″. This figure was used in all almanacs until 1968, when it was replaced by a value of 8.794″, derived by radar echo methods and by observations made with a *Mariner* space probe. With the heliometer he also measured the

distances of 20 of the brighter and nearer Southern stars.

The bright comet of 1882 was of great interest to astronomers. But it was on seeing a photograph of it that Gill realized it should be possible to chart and measure star positions by photography. At once he initiated a vast project, with the help of other observatories, to produce the *Cape Durchmusterung*, which gives the positions and brightness of more than 450,000 Southern stars. This was the first important astronomical work to be carried out photographically. Gill also served on the original council for the *International Astrographic Chart and Catalogue*, which was to give precise positions for all stars to the 11th magnitude. It was not completed until 1961, although all the photographs had been taken by 1900.

Gingerlich, Owen Jay (*1930–*), is an American astrophysicist who is perhaps better known as an author, editor and historian on astronomical themes.

Gingerlich was born in Washington, Iowa, on 24 March 1930, and was educated at Goshen College, where he obtained a BA in 1951. He then went to Harvard University and gained his MA in 1953. From 1955 to 1958 he was at the American University in Beirut, first as an Instructor, then as Assistant Professor of Astronomy, and finally as Director of the Observatory there. The following year he became Lecturer in Astronomy at Wellesley College, New York City. Since 1969 he has been Professor of Astronomy and the History of Science at Harvard University while retaining, since 1961, a position as Astrophysicist at the Smithsonian Astrophysical Observatory.

Gingerlich has carried out considerable research into stellar atmospheres. In astronomical history he has made particularly thorough studies of the lives of Nicolaus Copernicus (1473–1543) and Johannes Kepler (1571–1630). As an editor he has put together several collections of articles from scientific journals, been responsible for a symposium commemorating the 500th anniversary of the birth of Copernicus, and translated a popular *Introduction to Astrophysics* from the French.

Ginsburg, Vitalii Lazarevich (*1916–*), is a Soviet scientist who has become one of the leading astrophysicists of the twentieth century.

Born in Moscow on 21 September 1916, Ginsburg completed his education at Moscow University, graduating in physics in 1938. He then studied as a postgraduate there and for a further two years at the Physics Institute of the Academy of Sciences. Since that time he has been a member of staff at the Physics Institute, from 1942 as Head of the Sub-Department of Theoretical Physics. A member of the Communist Party since 1944, Ginsburg has won several state prizes and honours, notably the Order of Lenin in 1966. He is also the author of books detailing his work.

Ginsburg's first major success was his use of quantum theory in a study of the Cherenkov radiation effect (in which charged particles such as electrons travel through a medium at a speed greater than that of light in that medium) in 1940. This work was important for the development of nuclear physics and the study of cosmic radiation, and Ginsburg continued to theorize in this field. Seven years later, with Igor Tamm (1895-1971, one of the original interpreters of the Cherenkov effect), he formulated the theory of a molecule containing particles with varying degrees of motion, for which he devised the first relativistically invariant wave equation. With Lev Landau (1908-1968), his former teacher, Ginsburg posited a phenomenological theory of conductivity. After 1950 he concentrated on problems in thermonuclear reactions. His work on cosmic rays – he was one of the first to believe that background radio-emission came from farther than within our own galaxy – led him to a hypothesis about their origin and to the conclusion that they can be accelerated in a supernova.

Since 1958 he has been researching into the theory of excitons and into crystallo-optics.

Gold, Thomas (*1920-*), is an Austrian-born astronomer and physicist who has carried out research in several fields but remains most famous for his share in formulating, with Fred Hoyle (1915-) and Hermann Bondi (1919-), the Steady State theory regarding the creation of the Universe.

Gold was born in Vienna on 22 May 1920. He received his university training at Cambridge University, where he earned his bachelor's degree in 1942. Elected a Fellow of Trinity College, Cambridge, in 1947, he lectured in physics at Cambridge until 1952. From then until 1956 he was Chief Assistant to Martin Ryle (1956-), the discoverer of quasars, later to become Astronomer Royal. In 1956, Gold emigrated to the United States where, two years later, he became Professor of Astronomy at Harvard. Moving to Cornell University in 1959, he took up the posts of Professor of Astronomy, Chairman of the Department, and Director of the Centre for Radiophysics and Space Research. Gold has served as an adviser to NASA and is a member of the Royal Astronomical Society, the Royal Society and the National Academy of Sciences.

The question of the conditions surrounding the

beginning of the Universe has fascinated astronomers for many centuries. The "hot big bang" theory, developed by George Gamow (1904-1968) and others, was parallelled in 1948 by the Steady State hypothesis put forward by Gold, Bondi and Hoyle.

The Steady State theory assumes an expanding Universe in which the density of matter remains constant. It postulates that as galaxies recede from one another, new matter is continually created (at an undetectably slow rate). The implications that follow are that galaxies are not all of the same age, and that the rate of recession is uniform.

Evidence began to accumulate in the 1950s, however, that the density of matter in the Universe had been greater during an earlier epoch. In the 1960s, microwave background radiation (at 3K) was detected, which was interpreted by most astronomers as being residual radiation from the primordial "Big Bang". Accordingly, the Steady State hypothesis was abandoned by most cosmologists in favour of the Big-Bang model.

Gold has also carried out research on a variety of processes within the Solar System, including studies on the rotation of Mercury and of the Earth, and on the Moon. In addition he has published some work on relativity theory.

Goldberg, Leo (*1913-*), is an American astrophysicist who has carried out research, generally as one of a team, into the composition of stellar atmospheres and the dynamics of the loss of mass from cool stars.

Goldberg was born in Brooklyn, New York, on 26 January 1913. Completing his education, he gained his bachelor's degree in 1934 at Harvard University, where he immediately became Assistant Astronomer. Three years later he received his master's degree and moved to the University of Michigan, where he was Special Research Fellow from 1938 to 1944. At the end of that time he was made a Research Associate both at Michigan University and at the McMath and Hulbert Observatory. Between 1945 and 1960 he rose from Assistant Professor to Professor of Astronomy, and for almost all of that time he was also Chairman of the Department of Astronomy in the university and Director of the Observatory. In 1960 he was appointed Higgins Professor of Astronomy at Harvard, a position he held until 1973. He was Chairman of the Department of Astronomy and Director of Harvard College Observatory from 1966 to 1971. From 1971 to 1977 he was Director – and since 1977 he has been Emeritus Research Scientist – of the Kitt Peak National Observatory in Arizona.

Goldberg's main subject of research has been

the Sun. As one of a team at the McMath and Hulbert Observatory, he contributed towards some spectacular films of solar flares, prominences and other features of the Sun's surface. At Harvard, he and his colleagues designed an instrument that could function either as a spectrograph or as a spectroheliograph (a device to photograph the Sun using monochromatic light), that formed part of the equipment of Orbital Solar Observatory IV, launched in October 1967. He has also carried out research on the temperature variations and chemical composition of the Sun and of its atmosphere, in which he succeeded in detecting carbon monoxide (as predicted by Henry Russell).

Greenstein, Jesse Leonard (*1909-*   ), has made important astronomical discoveries by combining his observational skills with current theoretical ideas and techniques. His early work involved the spectroscopic investigation of stellar atmospheres; later work included a study of the structure and composition of degenerate stars. He took part in the discovery of the interstellar magnetic field and in the discovery and interpretation of quasi-stellar radio sources - quasars.

Greenstein was born in New York City on 15 October 1909. He developed an interest in astronomy from an early age, although when he was young there were few popular astronomy textbooks and almost no professional astronomers in the United States. His grandfather, however, had an excellent library and from the age of eight the young Jesse began to use it; he was also encouraged by the gift of a small telescope. Greenstein admits that its location, overlooking New York City, was not ideal for observational purposes, but he nevertheless retained his childhood enthusiasm for astronomy throughout his life. He studied at Harvard and wrote a thesis on interstellar dust for his PhD, which he received in 1937. For the following two years he was a fellow of the National Research Council. In 1939 he accepted a post at the University of Chicago where, besides his teaching, he continued his research career at the Yerkes Observatory; he held this post for nine years, with a brief interlude during World War II, during which time he was involved in designing specialized optical instruments. In 1948 he joined the California Institute of Technology and also became a staff member of the Mount Wilson and Palomar Observatories. Soon after joining the California Institute of Technology, he initiated its Graduate School of Astrophysics; he became Chairman of the Faculty in 1965 and Lee A. Dubridge Professor of Astrophysics in 1971. He has been awarded several medals, including the Gold Medal of the Royal Astronomical Society, the Gold Medal of the Astronomical Society of the Pacific and NASA's Distinguished Public Service Medal. Greenstein has now retired but continues to write prolifically and carries on with his observational research work.

Greenstein began his career by spectroscopically studying stellar atmospheres to try to explain anomalies in the spectra of some stars. Using the spectrographs at the McDonald Observatory and later the Mount Wilson and Palomar Observatories (now Hale), Greenstein developed a method of analysing the spectra of "peculiar" stars by comparing them with the spectra of other average stars such as the Sun. His spectroscopic programme was closely linked with a parallel growth of new ideas in nuclear astrophysics that eventually led to the currently accepted theories of stellar evolution. In connection with the development of these theories, Greenstein independently suggested that the neutron-producing reaction in red giant stars was required for the production of heavy elements.

Greenstein rekindled his early postgraduate interest in the properties of interstellar dust by studying the nature of the interstellar medium with Leverett Davis. He developed the idea that space was pervaded by dominantly regular magnetic fields which aligned non-spherical, rapidly spinning, paramagnetic dust grains and so produced the interstellar polarization of light.

Greenstein was one of the leading figures in the explosive post-World War II development of radio astronomy in the United States. The rapid growth in this field resulted in the discovery of quasars in 1964, and Greenstein played a key role in the story of their discovery. He confirmed Maarten Schmidt's hypothesis that the emission lines of these peculiar bluish stellar objects could be explained by a shift in wavelength and he found this to be true of the spectrum of 3C 48. He found that the lines were due to hydrogen provided that the velocity with which 3C 48 was receding was just over 70,000 miles (110,000 km) per second. In collaboration with Schmidt, Greenstein proposed a detailed physical model of the size, mass, temperature, luminosity, magnetic field and high-energy particle content of quasars. The nature of quasars, the most luminous and enigmatic objects in the Universe, still remains debatable, however.

During the 1970s Greenstein spent most of his time studying white dwarf stars. He collected quantitive information on their size, temperature, motion and composition and by 1978 he had discovered some 500 of these degenerate stars. His research enabled him to pinpoint the problems of explaining the evolutionary sequence that links red giant stars with white dwarfs, thus initiating spectroscopic studies of such stars from space.

Greenstein is a leading figure in modern astronomy. During the 1970s he guided both NASA and the National Academy of Sciences in their future policies and by chairing the board of directors of the Association of Universities for Research in Astronomy from 1974 to 1977 he has been influential in the research programmes of the Kitt Peak and Cerro Tololo Observatories. He is the author of more than 380 technical papers and has edited several books, including *Stellar Atmospheres* (1960). During his career, Greenstein has changed fields of specialization many times, with the personal goal of applying new branches of physics to the study of the Universe.

Hale, George Ellery (*1868–1938*), was one of the finest American astronomers. Much of his life, however, was spent organizing and arranging funds to be made available for the construction of large telescopes, including the 60-inch (1.5 m) and 100-inch (2.5 m) reflectors at Mount Wilson, and the 200-inch (5 m) Mount Palomar telescope. Principally he was an astrophysicist, and he distinguished himself in the study of solar spectra and sunspots. He developed a number of important instruments for the study of solar and stellar spectra, including the spectroheliograph and the spectrohelioscope.

Hale was born in Chicago on 29 June 1868, the son of a man of considerable means. He began his education at the Oakland Public School and continued at Adam Academy, Chicago, before going on to the Massachusetts Institute of Technology to study physics, chemistry and mathematics.

In 1892 Hale was appointed Professor of Astronomy at the University of Chicago, and at once set about the establishment of a new observatory. He persuaded C.T. Yerkes, a Chicago industrialist, to donate a large sum of money which was to be used to build the 40-inch (1 m) Yerkes refractor telescope. When this was completed in 1897, Hale moved in his astrophysical instruments from his own laboratory at Kenwood.

For a while in 1893 he worked with the physicists Helmholtz, Planck and Kundt at the University of Berlin. However, he eventually abandoned his plans to take a doctorate and never found the time afterwards to work towards this

goal. He was, even at this time, a very distinguished man of science and later (1899) he was instrumental in the founding of the American Astronomical Society.

From 1904 Hale was the Director of the Mount Wilson Observatory. Eventually, however, overwork forced him to resign in 1923. Nevertheless, he persisted in pursuit of his goal of a 200-inch telescope. Through his inspiration in the conception of the telescope, and his efforts in securing from the Rockefeller Foundation the vast amount of money necessary for its construction, the 200-inch reflecting telescope on Mount Palomar came into being. He did not see the completion of his greatest dream, for he died in Pasadena on 21 February 1938; but ten years later, when it was completed, the telescope was dedicated to him.

Even when he was quite young his interest in astronomy was enormous. Through a friendship with the amateur astronomer Sherburne Burnham (1838–1921) he bought a second-hand 4-inch (10 cm) refracting telescope. Another friendship with Hough (1836–1909) allowed him to view the heavens, from time to time, through the old 18½-inch (47 cm) refractor at the University of Chicago. Long before he became a student he constructed spectroscopes. When his father bought him a spectrometer he accurately measured the principal Fraunhofer lines in the solar spectrum. While he was a student he continued his observations and developed the idea of the spectroheliograph – a means of surveying the occurrence of a particular line in the Sun's spectrum. The instrument he constructed did not fit well on to his 4-inch telescope, so his father bought him a 12-inch (30.5 cm) refractor and also equipped a solar laboratory for him. From 1891 to 1895 he used this observatory extensively and made improvements to his instruments.

Hale's work on solar spectra was the stimulus for the construction by him of a number of specially designed telescopes, the most important of which was the Snow telescope (named after the benefactor, Miss Helen Snow) eventually installed on Mount Wilson. Later Hale was also to seek benefactors to build a 60-inch (150 cm) reflector (completed in 1908) using the mirror blank his father bought, and later still he managed to persuade J.D. Hooker, a Los Angeles businessman, to finance the construction of the 100-inch (250 cm) reflector (completed in 1918).

Meanwhile he surveyed the solar chromosphere as well as the rest of the Sun. In 1905 he obtained photographs of the spectra of sunspots which suggested that sunspots were colder – rather than hotter, as had been suspected – than the surrounding solar surface. Three years later he detected a fine structure in the hydrogen lines of the sunspot spectra. By comparing the split spectral lines of sunspots with those lines produced in the laboratory by intense magnetic fields (exhibiting the Zeeman effect) he showed the presence of very strong magnetic fields associated with sunspots. This was the first discovery of a magnetic field outside the Earth. In 1919 he made another important discovery relating to these magnetic fields by showing that they reverse polarity twice every 22–23 years.

Hale had to resign as Director of the Mount Wilson Observatory because of overwork, but he was not a man to rest, and shortly afterwards he adapted his spectroheliograph to allow an observer to view the spectra with his eye. This adaptation, which created the spectrohelioscope, involved much more than merely the replacement of photographic film by any eyepiece.

As is evident from his creation of numerous telescopes and observatories, Hale was a highly successful organizer. At one time he was elected to the governing body of Throop Polytechnic Institute in Pasadena, and through his influence this initially little-known institute with a few hundred students developed into the California Institute of Technology, now famous throughout the world for its research and scholarship.

Hall, Asaph (*1829–1907*), was an American astronomer who discovered the two Martian satellites, Deimos and Phobos. He is also noted for his work on satellites of other planets, the rotation of Saturn, the mass of Mars and double stars.

Hall was born in Goshen, Connecticut on 15 October 1829, into a well-established and once-prosperous New England family. His father, a clock manufacturer, also called Asaph Hall, died in 1842 and to alleviate the family's financial difficulties the young Asaph became a carpenter's apprentice at the age of 16. However by 1854 he wanted to continue his education and so he enrolled at the Central College in McGrawville, New York. There he met his future wife, a determined suffragist, Chloe Angeline Stickney, and soon after their marriage in 1856, Hall, who by this time was determined to become an astronomer, took an extremely low-paid job at the Harvard College Observatory in Cambridge, Massachusetts. His status soon rose to that of an observer and being an expert computer of orbits he managed to supplement his meagre income by compiling almanacs and observing culminations of the Moon. In 1862 Hall accepted a post as assistant astronomer at the United States Naval Observatory in Washington and within a year of his arrival he was given a professorship.

In 1877, Hall discovered that Mars had two satellites and this achievement won him the Lalande Prize, the Gold Medal of the Royal Astronomical Society in 1879 and the Arago Medal in 1893. He was elected to the National Academy of Sciences in 1875 and served as its Home Secretary for twelve years and its Vice-President for six years. In 1902 he served as President of the American Association for the Advancement of Science and from 1897 to 1907 he was associate editor of the *Astronomical Journal*. Following his retirement from the United States Naval Observatory at the age of 62, he continued to work as an observer in a voluntary capacity until 1898, when he went to Harvard to take up a teaching post in celestial mechanics. After five years of teaching he retired to his rural home in Connecticut where he lived until his death on 22 November 1907.

Hall's first years at the United States Naval Observatory were troubled by the unwholesome climate of the American Civil War. He spent this inital period, from 1862 to 1875, as an assistant observer of comets and asteroids. However, in 1875 Hall was given responsibility for the 26-inch (66-cm) apertrefracting telescope that had been built by Alvan Clark, specifically for the United States Naval Observatory and, at the time, it was the largest refractor in the world. Hall's first discovery using this telescope was a white spot on the planet Saturn which he used as a marker to ascertain Saturn's rotational period.

In the year 1877, Hall decided to use the superb image-forming qualities of the 26-inch (66 cm) refractor in a search for possible moons of Mars. It was a particularly good year for such a search because of the unusually close approach of Mars and Hall was guided by the parameters set by his theoretical calculations that indicated the possibility of a Martian satellite being close to the planet itself. Hall's first glimpse of a Martian moon later named Deimos, occurred on 11 August 1877. By 17 August Hall had convinced himself that the object was definitely a satellite and on that same day he found the second satellite, Phobos. He disclosed his observations to Simon Newcomb, the Scientific Head of the Observatory, who erroneously believed that Hall failed to recognize that the "Martian stars" were satellites. Hence Newcomb took the undeserved credit for their discovery in the wide press coverage that followed.

During the following years Hall continued to work on the orbital elements of planetary satellites. In 1884 he showed that the position of the elliptical orbit of Saturn's moon, Hyperion, was retrograding by about 20 degrees per year. In addition to his planetary satellite studies, Hall made numerous investigations of binary star orbits, stellar parallaxes, and the position of the stars in the Pleiades cluster. Owing to his discoveries and to the clarity and precision of his work on the satellites of Mars, Saturn, Uranus and Neptune, which has been compared with that of Bessel, Hall has become generally known as "the caretaker of the satellites".

Halley, Edmond (or Edmund) (*1656–1742*), was an English mathematician, physicist and astronomer who not only identified the comet later to be known by his name, but also compiled a star catalogue, detected stellar motion using historical records, and began a line of research that – after his death – resulted in a reasonably accurate calculation of the astronomical unit.

Halley was born at Haggerton, near London, on 8 November 1656. The son of a wealthy businessman, he attended St Paul's School (in London) and then Oxford University, where he wrote and published a book on the laws of Johannes Kepler (1571–1630) that drew him to the attention of the Astronomer Royal, John Flamsteed (1646–1719). Flamsteed's interest secured for him, despite his leaving Oxford without a degree, the opportunity to begin his scientific career by spending two years on the island of St Helena, charting (none too successfully) the hitherto unmapped stars of the Southern hemisphere. The result was the first catalogue of star positions compiled with the use of a telescope. On his return in 1678, Halley was elected to the Royal Society: he was 22 years old. For some years he then travelled widely in Europe, meeting scientists – particularly astronomers – of international renown, including Johannes Hevelius (1611–1687) and Giovanni Cassini (1625–1712), before finally returning to England to settle down to research. He also became a firm friend of Isaac Newton (1642–1727). It may have been through Newton's influence that Halley in 1696 took up the post of Deputy Controller of the Mint at Chester. Two years later he accepted command of a Royal Navy warship, and spent considerable time at sea. In 1702 and 1703 he made a couple of diplomatic missions to Vienna before, in the latter year, being appointed Professor of Geometry at Oxford. His study of comets followed immediately. He succeeded Flamsteed as Astronomer Royal in 1720 and held the post until his death, at Greenwich, on 14 January 1742.

In St Helena, Halley first observed and timed a transit of Mercury, realizing as he did so that if a sufficient number of astronomers in different locations round the world also timed their observations and then compared notes, it would be possible to derive the distance both of Mercury and of the Sun. Many years later he prepared extensive notes on procedures to be followed by

astronomers observing the expected transit of Venus in 1761; he published the notes of 1716. No fewer than 62 observing stations noted the 1761 transit, and from their findings the distance of the Sun from the Earth was calculated to be 153 million kilometres – remarkably accurate for its time (the modern value is 149.6 million km).

Astronomy was always Halley's major interest. In the 1680s and 1690s he prepared papers on the nature of trade winds, magnetism, monsoons, the tides, the relationship between height and pressure, evaporation and the salinity of inland waters, the rainbow, and a diving bell; for some of the years he was also helping Newton both practically and financially to formulate his great work, the *Principia*; but these activities were all incidental to the pleasure he took in observing the heavens.

One of Halley's first labours as Professor at Oxford was to make a close study of the nature of comets. Twenty years earlier, the appearance of a comet visible to the naked eye had aroused great popular excitement; yet somehow Newton's *Principia* had ignored the subject. Now Halley, with Newton's assistance, compiled a record of as many comets as possible and charted their progress through the heavens. A major difficulty in determining the path of a comet arose from their being visible for only short periods, leaving by far the greater part of their journey explicable by any number of hypotheses. Some authorities of the time believed that comets travelled in a straight line; some in a parabola (as Newton) or a hyperbola; others suggested an ellipse. In the course of his investigations Halley became convinced that the cometary sightings reported in 1456, 1531, 1607 and, most recently, in 1682, all represented reappearances of the same comet. Halley therefore assumed that such a traveller through space must follow a very elongated orbit around the Sun, taking it at times farther away than the remotest of the planets. On the parabolic path that he calculated it should follow – and making due allowance for deviations from its "proper" path through the attraction of Jupiter – Halley declared that this comet would appear again in December 1758. When it did, public acclaim for the astronomer (who by that time had been dead 16 years) was such that his name was irrevocably attached to it.

In 1710 Halley began to examine the writings of Ptolemy, the Alexandrian astronomer of the second century AD. Throughout his life Halley was always keenly interested in classical astronomy (he made outstanding translations of the *Conics* of Apollonius and the *Sphaerica* of Menelaus of Alexandria), and having catalogued stars himself he paid special attention to Ptolemy's stellar catalogue. This was not Ptolemy's original; it was in fact 300 years older than it appeared to be, being a direct borrowing of the list compiled by Hipparchus in the third century BC. For all Ptolemy's shortcomings, however, Halley could not believe that he had been so negligent as to credit the stars with positions wildly at variance with the bearings they now occupied, 15 centuries later. The conclusion that Halley was forced to come to was that the stars had moved. Later Halley was able to detect such movements in the instances of three bright stars: Sirius, Arcturus and Procyon. He was correct, too, in assuming that other stars farther away and consequently dimmer underwent changes of position too small for the naked eye to detect. More than a century had to pass before optical instruments achieved a sophistication sufficient to be able to detect such movement.

Hanbury-Brown, Robert (*1916–*), is a British radio-astronomer who was involved with the early development of radio-astronomy techniques and who has since participated in designing a radio interferometer which permits considerably greater resolution in the results provided by radio telescopes.

Hanbury-Brown was born on 31 August 1916 in Aruvankadu, India. After studying engineering at Brighton Polytechnic College (Sussex), he was awarded an external degree by the University of London. He went on to do some postgraduate research at the City and Guild College before joining a radar research team under the auspices of the Air Ministry in 1936. During World War II Hanbury-Brown took an active part in the radar research programme; a member of the British Air Commission, he also worked at the Naval Research Laboratory, Washington DC. At the conclusion of the war, he briefly became a private radar consultant, but in 1949 he joined the staff at the Jodrell Bank Observatory in Cheshire, and began to carry out research into radio-astronomy. In 1960 he was made a Fellow of the Royal Society and appointed Professor of Radio-astronomy at the Victoria University, Manchester, where he remained until 1962. He then took up the Chair of Astronomy at the University of Sydney, where there is an active radio-astronomy observatory at Parkes.

Radio waves of cosmic origin were first detected accidentally by Karl Jansky (1905–1950) in 1931 while he was investigating a problem in communications for the Bell Telephone Company. Eighteen years later at Jodrell Bank Observatory, then under the direction of Bernard Lovell (1913–), Hanbury-Brown joined a team actively engaged in using radio methods for the investigation of the origin of meteor showers. He became one of the first astronomers to construct a radio map of the sky. Such a map could be compiled using data collected at night or during the day (unlike optical astronomy, which requires clear night-time conditions for observation purposes), and revealed features quite different from those found using optical telescopes.

In addition to the examination of radio emission from structures within the Solar System and our own Galaxy, Hanbury-Brown investigated possible emissions from extragalactic sources. In 1949, with C. Hazard, he detected radio waves emanating from M31, the Andromeda nebula, at a distance of 2.2 million light-years. But radio telescopes of the time lacked sufficient resolution to pinpoint a radio source accurately enough to identify that source through an optical telescope. It took three years more for Hanbury-Brown and his colleagues to devise the radio interferometer, which greatly improved resolution. Using the device, Hanbury-Brown measured the size of Cassiopeia A and Cygnus A – both very strong radio sources. Walter Baade (1893–1960) and Rudolph Minkowski (1895–1976) were then able to relate the more accurate radio locations given to their own optical observations, and as a result Cygnus A became the first radio source traced to a definite optical identification – even though it had a magnitude (brightness) of only 17.9.

In 1956 Hanbury-Brown devised a further re-

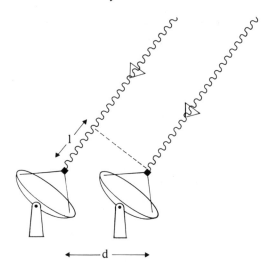

Hanbury-Brown developed interferometry in radio-astronomy, which employs two (or more) radio telescopes at which the path length of waves from a radio source differ (by l) and, if out of phase, result in interference when they are combined. Usually one of the telescopes is mounted on rails so that it can be moved to vary the base-line d.

finement to radio-astronomy, in the form of the technique of intensity interferometry. Since then he has used the stellar interferometer at Narrabi Observatory (in Australia) to study the sizes of hotter stars.

The early work carried out by Hanbury-Brown at Jodrell Bank contributed to the development of the 76 m radio telescope, for a long time the largest steerable radio telescope in the world. Other types of radio telescopes have been developed since then, such as the 300 m dish at Arecibo, in Puerto Rico, the 5 km radio telescope at Cambridge (consisting of eight-in-line 13 m dishes), and the VLA (Very Large Array) in the United States.

Hawking, Stephen William (*1942-*), is a British theoretical physicist and mathematician whose main field of research has been the nature of space–time and those anomalies in space–time known as singularities.

Hawking was born in Oxford on 8 January 1942, and from an early age he showed exceptional talent in mathematics and physics. At Oxford University he became especially interested in thermodynamics, relativity theory and quantum mechanics – interests that were encouraged by his attending a summer course at the Royal Observatory in 1961. Accordingly, when he completed his undergraduate course in 1962 (receiving a First Class Honours degree in physics), he enrolled as a research student in General Relativity at the Department of Applied Mathematics and Theoretical Physics at the University of Cambridge.

During this postgraduate programme, Hawking was diagnosed as suffering from an incurable and progressive neuromotor disease that affects various voluntary and involuntary brain functions, particularly the capacity for sequence of thought. He was nevertheless able to continue his studies and to embark upon a distinguished and productive scientific career: he was elected Fellow of the Royal Society in 1974, and became Lucasian Professor of Mathematics at Cambridge University in 1980.

From its earliest stages, Hawking's research has been concerned with the concept of singularities – breakdowns in the space–time continuum where the laws of physics might no longer apply. The prime example of a singularity is a black hole, the final form of a collapsed star. During the later 1960s, Hawkins – relying on various assumptions about the properties of matter, and incidentally developing a mathematical theory of causality in curved space–time – proved that if Einstein's General Theory of Relativity is correct, then a singularity must also have occurred at the Big Bang, the beginning of the Universe and the birth of space–time itself.

In 1970 Hawking's research turned to the examination of the properties of black holes. A black hole can be created when a star has spent so much of its energy that the pressure produced by the remaining stellar nuclear reactions is insufficient to sustain the star against the force of its own gravity. It then collapses into a minute, enormously dense singularity, with so strong a gravitational field that its escape velocity requires a speed faster than that of light. A black hole is a chasm in the fabric of space–time, and its boundary is called the event horizon. Continuing his research, Hawking realized that the surface area of the event horizon around a black hole could only increase or remain constant with time – it could never decrease. This meant, for example, that when two black holes merged, the surface area of the new black hole would be larger than the sum of the surface areas of the two original black holes.

Over the next four years, Hawking – with B. Carter, W. Israel and D. Robinson – provided mathematical proof for the hypothesis formulated by John Wheeler (1911-), known as the "No Hair Theorem". This stated that the only properties of matter that were conserved once it entered a black hole were its mass, its angular momentum and its electric charge; it thus lost its shape, its "experience", its baryon number and its existence as matter or antimatter.

Since 1974, Hawking has studied the behaviour of matter in the immediate vicinity of a black hole, from a theoretical basis in quantum mechanics. He found, to his initial surprise, that black holes – from which nothing was supposed to be able to escape – could emit thermal radiation. Several explanations for this phenomenon were proposed, including one involving the creation of "virtual particles". A virtual particle differs from a "real" particle in that it cannot be seen by means of a particle detector, but can be observed through its indirect effects. "Empty" space is thus full of virtual particles being fleetingly "created" out of "nothing", forming a particle and antiparticle pair which immediately destroy each other. (This is a violation of the principle of conservation of mass and energy, but is permitted – and predicted – by the "uncertainty principle" of Werner Heizenberg.) Hawkings proposed that when a particle pair is created near a black hole, one half of the pair might disappear into the black hole, leaving the other half which might radiate away from the black hole (rather than be drawn into it). This would be seen by a distant observer as thermal radiation.

Hawking's present objective is to produce an

overall synthesis of quantum mechanics and relativity theory, to yield a full quantum theory of gravity. Such a unified physical theory would incorporate all four basic types of interaction: strong nuclear, weak nuclear, electromagnetic and gravitational. The properties of space–time, the beginning of the Universe, and a unified theory of physics are all fundamental research areas of science. Hawking has made, and continues to make, major contributions to the modern understanding of them all.

Hayashi, Chushiro (*1920–*), is a Japanese physicist whose research in 1950 exposed a fallacy in the "hot big bang" theory proposed two years earlier by Ralph Alpher (1921–), Hans Bethe (1906–) and George Gamow (1904–1968). Since that time, Hayashi has published many papers on the origin of the chemical elements in stellar evolution and on the composition of primordial matter in an expanding Universe.

Hayashi was born in Kyoto, Japan, on 25 July 1920. Completing his education at the University of Kyoto, from which he received a BSc in 1942, he became a Research Associate at the University of Tokyo for four years, before returning to Kyoto as Research Associate from 1946 to 1949. He then spent five years as Assistant Professor at Naniwa University, Osaka, until he once again returned to Kyoto University as a member of the Physics Faculty, becoming Professor of Physics in 1957.

It was George Gamow who, in 1946, proposed that the early dense stages of the Universe were hot enough to enable thermonuclear reactions to occur. The first detailed calculation of the formation of helium in this way, in the "hot big bang", was published two years later. The three collaborators hoped that their work might account not only for the observed abundance of helium in the universe but also for the distribution of other, heavier, elements. This theory assumed that matter was originally composed of neutrons which, at very high temperature and if the matter was of great enough density, combine with protons.

But Hayashi pointed out that at times in the Big Bang earlier than the first 2 seconds, the temperature would have been greater than 10^{10} K, which is above the threshold for the making of electron–positron pairs. The creation of one pair requires about 1 MeV of energy, and at 10^{10} K many protons have this much energy. The effect of this is radically to change the timescale of the α-β-γ theory. Neutrons can react with the thermally excited positrons through the so-called weak interactions to produce protons and antineutrinos, and the reaction time for this to happen (at temperatures above 10^{10} K) is less

about 1 second. Hayashi proposed that at such a temperature there was complete thermal equilibrium between all forms of matter and radiation. Below that temperature, the weak interactions cannot maintain the neutrons in statistical balance with the protons because the concentration of electron pairs is falling abruptly. This means that the ratio of neutrons to protons is "frozen in" until a few hundred seconds have gone by and neutron decay becomes appreciable. The frozen-in ratio at a temperature below 10^{10} K is about 15 per cent – and such a change in the ratio affects the helium abundances. The frozen-in abundance of neutrons does not depend on the material density but on the temperature and the properties of the weak interactions. So provided the density is great enough for the combining reaction between neutrons and protons to occur faster than the expansion rate, a fixed concentration of neutrons will be incorporated into helium nuclei, however great the material density is, producing a "plateau" in the relationship between helium abundance and material density.

Hayashi derived a percentage value for the abundance plateau, but more recent research by physicists such as Fred Hoyle (1915–), William Fowler (1911–) and R. Wagoner suggests that his value is too high.

Research continues. As yet there is not enough evidence of the primeval build-up of heavier elements. In any case, it now appears that the concentration of such elements in the galaxy has changed with time – older stars, for instance, tend to have a lower metal content than young stars. Astrophysicists are at present trying to correlate element abundance, stellar type and motion, and galactic location. It is to be hoped that such work will lead to an improved understanding of the way in which the heavier elements have been formed.

Heraklides of Pontus (*388–315* BC), was an ancient Greek philosopher and astronomer who is remembered particularly for his teaching that the Earth turns on its axis, from west to east, once every 24 hours.

Born at Heraklea, near the Black Sea, Heraklides migrated to Athens and became a pupil of Speusippus, under the direction of Plato, in the Academy. Nearly elected to succeed Speusippus as head of the Academy, Heraklides was at one stage left temporarily in charge of the whole establishment by Plato. He is said also to have attended the schools of the Pythagorean philosophers, and would thus have come into contact with his contemporary, Aristotle (384–322 BC). Although all his writings are lost, it is clear from those of his contemporaries that his astronomical theories were more advanced than those of other scientists of his age.

In proposing the doctrine of a rotating Earth, Heraklides contradicted the accepted model of the Universe put forward by Aristotle. Aristotle had accepted that the Earth was fixed, and said that the stars and the planets in their respective spheres might be at rest. Heraklides thought it highly impossible that the immense spheres of the stars and planets rotated once every 24 hours. He also thought that the observed motions of Mercury and Venus suggested that they orbited the Sun rather than the Earth. He did not completely adopt the heliocentric view of the Universe stated later by Aristarchos (in around 280 BC). He proposed instead that the Sun moved in a circular orbit (in its sphere) and that Mercury and Venus moved on epicycles around the Sun as centre.

Apart from his astronomical work, Heraklides contributed to literary criticism and musicology. His less scientific interests included phenomena of the occult – trances, visions, prophesies and portents – breakdowns in health, which he attempted to interpret in terms of the retribution of the gods, and reincarnation.

Herbig, George Howard (*1920–*), is an American astronomer who specializes in spectroscopic research into irregular variable stars, notably those of the T-Tauri group.

Born on 20 January 1920 in Wheeling, West Virginia, Herbig was educated at the University of California in Los Angeles, graduating in 1943. In 1944 he became a member of the staff at the Lick Observatory, California, beginning as an assistant. From Junior Astronomer he progressed to Assistant Astronomer, Astronomer and, from 1960 to 1963, Assistant Director; in 1966 he became Professor of Astronomy.

Herbig's main area of research has been the nebular variables of which the prototype is T-Tauri. It is believed that the members of this group are in an early stage of stellar evolution. Most of them are red and fluctuate in light intensity; their associated nebulosities are also variable in brightness and structure, although the reason for this is not known.

With Bidelman and Preston, Herbig has worked on the spectra of these and other variable stars. In 1960 he drew attention to the fact that many of them have a predominance of lithium lines, similar to the abundance of lithium on Earth and in meteorites (although considerably more abundant than in the Sun). He concluded that both the planetary and T-Tauri abundance of lithium might represent the original level of this element in the Milky Way, but that the lithium in the Sun and other stars may have largely

been lost through nuclear transformation. Herbig also showed that there seems to be a conservation of angular momemtum in such young, cool variable stars, and that T-Tauri variables move together in parallel paths within the obscuring cloud in which they were formed.

Herbig also worked on binary stars, which are in relative orbital motion because of their proximity and mutual gravitational attraction. He investigated the binary of shortest known orbital period, VV Puppis, which is an eclipsing binary of period 100 minutes.

Herbig has also investigated the spectra of atoms and molecules that originate in interstellar space. In 1904, Johannes Hartmann (1865-1936) found that the absolute lines of Ca(II) in the spectrum of Delta Orionis do not take part in the periodic oscillation of other lines. Since then other atoms and molecular combinations have been discovered to have originated in interstellar space, such as Na(I), Ca(I), K(I), Ti(II), CN and CH. There are also a number of diffuse interstellar absorption lines which are as yet unidentified but which Herbig has succeeded in resolving into band lines.

Herschel, Frederick William (*1738–1822*), was a German-born English astronomer who contributed immensely to contemporary scientific knowledge. Through determined efforts to improve the quality of his telescopes, he was able to use the finest equipment of his time, which in turn permitted him to make many significant discoveries about the nature and distribution of stars and other bodies, both within the Solar System and beyond it. He was the most influential astronomer of his day.

Herschel was born in Hanover (now in West Germany) on 15 November 1738. At the age of 14 he joined the regimental band of the Hanoverian Guards as an oboist (as his father had before him), and four years later he visited England with the band. In 1757 he emigrated to Britain, going first to Leeds – where he earned his living copying music and teaching – and then, three years later, by commission from the Earl of Darlington, to Durham to become conductor of a military band there. From 1761 to 1765 Herschel worked as a teacher, organist, composer and conductor in Doncaster. He then did similar work in Halifax for a year. In 1766 he was hired as organist at the Octagon Chapel in Bath, where he remained for the next 16 years; during this time he ran a tutorial service that helped to finance his growing interest in astronomy. In 1772 he revisited Hanover in order to bring his sister Caroline back to England. She too became fascinated by astronomy and helped Herschel enormously both in the delicate task of preparing instruments and in making observations. The serious astronomical work began in 1773, with the building of telescopes and the grinding of mirrors. Herschel's first large reflector was set up behind his house in 1775.

Herschel's discovery of the planet Uranus in 1781 – the first planet to have been discovered in modern times – created a sensation: it signalled that Newton's work had not covered everything there was to know about the Universe. Herschel originally named the new planet "Georgium Sidum" (George's Star) in honour of King George III, but the name Uranus – proposed by Johann Bode (1747-1826) of the Berlin Observatory – was ultimately accepted. Nevertheless, the King was flattered, and Herschel received a royal summons to bring his equipment to court for inspection. In the same year the Royal Society elected Herschel a Fellow, and awarded him the Copley Medal. In 1782 he was appointed court astronomer, a post that carried with it a pension of 300 guineas per year. This enabled him to give up teaching and to move from Bath to Windsor, and then to Slough, although he continued to make telescopes for sale in order to supplement his income until 1788 (when he married a wealthy widow). In addition, the King provided grants for the construction of larger instruments; for instance, he provided £4,000 for a telescope with a focal length of more than 40 ft (12 m) and a reflector that was $3\frac{1}{2}$ ft (100 cm) in diameter. (This telescope proved rather cumbersome and was not used after 1811, although for many years it remained the largest in the world.)

Herschel visited Paris in 1801, meeting Pierre Laplace (1749-1827) and Napoleon Bonaparte. Many honours were conferred upon him (he was knighted in 1816), and he was a member of several important scientific organizations. He became ill in 1808, but continued to make observations until 1819. In that year his only son, John (1792-1871), finished his studies at Cambridge and came to take over his father's work. Herschel died in Slough on 25 August 1822.

Herschel's first large telescope was a 6-foot (1.8 m) Gregorian reflector that he built himself in 1774. In many ways it was better than other existing telescopes, and Herschel decided that its primary use would be to make a systematic survey of the whole sky. His first review was completed in 1779, when he immediately began a second survey with a 7-foot (2.1 m) reflector. In this project he concentrated on noting the positions of double stars, that is, stars that appear to be very close together, perhaps only as a consequence of chance alignment with the observer. His first catalogue of double stars was published in 1782

(with 269 examples); a second catalogue (with 434 examples) appeared in 1785; and a third was issued in 1821, bringing the total number of double stars recorded to 848. Galileo (1564-1642) and others had suggested that the motion of the nearer (and it was presumed therefore brighter) star relative to the more distant (thus fainter) star could be used to measure annual movements of the stars. Herschel's observations in 1793 demonstrated that a correlation between dimness and distance did not apply in all cases, and that in fact some double stars were so close together as to rotate round each other, held together by an attractive force. This was the first indication of gravity acting on bodies outside the Solar System.

Herschel's work on bodies within the Solar System included an accurate determination of the rotation period of Mars (in 1781): 24 hours, 39 minutes and 21.67 seconds – only two minutes longer than the period now accepted. By inventing an improved viewing apparatus for his telescope, particularly valuable when little light was available, in 1787 he discovered Titania and Oberon, two satellites of Uranus. Incorporating the "Herschelian arrangement" into a massive telescope 12 metres long, Herschel then discovered two further satellites of Saturn (Enceladus and Mimas) on its first night of use. Saturn continued to be an object of great interest to him.

During the 1780s Herschel published a number of papers on the evolution of the Universe from a hypothetical uniform initial state to one in which stars were clumped into galaxies (seen as nebulae). Herschel had become interested in nebulae in 1781, when he was given a list of a hundred of these indistinct celestial bodies compiled by Charles Messier (1730-1817). Herschel began looking for more nebulae in 1783, and the improved resolving power of his telescopes enabled him to see them as clusters of stars. His first catalogue of nebulae (citing no fewer than 2,500 examples) was published in 1802; an even longer catalogue (with 5,000 nebulae) appeared in 1820.

In 1800 Herschel examined the solar spectrum using prisms and temperature-measuring equipment. He found that there were temperature differences between the various regions of the spectrum, but that the hottest radiation was not within the visible range, but in the region now known as the infra-red. This was the beginning of the science of stellar photometry. Using data published by Nevil Maskelyne (1732-1811) on seven particularly bright stars, Herschel demonstrated that if the Sun's motion towards Argelander (a star in the constellation Hercules) was accepted, then the "proper motion" of the seven stars was a reflection of the motion of the observer. This relegation of the Solar System from the centre of the Universe was, in its way, analogous to the dethronement of the Earth from the centre of the Solar System by Copernicus. Herschel also measured the velocity of the Sun's motion.

An industrious and dedicated astronomer, and a very practical man, Herschel contributed enormously to the advance of scientific progress.

Herschel, John Frederick William (*1792-1871*), was the first astronomer to carry out a systematic survey of the stars in the Southern hemisphere and to attempt to meaure, rather than estimate, the brightness of stars. Besides this, he continued his father's studies of double stars, nebulae and the Milky Way.

John Herschel was born in Slough, England, on 7 March 1792, the only child of the astronomer William Herschel. Unsurprisingly, the young Herschel's career was strongly influenced by the fact that he was brought up by his father and his Aunt Caroline, who were both devoted to astronomy. From the age of eight, after a short spell at Eton, Herschel was educated at a local private school. He then went to St John's College, Cambridge, to read mathematics. From 1816 to 1850 Herschel had no permanent paid post, but his scientific life was closely bound up with two Royal Societies. He became a fellow of the Royal Society in 1813, served as its Secretary from 1824 to 1827, and won its Copley Medal in 1821 and 1847 and its Royal Medal in 1833, 1836 and 1840. He received the Lalande Prize of the French Academy in 1825 and the Gold Medal of the Astronomical Society in 1826 for the catalogue of double stars which he compiled with James South. When Herschel died on 11 May 1871 he was mourned by the whole nation, not only as a great scientist, but also as a remarkable public figure.

After completing his studies and taking his MA in 1816, Herschel embarked on his scientific career. As one of his obituarists noted, he may well have taken up astronomy out of a sense of "filial devotion". His first paper, on the computation of lunar occultation, appeared in 1822, by which time he had moved on to systematically observing double stars. This work, a continuation of one of his father's projects, was carried out in collaboration with James South, who possessed two excellent refracting telescopes in London. William Herschel had demonstrated that the orbital motion of binary stars was due to their mutual attraction; John Herschel studied new and known double star systems, especially Gamma Virginis, in order to establish a method for determining their orbital elements.

Soon after his marriage to Margaret Brodie Stewart, in 1829, Herschel planned an expedition to the Southern hemisphere. He chose to go to the Cape of Good Hope, partly because of its excellent astronomical tradition, built up as a result of Lacaille's work in the 1850s, partly because, being located on the same meridian of longitude as eastern Europe, it made co-operative observations easier. Herschel arrived in Cape Town with his wife and the first three of his twelve children on 16 January 1834 and set himself the mammoth task of mapping the southern skies. By 1838 he had catalogued 1,707 nebulae and clusters, listed 2,102 pairs of binary stars and carried out star counts in 3,000 sky areas. Besides simply mapping the stars, he made accurate micrometer measurements of the separation and position angle of many stellar pairs and produced detailed sketches of the Orion region, the Magellanic Clouds, and extragalactic and planetary nebulae. He also recorded the behaviour of Eta Carinae (whose nature is still not entirely understood) when it underwent a period of dramatic brightening in December 1837.

To ascertain the brightness of the stars he catalogued, Herschel invented a device called an astrometer. It enabled him to compare the light output of a star with an image of the full moon, whose brightness could be varied to match the star under observation with the main telescope. This attempt to ascertain absolute magnitude was a major step forward in stellar photometry. Besides his personal research work, Herschel also collaborated with Thomas Maclear, Director of the Cape Observatory, in the Observatory's routine geodetic and tidal work and in observations of Encke's and Halley's comets.

On his return to London on 15 May 1838, Herschel began to prepare the results of his African trip for publication. At the same time he pursued his interest in the art of photography. His interest in the subject led him to invent much of the vocabulary - positive, negative and snapshot - that is associated with the craft today. His massive *Results of Astronomical Observations Made During the Years 1834-38 at the Cape of Good Hope* was published in 1847; two years later he produced *Outlines of Astronomy*, which became a standard textbook for the following decades. His *General Catalogue of Nebulae and Clusters*, now known as the NGC, still remains the standard reference catalogue for these objects. The last of his ambitious projects, *General Catalogue of 10,300 Multiple and Double Stars*, was published posthumously.

John Herschel was a celebrated scientist throughout his life and his name epitomized science to the public in much the same way as Einstein's did in the following century. After his death his reputation suffered a decline, and it rose again only when astronomers began to realize that he occupied the same commanding and innovative position for astronomers in the Southern hemisphere as his father William did for astronomers in the north.

Hertzsprung, Ejnar (*1873-1967*), was a Danish astronomer and physicist who, having proposed the concept of the absolute magnitude of a star, went on to describe for the first time the relationship between the absolute magnitude and the temperature of a star, formulating his results in the form of a graphic diagram that has since become a standard reference.

Hertzsprung was born in Frederiksberg, Denmark, on 8 October 1873. His father was interested in astronomy and stimulated a similar fascination for the subject in his son, but the poor financial prospects of an aspiring astronomer led Hertzsprung initially to choose chemical engineering as his career. He graduated from the Frederiksberg Polytechnic in 1898 and then went to St Petersburg (now Leningrad), where he worked as a chemical engineer until 1901. Returning to Copenhagen via Leipzig, he studied photochemistry under Wilhelm Ostwald (1853-1932) and began to work as a private astronomer at the observatory of the University of Copenhagen and the Urania Observatory in Frederiksberg. Under the generous tutelage of H. Lau, Hertzsprung rapidly acquired the skills of contemporary astronomy.

Following a correspondence with Karl Schwarzschild (1873-1916) at the University of Göttingen, Hertzsprung was invited to take up the post of Assistant Professor of Astronomy at the Göttingen Observatory in 1909. When Schwarzschild moved on to the Potsdam Astrophysical Observatory later in that same year, Hertzsprung went with him. Willem de Sitter (1872-1934) was appointed Director of the Leiden Observatory (in the Netherlands) in 1919, and he appointed Hertzsprung head of the Department of Astrophysics. Within a year, Leiden University appointed Hertzsprung a Professor, and on the death of de Sitter he also became Director of the Leiden Observatory. He retired in 1945 and returned to Denmark, but he did not cease his astronomical research until well into the 1960s.

Hertzsprung's outstanding contributions to astrophysics were recognized by his election to many prestigious scientific academies and societies and with the award of a number of honours. He died in Roskilde, Denmark, on 21 October 1967.

It was quite early in his work at the Observatory in Copenhagen that Hertzsprung realized the importance of photographic techniques in astronomy. He was extremely well qualified to apply these methods and did so with great precision and energy. In 1905 he published the first of two papers (the second appearing in 1907) in a German photographic journal on the subject of stellar radiation. He proposed a standard of stellar magnitude (brightness) for scientific measurement, and defined this "absolute magnitude" as the brightness of a star at the distance of ten parsecs (32.6 light-years). As a further innovation, he described the relationship between the absolute magnitude and the colour – i.e. the spectral class or temperature – of a star. During the following year (1906), Hertzsprung plotted a graph of this relationship in respect of the stars of the Pleiades. Later, he noticed that there were some stars of the same spectral class that were much brighter, and some that were much dimmer, than the sun. He named these the red giants and the red dwarfs respectively.

Publication of his papers in a photographic journal, and refusal altogether to publish his diagrammatic material (because of diffidence in the quality of his own observations), meant that his discoveries were simply not known by Hertzsprung's fellow astronomers. And in 1913 Henry Russell (1877-1957), an American astronomer, presented to the Royal Astronomical Society a diagram depicting the relationship that Hertzsprung had previously and independently discovered, between the temperature and absolute magnitude of stars. Credit was eventually accorded to both astronomers equally and the diagram named after both of them.

The Hertzsprung-Russell diagram, one of the most important tools of modern astronomy, consists of a log-log plot of temperature versus absolute magnitude. As plotted, the stars range themselves largely along a curve running from the upper left (the blue giant stars) to the lower right (the red dwarf stars) of the graph. This apparent arrangement is simply a reflection of the mass of each star, which is responsible for its temperature and luminosity. Approximately 90 per cent of stars belong to this "main sequence"; most of the rest are red giants, blue dwarfs, Cepheid variables or novae. The blue giant stars are giant hot stars, the red dwarfs are compact cooler stars. Our Sun lies near the middle of the main sequence, and is classed as a yellow dwarf.

One of the earliest uses of the Hertzsprung-Russell diagram was devised in 1913, when Hertzsprung developed the method of "spectroscopic parallax" (as distinct from "trigonometric parallax") for the determination of the distances of stars from the Earth. His method relied on data for the proper motions of the nearest (galactic) Cepheids and on Henrietta Leavitt's data for the periods of the Cepheids (which are variable stars) in the Small Magellanic Clouds (which are, it turned out, extragalactic). He deduced the distances of the nearest Cepheids from their proper motions and correlated them with their absolute magnitude. He then used Henrietta Leavitt's data on the length of their periods to determine their absolute magnitude and hence their distance. He found the Small Magellanic Cloud Cepheids to be at an incredible distance of 10,000 parsecs. His method was excellent, but there was a serious source of error, which led to an overestimation of the distance: he had not accounted for the effect of galactic absorption of stellar light. Nevertheless, this work earned Hertzsprung the Gold Medal of the Royal Astronomical Society.

The Hertzsprung–Russell diagram has also been essential to the development of modern theories of stellar evolution. As stars age and deplete their store of nuclear fuel, they are believed to leave the main sequence and become red giants. Eventually they radiate so much energy that they then cross the main sequence and collapse into blue dwarfs. Larger stars may follow a different pattern and explode into novae, or collapse to form black holes, at the end of their lifespans.

In 1922 Hertzsprung published a catalogue on the mean colour equivalents of nearly 750 stars of magnitude greater than 5.5. This catalogue was notable for the particularly elegant manner in which Hertzsprung managed to analyse the data to uncover a linear relationship.

Most of Hertzsprung's later work was devoted to the study of variable and of double stars. He worked on variable stars (especially Polaris) at Potsdam in 1909, and later in Johannesburg (from 1924 to 1925) and at the Harvard College Observatory (1926) and at Leiden.

Hevelius (or Hewel or Hewelcke), **Johannes** (*1611–1687*), was a German astronomer, most

Selenographia, *published in Danzig in 1647, was one of the first definitive works on the Moon and contained Moon maps originally drawn by Hevelius. (Ann Ronan Picture Library)*

famous for his careful charting of the surface of the Moon.

Hevelius was born at Danzig (how Gdansk) in northern Poland on 28 January 1611. A wealthy brewing merchant, he had a well-equipped observatory installed on the roof of his house in 1641, and was one of the most active observers of the seventeenth century. During the daytime he worked in his business and some evenings he took his seat on the City Council, but most of the rest of his free time he was up on his roof, observing, noting and cataloguing. His wife, Elizabeth, shared his interests and assisted him greatly in the study of the Moon, his catalogue of the stars and his work on comets. After his death, she edited and published his most famous work, *Prodromus Astronomiae* (1690).

Between 1642 and 1645, Hevelius deduced a fairly accurate value for the period of the solar rotation and gave the first description of the bright ideas in the neighbourhood of sunspots. The name he gave to them, *faculae*, is still used. He also made observations of the planets, particularly of Jupiter and Saturn. On 22 November 1644 he observed the phases of Mercury, which had been predicted by Copernicus.

In 1647, Hevelius published the first comparatively detailed map of the Moon, based on ten years' observations. It contained diagrams of the different phases for each day of lunation. He realized that the large, uniform grey regions on the lunar disc consisted of low plains, and that the bright contrasting regions represented higher, mountainous relief. He obtained better values for the heights of these lunar mountains than had Galilei Galileo (1564–1642) a generation before. His *Selenographia* also has an appendix that contains his observations of the Sun from 1642 to 1645.

Hevelius was interested in positional astronomy and planned a new star catalogue of the Northern hemisphere, which was to be much more complete than that of Tycho Brahe (1546–1601). He began in 1657, but his observatory, with some of his notes, was destroyed by fire in 1679. Nevertheless, his observations enabled him to catalogue more than 1,500 stellar positions. The resulting *Uranographia* contains an excellent celestial atlas with 54 plates, but Hevelius's practice of using only the naked eye to observe positions (despite representations by no less a man than Edmund Halley) considerably reduces the value of his work. Hevelius used telescopes for details on the Moon and planets, but refused to apply them to his measuring apparatus.

Hevelius discovered four comets – he called them "pseudo-planetae" – and suggested that these bodies orbited in parabolic paths about the Sun. Many later writers have declared that this suggestion indicates that he knew the nature of comets earlier than did either Halley or Newton.

A few of the names he gave to features of the Moon's surface are still in use today, particularly those that reflect geographical names on Earth. For his charting of the lunar formations, Hevelius has come to be known as the founder of lunar topography.

Hewish, Anthony (*1924–*), is a British astronomer and physicist whose research into radio scintillation resulted in the discovery of pulsars. For this achievement, and for his continued work in the field, he was awarded the 1974 Nobel Prize in Physics (jointly with Martin Ryle).

Hewish was born on 11 May 1924 in Fowey, Cornwall, and attended King's College, Taunton, before going to Gonville and Caius College at Cambridge. Graduating in 1948, Hewish worked at the Telecommunications Research Establishment in Malvern, where he met Martin Ryle (1918–), who was later to become Astronomer Royal. With Ryle, Hewish then became part of a team undertaking solar and interstellar research by radio at the Cavendish Laboratory, in Cambridge, and carrying out a series of intensive surveys known respectively, when published, as the *First, Second, Third,* and *Fourth Cambridge Catalogues*. In the later 1960s, he initiated research into radio scintillation at the Mullard Observatory; the discovery of the first pulsar – and then another three – followed. Made Reader at Cambridge University in 1969, he became Professor of Radio-astronomy there in 1972.

Before 1950, Hewish's experimental work using radio telescopes was directed in the main to the study of solar atmosphere. He used simple corner reflectors to examine the Sun's outer corona in order to discover the electron density in its atmosphere, and to study the irregular hot gaseous clouds of plasma surrounding the Sun. After 1950, when – mainly through the efforts of Ryle – new instruments became available, radio observations were extended to sources other than the Sun. In particular Hewish examined the fluctuation in such sources of the intensity of the radiation (the scintillation) resulting from disturbances in ionized gas in the Earth's atmosphere, within the solar system, and in interstellar space. Engaged in this research at Mullard Observatory one day in 1967, Hewish's attention was drawn by a research student, Jocelyn Bell, to some curiously fluctuating signals being received at regular intervals during the sidereal day. Installation of a more sensitive high-speed recorder revealed, on 28 November 1967, the first indication of a pulsed emission whose fixed celestial direction ruled out the possibility of an artificial source. The November results were confirmed in early December, and verified that Hewish and Bell had discovered pulsating radio stars, or pulsars.

The results of a more detailed investigation by Hewish were published in February 1968, by which time three more pulsars had been identified. This investigation showed that pulsars are sources of radio emission in our galaxy which give out radiation in brief pulses. Although each pulsar emits radiation with nearly constant pulsation periods, the rate of emission differs between pulsars, as does the "shape" of the pulse. Pulses can be single-, double-, or even triple-peaked. Shapes can differ within each pulsar, but the mean pulse shape changes only very slightly – generally to decrease the interval – over many months. Comparative studies of successive shapes have shown that each pulse itself is made up of two pulsatory constituents: a regular (class 1) one, and another (class 2) pulsating at irregular frequency within the first one.

It is now generally accepted – as originally proposed by Thomas Gold (1920–   ) and others – that pulsars are rotating neutron stars (stars that are nearing the end of their stellar life, having practically exhausted their nuclear energy). It remains less clear how rotational energy is converted to emission of such shapes and such intensity as have been discovered, although many hypotheses have been put forward.

Hewish's initial discovery of four pulsars began a period of intensive research, in which more than 170 pulsars have been found since 1967. In the meanwhile, Hewish has patented a system of space navigation using three pulsars as reference points, that would provide "fixes" in outer space accurate up to a few hundred kilometres. He continues to work in radio-astronomy.

Hey, James Stanley (*1909–   *), is a British physicist whose work in radar led to pioneering research in radio-astronomy.

Hey was born on 3 May 1909 in the Lake District. Reading physics at Manchester University, he gained his master's degree in X-ray crystallography in 1931. From 1940 to 1952 he was on the staff of an Army Operational Research Group, for the last three years as the Head of the establishment. He then became a Research Scientist at the Royal Radar Establishment, being promoted in 1966 to Chief Scientific Officer. He retired in 1969, although he continued to write about astronomy from his home in Sussex. Hey was made a Fellow of the Royal Society in 1978.

Between 26 and 28 February 1942, during World War II, the British early-warning coastal defence radar became severely jammed. At first the jamming was attributed to enemy counter-measures but Hey, noting that the interference began as the Sun rose and ceased as it set, concluded that the spurious radio radiation emanated from the Sun and that it was related to solar activity. And he further proposed that the radiation – in strength about 10^5 of the calculated black-body radiation – was associated with a large solar flare that had just been reported.

At the end of World War II, research began in earnest at the Royal Radar Establishment in Malvern. For some years, Grote Reber (1911–   ) had been working along the same lines in the United States, and he had published his discovery of intense radio sources located in the Milky Way, notably in the constellations Cygnus, Taurus and Cassiopeia. The announcement in 1946 by Hey and his colleagues that they had narrowed down the location of the radiation source in Cygnus to "a small number of discrete sources" (in fact, to Cygnus A) stimulated a search for other discrete sources around the world. Attempts were also made to devise methods to achieve better resolution in the locating of radio sources so that, eventually, it would be possible to identify such sources as optically observed objects.

Hey and his team also returned to a study of the Sun as a radio source. They discovered that large sunspots were powerful ultra-shortwave radio transmitters and that, although the Sun was constantly emitting radio waves, they were of unexpected strength.

Using radio, the team noted that they could detect and follow meteors more accurately than ever before.

Hipparchus (fl. *c. 146–c.127* BC), was a Greek astronomer and mathematician whose careful research and brilliant deductions led him to many discoveries that were to be of importance and relevance even two thousand years later.

Hipparchus was born in Nicaea, in Bithynia (now in Turkey), in about 146 BC. What little is known about him and his life is contained in the writings of Strabo of Amasya and Ptolemy of Alexandria, both of whom were writing well over 100 years after Hipparchus' death. But it is recorded that Hipparchus carried out his astronomical observations in Bithynia, on the island of Rhodes, and in Alexandria.

In 134 BC Hipparchus noticed a new star in the constellation Scorpio, a discovery which inspired him to put together a star catalogue – first of its kind ever completed. He entered his observations of stellar positions using a system of celestial latitude and longitude, making his measurements with greater accuracy than any observer before him, and taking the precaution wherever possible to state the alignments of other stars as a check on present position. His finished work, completed in 129 BC, listed about 850 stars classified not by location, but by magnitude (brightness), for which classification he devised a system very close to the modern one. The resulting catalogue was thus so excellent that it was not only plagiarized *en bloc* by Ptolemy, but was used by Edmund Halley 1,800 years later.

Hipparchus was troubled by the fact that the Babylonians had had a different number of days in their year. In trying to resolve this problem he studied the motions not only of the Sun and the Moon, but also of the Earth. In his star catalogue he noted that the star Spica was measured at 6° from the autumn equinox – whereas in the records of Timocharis of Alexandria 150 years earlier it had plainly been at 8°. He came to the conclusion that it was not Spica that was moving, but an east-to-west movement (or precession) of the Earth, and he managed to calculate a value for the annual precession of 45″ or 46″, which, considering the now accepted rate of 50.26″ per year, was an amazing feat of accuracy with the simple instruments available to him at the time. (Ptolemy credits Hipparchus with the invention of an improved kind of theodolite.) The definition of the precession of the equinoxes is usually said to be Hipparchus' most significant work. Using his knowledge of the equinoxes, Hipparchus calculated the terrestrial year to be $365\frac{1}{4}$ days, diminishing annually by a three-hundredth of a day (in which he was again astonishingly accurate), and the lunar period to be 29 days 12 hours 44 minutes and $2\frac{1}{2}$ seconds (which was only 1 second too short). From Hipparchus' time, eclipses of the Moon could be predicted to within one hour, and those of the Sun less accurately.

With such knowledge, it is surprising that Hipparchus accepted the notion of the geocentric Universe, declaring that the Sun orbited the Earth in a circle of which Earth was not quite at the centre. The Moon was said to do the same, except that the centre of its orbit was itself moving (a "moving eccentric").

Hipparchus' astronomical work led him to various areas of mathematics. He was one of the earliest formulators of trigonometry, for which he devised a table of chords. The theorem that provides a basis for the field of plane geometry was also proposed by him, although later attributed to Ptolemy (whose name is still generally attached to it).

Until Copernicus (1473–1543), there was no greater astronomer than Hipparchus.

Hoyle, Fred (*1915–*), is a British cosmologist and astrophysicist, distinguished for his work on the evolution of stars, the development of the Steady State Theory of the Universe, and a new theory on gravitation.

Hoyle was born in Bingley, Yorkshire, on 24 June 1915. He attended the local grammar school and then went to Emmanuel College, Cambridge. In 1939 he was elected a Fellow of St John's College, Cambridge, and in 1945 he became a lecturer in mathematics at the University. Three years later he developed the Steady State Theory as a cosmological model to explain the structure and properties of the Universe. In 1956 he left Britain for the United States to join the staff of the Hale Observatory. He returned to Britain ten years later to become Director of the Institute of Theoretical Astronomy at Cambridge. Having been a Fellow of the Royal Society for some years, he was elected President of the Royal Astronomical Society.

According to Hoyle's new theory on gravitation, matter is not evenly distributed throughout space, but forms self-gravitating systems. These systems may range in diameter from a few kilometres to a million light-years and they vary greatly in density. They include galaxy clusters, single galaxies, star clusters, stars, planets and planetary satellites. Hoyle argues that this variety need not imply that the self-gravitating systems were formed in diverse ways, but rather that there is no significant intrinsic difference between one place in the Universe and another or between one time and another.

To explain this structure of a Universe composed of clusters of matter of different size and to explain its formation, Hoyle calculated the theoretical thermal conditions under which a large cloud of hydrogen gas would contract under the influence of its own gravitation. He found that a contracting cloud whose temperature is less than that required for it to exist in equilibrium will break up into self-gravitating fragments small enough to be at equilibrium in the new, increased density of the cloud fragments. Moreover, such fragmentation will continue until the formation of opaque fragments dense enough for gravitational contraction to offset radiation loss and to maintain the temperature at the necessary equilibrium.

To account for the origin of the elements in the Universe, Hoyle, in collaboration with his colleague, William Fowler (1911–), proposed that all the elements may be synthesized from hydrogen in eight separate processes that occur in different stages of the continual process by which hydrogen is converted to helium by successive fusions of hydrogen with hydrogen. The second stage occurs when the supply of hydrogen is exhausted and the cloud of gas heats up to allow the helium-burning stage, in which helium nuclei interact, to proceed. The third stage is the alpha process, whereby the cloud contracts further to reach temperatures of 10^9 K until (Ne^{20}) nuclei built up by the helium-burning stage can interact, releasing particles that in turn are used to build up nuclei of new elements, and so on, until only the element iron is left. Although alternative approaches continue to be explored, there is considerable evidence confirming such an account for the abundant distribution of the elements. But new observations and evidence supplied by interplanetary exploration, such as that from the American Voyager probes, will in future be of great importance in revealing the history of chemical elements.

The Steady State theory was expounded, in collaboration with Thomas Gold and Hermann Bondi, as a model to explain the structure and properties of the Universe. It postulated that the Universe is expanding, but that its density remains constant at all times and places, because matter is being created at a rate fast enough to keep it so. According to this model the creation of matter and the expansion of the Universe are interdependent. It calls for no new theory of space-time. Hoyle was able to propose a mathematical basis for his theory which could be reconciled with the theory of relativity.

New observations of distant galaxies have, however, led Hoyle to alter some of his initial conclusions. According to his theory, because no intrinsic feature of the Universe depends on its distance from the observer, the distant parts of the Universe are the same in nature as those parts that are near: But the detection of some radio galaxies indicates that in fact the Universe is very different at different distances, evidence which directly contradicts the fundamental hypotheses of the Steady State theory.

Hoyle is a prolific writer of science fiction as well as popular books on science; these latter include *Of Man and the Galaxies* (1966), *Astronomy Today* (1975) and *Energy and Extinction: the Case for Nuclear Energy* (1977).

Hubble, Edwin Powell (*1889–1953*), was an American astronomer who studied extragalactic nebulae and demonstrated them to be galaxies like our own. He found the first evidence for the expansion of the Universe, in accordance with the cosmological theories of George Lemaître and Willem de Sitter, and his work led to an enormous expansion of our perception of the size of the Universe.

Hubble was born in Marshfield, Missouri, on 20 November 1889. He went to High School in Chicago and then attended the University of Chicago where his interest in mathematics and astronomy was influenced by George Hale and Robert Millikan (1868–1938). After receiving his bachelors degree in 1910, he became a Rhodes Scholar at Queen's College at Oxford University, where he took a degree in jurisprudence in 1912. When he returned to the United States in 1913, he was admitted to the Kentucky Bar, and he practised law for a brief period before returning to Chicago to take a research post at the Yerkes Observatory from 1914 to 1917.

In 1917 Hubble volunteered to serve in the United States Infantry and was sent to France at the end of World War I. He remained on active service in Germany until 1919, when he was able to return to the United States and take up the earlier offer made to him by Hale of a post as astronomer at the Mount Wilson Observatory near Pasadena, where the 100-inch (2.5 m) reflecting telescope had only recently been made operational. Hubble worked at Mount Wilson for the rest of his career, and it was there that he carried out his most important work. His research was interrupted by the outbreak of World War II, when he served as a ballistics expert for the US War Department. He was awarded the Gold Medal of the Royal Astronomical Society in 1940, and received the Presidential Medal for Merit in 1946. He was active in research until his last days, despite a heart condition, and died in San Marino, California, on 28 September 1953.

While Hubble was working at the Yerkes Observatory, he made a careful study of nebulae, and attempted to classify them into intra- and extragalactic varieties. At that time there was great interest in discovering what other structures, if any, lay beyond our Galaxy. The mysterious gas clouds, known as the smaller and larger Magellanic Clouds, which had first been systematically catalogued by Messier and called "nebulae", were good extragalactic candidates and were of great interest to Hubble. He had been particularly inspired by Henrietta Leavitt's work on the Cepheid variable stars in the Magellanic Clouds; and the later work by Harlow Shapley, Henry Russell and Ejnar Hertzsprung on the distances of these stars from the Earth had demonstrated that the Universe did not begin and end within the confines of our Galaxy. Hubble's doctoral thesis was based on his studies of nebulae, but he found it frustrating because he knew that more definite information depended upon the availability of telescopes of greater light-gathering power and with better resolution.

After World War I, with the 100-inch (2.5 m) reflector at Mount Wilson at his disposal, Hubble was able to make significant advances in his studies of nebulae. He found that the source of the light radiating from nebulae was either stars embedded in the nebular gas or stars that were closely associated with the system. In 1923 he discovered a Cepheid variable star in the Andromeda nebula. Within a year he had detected no fewer than 36 stars within that nebula alone, and found that 12 of these were Cepheids. These 12 stars could be used, following the method applied to the Cepheids that Leavitt had observed in the Magellanic Clouds, to determine the distance of the Andromeda nebula. It was approximately 900,000 light-years away, much more distant than the outer boundary of our own Galaxy – then known to be about 100,000 light-years in diameter.

Hubble discovered many gaseous nebulae and many other nebulae with stars. He found that they contained globular clusters, novae and other stellar configurations that could also be found within our own Galaxy. In 1924 he finally proposed that these nebulae were in fact other galaxies like our own, a theory which became known as the "island universe". From 1925 onwards he studied the structures of the galaxies and classified them according to their morphology into regular and irregular forms. The regular nebulae comprised 97 per cent of them and appeared either as ellipses or as spirals, and the spirals were further divided into normal and barred types. All the various shapes made up a continuous series, which Hubble saw as an integrated "family". The irregular forms comprised only 3 per cent of the nebulae he studied. By the end of 1935, Hubble's work had extended the horizons of the Universe to 500 million light-years.

Having classified the various kinds of galaxies that he observed, Hubble began to assess their distances from us and the speeds at which they were receding. The radial velocity of galaxies had been studied by several other astronomers, in particular by Vesto Slipher (1875–1969). Hubble analysed his data, and added some new observations. In 1929 he found, on the basis of information for 46 galaxies, that the speed at which the galaxies were receding (as determined from their spectroscopic red shifts) was directly correlated with their distance from us. He found that the more distant a galaxy was, the greater was its speed of recession - now known as Hubble's Law. This astonishing relationship inevitably led to the conclusion that the Universe is expanding, as Lemaître had also deduced from Einstein's General Theory of Relativity.

This data was used to determine the portion of the Universe which we can ever come to know, the radius of which is called the Hubble radius.

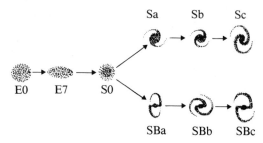

Hubble's classification, still used today, is based on a galaxy's shape. Elliptical galaxies range from the almost spherical E0 type to the markedly elliptical E7. Type S0 – a spiral disc without arms – marks the transition from elliptical to spiral types. Types Sa, Sb and Sc are normal spirals with progressively looser arms. Barred spirals, types SBa, SBb and SBc, are also differentiated by the degree of openness of their arms.

Beyond this limit, any matter will be travelling at the speed of light, and so communication with it will never be possible. The data on galactic recession was also used to determine the age and the diameter of the Universe, although at the time both of these calculations were marred by erroneous assumptions, which were later corrected by Walter Baade (1893–1960). The ratio of the velocity of galactic recession to distance has been named the Hubble constant, and the modern value for the speed of galactic recession is 530 km/sec/10^6 parsecs (1 parsec = 3.26 light-years) – very close to Hubble's original value of 500.

During the 1930s, Hubble studied the distribution of galaxies and his results supported the idea that their distribution was isotropic. They also clarified the reason for the "zone of avoidance" in the galactic plane. This effect was caused by the quantities of dust and diffuse interstellar matter in that plane.

Among his later studies was a report made in 1941 that the spiral arms of the galaxies probably did "trail" as a result of galactic rotation, rather than open out. After World War II Hubble became very much an elder statesman of American astronomy. He was involved in the completion of the 200-inch (5 m) Hale telescope at Mount Palomar, which was opened in 1948. One of the original intentions for this telescope was the study of faint stellar objects, and Hubble used it for this purpose during his few remaining years.

Huggins, William (*1824–1910*), was a British astronomer and pioneer of astrophysics. He revolutionized astronomy by using spectroscopy to determine the chemical make-up of stars and by using photography in stellar spectroscopy. With these techniques he investigated the visible spectra of the Sun, stars, planets, comets and meteors and discovered the true nature of the so-called "unresolved" nebulae.

As a young boy he had been given a microscope, which helped to develop his first interest in physiology. Then when he was about 18 he bought himself a telescope and became increasingly interested in astronomy, although London, even at that time, was a poor place for making observations. It was intended that he should go to Cambridge University, but when the time came his family persuaded him to take charge of their drapery business in the City of London. He diligently followed this trade from 1842 to 1854, when he sold the business and moved with his parents to a new home south of London in Tulse Hill, where he built his own private observatory. Although he had continued to make observations whilst in business, it was only after he moved that he devoted his time entirely to science.

Huggins was elected a Fellow of the Royal Society in 1865 and was President from 1900 to 1905. He also served terms as President of the British Association for the Advancement of Science and the Royal Astronomical Society. His country honoured him by making him a Knight Commander of the Order of Bath and he was also one of the original members of the Order of Merit in 1902. From 1890 he received a Civil List pension (of £150). Huggins died at his home in Tulse Hill on 12 May 1910.

Huggins spent his first two years of research from 1858 to 1860, observing the planets with an 8-inch (20 cm) refracting telescope. He was looking for a new line of action when, in 1859, Gustav Kirchoff (1824–1887) and Robert Bunsen (1811–1899) published their findings on the use of spectroscopy to determine the chemical composition of the Sun. Huggins, together with his friend W.A. Miller (who was Professor of Chemistry at King's College, London), designed a spectroscope and attached it to the telescope. They began to observe the spectra of the Sun, Moon, planets and brighter stars. They compared the spectral lines which they observed with those produced by various substances in the laboratory, and in this way they were able to draw conclusions about the composition of the stars and planets. They published their results in 1863 in a paper presented to the Royal Society: *Lines of the Spectra of some of the Fixed Stars.*

It showed that the brightest stars had elements in common with those of the Earth and the Sun, although there was a diversity in their proportions. In the same paper they suggested that starlight originated in the central part of a star and then passed through the hot gaseous envelope that surrounds it.

Following this initial success, other great achievements were to come. Some of the tiny indistinct objects known as nebulae had been observed to be faint clusters of stars. Others could not be resolved but it was believed that eventually more powerful telescopes would show up the individual stars and confirm that they were similar to those already resolved. Huggins realized that those nebulae of stellar origin would give a characteristic stellar spectrum. When he observed the unresolved nebulae in the constellation of Draco in 1864 this was not the case. Only a single bright line was observed. Seeing this, he understood the nature of these objects – they were clouds of luminous gas and not clusters of stars. In the same year he observed the great nebula in Orion and saw two unknown lines in its spectrum. Huggins postulated the existence of a previously undiscovered element, "nebulium", but in 1927 Ira Bowden (1898–1973) showed that the lines were caused by ionized oxygen and nitrogen. Although Huggins had discovered the gaseous nature of nebulae, which suggested that they may be the "parents" of stars, his cautious nature prevented him from stating it as a fact. Like other scientists of his day, he believed that chemical elements were unchangeable.

On 18 May 1866 Huggins made his first spectroscopic observation of a nova and found that, superimposed on a solar-type spectrum, there were a number of bright hydrogen lines which suggested that the outburst occurred with an emission of gas with a higher temperature than that of the star's surface. He then showed that the

Huggins used a two-prism spectroscope to produce stellar spectra with an 8-inch (20 cm) telescope at his observatory in Tulse Hill, South London. (Ann Ronan Picture Library)

bands of this gas were coincident with those obtained from a candle flame in the laboratory and therefore arose from carbon vapours.

In 1868 Huggins spectroscopically measured the velocity of the star Sirius by observing the Doppler shift of the F line of hydrogen towards the red end of the spectrum. Since the measurements that he was making were tiny, his result of 47.1 km/sec (29.4 miles per second) was high compared with the modern figure, but it was as accurate as his purely visual observations would allow. In the same year he examined the spectrum of a comet and found that its light was largely due to luminous hydrocarbon vapour. He went on to more observational successes with a pair of large telescopes lent to him by the Royal Society in 1870 and he made the first ultraviolet spectrograph. In 1899 he and his wife jointly published an *Atlas of Representative Stellar Spectra*.

Besides his interest in astronomy, Huggins was also a keen violinist and fisherman. He worked briefly with the chemist and physicist William Crookes (1832–1919) on the investigation of spiritualism, but became disillusioned as his suspicion of trickery increased.

Huggins was a pioneer, and as such he was often hampered by the inadequacy of his instruments and perhaps frustrated because he knew that more accurate observations and measurements could be made when better and more powerful equipment became available.

Part of Huggins' talent lay in his ability to foresee the possibilities in new ideas that were being initiated by his contemporaries. The three fundamental discoveries that made him famous within various fields of astronomy were made with his modest 8-inch (20 cm) refracting telescope. He established that elements such as hydrogen, calcium, sodium and iron were to be found in the stars and that the Universe was made up of well-known elements. He resolved the long debate as to whether all nebulae were clusters of stars by proving that some, like that in Orion, were gaseous and he used the spectroscope to detect the motion of stars and to measure their compositions and velocities.

Humason, Milton Lasell (*1891–1972*), was an American astronomer famous for his investigations, at Mount Wilson Observatory, into distant galaxies. Humason was born at Dodge Centre, Minnesota on 19 August 1891. There is no great list of educational achievements for Humason because he entered astronomy by an unusual route. When he was 14, his parents sent him to a summer camp on Mount Wilson and he so enjoyed it that when he had been back at High

School for only a few days, he obtained permission from his parents to take a year off school and return there. He extended his "year" well beyond twelve months and became one of astronomy's most notable educational dropouts. Sometime between 1908 and 1910, after his voluntary withdrawal from higher education, he became a mule driver for the packtrains that travelled the trail between the Sierra Madre and Mount Wilson during construction work on the Observatory. He brought up much of the timber and other building materials for the telescope's supporting structure, the local cottages and the scientists' quarters.

He became engaged to the daughter of the Observatory's engineer and married her in 1911. In the same year he gave up his job as driver of the packtrains and went to be foreman on a relative's range in La Verne. But he still loved Mount Wilson and in 1917, when a janitor was leaving, his father-in-law suggested that this might be an opening for better opportunities. So Humason initially joined the staff of Mount Wilson Observatory as a janitor. His position was soon elevated to night assistant. George Hale (1868–1938), the Director of the Observatory at the time, recognized Humason's unusual ability as an observer and in 1919 he was appointed to the scientific staff. There was considerable opposition to this appointment, partly because Humason had had no formal education after the age of 14 and partly because he was a relative of the Observatory's engineer.

Humason was Assistant Astronomer from 1919 to 1954 and then Astronomer at both the Mount Wilson and Palomar Observatories. In 1947 he was appointed Secretary of the Observatories, a position which involved him in handling public relations and administrative duties. In 1950 he was awarded the honorary degree of Doctor of Philosophy by the University of Lund in Sweden. He was a quiet, friendly man who was often consulted on administrative and personal problems. He died suddenly at his home near Mendocino, California, on 18 June 1972.

At Mount Wilson Observatory Humason took part in an extensive study of the properties of galaxies that had been initiated by Edwin Hubble. The research programme began in 1928 and consisted of making a series of systematic spectroscopic observations to test and extend the relationship that Hubble had found between the red shifts and the apparent magnitudes of galaxies. But because of the low surface brightness of galaxies there were severe technical difficulties. Special spectroscopic equipment, including the Rayton lens and the solid-block Schmidt camera, was designed. With these instruments it became possible to obtain a spectrum of a galaxy too faint to be picked up visually with the telescope used. The method was to photograph the field containing the galaxy and accurately measure the position of its image with respect to two or more bright stars. Guide microscopes were then set up at the telescope with exactly the same offsets from the slit of the spectrograph. It was a tedious task and often took several nights of exposure to produce a spectrum on a 12.7 mm (half-inch) plate.

Humason undertook this exacting programme. He personally developed the technique and made most of the exposures and plate measurements. During the period from 1930 to his retirement in 1957, the velocities of 620 galaxies were measured. He used the 100-inch (2.5 m) telescope until the 200-inch (5 m) Hale telescope was completed and the programme transferred to that instrument. Humason's results were published jointly with those of N.U. Mayall and A.R. Sandage in "Redshifts and Magnitudes of Extragalactic Nebulae", which appeared in the Astronomical Journal of 1956. This data still represents the majority of known values of radial velocities for normal galaxies, including most of the large values.

Humason applied the techniques he had developed for recording spectra of faint objects to the study of supernovae, old novae that were well past peak brightness, and faint blue stars (including white dwarfs). One by-product of his studies on galaxies was his discovery of Comet 1961e, which is notable for its large perihelion distance and its four-year period of visibility with remarkable changes in form.

Humason is remembered for his ability to handle instruments with meticulous care and great skill. He provided criteria for studying various models of the Universe. He became internationally famous for his work on galaxies and, in spite of his lack of formal training, won a leading role in American astronomy.

Huygens, Christiaan (*1629-1695*), was a Dutch scientist whose work had a significant effect on the development of optics - particularly telescopes and microscopes - and on the general development of astronomy and physics.

Huygens was born into a prominent Dutch family on 14 April 1629, at The Hague. His family combined a tradition of diplomatic service with a strong inclination towards education and culture. René Descartes was a frequent guest at the family house. Huygens' father, Constanijn, was a versatile man - a diplomat, a prominent Dutch and Latin poet, and a composer. The young Christiaan was educated at home before being sent to the University of Leiden in 1645 to study

mathematics and law, followed by two years of studying law at Breda.

Eschewing his expected career in diplomacy, Huygens returned to his home in 1651 and for the next 16 years he lived on an allowance from his father. He was thus able to devote himself to his chosen task - the scientific study of nature - and this long period of near-seclusion was the most fruitful period of his career.

In 1666, on the foundation of the Académie Royale des Sciences in Paris, Huygens was invited to live and work at the Bibliothèque Royale. He did so for 15 years until his delicate health and the changing political climate took him back to his home. There he continued to experiment and very occasionally he ventured abroad to meet other great scientists of the time (in 1689 he visited England to meet Newton in London). During his stay in Paris, Huygens had twice been forced to return home for health reasons. In 1694 he fell ill again but this time did not recover and he died the following summer at The Hague on 8 June.

Through working with his brother, Constantijn, Huygens became skilful in grinding and polishing lenses, and the telescopes that the two brothers constructed were the best of their time. Huygens' comprehensive study of geometric optics led to the invention of a telescope eyepiece that reduced chromatic aberration. It consisted of two thin plano-convex lenses, rather than one fat lens, with the field lens having a focal length three times greater than that of the eyepiece lens. Its main disadvantage was that cross-wires could not be fitted to measure the size of an image. To overcome this problem Huygens developed a micrometer, which he used to measure the angular diameter of celestial objects.

Having built (with his brother) his first telescope, which had a focal length of 3.5 m, Huygens discovered Titan, one of Saturn's moons, in 1655. Later that year he observed that its period of revolution was about 16 days and that it moved in the same plane as the so-called "arms" of Saturn. This phenomenon had been somewhat of an enigma to many earlier astronomers, but because of Huygens' superior 7 m telescope, and a piece of sound if not brilliant deduction, he partially unravelled the detail of Saturn's rings. In 1659 he published a Latin anagram which, when interpreted, read "It (Saturn) is surrounded by a thin flat ring, nowhere touching and inclined to the ecliptic". The theory behind Huygens' hypothesis followed later in Systema Saturnium, which included observations on the planets, their satellites, the Orion Nebula and the determination of the period of Mars. The content of this work amounted to an impressive defence of the Copernican view of the Solar System. More sig-

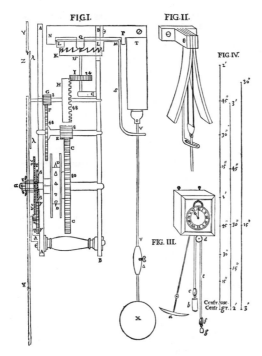

FIG.I.   FIG.II.

FIG.IV.

FIG.III.

Huygens' design for a pendulum clock – to prove of great value to astronomers – appeared in his Horologium Oscillatorium, *published in Paris in 1673. (Ann Ronan Picture Library/E.P. Goldschmidt & Co Ltd)*

nificantly, between the period 1655 to 1659, Huygens invented an important astronomical instrument – the pendulum clock. This was a significant innovation because astronomers need an accurate clock to keep track of the positions of the stars as the Earth turns. It was also of great importance in helping navigators to find longitudes.

Huygens went on to study "centrifugal" force and to show its relationship to gravitational force, although he lacked the Newtonian concept of acceleration. Both in the early and later part of his career he considered projectiles and gravity, developing the mathematically primitive ideas of Galileo and finding a remarkably accurate value for the distance covered by a falling body in the first one second. In fact his gravitational theories deal successfully with some difficult points that Newton carefully avoided.

The culmination of Huygens' many years of research in optics was published in 1678 in *Traité de la Lumière*. It included his wave or pulse theory of light and became the foundation of many subsequent advances in astronomy and optics. The essence of his theory is that light is transmitted as a pulse and has a tendency to move in the "ether" as a kind of serial displacement. Two years earlier

he had used this wave theory to explain reflection and refraction. But, although Huygens' analysis of the double refraction occurring in crystals of quartz is impressive, he failed to elucidate the phenomenon of the polarization which occurs when the refracted ray is directed through a second crystal.

The impact of Huygens' work in his own time and in the eighteenth century was much less than his genius deserved. He was essentially a solitary man who did not attract students or disciples, and he was slow to publish his findings. Also, as he lived in an age of such revolutionary figures as Descartes, Newton and Leibniz, his work often appeared to be conservative in comparison with theirs, partly because of his suspicion of ideas which seemed more occult than purely mechanistic. This scepticism accounts for his refusal to accept Newton's theory of mutual attraction between two bodies. The two devices that Huygens did develop – the telescope and the clock – have been fundamental tools in astronomy ever since.

J

Jansky, Karl Guthe (*1905–1950*), was an American radio engineer whose discovery of radio waves of extraterrestrial origin led to the development of radio-astronomy.

Jansky was born at Norman, Oklahoma, on 22 October 1905. He was educated at the University of Wisconsin, where his father was a member of the Faculty. He spent a year as an instructor before beginning his career as an engineer with the Bell Telephone Laboratories in 1928. His fundamental discovery of the existence of extraterrestrial radio waves was made and published by 1932. Thereafter Jansky did not continue this kind of scientific work. He became more involved with engineering and left the research in astronomy to others. Jansky died at an early age, of a heart complaint, at Red Bank, New Jersey, on 14 February 1950.

When Jansky joined the Bell Telephone Company as a research engineer, he was assigned the task of tracking down and identifying the various types of interference from which radio telephony and radio reception were suffering. The company was particularly concerned with the interference that occurred at short wavelengths of around 15 m (then being used for ship-to-shore radio communications). It was well known that some of the static interference was caused by thunderstorms, nearby electrical equipment or aircraft, but, by building a high quality receiver and aerial system that was set on wheels and could be rotated in various directions, Jansky was able to detect a new and unidentifiable kind of static. After months of study Jansky associated the source of the unidentified radio interference with the stars. He had noticed that the background hiss on a loudspeaker attached to the receiver and antenna system reached a maximum intensity every 24 hours. From overhead, it seemed to move steadily with the Sun but gained on the Sun by four minutes per day. This amount of time correlates with the difference of apparent motion, as seen on Earth, between the Sun and the stars, and so Jansky surmised that the source must lie beyond the Solar System. By the spring of 1932, he had concluded that the source lay in the direction of Sagittarius. This was the direction which the American astronomer, Harlow Shapley (1885–1972), and the Dutch astronomer, Jan Oort (1900–   ), had confirmed as being the direction of the centre of our Galaxy. Jansky published his results in December 1932. In the same month Bell Telephone Laboratories issued a press release on Jansky's discovery to the New York Times and it made front-page news. This was the birth of radio-astronomy. There was now a second region of the electromagnetic spectrum in which it was possible to study the stars – a radio window on the Universe. There was no immediate follow-up to Jansky's discovery, however, and it was left to an amateur American astronomer, Grote Reber, to pursue the matter. It was not until the end of World War II that the importance of radio-astronomy began to be recognized.

Although Jansky died at an early age, he did live long enough to see radio-astronomy develop into an important tool of modern astronomical research. By their ability to penetrate the Earth's atmosphere and dust clouds in space, radio telescopes enable the study of celestial objects that are impossible to detect by optical means. In honour of Karl Jansky the International Astronomical Union named the unit of strength of a radiowave emission a jansky (symbolized Jy), in 1973.

Janssen, Pierre Jules César (*1824–1907*), was a French astronomer, famous for his work in physical astronomy and spectroscopy.

Janssen was born in Paris on 22 February 1824. His father was a musician of Belgian descent and his maternal grandfather was a well-known architect. In his early life he had an accident which left him permanently lame, and as a result he never went to school. Because of financial difficulties he went out to work at an early age. He worked in a bank from 1840 to 1848, but educated himself at the same time and took his Baccalau-

reat at the age of 25. He studied mathematics and physics at the Faculty of Sciences in Paris and gained his Licence des Sciences in 1852. He worked for a while as a substitute teacher in a lycée, before being sent on the first of his scientific missions – to Peru – in 1857. He returned with a bad attack of dysentery and became a tutor to the wealthy Schneider family who owned iron and steel mills in Le Creusot. He was awarded his doctorate in 1860, and in 1862 began work with E. Follin of the Faculty of Medicine. In 1865 he was made Professor of Physics at the École Spéciale d'Architecture. He was elected to the Academy of Sciences in 1873 and to the Bureau of Longitudes in 1875. He was appointed Director of the new astronomical observatory, established by the French government at Meudon in 1875, a position he held until his death in Paris on 23 December 1907.

Although Janssen travelled to Peru to measure the magnetic equator, his first real research work was in the field of ophthalmology. He went on to work on the construction of an ophthalmoscope at the Faculty of Medicine in Paris. But ever since he had heard that Gustav Kirchoff (1824–1887) had demonstrated the presence of terrestrial elements in the make-up of the Sun in 1859, Janssen had decided that his real passion was for physical astronomy. He built himself an observatory on the flat roof of his wife's house in Montmartre and began to work on the nature of the dark bands in the solar spectrum. He found that these bands were most noticeable at sunrise and sunset. For his research he constructed a special spectroscope with a high dispersive power, to which he attached a device for regulating luminous intensity. By 1862 he was able to show that these bands can be resolved into rays and that they are always present. In 1864 he travelled to Italy and there he was able to show that the intensity of the rays varied during the course of a day in relation to the terrestrial atmosphere. He showed that the origin of the phenomenon was terrestrial and called the rays "telluric rays". To prove his point that the intensity of telluric rays would be less in thinner air, he travelled to the Bernese Alps to measure the rays at a height of 2,700 m. They were even weaker than he expected, and so he attributed the extra effect to the dryness of the air, and went to the shores of Lake Geneva to study the effect of humidity on the strength of the rays. In 1867 he spent time in the Azores, carrying out optical and magnetic experiments which concluded that water vapour was present in the atmosphere of Mars.

In 1868 Janssen went to India to observe the total eclipse of the Sun which occurred on 18 August. Together with other scientists, he noted that there were a number of bright lines in the spectrum of the solar chromosphere. He demonstrated the gaseous nature of the red prominences, but he was unable to correlate the exact positions of the lines in the solar spectrum with wavelengths of any known elements. Janssen continued to observe the unobscured Sun for 17 days after the eclipse and he reported his findings to the French Academy of Sciences by telegram. In October of the same year, Norman Lockyer (1836-1920), an English astronomer and physicist, observed the chromosphere through a special telescope designed by him in 1866. He noted, as Janssen had, that there was a third yellow line in the spectrum, which did not correspond to either of the two known lines of sodium. He immediately reported his findings to the French Academy of Sciences and a letter from Janssen, also reporting that a new element must be responsible for the yellow line, arrived at the same time as the letter from Lockyer. The two scientists became firm friends, because of the coincidence of their discovery, and a medallion was struck by the French Academy of Sciences bearing their profiles and names. Lockyer went on to discover that the new line represented a substance that was later christened helium.

In the same year, 1868, Janssen developed a spectrohelioscope so that he could observe the Sun and solar prominences spectroscopically in daylight conditions. With it he attempted to ascertain whether or not the Sun contains oxygen. He realized it would help his research if he could eliminate some of the obscuring effects of the Earth's atmosphere, and for this reason he established an observatory on Mont Blanc. By this time his health was not good, and to overcome his disability he invented a device which enabled him to be carried up Mont Blanc; even so, the journey in this conveyance took 13 hours. Janssen went to any lengths to continue his observations. In order to observe the eclipse on 22 December 1870, he travelled to Algeria by balloon, despite the Franco-Prussian War. He later devised an aeronautical compass which was capable of instantly indicating the direction and speed of flight.

From 1876 to 1903 Janssen summarized the history of the surface of the Sun by means of solar photographs. These were made at the astrophysical observatory in Meudon and were collected together in his *Atlas de Photographies Solaires* (1904). In order to observe the transit of Venus in 1882, he took a series of photographs in rapid succession which enabled him to measure successive positions of the planet. He obtained a series of separate images, laid out in a circle on the photographic plate. Here Janssen had anticipated one of the operations necessary for cinematography, which was to be invented 20 years later. He also invented another device of historical interest, the photographic revolver, in 1873.

Jeans, James Hopwood (*1877-1946*), was a British mathematician and astrophysicist who made important contributions to cosmogony – particularly his theory of continuous creation of matter – and became known to a wide public through his popular books and broadcasts on astronomy.

Jeans was born at Ormskirk, Lancashire, on 11 September 1877, but moved at the age of three to Tulse Hill, London, where he spent his childhood. His interests in science and his literary bent disclosed themselves at an early age. When he was only nine years old he wrote a handbook on clocks which included an explanation of the escapement principle and a description of how to make a clock from pieces of tin. He was educated at Merchant Taylors' School, London, from 1890 to 1896 and then went to Cambridge to study mathematics at Trinity College. He graduated in 1900 and was awarded a Smith's Prize. In 1901 Jeans was appointed a Fellow of Trinity and from 1905 to 1909 he was Professor of Applied Mathematics at Princeton University in the United States. From 1910 to 1912 he was Stokes Lecturer in Applied Mathematics at Cambridge. Thereafter he held no university post, but devoted himself to private research and writing, although he was a research associate at the Mount Wilson Observatory, California, from 1923 to 1944. In 1928 Jeans stated his belief that matter was continuously being created in the Universe. He never developed this idea (a forerunner of the Steady State theory), however, for in that year his career as a research scientist came to an end. After that time he concentrated on broadcasting and writing popular books on science. He was awarded the Royal Medal of the Royal Society in 1919 and was knighted in 1928. He died on 1 September 1946 at Dorking, Surrey.

The first years of Jeans' research career were spent on problems in molecular physics, in particular on the foundations of the kinetic molecular theory. His *Dynamical Theory of Gases* (1904), which contained his treatment of the persistence of molecular velocities after collisions (that is, the tendency for molecules to retain some motion in the direction in which they were travelling before collision), became a standard text.

Jeans next worked on the problems of equipartition of energy in its application to specific heat capacities and black-body radiation. In 1905 he corrected a numerical error in the derivation of the classical distribution of black-body radiation made by John Rayleigh (1842–1919) and formulated the relationship known as the Rayleigh-Jeans law, which describes the spectral distribution of black-body radiation in terms of wavelength and temperature. For some time thereafter Jeans investigated various problems in quantum theory, but in about 1912 he turned his attention to astrophysics.

Jeans had been interested in astrophysics since his student days. In an undergraduate prize-winning essay he had treated compressible and incompressible fluids at a deeper level than had Henri Poincaré (1854–1912), and this work led directly to a consideration of the origin of the universe, or cosmogony. Jeans distinguished two extremes: an incompressible mass of fluid and a gas of negligible mass surrounding a mass concentrated at its centre. He argued that if an incomprehensible mass were to contract or be subjected to an increase in angular momentum, it would evolve into an unstable pear-shaped configuration and then split in two. Double stars could be formed in this way. At the other extreme, gas of a negligible mass could evolve through ellipsoidal figures to a lenticular shape and then eject matter from its edge; spiral nebulae could be formed in this way. Jeans concluded that the rotation of a contracting mass could not give rise to the formation of a planetary system. He himself favoured a tidal theory of the Solar System's origins, in which planetary systems were created during the close passage of two stars. This theory is no longer held in much favour, but Jeans did point out the errors in the nebular theory by which Laplace (1749–1812) attempted to explain the origin of the Solar System.

Jones, Harold Spencer (*1890–1960*), was a British astronomer, the tenth Astronomer Royal. He is noted for his study of the speed of rotation of the Earth, the motions of the Sun, Moon and planets and his determination of solar parallax.

Jones was born in London on 29 March 1890, the third child of an accountant. He attended Hammersmith Grammar School and Latymer Upper School, where he excelled at mathematics. He won a scholarship to Jesus College, Cambridge. Following his graduation in 1913 he was awarded a research fellowship to Jesus College. In the same year he was appointed Chief Assistant at the Royal Observatory, Greenwich, to succeed Arthur Eddington (1882–1944), who had gone to Cambridge as Plumian Professor. Ten years later, in 1923, Jones was appointed His Majesty's Astronomer on the Cape of Good Hope. In 1933 he returned to England to become Astronomer Royal. He held this position until his retirement in 1955. He was President of the International Astronomical Union from 1944 to 1948 and Secretary General of the Scientific Union from 1955 to 1958. He had been President of the Royal Astronomical Society from 1938 to 1939 and was knighted in 1943. Jones died in London on 3 November 1960.

Jones' first period of research began when he went to Russia in 1914 to observe an eclipse. He wrote several papers on the variation of latitude, as observed using an instrument known as the Cookson floating telescope. During this time he also made determinations of the photographic magnitude scale of the North Polar Sequence (the stars located near the Celestial North Pole). While at the Cape of Good Hope, he published an important catalogue containing the radial velocities of the southern stars, calculated the orbits of a number of spectroscopic binary stars, and made a spectroscopic determination of the constant of aberration. In 1924 he made extensive observations of Mars, using a 7-inch (18 cm) heliometer – a refracting telescope for measuring the angular diameter of celestial objects – and these observations were later used to obtain the value for solar parallax. In 1925 he obtained and described a long series of spectra of a nova which had appeared in the constellation of Pictor.

While Jones was working at the Cape of Good Hope, he had collected more than 1,200 photographic observations towards the solar parallax programme and as a result, by international agreement in 1931, he was entrusted with dealing with all results of the observations of Eros. Eros was discovered in 1898, a minor planet whose orbit brings it to within 24 million km of Earth. From photographic observations in both hemispheres, Jones derived a figure for the solar parallax that corresponded to a distance of 149,670,000 km and published his results in 1941. By 1967 the distance of the Earth from the Sun had been obtained using direct measurements by radar. The result, a distance of 149,597,890 km, is ten times as accurate (though the difference is only 0.05 per cent) as that which Jones had originally derived using parallax. Any improvements on this value hinges on the limitations of our present knowledge of the velocity of light. It was unfortunate that Jones' painstaking and time-consuming work on determining the mean distance of the Earth from the Sun came just before the use of automatic computing equipment made his methods and instruments redundant.

Besides his work on solar parallax, Jones' principal contributions to astronomy were his work on the motions and secular acceleration of the Sun, Moon and planets and the rotation of the Earth. He proved that fluctuations in the observed longitudes of these celestial bodies are due not to any peculiarities in their motion, but to fluctuations in the angular velocity of rotation of the Earth. He also successfully investigated geophysical phenomena such as the rotation of the Earth, its magnetism and oblateness and he estimated the mass of the Moon. As Astronomer Royal, Jones campaigned for the Royal Observatory to be moved from Greenwich, because the increasing smoke and lights of London hindered observation. It was not until after World War II, however, that a new site was procured at Herstmonceux Castle, Sussex, and the new Observatory was not completed until 1958, three years after Jones' retirement.

Joy, James Harrison (*1882–1973*), was an American astronomer, most famous for his work on stellar distances, the radial motions of stars and variable stars.

Joy was born on 23 September 1882 in Greenville, Illinois, the son of a merchant of New England ancestry. He was educated locally and then attended Greenville College, obtaining a PhD degree in 1903. From 1904 to 1914 he worked at the American University of Beirut, in Lebanon, first as a teacher and then as Professor of Astronomy and Director of the Observatory. He returned to the United States in 1914, worked at the Yerkes Observatory as an instructor for a year, and then joined the staff of Mount Wilson Observatory, where he remained until 1952. He was Vice-President of the American Astronomical Society in 1946 and President in 1949.

When Joy joined the staff of the Yerkes Observatory in 1914, he took part in a programme of measuring stellar distances, using the 40-inch (1 m) Yerkes refractor, by direct photography and parallax measurements, an extremely tedious and out-of-date method. After 1916, he began to make spectroscopic observations at Mount Wilson Observatory and he was subsequently invited to take part in their research programme to obtain stellar distances.

The new method of finding the distance to stars was to compare the apparent magnitude of the star with its absolute magnitude. Joy continued with this programme, in collaboration with his colleagues Walter Adams (1876–1956) and Milton Humason (1891–1972), for more than 20 years and their results enabled them to ascertain the spectral type, absolute magnitude, and stellar distance of more than 5,000 stars.

Joy and his colleagues also studied the Doppler displacement of the spectral lines of some stars to determine their radial velocities. By noting the variations in radial velocity, Joy and his team were able to show that many stars are spectroscopic binary stars and that their period and orbit

could therefore be elucidated. From their observations of eclipsing binary stars they deduced the absolute dimensions, masses and orbital elements of some specific stars within eclipsing binary systems. Using radial velocity data of 130 Cepheid variable stars, Joy determined the distance and direction of the centre of the Galaxy and calculated the rotation period for bodies moving in circular orbits at the distance of the Sun, with a view to calculating the rotation period of the Galaxy.

Joy also spent many years of his life observing variable stars and classifying them according to their characteristic spectra. While studying the long-period variable star, Mira Ceti, Joy observed the spectrum of a small hot companion object. It was later named Mira B and shown to be a white dwarf; it can be observed visually today. Joy later became interested in the parts of the Galaxy where dark, absorbing clouds of gas and dust exist, and by carefully observing these areas he found examples of a particular kind of variable star, called a T-Tauri star, which is strongly associated with these areas. T-Tauri stars have a wide range of spectral types combined with characteristically low magnitudes. Joy showed that these characteristics indicated that they were very young stars in an early stage of their evolutionary history.

K

Kant, Immanuel (*1724–1804*), is more generally regarded as a philosopher than an astronomer, but his theoretical work in astronomy inspired cosmological theories and many of his conjectures have been confirmed by observational evidence.

Kant was born in Königsberg (now Kaliningrad in the Soviet Union) on 27 April 1724 and he lived there or nearby for all of his life. His grandfather was an immigrant from Scotland, called Cant, whose name was Germanized. Kant's father was a saddlemaker of modest means and conventional religious beliefs and his mother was a member of a pietist Protestant sect.

At the age of ten Kant entered the Collegium Fridericianum, where he was expected to study theology. Instead, he concentrated on the classics and then went to the University of Königsberg to study mathematics and physics. Six years after he entered university, his father died and he was forced to work as a private tutor to three of Königsberg's leading families in order to support his brothers and sisters. He did not return to the

University until 1755, when he gained his PhD and became an unpaid lecturer. Fifteen years later, Kant was offered the Chair in Logic and Metaphysics, a post he held for 27 years. He died in Königsberg on 12 February 1804.

Kant's most important work was a philosophical text, the *Critique of Pure Reason*, published in 1781 when he was in his late fifties. In his early pre-*Critique* work, however, he dealt with various scientific subjects, including a consideration of the origin and natural history of the Universe. Kant was not an experimental scientist in any sense and he has sometimes been accused of being merely an "armchair scientist". Yet he was not ignorant of the scientific advances of his day and his theoretical works on astronomy were deeply affected by his studies of Newtonian and Leibnizian physics. The hypotheses Kant put forward inspired other theories, notably those propounded by Carl von Weizsäcker (1921-) in the Gifford Lectures of 1959-60 and by Gerard Kuiper (1905-1973) of the Yerkes Observatory in the United States. They also coincided with another more empirical work on the nature of the Universe that later became known as the Kant-Laplacian theory.

Besides being indebted to Newton, Kant's thought on astronomy and cosmology was also influenced by a work entitled *Original Theory or a New Hypothesis of the Universe*, published by Thomas Wright in 1758. Kant's pre-Critique *Universal Natural History and Theory of the Heavens* was based on the theories of Newton and Wright. It also anticipated facts of astronomy that were later confirmed only by advanced observational techniques. Kant proposed that the Solar System was part of a system of stars constituting a galaxy and that there were many such galaxies making up the whole Universe. His conjecture that nebulous stars were also separate galaxies similar to our own was confirmed only in the twentieth century.

Although Kant accepted the religious claim that God created the world, in the *Natural History* he concerned himself with explaining how the Universe evolved once it had been created. In contrast with the idea that planets were formed as a result of tidal forces set off in the Sun when some large celestial body passed close by, he argued, in the theory that came to be associated with one put forward by Laplace, that planetary bodies in the Solar System were formed by the condensation of nebulous, diffuse primordial matter that was previously widely distributed in space. He used the Newtonian theory of the attraction and repulsion of materials to account for the fact that the Solar System, like other celestial systems, is flattened out like a disc. He also sup-

posed that action at a distance was possible, explaining the gravitational attraction that held the moons and planets in their orbits. Moreover, Kant argued that the Universe continues to develop: its parts come together and disperse with the condensation and diffusion of matter in the infinity of time and space.

Kant's most famous work, *Critique of Pure Reason*, inaugurated the "Copernican Revolution" in philosophy, turning attention to the mind's role in constructing our knowledge of the objective world. He examined the legitimacy and objectivity of cognition and science, an investigation which led him to doubt a number of the presuppositions necessary to the theories put forward in *Natural History*. For example, one of the self-contradictory conclusions considered in the *Critique* showed that we cannot, with certainty, make assertions concerning the finite or infinite nature of space and time. But even with this qualification it is amazing that, based only on Newtonian principles and information gleaned from reading an abstract of the book by Wright, Kant's hypotheses coincide so well with later cosmological theories.

Kapteyn, Jacobus Cornelius (*1851-1922*), was a Dutch astronomer who analysed the structure of the Universe by studying the distribution of stars using photographic techniques. To achieve more accurate star counts in selected sample areas of the sky he introduced the technique of statistical astronomy. He also encouraged fruitful international collaboration among astronomers.

Kapteyn was born in Barneveld, The Netherlands, on 19 January 1851. He was born into a large and talented family and he displayed great academic abilities early in his life. He began his studies at the University of Utrecht in 1868 when he was 17, although he had already satisfied the University's entrance requirements a year earlier. Kapteyn concentrated his studies on mathematics and physics and earned his doctorate for a thesis on vibration.

Kapteyn's career in astronomy began when he was employed by the astronomical observatory at Leiden in 1875. Three years later he was appointed as the first Professor of Astronomy and Theoretical Mechanics at the University of Groningen. He was a member of the French Academy of Science and a Fellow of the Royal Society. He was active in the organizational work which eventually led to the establishment of the International Union of Astronomers. He retired from his post at Groningen in 1921, but continued to work and publish his results. He died in Amsterdam on 18 June 1922.

Initially there was a lack of appropriate facilities at the University of Groningen, but this did not deter Kapteyn. He proposed a cooperative arrangement with Sir David Gill at Cape Town Observatory in South Africa, whereby photographs of the stars in the Southern hemisphere were analysed at Groningen. This early collaborative work with Gill resulted in the publication during the years 1896 to 1900 of the *Cape Photographic Durchmusterung*. It was welcomed as an essential complement to Argelander's monumental *Bonner Durchmusterung* (1859-1862), because it presented accurate data on the brightness and positions of nearly 455,000 stars in the less-studied Southern hemisphere. The catalogue included all stars of magnitude greater than 10 which lay within 19 degrees of the South Pole, and it encouraged Edward Pickering's team of astronomers from the Harvard Observatory, who set up a research station in Chile, to expand their observations of stars in the southern skies.

Kapteyn's next project was to improve the technique of trigonometric parallax so that he could obtain data of a higher quality on the proper motions of stars. Although proper motion had been observed for many years, its explanation was unknown. It had been assumed by most astronomers that there was no pattern in the proper motion of stars, that they resembled the random Brownian motions of gas molecules. In 1904 Kapteyn reported that there was indeed a pattern. He found that stars could be divided into two streams, moving in nearly opposite directions. The notion that there was this element of order in the Universe was to have a considerable impact, although its significance was not realized at the time.

Arthur Eddington and Karl Schwarzschild extended Kapteyn's work and confirmed his results, but they missed the underlying importance of their observations. It was not until 1928 that Jan Oort and Bertil Lindblad, greatly aided by recent discoveries on the characteristics of extragalactic nebulae, proposed that Kapteyn's results could be readily understood if they were considered in the contest of a rotating spiral galaxy. Kapteyn's data had been the first evidence of the rotation of our Galaxy (which at that time was not understood to be in any way distinct from the rest of the Universe), although it was not recognized as such at the time.

F.W. Herschel had investigated the structure of stellar systems by counting the number of stars in different directions. Kapteyn decided to repeat this analysis with the aid of modern telescopes. He selected 206 specific stellar zones, and in 1906 he began a vast international programme to study them. His aim was to ascertain the magnitudes of all the stars within these zones, as well as to collect data on the spectral type, radial velocity, proper motion of the stars and other astronomical parameters. This enormous project was the first co-ordinated statistical analysis in astronomy and it involved the co-operation of over 40 different observatories. The project was extended by Edward Pickering to include 46 additional stellar zones of particular interest.

The analysis of data collected for the programme was a colossal task and took many years to complete. In 1922, only weeks before his death, Kapteyn published his conclusions based on the analysis he had completed. His overall result was strikingly similar to that obtained by Herschel. He envisaged an island Universe, a lens-shaped aggregation of stars that were densely packed at the centre and thinned away as empty space outside the Galaxy was reached. The Sun lay only about 2,000 light-years from the centre of a structure which spanned some 40,000 light-years along its main axis.

A fundamental error in the construction of "Kapteyn's Universe" was his neglect of the possibility that interstellar material would cause stellar light from a distance to be dimmed. This placed a limit on the maximum distance from which data could be obtained. Kapteyn had, in fact, considered this possibility, and he tried unsuccessfully to detect its effect. The effect Kapteyn had sought was observed by Robert Trumpler nearly ten years after Kapteyn's death. Harlow Shapley's model for the structure of our Galaxy soon replaced that proposed by Kapteyn. Today the Galaxy is thought to span some 100,000 light-years (9.5×10^{17} km) and to be shaped like a pancake which thickens considerably towards the centre. Our Solar System lies quite a long way out along one of the spiral arms, 30,000 light-years from the centre of the Galaxy – which lies in the direction of the constellation Sagittarius.

Keeler, James Edward (*1857-1900*), was an American astrophysicist noted for his work on the rings of Saturn and on the abundance and structure of nebulae.

Keeler was born in La Salle, Illinois, on 10 September 1857. He did not attend school between the ages of 12 and 20, but during these years he developed a keen interest in astronomy. He made a variety of astronomical instruments and spent long hours studying the Solar System. A benefactor enabled him to study at Johns Hopkins University, where he earned his bachelors' degree in 1881. While a student he participated in an expedition to Colorado to study a solar eclipse. In 1881 he began his career as assistant to Samuel Langley (1834-1906), Director of the Allegheny Observatory, and he took part in that year's expedition to the Rocky Mountains to measure solar infrared radiation.

In 1883 Keeler went to Germany to study at the Universities of Heidelberg and Berlin. A year later he returned to the Allegheny Observatory and in 1886 he went to Mount Witney, the future site of the Lick Observatory. He was appointed Astronomer at the Lick Observatory upon its completion in 1888. Keeler became Professor of Astrophysics and Director of the Allegheny Observatory in 1891, but returned to the Lick Observatory as Director in 1898. He was elected Fellow of the Royal Astronomical Society of London in 1898 and made a member of the National Academy of Sciences in 1900. He died suddenly in San Francisco on 12 August 1900.

Keeler's earliest work was a spectroscopic demonstration of the similarity between the Orion nebula and stars. In 1888, using the 35-inch (91 cm) refracting telescope at Lick Observatory and an improved spectroscopic grating, he demonstrated that nebulae resembled stars in their pattern of movement. He also studied the planet Mars, but he was unable to confirm Schiaparelli's observation that the Martian surface was etched with a pattern of "canals". In 1895 Keeler made a spectroscopic study of Saturn and its rings, in order to examine the planet's period of rotation. He found that the rings did not rotate at a uniform rate, thus proving for the first time that they could not be solid and confirming James Clerk Maxwell's theory that the rings consist of meteoritic particles.

After 1898 Keeler devoted himself to a study of all the nebulae that William Herschel had catalogued a hundred years earlier. He succeeded in photographing half of them, and in the course of his work he discovered many thousands of new nebulae and showed their close relationship to stars. Keeler was not only a keen and successful observer of astronomical phenomena; he was also skilled at designing and constructing instruments. These included modifications to the Crossley reflecting telescope and a spectrograph in which spectral lines were recorded with the aid of a camera.

Kepler, Johannes (*1571–1630*), was a German astronomer who combined great mathematical skills with patience and an almost mystical sense of universal harmony. He is particularly remembered for what are now known as Kepler's Laws of Motion. These had a profound influence on Newton and hence on all modern science. Kepler was also absorbed with the forces that govern the whole Universe and he was one of the first and most powerful advocates of Copernican heliocentric (Sun-centred) cosmology.

Kepler was born on 27 December 1571 in Weil der Statt near Stuttgart, Germany. He was not a healthy child and since it was apparently thought that he was capable only of a career in the ministry, he was sent for religious training in Leonberg, Adelberg and Maulbronn. One event that impressed him deeply during his early years was the viewing of the "great" comet of 1577 and his interest in astronomy probably dates from that time. He passed his baccalaureate at the University of Tübingen in 1588 and then returned to Maulbronn for a year. From 1589 to 1591 he studied philosophy, mathematics and astronomy under Michael Mästlin at the University of Tübingen; yet although he showed great aptitude and promise and obtained his MA in 1591, he then embarked on a three-year programme of theological training. This was interrupted in the last year when he was nominated for a teaching post in mathematics and astronomy in Graz. It was during this teaching period that he abandoned his plans for a career in the ministry and concentrated on astronomy. He wrote his first major paper while at Graz and attracted the attention of other notable astronomers of the time, particularly Tycho Brahe and Galileo.

Kepler was a Lutheran and so was frequently caught up in the religious troubles of his age. In 1598 a purge forced him to leave Graz. He travelled to Prague and spent a year there before he returned to Graz; he was expelled again and arrived back in Prague, where he became Tycho Brahe's assistant in 1600. Brahe died a few months later, in 1601, and Kepler succeeded him as Imperial Mathematician to Emperor Rudolph II. On his deathbed Brahe requested that Kepler complete the Rudolphine Astronomical Tables, a task which Kepler finished in 1627.

Kepler lived in Prague until 1612 and produced what was perhaps his best work during those years. He was given a telescope in 1610 by Elector Ernest of Cologne and studied optics, telescope design and astronomy. In 1611 Emperor Rudolph was deposed, but Kepler was retained as Imperial Mathematician. In 1612, upon Rudolph's death, Kepler became District Mathematician for the States of Upper Austria and moved to Linz. But personal problems plagued him for the next ten years – the arrest and trial of his mother, who was accused of witchcraft in 1615 but exonerated in 1621, being particularly distressing.

It was in Linz that Kepler published three of his major works. In 1628 he became the private mathematician to Wallenstein, Duke of Friedland and Imperial General, partly because of the Duke's promise to pay the debt owed Kepler by the deposed Emperor Rudolph. In 1630 religious persecution forced Kepler to move once again. He fell sick with an acute fever, and died en route to Regensburg, Bavaria, on 15 November 1630.

Kepler's work in astronomy falls into three main periods of activity, at Graz, Prague and Linz. In Graz Kepler did some work with Mästlin on optics and planetary orbits, but he devoted most of his energy to teaching. He also produced a calendar of predictions for the year 1595 which proved so uncanny in its accuracy that he gained a degree of local fame. Kepler found the production of astrological calendars a useful way of supplementing his income in later years, but he had little respect for the art. More important, in 1596 he published his *Mysterium Cosmographicum*, in which he demonstrated that the five Platonic Solids, the only five regular polyhedrons, could be fitted alternately inside a series of spheres to form a "nest" which described quite accurately (within 5 per cent) the distances of the planets from the Sun. Kepler regarded this discovery as a divine inspiration which revealed the secret of the Universe. It was written in accordance with Copernican theories and it bought Kepler to the attention of all European astronomers.

Before Kepler arrived in Prague and was bequeathed all Tycho's data on planetary motion, he had already made a bet that, given Tycho's unfinished tables, he could find an accurate planetary orbit within a week. It took rather longer, however. It was five years before Kepler obtained

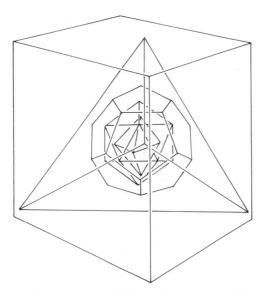

Kepler adopted Plato's idea of five nesting regular solids (from the centre: octahedron, icosahedron, dodecahedron, tetrahedron and cube) and suggested that the planetary orbits fitted between them.

his first planetary orbit, that of Mars. In 1604 his attention was diverted from the planets by his observation of the appearance of a new star, "Kepler's nova", to which he attached great astrological significance.

In 1609 Kepler's first two laws of planetary motion were published in *Astronomia Nova*, which is a long text and as unreadable as it is important. The First Law states that planets travel in elliptical rather than circular or epicyclic orbits and that the Sun occupies one of the two foci of the ellipses. What is now known as the Second Law, but was in fact discovered first, states that the line joining the Sun and a planet traverses equal areas of space in equal periods of time, so that the planets move more quickly when they are nearer the Sun. This established the Sun as the main force governing the orbits of the planets. Kepler also showed that the orbital velocity of a planet is inversely proportional to the distance between the planet and the Sun. He suggested that the Sun itself rotates, a theory which was confirmed by using Galileo's observations of sunspots, and he postulated that this established some sort of "magnetic" interaction between the planets and the Sun, driving them in orbit. This idea, although incorrect, was an important precursor of Newton's gravitational theory. The *Astronomia Nova* had virtually no impact at all at the time, and so Kepler turned his attention to optics and telescope design. He published his second book on optics, the *Dioptrice*, in 1611. That year was a difficult one, because Kepler's wife and sons died. Then, in 1612, the Lutherans were thrown out of Prague so Kepler had to move on again to Linz.

In Linz Kepler produced two more major works. The first of these was *De Harmonices Mundi*, which was almost a mystical text. The book was divided into five chapters and buried in the last was Kepler's third Law. In this Law he describes in precise mathematical language the link between the distances of the planets from the Sun and their velocities – a feat which afforded him extraordinary pleasure and confirmed his belief in the harmony of the Universe. The second major work to be published during his stay in Linz, the *Epitome*, intended as an introduction to Copernican astronomy, was in fact a very effective summary of Kepler's life's work in theoretical astronomy. It was a long treatise of seven books, published over a period of four years, and it had more impact than any other astronomical text of the mid-seventeenth century.

Soon after its publication, Kepler's Lutheran background caused yet another expulsion and this time he went to Ulm, where he finally completed the Rudolphine Tables. They appeared in

1627 and brought Kepler much popular acclaim. These were the first modern astronomical tables, a vast improvement on previous attempts of this kind, and they enabled astronomers to calculate the positions of the planets at any time in the past, present or future. The publication also included other vital information, such as a map of the world, a catalogue of stars, and the latest aid to computation, logarithms.

Kepler wrote the first science fiction story, *Solemnium*, which described a man who travelled to the Moon. It was published in 1631, a year after his death, although it had been written 20 years earlier. Kepler was a remarkable man and a brilliant scientist. He kept a steady eye on what he saw as his true vocation as a "speculative physicist and cosmologist" and, despite living in times of political unrest and religious turmoil, was never swayed by religious bigotry or political pressures. His new astronomy provided the basis on which Newton and others were to build, and to this day his three Laws of Motion are considered to be the basis of our understanding of the Solar System. His work and his strong support of Copernican cosmology mark a fundamental divide between two eras - that of the Ptolemaic Earth-centred view of the Universe that had been accepted for the previous 15 centuries, and the new age given birth by the Copernican heliocentric, or Sun-centred, view of the Solar System.

Kirkwood, Daniel (*1814–1895*), was an American astronomer who is known for his work on asteroids, meteors and the evolution of the Solar System.

Kirkwood was born in Hartford County, Maryland, on 27 September 1814. He became a teacher in 1833 and rose to become Principal of Lancaster High School from 1843 to 1849 and then of the Pottsville Academy from 1849 to 1851. He went on to become Professor of Mathematics at the University of Indiana. During this period of tenure, he had a two-year break which he spent as Professor of Mathematics and Astronomy at Jefferson College in Pennsylvania. In retirement Kirkwood moved to California and in 1891 he became a lecturer in astronomy at the University of Stanford. He died in Riverside, California, on 11 June 1895.

Kirkwood's first astronomical paper was published in 1849. It consisted of a dubious mathematical description of the rotational periods of the planets. He was more interested, however, in the distribution of the asteroids in the Solar System. As early as 1857 he had noticed that three regions of the minor planet zone, sited at 2.5, 2.95 and 3.3 astronomical units from the Sun, lacked

asteroids completely. In 1866 he published his analysis of this observation and proposed that the gaps, subsequently named "Kirkwood gaps", arose as a consequence of perturbations caused by the planet Jupiter. The effect of Jupiter's mass would be to force any asteroid that appeared in one of the asteroid-free zones into another orbit, with the result that it would immediately leave the zone. It has since been proposed that non-gravitational effects, such as collisions, may also play a role in the maintenance of these gaps. Since Kirkwood's time, several more such gaps have been recognized.

Kirkwood used the same theory to explain the non-uniform distribution of particles in the ring system of Saturn. He suggested that Cassini's division was maintained by the perturbing effect which Saturn's satellites - Mimas, Enceladus, Thetys, Dione and, to a lesser extent, Rhea and Titan - had on the orbits of the particulate material making up the rings. The gravitational forces of these satellites would prevent the ring material from entering the Cassini Division, the Encke's Division, and the gap between the Crêpe Ring and Ring B in a manner similar to the way in which Jupiter affected the asteroids.

Kirkwood is best known for his work on the "Kirkwood gaps", but he also carried out research into comets and meteors, made a fundamental critique of Laplace's work on the evolution of the Solar System, and carried out preliminary studies on families of asteroids.

Kuiper, Gerard Peter (*1905–1973*), was a Dutch-born American astronomer who is best known for his studies of lunar and planetary surface features and his theoretical work on the origin of the planets in the Solar System.

Kuiper was born on 7 December 1905 at Harenkarspel, The Netherlands. After completing his education in his own country, he emigrated to the United States in 1933 and four years later became a naturalized American citizen. He joined the staff of the Yerkes Observatory, which is affiliated to the University of Chicago. Between 1947 and 1949 he was Director of the Observatory, returning for a second term in this office from 1957 to 1960. From 1960 until his death in 1973 he held a similar position at the Lunar and Planetary Laboratory at the University of Arizona, and he was closely linked with the American space programme.

Kuiper's work on the origin of the planets stemmed from the theoretical discrepancies that arose from new twentieth-century hypotheses on galactic evolution. One of the more favoured of these theories is that stars, and presumably planets, are formed from the condensation products of interstellar gas clouds. For this condensation to take place, the gravitational effects pulling the cloud together must exceed the expansive effect of the gas pressure of the cloud. However, calculations of this hypothetical process showed that under given conditions of temperature and density, there was a lower limit to the size of the condensation products. In fact, it was found that this condensation theory was inadequate to account for the temperature or the amount of material that make up the bulk of the planets in the Solar System. To compensate for this, Kuiper and his colleagues proposed that the mass of the cloud from which the planets were formed was much greater than the present mass of the planets, and suggested that the mass of the original interstellar gas cloud was approximately one-tenth the mass of the Sun, or 70 times the total mass of the planets. The results of condensation according to these new conditions would produce "proto-planets". But the idea of the formation of proto-planets still appears to be unworkable, partly because it involves the condensation of only $1\frac{1}{2}$ per cent of the original interstellar gas cloud, thus leaving the rest of the material unaccounted for.

Kuiper's work on planetary features proved to be far more fruitful. In 1948 he predicted that carbon dioxide was one of the chief constituents of the Martian atmosphere – a theory he was able to see confirmed when the era of research into that planet began in 1965 with the Mariner space probes to Mars. He also discovered the fifth moon of Uranus in 1948, which he called Miranda; and in 1949 he discovered the second moon of Neptune, Nereid. Compared with Neptune's first moon, Triton, which has a diameter of 3,000 km, Nereid is a dwarf and has an eccentric orbit; its distance from Neptune varies by several million kilometres. Kuiper's spectroscopic studies of the planets Uranus and Neptune led to the discovery of features subsequently named "Kuiper bands", found at wavelengths of 7,500 Å, which have been identified as being due to the presence of methane.

During his working life, Kuiper instigated many planetary research programmes and he played a vital role in the United States' space-probe programme during the late 1960s and early 1970s. In recognition of his work, the International Astronomical Union has named a ray-crater on the planet Mercury after him.

L

Lacaille, Nicolas Louis de (*1713–1762*), was a French scientist, a positional astronomer who also contributed to advances in geodesy. His best-known work grew out of his four-year expedition to South Africa.

Lacaille was born in Rumigny, France, on 15 March 1713. Being destined for a career in the ministry, he entered the Collège Lisieux, Paris, in 1729, but by chance he became fascinated in books on mathematics and astronomy and decided to change the direction of his career. He contacted the French Academy of Sciences in 1736 and began to make astronomical observations in 1737. He participated in two Academy projects, in 1738 and 1739, and established his reputation as a thorough and talented scientist. This led to his election to the membership of the French Academy of Sciences and his appointment, at the age of only 26, as Professor of Mathematics at the Collège Mazarin, now the Institut de France, Paris. He was subsequently given an observatory for his personal research.

The stars of the Southern hemisphere were then relatively unknown compared with those of the Northern hemisphere, and so Lacaille proposed to the French Academy that a study be made of the southern skies. His suggestion was accepted, the government provided funding, and Lacaille was put in charge of the project. He left Paris in 1750 and sailed for the Cape of Good Hope. But the conditions under which he worked were poor, and he suffered from overwork and ill-health. He had completed his programme by 1753, and travelled back to France, via Mauritius and Réunion, where he continued his studies.

On his return to Paris in 1754, Lacaille quickly returned to his observatory to analyse the enormous quantity of data which he had collected. He continued his work schedule at a merciless pace and as a result died, prematurely, in Paris on 21 March 1762.

Lacaille's first serious scientific work was the task of obtaining an accurate plot of the French coastline between Nantes and Bayonne. It was assigned him by the French Academy of Sciences and was undertaken with the help of his colleague Giacoma Maraldi (1665–1729), Giovanni Cassini's nephew, in 1738. The next year Lacaille was appointed to the team of scientists who were trying to resolve a dispute which had been raging for decades. In opposition to Huygens, Newton and their followers, there was a school of thought, headed by Jacques Cassini (1677–1756) that insisted that the Earth was a distorted sphere which was flattened at the Equator rather than at the poles.

Lacaille and his team sought to confirm Cassini's measurement of the meridian of France which ran from Perpignan to Dunkirk. They discovered that Cassini had in fact been in error, and that his conclusions on the shape of the Earth were therefore invalid.

Upon assuming his post as Professor at the Collège Mazarin, Lacaille's primary interest was to collect a huge quantity of positional data for stars in the northern skies. He also devoted considerable energy to writing popular textbooks on mathematics and applied science. The turning point in his career came in October 1750, when he began his expedition to South Africa.

Despite the lack of equipment and poor research conditions Lacaille achieved an extraordinary number of observations. He determined the positions of nearly 10,000 stars, including a large number of seventh-magnitude stars that are invisible to the naked eye. He charted and named 14 new constellations, abandoning the traditional mythological naming system and instead choosing names of contemporary scientific and astronomical instruments. Lacaille measured the lunar parallax, with the aid of Joseph de Lalande (1732-1807) in Berlin. Their simultaneous observations provided them with a base-line longer than the radius of the Earth and gave an accurate measurement of the lunar parallax. It indicated that the average distance from the Earth to the Moon was approximately 60 times the radius of the Earth. Lacaille's determination of the solar parallax was less accurate, being underestimated by about 10 per cent.

Lacaille's other astronomical work during his stay in South Africa included the compilation of the first list of 42 "nebulous stars", estimates for the distances between the Earth and both Mars and Venus, and the observation that Alpha Centauri is a double star. He also performed a number of geodetic investigations, in particular he made the first measurement of the arc of meridian in the Southern hemisphere.

Soon after his return from Cape Town, Lacaille published his preliminary star catalogue which included a star map and a description of 2,000 of the stars he had studied in South Africa. Although this catalogue contained nearly five times as many southern stars as its most complete predecessor, it suffered from the inevitable inaccuracy resulting from Lacaille's reliance on small telescopes. The catalogue of all Lacaille's data, *Coelum australe stelliferum*, was published in 1763, a year after his death.

Lacaille's later work included a brief catalogue of 400 of the brightest stars, and the first accurate estimate of the distance between the Earth and the Moon in which the fact that the Earth is not a perfect sphere was taken into consideration (1761). His major work during the last years of his life was the analysis of the data he had collected during his visit to South Africa, but he also performed many long computations for other purposes (including the publication of tables of logarithms in 1760).

Lagrange, Guiseppe Lodovico (*1736-1813*), was a French-Italian mathematician who made notable contributions to the development of Newtonian celestial mechanics and attempted to explain some aspects of the Solar System.

Lagrange was born in Turin, Italy, on 25 January 1736. He studied at Turin College where he was taught physics by G. Beccaria (1716-1781) and geometry by Revelli. He became fascinated by algebra and in 1755 he began a correspondence with Leonhard Euler (1707-1783) which showed him to be an exceptionally skilled mathematician.

At the age of 19, Lagrange was appointed Professor of Mathematics at the Artillery School in Turin and the following year he was elected to the Berlin Academy of Sciences. His first opportunity to leave Turin and visit Paris arose in 1763, when he won a prize in a mathematics competition held by the French Academy. He won the same prize in 1766, 1771, 1774 and 1780. In 1776 Lagrange succeeded Euler as Director of the mathematics section of the Berlin Academy. He moved to Paris at the invitation of King Louis XIV in 1787 and was elected a Fellow of the Royal Society of London in 1791. He was given the chair of Mathematics at the École Polytechnique in 1795. He retired in 1799 and died on 10 April 1813.

Lagrange's work falls into three distinct periods: the first covers his years in Turin (1736-1766), the second his tenure in Berlin (1767-1787) and the last in Paris (1787-1813).

In Turin he devised a method of minima and maxima which was named by Euler as the "calculus of variations" and he applied it to astronomy to solve problems in celestial mechanics. In 1764 he wrote a paper, which he submitted to the French Academy for their competitions on astronomical problems, that dealt with the question of lunar libration. In 1766 he won the same competition for his work on the analysis of the gravitational interaction between Jupiter and its four known moons.

Lagrange was deeply interested in complex and subtle gravitational interactions and, while in Berlin in 1772, he wrote an important paper on the three-body problem. In it he explained how the configuration of two celestial bodies in orbit around a common gravitational centre was not necessarily the only stable arrangement. He theorized that in fact three bodies would be stable if they were arranged at the apices of an equilateral triangle, provided that the mass of one of these bodies was negligible. However, it was not until a century later that exactly such a stable three-bodied configuration was found to exist within the Solar System. A perfect example of such a system is the interaction between the asteroid named Achilles (number 588), which has a negligible mass and forms a completely stable three-bodied system, and the Sun and Jupiter.

In 1774 Lagrange went on to study the motion of the Moon. As well as accelerating over a long-term period in its orbital path around the Earth, the Moon varies slightly in its motion because of variations in the gravitational attraction of the Sun on the Earth–Moon system. In his later life, Lagrange also studied cometary and planetary problems, but most of his later work was concentrated on writing and developing his other interests.

Lagrange was an extraordinarily talented mathematician and astronomer who also made a fundamental contribution to the field of theoretical mechanics. His work has been particularly important to modern cosmology and the "Langrangian anchor" has become a basic tool in the study of space-time.

Lalande, Joseph Jérome le François de (*1732-1807*), was a French astronomer noted for his planetary tables, his account of the transit of Venus, and numerous writings on astronomy.

Lalande was born at Bourg-en-Bresse on 11 July 1732. He was the only child of relatively wealthy parents, his father being the director of both the local post office and a tobacco warehouse. Lalande was educated at the Jesuit College in Lyon in preparation for his joining the Order. Instead he went to Paris to continue his studies and it was during this time that he first became intrigued by astronomy. He was influenced by Joseph-Nicolas Delisle (1688-1768) and Charles le Monnier, both leading figures in the fields of astronomy and mathematical physics. Lalande was appointed Professor of Astronomy at the Collège de France in 1762 and during his tenure there he published his *Treatise of Astronomy*. In 1795 he was made Director of the Paris Observatory, where he concentrated on compiling a catalogue of stars in which he noted 47,000 stars in all, including the planet Neptune, without realizing that it was not a star; thus he had observed Neptune 50 years before it was formally discovered. Lalande died in Paris on 4 April 1807.

It was Lalande's involvement in calculating the distance to the Moon that earned him his initial acclaim. In those days the method used to calculate the distance to celestial objects was parallax. This meant that measurements had to be made simultaneously by two people from observatories sited on opposite sides of the Earth. Lalande's mentor, Monnier, generously suggested that La-

lande should participate in the parallax programme and so in 1751 he was despatched to Berlin, where he became a guest of the Prussian Observatory. At the same time, in collaboration with Lalande, another French venture led by Nicolas de Lacaille was mounted at the Cape of Good Hope. Its purpose was to note the position of the Moon at the time of its transit from different positions on the same meridian. The combined results of these two ventures greatly improved the accuracy of the value of the Moon's parallax. Having published the results of these observations, Lalande and Monnier disagreed over the allowance to be given to the flattening of the Earth's surface. It was eventually decided, by consensus, that Lalande's results were valid, but Monnier never quite recovered from the slight and chose to remain somewhat distant from his former pupil from that time onwards.

Lalande was at the height of his profession during the 1760s and so was fortunate enough to be able to participate in the observations of the two transits of Venus that occurred in 1761 and 1769. Such transits are a rare phenomenon that occur twice within a period of eight years only every 113 years, and the event offered eighteenth-century astronomers the chance to establish accurately the size of the Solar System. During the transit, which takes approximately five hours, Venus can be seen silhouetted across the face of the Sun; the distance of the Earth from the Sun can be deduced by measuring the different times that the planet takes to cross the face of the Sun when seen from different latitudes on Earth. A host of expeditions was organized with world-wide collaboration, and Lalande was made personally responsible for collecting the results of observations and co-ordinating expeditions to all corners of the world.

Lalande was a controversial person throughout his long life, often falling into arguments with fellow astronomers. Besides his particularly well-documented account of the transit of Venus, Lalande wrote numerous textbooks on astronomy.

Laplace, Pierre Simon (Marquis de) (*1749-1827*), was a French astronomer and mathematician who contributed to the fields of celestial mechanics, probability, applied mathematics and physics.

Laplace was born on 28 March 1749 at Beaumont-en-Auge, in Normandy, France. The family were comfortably well-off – his father was a magistrate and an administrative official of the local parish and was probably also involved in the cider business. When he was seven Laplace was enrolled at the Collège in Beaumont-en-Auge run by the Benedictines and he attended as a day-boy until the age of 16. Typically, a young man would go either into the Church or into the Army after such an education. His father intended him to go into the Church, but Laplace entered Caen University in 1766 and matriculated in the Faculty of Arts. Rather than take his MA, he went to Paris in 1768 with a letter of recommendation to Jean le Rond d'Alembert (1717–1773). The story is that d'Alembert gave him a problem and told him to return with the solution a week later. It is said that Laplace returned with the solution the next day and that d'Alembert immediately employed him at the École Militaire.

Laplace was elected to the Academy of Sciences in 1773 and was fairly well-known by the end of the 1770s. By the late 1780s, he was recognized as one of the leading people at the Academy. In 1784, the Government appointed him to succeed E. Bezout (1730–1783), the French mathematician, as examiner of cadets for the Royal Artillery. At the same time Gaspard Monge (1746–1818), the French mathematician who invented descriptive geometry, was appointed to examine naval cadets. When Napoleon became first consul in 1799, he appointed Laplace as Minister of the Interior, but dismissed him shortly afterwards and elevated him to the Senate. In 1814 Laplace voted for the overthrow of Napoleon in favour of a restored Bourbon monarchy, and so after 1815 he became an increasingly isolated figure in the scientific community. He remained loyal to the Bourbons until he died. In 1826 he was very unpopular with the Liberals for refusing to sign the declaration of the French Academy supporting the freedom of the press. After the restoration of the Bourbons, he was made a Marquis. Laplace died on 5 March 1827.

Laplace's contribution to astronomy began in 1773, when he examined the orbit of Jupiter to ascertain why it seemed to be continually shrinking, whereas Saturn's orbit seemed to be continually expanding. This was a problem that had until then been unsolvable in terms of Newtonian gravitation. Laplace produced a brilliant paper, in three parts, that was published by the Academy of Sciences between 1784 and 1786; in it he showed that this phenomenon had a period of 929 years and explained the reasons for its occurrence. The main purpose of the paper, however, was to establish the permanence of the Solar System, once and for all. Newton had concluded that because there were so many mutual gravitational interactions between the component bodies of the Solar System, there must be some divine intervention, needed from time to time, to preserve the system in its existing state and there had been no advances on this concept until Laplace

tackled the problem again more than 50 years later.

With the help of Lagrange, Laplace showed that, because all the planets orbit around the Sun in the same direction, the eccentricities and inclinations of their orbits to each other will always remain small. His investigation presupposed that the Solar System is isolated in space and completely free from diffuse matter. He also assumed that the Sun could exist indefinitely in its present physical state.

In 1787 Laplace wrote a paper to the Academy of Sciences on a problem that Joseph Lagrange failed to solve, concerned with the average angular velocity of the Moon about the Earth. Laplace found that although the mean motion of the Moon round the Earth depends mainly on the gravitational attraction between them, it is slightly reduced by the pull of the Sun on the Moon. This action by the Sun, in turn, depends on the changes in eccentricity of the Earth's orbit due to perturbations caused by the other planets. The result is that the Moon's mean motion is accelerated while the Earth's orbit tends to become more circular.

Between 1799 and 1825, Laplace wrote volumes of *Traité de Mécanique Céleste*. In the first part he gave the general principles of the equilibrium and motion of bodies. By applying these principles to the motion of the planetary bodies, he obtained the law of universal attraction – the law of gravity as applied to the Earth. By analysis he was able to obtain a general expression for the motions and shapes of the planets and for the oscillations of the fluids with which they are covered. From these expressions, he was able to explain and calculate the ebb and flow of tides, the variations in the length of a degree of latitude and the associated change in gravitational force, the precession of the equinoxes, the way the Moon turns slightly to each side alternately (so that over a period slightly more than half of its surface is visible), and the rotation of Saturn's rings. He tried to show why the rings remain permanently in Saturn's equatorial plane. From the same gravitational theory he deduced equations for the principle motions of the planets, especially Jupiter and Saturn.

In 1796, Laplace published his *Exposition du Système du Monde*, a popular work which was widely read because it gave a theory designed to explain the origin of the Solar System. It suggested that the Solar System resulted from a primitive nebula which rotated about the Sun and condensed into successive zones or rings from which the planets themselves are supposed to have been formed. This theory was generally accepted through the nineteenth century. Since then, however, it has been shown that it is impossible for planets to form in this way because new eccentricities were later discovered which could not be explained by Laplace's concept. Laplace suggested that, as the nebula rotated and contracted, its speed of rotation would increase until the outer parts were moving too quickly for the nebula's gravitational pull to hold them. The remainder of the nebula would then shrink further, rotate faster and another planet would form. This would be repeated until only enough material to form a stable Sun was left at the centre. This theory of planetary formation does not account for the retrograde spin of Venus and the eccentric orbit of Pluto. Also, the theory fails to explain how the energy from the Sun is being continuously created.

Laplace was one of the most influential of eighteenth-century scientists, whose work confirmed earlier Newtonian theories and finally affirmed the permanence and stability of the Solar System. He also compiled considerably improved astronomical tables of the planetary motions, tables that remained in use until the mid-nineteenth century. Together with Lagrange, he was largely responsible for the development of positional astronomy in the eighteenth and nineteenth centuries.

Leavitt, Henrietta Swan (*1868-1921*), was an American astronomer, an expert in the photographic analysis of the magnitudes of variable stars. Her greatest achievement was the discovery of the period–luminosity relationship for variable stars, which enabled Ejnar Hertzsprung and Harlow Shapley to devise a method of determining stellar distance.

Leavitt was born in Lancaster, Massachusetts, on 5 July 1868. She studied at the Society for the Collegiate Instruction of Women, which later became Radcliffe College and associated with Harvard. She earned her bachelor's degree in 1892, but continued her studies there for an additional year. Her first work in astronomy was in a voluntary capacity at the Harvard College Observatory, where she was an assistant in the programme which Edward Pickering had initiated on the measurement of stellar magnitudes. In 1902 Leavitt was given a permanent appointment to the staff of the Observatory, and was ultimately appointed Head of the department of photographic stellar photometry. She died prematurely of cancer on 12 December 1921, in Cambridge, Massachusetts.

Leavitt's work was a direct outgrowth of Pickering's overall research programme at the Observatory. She was extensively involved with the establishment of a standard photographic sequence of stellar magnitudes, and besides discovering a total of 2,400 new variable stars, she also discovered four novae. Her most far-reaching discovery, however, was that the periods of some variable stars is directly related to their magnitudes.

Leavitt spent many years studying a kind of variable star called the Cepheid variable, named after the first of the type to be discovered, Delta Cephei in the Magellanic Clouds. These star collections were photographed by the astronomers at the Harvard Observatory in Arequipa, Peru. As early as 1908, when she published a preliminary report of her findings, Leavitt suspected that there was a relationship between the length of the period of variation in brightness and the average apparent magnitude of the Cepheids. In 1912 she published a table of the length of the periods, which varied from 1.253 to 127 days, with an average of around 5 days, and the apparent magnitudes of 25 Cepheids. There was a direct linear relationship between the average apparent magnitude and the logarithm of the period of these variable stars.

The reason Leavitt was able to notice this relationship for the variable stars in the Magellanic Clouds, while it had remained unnoticed for other variable stars, lies in the close grouping of these Cepheids in terms of their distances from each other in contrast to their enormous distance from the Earth. A nearby, albeit dim, variable star might seem to be brighter than a more distant star of greater magnitude. It has since become apparent that the period–luminosity relationship discovered by Leavitt applies only for Cepheids which lie in "dust-free" space.

At the time this undiscovered factor did not prevent Hertzsprung and Shapley from independently applying the period–luminosity relationship to the determination of stellar distances. All of the Cepheids were too far from the Earth for their distances to be determined using the standard parallax method, pioneered by Friedrich Bessel. But Hertzsprung and Shapley were able to convert Leavitt's period–luminosity curve so that it could be read in terms of absolute rather than apparent magnitude. Then, once they had determined the period of any Cepheid, they could return to the curve and read off its absolute magnitude. By comparing a Cepheid's apparent magnitude with its absolute magnitude, the distance of the star from the Earth could be deduced.

Their results were nothing short of astonishing for contemporary astronomers. They found that the Magellanic Clouds were approximately 100,000 light-years away, a distance which was almost beyond the comprehension of their colleagues. Shapley revised these figures in 1918,

Leavitt studied the Large Magellanic Cloud, shown here in an infrared photograph, and found it to be about 100,000 light-years away. (*Royal Astronomical Society*)

finding the smaller Magellanic Cloud to be 94,000 light-years away.

When Leavitt first began studying the stars in the two hazy areas of the sky, the large and small Magellanic Clouds, she did not realize that they were extra-galactic. But, due to her work, it is now known that the Magellanic Clouds are in fact two irregular galaxies, companions of our own Galaxy. Thus Leavitt's vital contribution to astronomy was to provide the critical impetus for the discovery of the first technique capable of measuring large stellar distances.

Ledoux, Paul (*1914–*), is a Belgian astrophysicist whose main interest has been the factors that influence the stability of stars' composition.

Born in Forrières on 8 August 1914, Ledoux studied at the University of Liège, graduating in physics in 1937. For the next ten years he worked in several research posts abroad. After two years in Scandinavia, he received a Fellowship from the Belgian-American Foundation which enabled him to work in the United States at the Yerkes Observatory at Williams Bay, Wisconsin, from 1940 to 1941. After World War II Ledoux was awarded his doctorate of sciences from the University of Liège, and he returned to the Yerkes Observatory for a further year's study. In 1947 he was appointed as an assistant at the University of Liège, where he has remained ever since; he was made Professor in 1959.

Ledoux's research has concentrated on problems of stellar formation and structure: factors affecting the stability of stars – such as gravitation and the effects of relativity – have been of particular interest to him. He has investigated the influence that internal nuclear reactions have on the structure of stable stars, and he has also devoted considerable attention to the study of variable stars and their rotation.

Lemaître, Georges Édouard (*1894–1966*), was a Belgian cosmologist who – perhaps because he was also a priest – was fascinated by the Creation, the beginning of the Universe, for which he devised what later became known as the "Big-Bang" theory.

Lemaître was born in Charleroi on 17 July 1894. Trained as a civil engineer, he served as an artillery officer with the Belgian army during World War I. After the war he entered a seminary, where he was ordained a priest in 1923. He nevertheless maintained an unwavering interest in science, and from 1923 to 1924 he visited the University of Cambridge, where he studied solar physics and met Arthur Eddington (1882–1944). Afterwards he spent two years at the Massachusetts Institute of Technology in the United States, and it was while he was there that he became influenced by the theories of Edwin Hubble (1889–1953) and the Harvard astronomer Harlow Shapley (1885–1972) concerning the likelihood of an expanding Universe.

Having returned to his native country with better insight into the thinking of his contemporaries, Lemaître was made Professor of Astrophysics at the University of Louvain from 1927. In 1933 he published his *Discussion on the Evolution of the Universe*, which stated the theory of the Big Bang, and he followed this in 1946 with his *Hypothesis of the Primal Atom*. He died at Louvain on 20 June 1966.

The main feature of Lemaître's theory of the beginning of the universe stemmed from his belief in the "primal atom", formulated first in 1931. He visualized this atom as a single unit, an incredibly dense "egg" containing all the material for the Universe within a sphere about thirty times larger than the Sun. Somewhere between 20,000 and 60,000 million years ago, in his view, this atom exploded, sending out its matter in all directions. There then took place a balancing act between expansion and contraction. Ultimately expansion won, since when (around 9,000 million years ago) the galaxies have been drifting away from each other. The significance of this theory is not so much its affirmation of the expansion of the Universe as its positing of an event to begin the expansion.

In 1946 George Gamow (1904–1968) improved on Lemaître's basic theory, considering the Big Bang from just before the event to just after, thus giving the Big Bang itself a definite beginning and a definite end (and a scientific existence in between). However, Lemaître's and Gamow's solutions were for a time somewhat overshadowed by the invention of the radio telescope, which began to reveal aspects of the Universe previously unknown. Hermann Bondi (1919–   ), Thomas Gold (1920–   ) and Fred Hoyle (1915–   ), working at Cambridge, put forward their "Steady State" theory, in which they saw the Universe as having no beginning and no end: stars and galaxies were created, went through a life-cycle, and died, to be replaced by new matter being created out of "nothingness" (possibly hydrogen atoms).

For a time during the late 1940s and early 1950s the Steady State theory was a serious rival to Lemaître's and Gamow's Big Bang, but more recently the Steady State theory has been virtually abandoned. Research by Martin Ryle (1918–   ) and others has shown that the Universe may simply undergo periods of total expansion and total contraction that will go on indefinitely.

Le Verrier, Urbain Jean Joseph (*1811–1877*), was a French astronomer who, as well as being a trained chemist, became an authority in France on many aspects of astronomy and is chiefly remembered for his contribution to the discovery of the planet Neptune. Le Verrier was also instrumental in the establishment of the meteorological network across continental Europe.

He was born in St Lô, Normandy, on 11 March 1811, and went first to local schools before attending the Collège de Caen (1828–1830) and then the Collège de St Louis in Paris. There, in 1831, he won a prize in mathematics and entered the École Polytechnique. After a short time doing research in chemistry under the direction of Joseph-Louis Gay-Lussac (1778–1850) at Administration Tobaccos, he began teaching, both privately and at the Collège Stanislas in Paris. He applied for the post of Demonstrator in Chemistry at the École Polytechnique in 1837, but was instead offered a post in astronomy which, having already published some work in this subject, he accepted. Le Verrier was soon recognized as an astronomer of distinction. After the discovery of Neptune, he was elected to the Academy of Sciences in Paris (in 1846) and made a Fellow of the Royal Society in London (1847) which also awarded him the Copley Medal. A new Chair of Astronomy was created for him at the Faculty of Science in 1847, and in 1849 the Chair of Celestial Mechanics was established for him at the Sorbonne. He was politically active in the revolution of 1848, serving as a member of the legislative assembly in 1849, and later in 1852 as a senator. In 1854 Le Verrier took over the Directorship of the Paris Observatory after the death of his friend and colleague Dominique Arago (1786-1853). He was not a popular administrator (evidently he kept a tight rein on both the direction of research and its funding) and he was eventually dismissed from the post in 1870. The untimely death of his successor (Charles Delaunay), however, brought him back to the Observatory, albeit with some restrictions imposed. Thereafter, during the last few years of his life, Le Verrier was plagued with a progressive deterioration in his health. He died in Paris on 23 September 1877.

Le Verrier's first paper in astronomy, which dealt with shooting stars, was published in 1832. At the École Polytechnique his first major investigation (1838-1840) was into the stability of the Solar System. He made calculations based on minor variations in the planetary orbits and extended them to cover a period of more than 200,000 years, intending to demonstrate how little variation over time does actually occur. Through this exercise, however, he became fascinated by the notion of tracing the cause of the perturbations he had recorded, and he immediately began a study designed to identify the periodic comets and other bodies within the Solar System whose gravitational pulls might affect the planets in their orbits.

It was already known that the point of the planet Mercury's orbit closest to the Sun was progressively 38 seconds per century greater than would be predicted on the basis of Newtonian mechanics. In 1845 Le Verrier attempted to resolve this by proposing the existence of a planet – which he named Vulcan – lying 30 million kilometres from the Sun, *inside* the orbit of Mercury. (Le Verrier was by no means the only astronomer of the time, or since, to be seeking an "intramercurial" planet. Heinrich Schwabe (1789-1875), for instance, also had the idea. However, all attempts optically to detect a planet in this location have failed – and in any case, the anomaly in Mercury's orbit was later used by Karl Schwarzschild in 1916 to support Einstein's General Theory of Relativity, which predicted such an advance in Mercury's perihelion.)

In the same year Dominique Arago pointed out to Le Verrier that there was another discre-

pancy between the predicted and the observed behaviour of a planet, in the solar system. Alexis Bouvard (1767-1843) had produced tables on the planet Uranus in 1821, and fewer than 25 years later they were already grossly inaccurate. This suggested to Le Verrier that some planet outside Uranus's orbit was having a profound influence (although the possibility that another planet might exist beyond Uranus had in fact already been suggested by William Herschel and by Friedrich Bessel). Accordingly, Le Verrier published three papers on the subject during 1846, in the last of which he gave a prediction for the position and apparent diameter of the hypothetical planet.

Unknown to Le Verrier, a young English astronomer, John Couch Adams (1819-1892), had carried out virtually identical calculations a year earlier at Cambridge and had sent them to the Astronomer Royal, George Airy. For various reasons, Airy had left Adams' communication unread – until he perused Le Verrier's second publication on the matter. By that time Le Verrier had written to a number of observatories and asked them to test the prediction contained in his third paper. It happened that Johann Galle and Louis d'Arrest at the Berlin Observatory had just received a new and accurate star map of the relevant sector, and in order to test it, were glad to oblige. On the very first night of observation the new planet was found within 1° of Le Verrier's co-ordinates.

The argument that then ensued over who should receive the credit for the planet's discovery was aggravated by somewhat chauvinistic debate in the popular presses of both France and Britain. It extended to the question of naming the new planet. Dominique Arago wanted it to be named after Le Verrier, but (perhaps because of its optically greenish hue) he finally proposed that it should be called Neptune.

Thereafter, at the Paris Observatory, Le Verrier saw it as his life's work to compile a comprehensive analysis of the masses and the orbits of the planets of the Solar System, taking special note of their mutual influences. The work on Mercury, Venus, the Earth and Mars was carried out during the 1850s; that on Jupiter, Saturn, Uranus and Neptune during the 1870s. The whole was published only after Le Verrier's death, in the *Annals* of the Paris Observatory.

Lindblad, Bertil (*1895-1965*), was a Swedish expert on stellar dynamics whose chief contribution to astronomy lay in his use of the work of Jacobus Kapteyn (1851-1922) and Harlow Shapley (1885-1972) to demonstrate the rotation of our Galaxy.

Lindblad was born in Örebro in southern central Sweden on 26 November 1895. He completed his education at Uppsala University, where he studied mathematics, astronomy and physics. He graduated in 1920, having earned his PhD for research on radiative transfer in the solar atmosphere. He spent a two-year postdoctoral research period in the United States, visiting the Lick, Harvard and Mount Wilson Observatories. Lindblad returned to Sweden in 1922, and continued his work first in Uppsala and, from 1927, in Stockholm. He was appointed Director of the new Stockholm Observatory in 1927, and made Professor of Astronomy at the Royal Swedish Academy of Sciences.

Lindblad's original research earned him international recognition, and he was accorded many professional honours, including the Gold Medal of the Royal Astronomical Society. He died in Stockholm on 26 June 1965.

Lindblad's early research was concentrated in the field of spectroscopy, but he soon became interested in stellar dynamics. At that time there was a vigorous astronomical debate on the subject of the structure of the galaxy. Jacobus Kapteyn had proposed a model based on his observations on stellar motion, which suggested to him that the Solar System lay near the centre of the Galaxy. Harlow Shapley alternatively proposed that the centre of the Galaxy was some 50,000 light years away in the direction of the constellation Sagittarius.

Lindblad analysed Kapteyn's results and suggested that the two streams of stars which Kapteyn had observed could in fact represent the rotation of all the stars in our Galaxy in the same direction, around a distant centre; he thus confirmed Shapley's hypothesis that the centre lay in the direction of Sagittarius. But he also went on to stipulate that the speed of rotation of the stars in the Galaxy was a function of their distance from the centre (the "differential rotation theory"). Such an interpretation of Kapteyn's work was supported by an analysis put forward by Jan Oort (1900–   ), published shortly thereafter.

Stellar motion continued to be the dominant theme in Lindblad's research. He inspired many other Swedish astronomers, including his son, P. Lindblad, who succeeded him as Director of the Stockholm Observatory.

Lockyer, Joseph Norman (*1836–1920*), was a British scientist whose interests and studies were wide-ranging, but who is remembered mainly for his pioneering work in spectroscopy, through which he discovered the existence of helium,

although it was not to be isolated in the laboratory until nearly 30 years later.

Lockyer was born at Rugby on 17 May 1836. After his schooling in the Midlands he worked briefly as a civil servant in the War Office. The high reputation he was meanwhile gaining as an amateur astronomer led to his becoming (temporarily) secretary to the Duke of Devonshire's commission on scientific instruction. He was then appointed to a permanent post in the Science and Art department and in 1890 he became Director of the Solar Physics Observatory in South Kensington. He remained in this post until 1911, when he resigned rather than move with the Observatory to Cambridge.

Elected to the Royal Society in 1869 – the year in which he founded the scientific journal *Nature*, which he was to edit for 50 years – he was awarded its Rumford Medal in 1874. He was knighted in 1897, after the element he had named helium so many years before had finally been isolated in the laboratory by William Ramsay (1852–1916). Lockyer died in Salcombe Regis, Devon, on 16 August 1920.

A primary influence on Lockyer's researches was the newly discovered science of spectroscopy initiated in 1859 when Gustav Kirchhoff (1824–1887), together with his colleague Robert Bunsen (1811–1899), showed how the lines in the spectrum of a substance could indicate the actual composition of that substance. Throughout his life Lockyer was especially interested in solar phenomena. In 1868 he attached a spectroscope to a 6¼ in (15 cm) telescope and made a major breakthrough by observing solar prominences at times other than during a total solar eclipse. The success of Lockyer's experiment was ensured by his use of an instrument that could breach the spectrum of the diffused sunlight in the atmosphere, and thereby make visible the bright lines of the prominence spectrum. Although Lockyer had been the first to think of it, the same idea had occurred to Pierre Janssen (1824–1907) – then working in India – and both men, in mutual ignorance, decided to put their theory to the test during the same eclipse. Accordingly, the French Academy of Sciences experienced the surprising coincidence of receiving a message from each man confirming the success of their experiments within minutes of each other. This remarkable event was duly commemorated with the issuing of a medal by the French government which bore the likenesses of both astronomers.

Almost simultaneously with their recording of prominence spectra, Lockyer and Janssen (this time working together) announced a more momentous discovery. While studying the spectrum of the Sun during the eclipse, Janssen had noticed a line he had not seen before. He forwarded his observations to Lockyer who, after comparing the reported position of the line with that of the known elements, concluded that it originated in some previously unknown element that possibly did not exist on Earth. This idea did not receive widespread support among the chemists of the day. Spectroscopy was a new science which in the opinion of many had still to prove the bold claims that were being made for it. Lockyer's claim however was to prove an exception to the general record of contemporary illusory "discoveries". He named the unknown element "helium", after the Greek word for the Sun.

In 1881 Lockyer declared that certain lines produced in a laboratory became broader when an element was strongly heated. It was his belief that at very high temperatures atoms disintegrated into yet more elementary forms. The truth was not so simple, but in the next 20 years it was discovered that the atom has a complex internal structure and that it can acquire an electrical charge through the systematic removal of electrons. Lockyer was also the first astronomer to study the spectra of sunspots.

Further subjects of Lockyer's interest and investigation were the mysterious megalithic monuments that occur in Brittany and England, the most celebrated being those at Carnac and Stonehenge. It had long been believed that these erections were primarily of religious significance, but Lockyer noticed that the geometrical axis of Stonehenge is oriented towards the north-east, the direction in which the sun rises at the time of the summer solstice. In the case of Stonehenge the central "altar stone" seemed out of alignment by some 1° 12″. Lockyer believed, however, that the original builders had not been guilty of any inaccuracy but that the apparent error could be explained by a gradual change in position of the solstitial sunrise. And because the only possible source of change was the minute but regular variation in the progress of the Sun's ecliptic, it would be possible to calculate how many years were needed to have achieved a difference of 1° 12″. By this means Lockyer dated Stonehenge from the year 1840 BC (plus or minus 200 years) – a reckoning that was virtually confirmed in 1952 when, by radiocarbon dating of charred wood found in post-holes, a date of 1848 BC (plus or minus 275 years) was indicated.

Lomonosov, Mikhail Vasilievich (*1711–1765*), was a distinguished and controversial Russian scientist of whom, for many years, little was known outside his own country.

Lomonosov was born the son of a fisherman, in Deniskova (now Lomonosov), near Khollo-

gorov in Arkhangelsk' Province, Russia, on 8 November 1711. He demonstrated a remarkable skill in ancient languages at school in Moscow, and entered the Unversity of St Petersburg (now Leningrad) in 1736. Later that same year he transferred to the University of Marburg, in Germany, to study chemistry under Christian Wolff (1679–1764) and D. Vissing. Three years later, in 1739, he went to the University of Freiburg for instruction in mineralogy and mining under J. Henckel, but the association became less than cordial, and Lomonosov left in 1740 to travel in Europe before returning permanently to St Petersburg.

Always a controversial and argumentative character, Lomonosov soon got into trouble with the St Petersburg Academy of Science and was obliged to serve eight months in prison in 1743 for slandering one of its members. The support of Leonhard Euler (1707–1783) for Lomonosov's scientific work brought him back into favour, however, and in 1745 he was appointed Professor of Chemistry at the Academy. Both Euler and Lomonosov were active in the establishment of Moscow University in 1755. During his later years, Lomonosov's reputation as a scientist distinguished in many fields began to spread outside Russia and he was elected to several foreign scientific academies. At the same time he became increasingly withdrawn and bitter, and less productive scientifically. He died in St Petersburg on 15 April 1765.

Lomonosov's achievements span the arts and the sciences: he was a poet, linguist, grammarian, chemist, physicist, geologist, astronomer, cartographer, and much more. He is best remembered, in the West, for espousing several scientific ideas long before they became universally accepted. In particular he favoured the atomic theory and the wave theory of light; he opposed the contemporary phlogiston theory and anticipated Rumford in seeing heat as being generated in motion; and he promoted the principle of the conservation of mass. In astronomy he was largely responsible for awakening Russia to the Copernican Revolution. He made observations on comets and other heavenly bodies, and is especially remembered for discovering the atmosphere of Venus – a planet that he observed during its solar transit in 1761, although he did not publish his findings. (It was not for 150 years that the credit for this discovery was accorded to Lomonosov outside Russia.)

Lomonosov was a colourful, talented and outspoken scientist, successful in almost all his many fields of endeavour.

Lovell, Alfred Charles Bernard (*1913–*   ), is a British astrophysicist and author whose experience with radar during World War II led to his applying radar to the detection of meteors and to his energetic instigation of the construction of the radio telescope at Jodrell Bank in Cheshire, where he has been Director for more than 30 years.

Lovell was born at Oldland Common, Gloucestershire, on 31 August 1913, the son of a lay preacher. Educated at the Kingswood Grammar School, Bristol, he then attended Bristol University where he read physics, graduating in 1933. Three years later he became Assistant Lecturer in Physics at Manchester University. During World War II he was in the Air Ministry Research Establishment in Malvern where, under his guidance, centimetric airborne radar was developed for use on "blind bombing" air-raids and submarine defence. At the end of the war, Lovell returned to Manchester as Lecturer in Physics and immediately began pressing the authorities to set up a radio-astronomy station at Jodrell Bank (about 20 miles (32 km) south of Manchester). He was appointed Senior Lecturer in 1947 and Reader in 1949, all the while agitating for his dream of a radio telescope at Jodrell Bank to be made a reality. Finally, in 1951, Manchester University created a special Chair of Radio-astronomy for him and, with the Government guaranteeing part of the financing of his radio telescope, made the Directorship of Jodrell Bank an official post. He was elected a Fellow of the Royal Society in 1955 and received the Royal Medal of the Society in 1960. He was knighted in 1961. The author of several books, a number of which popularized radio-astronomy, he has also published many articles in scientific journals.

Lovell's first post-war research used radar to show that echoes could be obtained from daylight meteor showers invisible to the naked eye. Significantly, he proved the worth of such radio techniques by observing the meteor shower as the Earth passed through the tail of a comet in 1946 – a meteor shower that was visible to the naked eye. Having established the value of radio in this way, he showed by further studies that it was possible to make determinations of the orbits and radiants of meteors and thus prove that all meteors originate within the Solar System. With the same equipment, Lovell investigated the loud solar radio outburst in 1946, and in 1947 began to examine the aurora borealis.

In 1950, Lovell discovered that galactic radio sources emitted at a constant wavelength (frequency) and that the fluctuations ("scintillation") recorded on the Earth's surface (the subject of considerable scientific speculation) were introduced only as the radio waves met and crossed the ionosphere.

The year 1951 saw the beginning of the construction of the Jodrell Bank radio telescope. Taking six years to build, under Lovell's close personal supervision, the gigantic dish has an alt-azimuth mounting with a parabolic surface of sheet steel; it remains the largest completely steerable radio telescope in existence. It was completed just in time to track the Soviet *Sputnik 1* (the first artificial satellite), thus confounding the criticism that too much money had been spent on the project. The Jodrell Bank radio telescope (now part of the Nuffield Radio Astronomy Laboratory) is still probably the most useful instrument in the world for tracking satellites.

From 1958 Lovell became interested in radio emission from flare stars. After two years at work, when his results were still inconclusive, he began a collaboration with Fred Whipple (1906–   ) of the Smithsonian Astrophysical Observatory in the United States. A joint programme was arranged for simultaneous radio and optical observations of flare stars using Baker Nunn cameras from the Smithsonian satellite tracking network. The first results were published in *Nature* in 1963; they opened up new avenues for the study of large-scale processes occurring in a stellar atmosphere. It was also shown at that time that the integrated radio emission from the flare stars may account for a few per cent of the overall emission from the Milky Way. These combined optical and radio observations have also led to the establishing of a new value for the constancy of the relative velocity of light and radio waves in space.

Lowell, Percival (*1855–1916*), was an American astronomer and mathematician, the founder of an important observatory in the United States, whose main field of research was the planets of the Solar System. Responsible for the popularization in his time of the theory of intelligent life on Mars, he also predicted the existence of a planet beyond Neptune which was later discovered and named Pluto.

Lowell was born in Boston, Massachusetts, on 13 March 1855 to a family that was prominent locally. His interest in astronomy began to develop during his early school years. In 1876 he graduated from Harvard University, where he had concentrated on mathematics, and he then spent a year in travel before entering his father's cotton business. Six years later, Lowell left the business and travelled to Japan. He spent most of the next ten years travelling around the Far East, partly for pleasure, partly to serve business interests, but also to hold a number of minor diplomatic posts.

Lowell returned to the United States in 1893 and soon afterwards decided to concentrate on astronomy. He set up an observatory at Flagstaff, Arizona, at an altitude more than 2,000 m above sea level, on a site chosen for the clarity of its air and its favourable atmospheric conditions. He first used borrowed telescopes of 12- and 18-inch (30 and 45 cm) diameters to study Mars, which at that time was in a particularly suitable position. In 1896 he acquired a larger telescope and studied Mars by night and Mercury and Venus during the day. Overwork led to a deterioration in Lowell's health, and from 1897 to 1901 he could do little research, although he was able to participate in an expedition to Tripoli in 1900 to study a solar eclipse.

He was made non-resident Professor of Astronomy at the Massachusetts Institute of Technology in 1902 and he gave several lecture series in that capacity. He led an expedition to the Chilean Andes in 1907 which produced the first high-quality photographs of Mars. The author of many books, and the holder of several honorary degrees, Lowell died in Flagstaff on 12 November 1916.

The planet Mars was a source of fascination for Lowell. Influenced strongly by the work of Giovanni Schiaparelli (1835–1910) – and possibly misled by the current English translation of "canals" for the Italian *canali* ("channels") – Lowell set up his observatory at Flagstaff originally with the sole intention of confirming the presence of advanced life forms on the planet. Thirteen years later the expedition to South America was devoted to the study and photography of Mars. Lowell "observed" a complex and regular network of canals and believed that he detected regular seasonal variations which strongly indicated agricultural activity. He found darker waves that seemed to flow from the poles to the equator and suggested that the polar caps were made of frozen water. (The waves were later attributed to dust storm and the polar caps are now known to consist, not of ice, but mainly of frozen carbon dioxide. Lowell's canal system also seems to have arisen mostly out of wishful thinking; part of the system does indeed exist, but it is not artificial and is apparent only because of the chance apposition of dark patches on the Martian surface.)

Lowell also made observations at Flagstaff of all the other planets of the Solar System. He studied Saturn's rings, Jupiter's atmosphere and Uranus's rotation period. Finding that the perturbations in the orbit of Uranus were not fully accounted for by the presence of Neptune, Lowell predicted the position and brightness of a planet that he called Planet X, but was unable to discover. (Nearly 14 years after Lowell's death Clyde Tombaugh found the planet – Pluto – on 12

March 1930; the discovery was made at Lowell's observatory and announced on the 75th anniversary of Lowell's birth.)

Lowell is remembered as a scientist of great patience and originality. He contributed to the advancement of astronomy through his observations and his establishment of a fine research centre and he did much to bring the excitement of the subject to the general public.

Lynden-Bell, Donald (*1935–*), is a British astrophysicist particularly interested in the structure and dynamics of galaxies.

Lynden-Bell was born the son of an army officer on 5 April 1935. Educated at Marlborough College, he went to the University of Cambridge, where he graduated from Clare College. In 1960, having completed his PhD, he was elected Harkness Fellow of the Commonwealth Fund and joined the California Institute of Technology to work with Allan Sandage (1926–), at the Hale Observatory, on the dynamics of galaxies. Two years later he returned to Cambridge to take up an appointment as Assistant Lecturer in Applied Mathematics. Afterwards he became Fellow and Director of Studies in Mathematics at Clare College. Since 1972 he has been Professor of Astrophysics and Director of the Institute of Astronomy. The author of a number of significant papers, he is a Fellow of the Royal Astronomical Society.

During his second period at CIT, Lynden-Bell published a paper on *Galactic Nuclei as Collapsed Old Quasars* (1969), which proposed that quasars were powered by massive black holes. Later, continuing this line of thought, he postulated the existence of black holes of various masses in the nuclei of individual galaxies. The presence of these black holes – objects optically invisible because their light is "imprisoned" by the object's own tremendously strong gravitational attraction – as power centres of galaxies would account for the large amounts of infra-red energy that emanate from a galactic centre. Lynden-Bell further argued that in the dynamic evolution of star clusters the core of globular star clusters evolves independently of outer parts, and that it is necessary to postulate a dissipative collapse of gas to account for that evolution. This is certainly compatible with the presence of a central black hole within a stellar system.

Lyot, Bernard Ferdinand (*1897–1952*), was a French astronomer and an exceptionally talented designer and constructor of optical instruments. He concentrated on the study of the solar corona, for which he devised the coronagraph and the photoelectric polarimeter, and he proved that some of the Fraunhofer lines in the solar spectrum represent ionized forms of known metals rather than undiscovered elements.

Lyot was born in Paris on 27 February 1897. He graduated from the École Supérieure d'Électricité in 1917 and in 1918 he was awarded a diploma in engineering. He worked under Alfred Pérot at the École Polytechnique in Paris as a demonstrator in physics from 1918 to 1929, and from 1920 he held the post of Assistant Astronomer at the Meudon Observatory. In 1930 Lyot was made joint Astronomer at the Observatory, where he began to work full-time. Lyot's advances in the study of polarized and monochromatic light soon earned him an international reputation. He was elected to the French Academy of Sciences in 1939 and in the same year was awarded the Gold Medal of the Royal Astronomical Society in London. He published several books that outlined his discoveries and innovations. Having become Chief Astronomer at the Meudon Observatory in 1943, Lyot travelled to the Sudan in 1952 to observe a total eclipse of the Sun. He suffered a heart attack on the train journey home and died near Cairo, Egypt, on 2 April 1952.

Most of Lyot's research during the 1920s was devoted to the study of polarized light, reflected to the Earth from the Moon and from other planets. In addition to designing a polariscope of greatly improved sensitivity, Lyot made a number of observations about the surfaces and atmospheric conditions on other planets. In 1924 he reported that the Moon was probably covered by a layer of volcanic ash and that duststorms were a common feature of the Martian surface. (He also claimed to have detected water vapour on the surface of Venus, but it was later demonstrated that what tiny amount of water vapour actually is there could not have been seen using Lyot's instruments.)

For centuries, astronomers wishing to study the solar corona had been restricted to the rare and brief occasions of total eclipses of the Sun. The main problem involved in using optical instruments at other times had always been the "scattering" of light – by even the slightest particle of dust or the minutest fault in the object lens – so that the corona, which has only one-millionth of the brilliance of the solar disc, was totally obscured. In 1930 Lyot designed a "coronagraph", which included three lenses. The object lens was as perfect as he could make it, with a diameter of 8 cm and a focal length of 2 m. He took the instrument to the clear air of the Pic du Midi Observatory, in the Pyrenees, at an altitude of 2,870 m, and for the first time in the history of astronomy was able to observe the corona in broad daylight.

During the 1930s Lyot improved upon his coronagraph: he increased the size and focal length of the object lens and fitted the device with a sophisticated monochromatic filter designed to enable him to concentrate on the most important wavelengths in the coronal light. By increasing the length of time during which the solar corona could be observed, the coronagraph also permitted the observation of continuous changes in the corona. This meant that the corona could be filmed, as Lyot demonstrated for the first time in 1935. Lyot also reported the rotation of the corona in synchrony with the Sun.

The coronagraph was also essential to Lyot's realization that some of the lines in the solar spectrum, believed to represent the unknown elements "coronium", "geocoronium" and others, did in fact represent the highly ionized forms of perfectly well-known elements on Earth.

Lyot's later work included the construction of the photoelectric polarimeter, which facilitated further research on the solar corona.

Lyttleton, Raymond Arthur, is a British astronomer and theoretical physicist whose main interest is stellar evolution and composition, although he has extended this in order to investigate the nature of the Solar System.

Lyttleton was born in Warley Woods, near Birmingham. Educated at King Edward School, Birmingham, he then went to Clare College, Cambridge. As a Visiting Fellow at Princeton University in the United States from 1935–1937, Lyttleton worked with Henry Russell (one of the originators of the Hertzsprung–Russell diagram) and was inspired while there to propose a theory of planetary formation that at the time received some critical acclaim. Upon his return to Cambridge in 1937, Lyttleton was awarded his PhD and appointed Research Fellow of St John's College; together with Fred Hoyle (1915–   ) he established an active research school there in theoretical astronomy. During World War II he served as an Experimental Officer with the Ministry of Supply (1940-1942) and as a Technical Assistant to Sydney Chapman as Scientific Adviser to the Army Council War Office (1942–1945). Lyttleton was then appointed Lecturer in Mathematics at Cambridge University, becoming Stokes Lecturer in Mathematics in 1954, and Reader in Theoretical Astronomy in 1959. During the 1960s he held a number of scientific posts including a position as Research Associate at the Jet Propulsion Laboratory in California (1960), and various visiting professorships. In 1967 he was an original member of the Institute of Astronomy at Cambridge, with which he is still associated. Lyttleton is the author of many papers and several books on astronomical subjects and a member of leading scientific societies. He was elected Fellow of the Royal Society in 1955, from whom he received a Royal Medal in 1965.

Lyttleton's research has spanned most areas of theoretical astronomy. His earliest work in the subject, his theory of planetary formation, was formulated at Princeton. It involved the possibility of a binary companion star to the Sun, dealt with the rotation of the planets and their satellites, and showed that Pluto may be an escaped satellite of Neptune.

Upon his return to Cambridge, Lyttleton began his long and fruitful association with Fred Hoyle, with whom he contributed to the growing knowledge of stellar evolution. In the early 1940s they applied the new advances in nuclear physics, as developed by Hans Bethe (1906–) and others, to the problem of energy generation in stars. They also published, in 1939, a paper which demonstrated the presence of interstellar hydrogen on a large scale, at a time when most astronomers believed space to be devoid of interstellar gas.

In 1953 Lyttleton published a book on cometary formation and evolution, based upon the accretion theory. In the same year he published an important monograph on the stability of rotating liquid masses.

Lyttleton has also made important contributions to geophysics. He postulated that the Earth's liquid core was produced by a phase-change resulting from the combined effects of intense pressure and temperature. This is of great significance in the determination of the rate of change of Earth's volume, and would be of considerable relevance to the mechanics of mountain-formation. Lyttleton also stressed the hydrodynamic significance of the liquid core in the processes of precession and nutation.

Lyttleton's other interests include celestial mechanics, and the electrostatic theory of the expanding universe, which he proposed in 1959 with Hermann Bondi (1919–). Lyttleton is now Emeritus Professor of Astronomy at Cambridge.

M

McCrea, William Hunter (*1904–*), is an Irish theoretical astrophysicist and mathematician whose main interest has been the evolution of galaxies and planetary systems. He has proposed several theories that have aroused considerable scientific speculation.

McCrea was born in Dublin on 13 December 1904. Educated at Chesterfield Grammar School,

Derbyshire (England), he went on to study at Trinity College, Cambridge. Graduating in 1926, McCrea then travelled to the University of Göttingen as part of his postgraduate research programme, before returning to receive his PhD at Cambridge in 1929. From 1930 to 1932 he lectured in mathematics at Edinburgh University, then moved to London to take up the position of Reader and Assistant Professor in the Department of Mathematics at Imperial College.

In 1936 McCrea became Professor of Mathematics at Queen's University, Belfast. Although he formally held this post until 1944, McCrea was a temporary Principal Experimental Officer with Operational Research of the Admiralty from 1943 to 1945. After World War II McCrea became Professor of Mathematics at the Royal Holloway College of the University of London, a post he held – with some visiting Professorships – until 1966, when he was appointed Research Professor of Theoretical Astronomy at the University of Sussex in Brighton. He became Emeritus Professor there in 1972, but has since remained active and travelled widely. A Fellow of the Royal Society, and a recipient of the Gold Medal of the Royal Astronomical Society, McCrea has written several influential books on physics.

In pursuit of his investigations into the evolution of galaxies, McCrea had studied the factors that would influence the earliest stages of this evolution, when "protostars" condense out of the primordial gas cloud (formed predominantly of hydrogen, but with some helium) and then disintegrate to form globular clusters that in turn disperse as older (or "Population II") stars, located mainly in dust-free zones of space. He has particularly focused his attention on what might happen to this process if it encountered interstellar matter that was itself in a state of turbulence. Such an encounter would be critical in regulating the instability of the condensing material. McCrea has also analysed the effect of angular momentum, since the spinning of the interstellar matter would tend to counter the gravitational forces which promote condensation. Magnetic forces may also be of significance in this process. As a corollary of this research, McCrea has proposed a theory for the mechanism by which planets and other satellites may form.

Together with Edward Milne (1896-1950), McCrea was the founder of modern "Newtonian" cosmology. Milne had devoted much effort to investigating alternatives to relativistic cosmology, and with McCrea he found that Newtonian dynamics could be advantageously applied to the analysis of the primordial gas cloud. The model relied on the assumption that the gas cloud would be "very large" rather than of infinite size, although for the purposes of observation it would be "infinite".

McCrea has also contributed to discussion of Paul Dirac's "Large Number Hypothesis", which deals – among other things – with the ratio of the electrical and gravitational forces between an electron and a proton. This number comes to 10^{39}, which is – strikingly – the age of the Universe in terms of atomic units. This may suggest some meaningful connection between the age of the Universe (which is always increasing) and either the (hitherto presumed to be constant) electrical or gravitational forces – or it may be coincidental.

Other areas of interest to McCrea include the formation of molecules in interstellar matter (the formation of clouds of hydrogen in a gas cloud originally made up predominantly of mono-atomic hydrogen), and the composition of stellar atmospheres. He has also investigated the fact that the emission of neutrinos from the Sun appears to be less than would be expected on the basis of predictions about the nuclear reactions taking place inside. This may simply mean, however, that thermal conditions in the Sun's interior are different from what has been so far deduced.

In physics the most notable of McCrea's contributions has been his work on forbidden (low-probability) transitions of electrons between energy states, analyses of penetration of potential barriers (for instance by "tunnelling"), and his writings on relativity theory.

McCrea's work has covered many scientific fields, including mathematics, quantum mechanics, stellar astronomy and cosmology. He has made fundamental contributions to all of these fields and is an important figure in contemporary science.

Maskelyne, Nevil (*1732–1811*), was an influential British astronomer, physicist and – like so many others of his time – priest. He was the founder of the *Nautical Almanac* and he became Astronomer Royal at the age of 32.

Maskelyne was born in London on 6 October 1732. Educated at Westminster School, he studied divinity at Trinity College, Cambridge, where he received his bachelor's degree in 1754. He was ordained a year later, but instead of taking up a living, he went to the Greenwich Observatory as an Assistant to James Bradley (1693–1762). He was awarded his master's degree by Trinity College in 1757 and elected a Fellow of the college. In the following year he was made a Fellow of the Royal Society, which sent him, with R. Waddington, to the island of St Helena to observe the 1761 transit of Venus. Four years later he was appointed Director of the Greenwich

Observatory and (the fifth) Astronomer Royal, although he continued to carry out his clerical duties in such parishes as Shrawardine, Shropshire, and North Runcton, Norfolk. Awarded the Royal Society's Copley Medal in 1775, he received a doctorate in divinity from Cambridge University in 1777 and was elected to the French Academy of Sciences in 1802. He died in Greenwich on 9 February 1811.

It was probably his early interest in solar eclipses that led Maskelyne into his career as an astronomer. His first major project in observational astronomy was the excursion to St Helena, under the auspices of the Royal Society, in order to study the solar parallax during the 1761 transit of Venus and thereby determine accurately the distance of the Earth from the Sun. At the appropriate moment, however, the weather turned bad and, in any case, he had lost confidence in the instruments he had brought with him. (It was not until 1772 that Maskelyne perfected his technique for observing transits – by which time another transit of Venus had occurred, in 1769.) Nevertheless, on the sea journey to and from St Helena, he developed an interest in marine navigation by astronomical methods (an interest that was to colour most of what he later achieved), and spent a considerable amount of effort trying to devise a better means of determining longitude at sea.

Maskelyne's interests were perfectly represented by his foundation, in 1767, of the *Nautical Almanac*. This comprised a compendium of astronomical tables and navigational aids and included many of the results of Maskelyne's studies of the Sun, the Moon, the planets and the stars. His observations of the proper motions of several of the brighter stars were used by William Herschel (1738–1822) to demonstrate the movement of the Sun, which until 1783 had been presumed stationary.

Maskelyne's experiment on plumb-line deflection in 1774 aroused great interest among fellow geodeticists, although it was one of many attempts to determine the gravitational constant, solve Newton's gravitational equation, and thus deduce the density of the Earth. To measure the gravitational effect an isolated mountain might exert, he travelled to Schiehallion, a mountain in Perthshire, and determined the latitude both north and south of the mountain both by using a plumb-line and by direct survey. He found that the mass of the mountain between the two points of measurement caused the plumb-line to be deflected, so that the separation of the points was 27 per cent greater than was found by direct geographical measurement. From the magnitude of the plumb-line's deflection. Making certain assumptions about the mass and volume of the mountain, Maskelyne deduced from the magnitude of the plumb-line's deflection a gravitational constant and came to the conclusion that the Earth had a density of between 4.56 and 4.87 times that of water. This was reasonably close to the value now accepted (approximately 5.52 times that of water).

Maskelyne's work in astronomy contributed to a number of fields of study, but perhaps his most enduring contribution was the establishment of the *Nautical Almanac.*

Mästlin, Michael (*1550-1631*), was a German scholar, author and teacher who was one of the first influential men to accept the theories of Copernicus (1473-1543), and to transmit them. One of Mästlin's pupils was Johannes Kepler (1571-1630).

Mästlin was born on 30 September 1550 in Goppengin, Germany. He attended the University of Tübingen and gained both a bachelor's and a master's degree there before joining a theological course. While still a student Mästlin compiled astronomical tables and wrote learned essays that were read by influential scientists of the age; he also began to put together the information for a popular textbook. His education completed, Mästlin became Assistant to Apian, the Professor of Mathematics at Tübingen. When Apian went on extended leave in 1575, Mästlin took over his duties. But the arrangement proved unsatisfactory and after only a year he became a local pastor instead. In 1580, however, he was appointed Professor of Mathematics at Heidelberg and when, four years later, Apian was dismissed from Tübingen for refusing to sign the oath of Protestant allegiance, Mästlin was reinstated there. The religious oath did not present Mästlin with a problem: never a fervent believer, his religious views were compatible enough with those required for professorship. He had already advised Protestant governments against accepting the Gregorian calendar because it seemed to him a papal scheme to regain power over lost territories. Consequently, all the Mästlin's books and writings appeared on the Index of Pope Sixtus V in 1590.

Mästlin taught at Tübingen for 47 years, during which period he was elected Rector of the College of Arts and Sciences no fewer than eight times. He remained at Tübingen until his death in 1631.

In 1573 Mästlin published an essay concerning the nova that had appeared the previous year. He had taken some care to establish the position of the nova, and its location in relation to known stars convinced him that the nova was a new star – which implied, contrary to traditional belief, that things could come into being in the spheres beyond the Moon. Mästlin's essay made ingenious use of relatively simple observations and it impressed his contemporary Tycho Brahe (1546-1601) enough for him to incorporate it into his own *Progymnasmata.*

Mästlin's great popular work, the *Epitome of Astronomy*, represented the fruits of his researches as a student. A general introduction to the subject for the layman, it ran quickly through seven editions after its publication in 1582. Yet it propounded a severely traditional cosmology based on the ancient system of Aristotle (because this was easier to teach) despite the fact that Mästlin's own research had convinced him that Aristotle was wrong.

Later, Mästlin was explicitly to argue against the ideas of Aristotle, on the basis of his own observations, not only of the 1572 nova, but also of the 1577 and 1580 comets. Traditionally it was supposed that comets were merely meteorological phenomena, existing between the Moon and the Earth. Observation of the comet of 1577, however, showed no perceptible parallax: changes in observation position should have resulted in a particular and apparent displacement of the comet. Together with other observations, this led Mästlin to the conclusion that the comet was located beyond the Moon, probably in the sphere of Venus. These conclusions, in turn, seemed to Mästlin to be better explained on the basis of Copernicus's cosmology than on the basis of the one propounded by Ptolemy. Mästlin's subsequent expositions of the superiority of Copernican cosmology were delivered as lectures at Tübingen. Kepler attended these lectures as a young man, was deeply influenced by them, and, while Mästlin remained cautious in his acceptance, went on to embrace and develop the new cosmology quite fully. As a result the teacher–pupil relation between Mästlin and Kepler matured into a life-long, affectionate friendship.

Masursky, Harold (*1922-*), is an American geologist who has conducted research into the surface of the Moon and the other planets of the solar system. From the early years of the American space programme, Masursky has been a senior member of the team at National Aeronautics and Space Administration (NASA) responsible for the surveying of lunar and planetary surfaces, particularly in regard to the choice of landing sites. He and his colleagues – it is a field in which teamwork is especially important – have participated from the very first in the *Ranger, Apollo, Viking, Pioneer* and *Voyager* programmes.

Masursky was born on 23 December 1922 at Fort Wayne, Indiana. He graduated from Yale University in 1943 and gained his master's degree in geology **there** in 1951. At the end of that year,

Masursky played a leading part in planning various NASA missions. This Titan-Centaur rocket carried Voyager 1 and launched it towards the outer planets in 1977. (NASA/Science Photo Library)

he joined the US Geological Survey, working in its fuels branch in the search for petroleum. Eleven years later, still with the Survey, he transferred to the branch for "Astrogeological" studies and began work at NASA. Since then Masursky has received four medals from NASA for Exceptional Scientific Achievement, and in 1979 was made a member of the Space Science Advisory Committee of NASA's Advisory Council. An associate editor of a popular astronomical journal, he has also published more than 100 technical papers and edited a couple of books for NASA on the *Apollo* missions.

As early as 1964, Masursky was a member of the *Ranger* 9 site selection programme and co-ordinated the *Ranger* 8 and 9 Science Reports published a year later. His interest in the lunar surface led him, two years afterwards, to become a member of the Lunar Orbiter site selection working group and of the *Apollo* Group for Lunar Ex-

ploration Planning that monitored and guided the Moon landing. The results gained from *Apollo* 8 and 10 about the chemical and "geological" composition of the Moon were studied by the Lunar Science Working Group under Masursky's chairmanship. His work on *Apollo* 14, 15, 16 and 17 was soon followed by involvement with teams exploring Mars and Venus.

Masursky participated in the *Mariner* Orbital (1971) and *Viking* Lander (1975) explorations of Mars. He led the team that selected and monitored observations of Mars made by the *Mariner* Orbital Craft, then selected landing sites on Mars for the *Viking* landing. Contrary to expectation, observations by *Mariner* and *Viking* showed the existence of craters and very high mountains (*Nix Olympia* rose 27 km above the mean surface level of Mars, compared with Mount Everest's 9 km). A more surprising discovery concerned thousands of small channels on the planet surface. These were not the "canals" observed by Giovanni Schiaparelli, but something new. They were mostly a few kilometres wide; themselves sinuous and twisting, they also had tributary systems and, in some photographs, were almost indistinguishable from orbital observations of rivers on Earth. According to Masursky, only the assumption that rainfall occurred on Mars can adequately account for the observed nature of these channels. Some of the tributaries are reckoned to be as young as a few hundred million years, suggesting further to Masursky that the process of their creation occurred repeatedly.

In 1978 Masursky joined the Venus Orbiter Imaging Radar Science Working Group. The surface of Venus, hidden from visual or televisual observation by its thick layer of cloud, was mapped on the basis of radar readings taken from *Pioneer*.

The pictures gained from *Voyager*'s passage past Saturn provided data for which "geological" interpretation has continued for a number of years.

As a senior scientist with the US Geological Survey and member of a number of work groups, Masursky is able to maintain his position in the forefront of space exploration.

Maury, Antonia Caetana de Paiva Pereira (*1866-1952*), was an American expert in stellar spectroscopy who specialized in the detection of binary stars. She also formulated a classification system to categorize the appearance of spectral lines, a system that was later seen to relate to the appearance of the stars themselves.

Maury was born on 21 March 1866, into a family of whom many members were already prominent scientists. Educated at Vassar, she became an Assistant at the Harvard College Observatory even before she graduated in 1887. Working under the direction of Edward Pickering (1846–1919) she rapidly mastered spectroscopy, to the extent that within four years she had devised her new classification scheme for spectral lines, and in 1896 published the results of her work, based on the examination of nearly 5,000 photographs and covering nearly 700 bright stars in the northern sky. For many years following the publication of her scheme, Maury lectured in astronomy in various US cities. She accepted private pupils and occasionally also took on teaching jobs. At the age of 42 she returned to Harvard as a Research Associate to study the complex spectrum of Beta Lyrae. Following her retirement in 1935, Maury became Curator of the Draper Park Museum at Hasting on Hudson while continuing her study of Beta Lyrae. She died at Dobbs Ferry, New York, on 8 January 1952.

Maury's first spectroscopic work was to assist Pickering in establishing that the star Mizar (Zeta Ursae Majoris) was in fact a binary star, with two distinct spectra. That successfully accomplished, Maury was the first to calculate the 104-day period of this star. In 1889 she discovered a second such star, Beta Aurigae, and established that it had a period of only 4 days. During the next year she was engaged in a project studying the spectra of bright stars. Previously the great variety in types of star, as judged by their spectra, had been classified according to the mere absence or presence of the Fraunhofer lines. Maury now found this system inadequate for representing all the characteristics she observed: it was also possible to make classifications according to the appearance of the lines – the intensity, the distinctions and the line width, for example. Maury assumed the existence of three major divisions among spectra, depending upon the width and distinctness of the spectral lines. She defined class (a) as having normal lines; class (b) had hazy or blurred lines; and class (c) had exceptionally distinct lines. These divisions and their combinations represented in many ways a better classification of stellar spectra than both the system previously used, and the "improved" version proposed – also at Harvard – by Annie Cannon (1863–1941) almost simultaneously.

Maury's system enabled Ejnar Hertzsprung (1873–1967), co-originator of the Hertzsprung-Russell diagram, to verify his discovery of two distinct varieties of star: dwarfs, which in Maury's scheme fall under (a) and (b), and giants (c).

Mayer, Christian (*1719–1783*), was a Moravian Jesuit priest, an astronomer, mathematician and physicist. His work was seriously interrupted by the Pope's dissolution of the Jesuit order in 1773, although he managed to continue his astronomical studies, researching particularly into double stars.

Mayer was born on 20 August 1719 in a district now known as Mederizenlin, in modern Czechoslovakia. Various sources suggest that he was educated in many centres of learning around Europe and that he excelled in Greek, Latin, philosophy, theology and mathematics, but all that is definitely known is that he left home in his early twenties because his father disapproved strongly of his determination to become a Jesuit. Mayer entered the novitiate at Mannheim, and by the age of 33 he had had such success in his chosen career that he was appointed Professor of Mathematics and Physics at Heidelberg, although his main interest remained astronomy. Consequently, when the Elector Palatine, Karl Theodor, built an observatory first at Schwetzingen, then another larger one at Mannheim, Mayer was appointed Court Astronomer and given responsibility for equipping both with the best available instruments. The effects of Pope Clement XIV's dissolution of his order, however, rendered Mayer's court position untenable and he was relieved of his duties before he had completed the furnishing of the observatories. He managed to continue his own astronomical work and became well known in Europe – and even in the United States – for the careful presentation of his discoveries and observations in international journals. He died in Heidelberg on 12 April 1783.

Mayer carried out important astronomical research both under Karl Theodor's patronage and before and after. His studies included measurement of the degree of the meridian, based on work conducted in Paris and in the Rhenish Palatinate, and observations of the transits of Venus in 1761 and 1769. (The latter observation was conducted in Russia at the invitation of Catherine II.)

Mayer also studied double stars. His equipment was unable to distinguish true binary stars (in orbit round each other) from separate stars seen together only by the coincidence of Earth's viewpoint, but Mayer was the first to investigate and catalogue stars according to their apparent "binary" nature. Later work was more critical and therefore more successful, but Mayer's pioneering contribution is important to the history of astronomy.

In the late 1770s Mayer turned his attention to observing the companions of fixed stars, mistakenly thinking that he had discovered more than a hundred planets of other stars. The controversy arising from this claim marks the inauguration of a period of methodologically more sound observation in the study of stars.

Mayer, Johann Tobias (*1723-1762*), was a German cartographer, astronomer and physicist who in his short life did much to improve contemporary standards of observation and navigation, although a considerable amount of his research was superseded shortly after his death.

Mayer was born in Marbach, near Stuttgart, on 17 February 1723, the son of a cartwright and the youngest of six children. Shortly after his birth, his family moved to Esslingen, where he grew up. When he was six both his parents died and Mayer went to live in an orphanage. He developed some skill in architectural drawing and surveying and, under the direction of a local artillery officer, in 1739 produced plans and drawings of military installations. Mayer's map of Esslingen and its surrounds – the oldest such map still extant – was made in the same year. Having taught himself mathematics (a subject not studied at his Latin school), he published his first book two years later, on the application of analytical methods to the solution of geometrical problems; he was 18 years old. Within the next few years, he also acquired some knowledge of French, Italian and English. In 1746 he began work for the Homann Cartographic Bureau, in Nuremberg, devoting much of his time to collating geographical and astronomical facts contained in Homann's archives. He became so interested in the astronomical side of his work that in 1750 he published a compilation called *Kosmographische Nachrichten und Sammlungen auf das Jahr 1748*. His reputation both as cartographer and astronomer earned him an invitation to take up the post of Professor at the Georg August Academy in Göttingen, which he accepted. Eleven years later he contracted gangrene, and he died on 20 February 1762.

At the Homann Cartographic Bureau, Mayer's most important work was the construction of some 30 maps of Germany. These established exacting new standards for using geographical data in conjunction with accurate astronomical details to determine latitudes and longitudes on Earth. To obtain some of the astronomical details, he observed lunar oscillations and eclipses using a telescope of his own design. But it was in Göttingen that he decided to produce a map of the Moon's surface, which entailed both theoretical and practical work never undertaken previously. By observing the Moon he concluded that it had no atmosphere, and continuous observations with his repeating (or reflecting) circle produced Mayer's Lunar Tables in 1753, the accuracy of which (correct to one minute of arc) gained him

international fame. After 1755 he used a superior instrument, a 6-foot (1.8 m) radius mural quadrant made by John Bird, with which he made improvements on his earlier stellar observations, enabling him to introduce correction formulae for meridian transits of stars.

Mayer also invented a simple and accurate method for calculating solar eclipses, compiled a catalogue of zodiacal stars and studied stellar proper motion. In the process of devising a method for finding geographical co-ordinates without using astronomical observations, he arrived at a new theory of the magnet, which provided a convincing demonstration of the validity of the inverse-square law of magnetic attraction and repulsion.

Acting upon one of his last requests, shortly after Mayer died, his widow submitted to the British Admiralty a method for computing longitude at sea. Although the tables resulting from this method were superseded not long after by more accurate data being compiled by James Bradley at Greenwich, Mayer's widow was awarded £3,000 by the British Government for her husband's claim to a prize offered for such a venture.

Menzel, Donald Howard (*1901-1976*), was an American physicist and astronomer whose work on the spectrum of the solar chromosphere revolutionized much of solar astronomy. He was one of the first scientists to combine astronomy with atomic physics and, as a teacher and writer he had a considerable influence on the development of astrophysics during the twentieth century.

Menzel was born on 11 April 1901 at Florence, Colorado, where his father was a railroad agent. When Menzel was four his father moved to Leadville, a remote mining centre where Menzel then lived until the age of 16, when he enrolled at the University of Denver. After graduation, he joined the staff of Princeton University as a Graduate Assistant and came under the benign influence of Henry Russell (1877-1957), the co-originator of the Hertzsprung-Russell diagram, who taught a course on basic astrophysics there. Menzel soon became fascinated by the combination of atomic physics, mathematics and relativity theory. Nevertheless, to gain more practical astronomical experience, he became Assistant Astronomer at the Lick Observatory in California in 1924. There priority was given to measuring visual binary stars and stellar radial velocity, but of more interest to Menzel was William Campbell's collection of solar chromospheric spectra and he took the opportunity to develop a quantitative spectroscopy using recently gained knowledge of the spectra of complex atoms and wave mechanics.

In 1932 Menzel joined Harvard University Observatory (where he was to become Director some 30 years later). After four years he began experimental work to study the solar corona outside eclipses. The coronagraph he constructed for this purpose was the beginning of High Altitude Observatory, which has since been developed into one of the leading institutions participating in solar physics research. At Harvard, Menzel established a course that included study of radiative transfer, the formation of spectra in stellar atmospheres and gaseous nebulae, and atomic physics and statistical mechanics, together with the study of dynamics, classical electromagnetic theory and relativity. (This comprehensive syllabus was later published as *Mathematical Physics*.)

During World War II Menzel served with the US Navy, advising on the effect of solar activity on radio communication and radar propagation. After the war, he became involved in raising funds for a number of observatories. The war had shown the value of radio communication, and the need for information about solar activity led the US Air Force to construct a solar observatory in New Mexico. Menzel supervised the design of several instruments for the laboratory, using the results obtained to further study solar prominences, low temperatures in sunspots and the origin of solar flares. Menzel was also Chairman of the National Radio Astronomy Observatory Advisory Committee; he participated in setting up the Kitt Peak National Observatory in Arizona; he was instrumental in bringing the Smithsonian Astrophysics Observatory from Washington to Cambridge; and he was a key figure in finding independent funding for the Solar Observatory in South Africa.

Menzel retired from Harvard in 1971 to become scientific director of a company manufacturing antennae for communications and radio astronomy. He died on 14 December 1976 after a prolonged illness.

At Princeton, Menzel and Henry Russell held a virtual monopoly on theoretrical astrophysics. But that was by no means Menzel's sole interest. He devised a technique for computing the temperature of planets from measurements of water cell transmissions and he made important contributions to atmospheric geophysics, radio propagation and even lunar nomenclature. He also held patents on the use of gallium in liquid ball bearings and on heat transfer in atomic plants. Further work included the development of a fluid clutch and the investigation of solar energy conversion into electricity.

In his early days at Harvard, Menzel returned to his favourite subject, the Sun. In observing eclipses he developed a means of taking photographs with very good height resolution. Examining more than 800 spectra, he then established a wholly new theoretical approach to the structure of the gaseous envelope surrounding the Sun and other stars. With Perkins, Menzel also calculated the theoretical intensities of atomic hydrogen's spectral lines – a work that became a standard reference on the subject. It was followed by a series of papers on *Physical Processes in Gaseous Nebulae*, which provided a framework for the quantitative analysis of nebular spectra.

Messier, Charles (*1730–1817*), was a French astronomer whose work on the discovery of comets led to a compilation of the locations of nebulae and star clusters – the Messier Catalogue – that is still of some relevance 200 years later.

Messier was born on 26 June 1730 in Badonviller, in the province of Lorraine. Little is known about his life until he joined the Paris Observatory as a draughtsman and astronomical recorder under the duration of one of the most famous men of the time, Joseph-Nicolas Delisle (1688–1768). Later he searched the night sky for comets, but he was continually hampered by encountering other rather obscure forms which he came to recognize as nebulae. During the period 1760 to 1784, therefore, Messier set about compiling a list of these nebulae and star clusters in order that he and other astronomers could more easily pinpoint (and thus ignore) these celestial features, in this way not only saving time but reducing the risk of any confusion with possible new comets.

At an early stage in Messier's career, his work was already being acknowledged for its importance and thoroughness, and in 1764 he was elected to the Royal Society in London. Six years later, in 1770, he was duly honoured by his own country and made a member of the prestigious Academy of Sciences in Paris. He died in Paris on 12 April 1817.

Initially, Messier's interest in comets stemmed from the predicted return of Halley's Comet; before he died (in 1740), Halley calculated that the comet's reappearance would take place around 1758 to 1759. Messier duly sighted its return on 21 January 1759, an experience which was to inspire him with the desire to go on discovering new comets for the rest of his life. (Although he is attributed with being the first person to resight the Halley comet from French soil, a German amateur astronomer is believed to have been the first to actually see it, on Christmas Day, 1758.)

Messier certainly earned his nickname, the "Comet Ferret", from Louis XV. He spent long hours of painstaking search, over many years, to discover ultimately between 15 and 21 new comets. (The actual numbers vary according to the source of information, but it is thought not in any case to be less than fifteen.) In the beginning, he was frustrated by nebulae and star clusters which were, on occasions, readily confused with comets and had to be investigated continuously, a process that was also time-consuming. Messier decided that the most sensible idea was to compile a list identifying each of these permanent objects, numbering them and noting their position.

The task he undertook was an extremely difficult one, given the equipment available at that time. Although a vast improvement had then recently been achieved with the development (during the first half of the 1700s) of the compound lens, the range and capability of the telescope was still in its infancy. Nevertheless, Messier began this work in earnest in 1760, and by 1771 he had completed a preliminary list of 45 nebulae and galaxies, giving each one an identifying M number. Within ten years he had compiled the majority of his catalogue, and by 1784 the list consisted of 103 numbers.

Basically, Messier's original catalogue is still relevant today with some additions - Pierre Méchain (1744-1804) added 6 more during Messier's lifetime - although doubts inevitably exist as to the reality of some he registered. But none can doubt the presence of such famous astronomical features as the Crab Nebula M1, Andromeda M31, and the Pleiades or Seven Sisters M45.

Milne, Edward Arthur (*1896-1950*), was a brilliant British astrophysicist, mathematician and theoreticist, most famous for his formulation of a theory of relativity parallel to Einstein's General Theory which he called Kinematics Relativity.

Milne was born in Hull, Yorkshire, on 14 February 1896. After attending local schools, he won scholarships to Hymer's College, Hull (where he showed exceptional talent in mathematics), and then to Trinity College, Cambridge, which he entered in 1914. Poor eyesight prevented him from taking up active service on the outbreak of World War I, but in 1816 he began work at the Anti-Aircraft Experimental Section of the Munitions Inventions Department, and he carried out important research there, surrounded by many of the country's leading mathematicians and physicists. It was during these years that Milne became interested in atmospheric theory. His research contributions during the war years were later recognized in the award of an MBE.

Milne returned to Cambridge in 1919 and wrote three papers that derived, in part, from the work he had been engaged in during the war. On the strength of these papers he was elected Prize Fellow of Trinity College in 1919 (a post he held until 1925). He was offered the post of Assistant Director of the Solar Physics Observatory at Cambridge in the same year, but deferred acceptance for a year while he made additional studies of the subject. From 1921 to 1924 he served as Lecturer in Astrophysics and from 1924 to 1925 as Lecturer in Mathematics at Cambridge. Milne then moved to Manchester University to take up the Chair of Applied Mathematics. He was elected Fellow of the Royal Society in 1926, at the age of 30. Three years later, he accepted the Rouse Ball Chair of Mathematics at Oxford University, where he was elected a Fellow of Wadham College. (He held both of these posts until his death.)

From 1939 to 1944, during World War II, Milne served as a member of the Ordnance Board at Chislehurst, part of the Ministry of Supply. There he carried out research very similar to the sort he had done during World War I. His later years were affected by deteriorating health and he died suddenly while at a conference in Dublin on 21 September 1950.

Milne received many honours in recognition for the contributions he made to astrophysics and to cosmology, including the Royal Medal from the Royal Society in 1941. A member of many prominent international scientific organizations, he was also the author of several books.

There were three main phases in the development of Milne's work: his research on stellar spectra and radiative equilibrium at Cambridge and Manchester; his study of stellar structure during his early years at Oxford; and his formulation and development of Kinematic Relativity during the later years at Oxford.

At Cambridge Milne collaborated with Ralph Fowler to extend earlier theoretical work by Meghnad Saha (1894-1956) on thermal ionization. Together they developed a temperature scale for stellar spectra that has been used to improve the understanding of stellar surface conditions. It was then recommended to Milne that he investigate stellar atmospheres, and he turned to the primary work done by Karl Schwarzschild (1873-1916) and Arthur Schuster (1851-1935) on radiative equilibrium. Interested in the balance between radiation pressure and gravity in the Sun's chromosphere, Milne found that under certain conditions there would be great instability, and that such instability could lead to the emission of atoms from the Sun at speeds as high as 1,000 km per second. Milne derived a mathematical method to describe the net amount of radiation passing through the atmosphere.

He continued to investigate the structure of stellar atmospheres and he was able to relate the optical depth (or opacity) to observations on spectral frequency. At the time of his move to Oxford, Milne began to re-examine some of the work done by Arthur Eddington (1882-1944) on stellar structure. His proposals for a number of changes to the theory were not generally accepted, but his critical approach to the subject prompted serious scientific reappraisal. It was at about this time that Milne suggested that a decrease in luminosity might cause the collapse of a star, and that this would be associated with nova formation.

In 1932 Milne began the development of his theory of Kinematic Relativity. He felt that kinematics could be used to explain the properties of the Universe, thus providing at least an equivalent, a parallel rendering, of Einstein's General Theory of Relativity. Basing his theory on Euclidean space and on Einstein's Special Theory of Relativity alone, Milne was able to formulate a system of theoretical cosmology (in which he was also able to derive a gravitational theory) and systems of dynamics and electrodynamics. Furthermore, he provided a more acceptable estimate for the overall age of the Universe (10,000 million years) than that provided by the General Theory of Relativity.

Kinematic Relativity has not in fact replaced the General Theory, largely because it cannot be used to resolve detailed issues. Nor does it provide any genuinely new insights into the physical nature of the Universe. Its approach to the problem of time and space-time did, however, stimulate considerable and creative interest.

Minkowski (or Minkowsky), Rudolph Leo (*1895-1976*), was a German-born American astrophysicist, responsible for the compilation of the incomparably valuable set of photographs found in every astronomical library, the National Geographic Society Palomar Observatory Sky Survey. A leading authority on novae and so-called planetary novae, he was a pioneer in the science of radio-astronomy.

Minkowski was born in Strasbourg (then in Germany, now in France) on 28 May 1895. His family was of Polish extraction, and after he had been educated in local schools, he attended the University of Breslau (Wrocław) and gained a PhD in optics in 1921. After a year on the physics teaching staff at Göttingen, he became Professor of Physics at Hamburg University. Increasing oppression of those of his racial background in Germany in 1935, however, caused him to emigrate to the United States, where he joined his friend and former colleague, Walter Baade (1893-1960), at Pasadena. Shortly afterwards, he found a position as Research Assistant at the

Mount Wilson Observatory, California; comfortably settled into a regular staff position, he remained there for more than 20 years before transferring to Palomar Observatory. Minkowski retired twice, first from the Mount Wilson and Palomar Observatories in 1959, then, after spending a year at the University of Wisconsin and another five at the University of California at Berkeley, again in 1965. He continued his observations and investigations, publishing scientific papers until well into the 1970s. He died on 4 January 1976.

Minkowski became one of the world's leading investigators of the Universe's more violent phenomena. One of his central interests during a long career was the examination of supernovae. He quickly distinguished between the two principle types of supernovae and studied the spectra of many individual types in other galaxies. In collaboration with Walter Baade he studied the remnants of the few supernovae known to have appeared in our own Galaxy. The Crab Nebula was the subject of a particularly stringent examination. Its importance in astrophysics has increased as it has been discovered successively to be a radio source, an X-ray source and a pulsar.

It was the collaboration between Minkowski and Baade that first identified a "discrete radio source", Cygnus A, in 1951 – the first time that an extragalactic radio source was optically identified, albeit as an extremely distant object. But because of the distance, the radio emission was seen to be of immense power. It was Baade's view (in which Minkowski, at least at the beginning, concurred) that Cygnus A represented the collision of two galaxies; the fact that two apparent nuclei were identifiable by their radio signals seemed evidence enough. (Later investigation, however, has failed to find the expected corroborative evidence and the theory of colliding galaxies is at the moment discredited.)

The nature of planetary nebulae (dense stars in the process of becoming white dwarfs and shedding mass to do so) was another of Minkowski's long-term interests. In addition to his analysis of these objects he set up a survey, using a 10-inch (25cm) telescope, that more than doubled the number of planetary nebulae then known. It was at this time that he took over supervision of the National Geographic Society Palomar Observatory Sky Survey.

During Minkowski's study of supernovae and disturbed galaxies, his investigation into the internal motions within elliptical galaxies was important; but it was superseded only 12 years later when new and improved observing equipment became available. Minkowski determined the optical red-shift of the radio source 3C 295 (which remained the farthest point on the velocity–distance diagram of cosmology for 15 years) in his last observing run at the Palomar 200-inch (500 cm) telescope.

Moore, Patrick (*1923–*), is a British broadcaster, writer and popularizer of astronomy. An extrovert character, Moore has presented the BBC Television series *The Sky At Night* since 1968, as a result of which he has become a national celebrity, in constant demand as a speaker and raconteur.

Moore was born on 4 March 1923. Privately educated because of his poor health, he nevertheless served with the RAF during World War II, and for seven years after the war he assisted at a training school for pilots. After 1952 his interest in astronomy and his talent for communication inspired him to become a freelance author, although for three years, beginning in 1965, he was Director of the Armagh Planetarium (in Northern Ireland). He was awarded the OBE in 1968 and the Royal Astronomical Society's Jackson-Gwilt Medal in 1977. He has also received many honours from abroad, such as honorary membership of the Astronomic-Geodetic Society of the Soviet Union (1971).

To Moore, astronomy was once merely an exciting hobby for the evenings and other times off work. Part of his immense appeal today is the fact that he has managed to retain the air of the enthusiastic amateur, while at the same time boldly entering areas of study and research that to most lay people are fraught with complexities. He has never himself been employed as an astronomer, but it is very evident from his books and his broadcasts that he is consistently up to date with all modern facets of astronomy and that he understands his subject so thoroughly as to be able to make even the most difficult concepts clear to ordinary people.

His books (now totalling well over 60, most of them also in translation) include *Moon Flight Atlas* (1969), *Space* (1970), *The Amateur Astronomer* (1970), *Atlas of the Universe* (1970), *Guide to the Planets* (1976), *Guide to the Moon* (1976), *Can You Speak Venusian?* (1977), *Guide to the Stars* (1977) and *Guide to Mars* (1977).

Müller, Johannes (*1436–1476*), known as **"Regiomontanus",** was a German astronomer who compiled astronomical tables, translated Ptolemy's *Almagest* from Greek into Latin, and assisted in the reform of the Julian Calendar.

Müller was born in Königsberg on 6 June 1436, the son of a miller. Nothing is known of him until he enrolled at the University of Vienna on 14 April 1450, under the name of "Johannes Moli-

The frontispiece of Regiomontanus' Epitome in Ptolemaei Almagestum, *published in Rome in 1496, shows Ptolemy and Regiomontanus seated below an armillary sphere encircled with the signs of the Zodiac. (Ann Ronan Picture Library)*

toris de Künigsberg". The name Regiomontanus is derived from a latinization of his birth place: Regio Monte, meaning King's Mountain. At the age of 15 he was awarded his bachelor's degree and, in 1457, was appointed to the Faculty of Astronomy at the University of Vienna. He died, probably of the plague, in Rome in 1476.

At Vienna Regiomontanus (as he was called by then) became a close friend and colleague of G. von Peuerbach, under whom he had studied astronomy. The course of their lives was deeply affected in 1460 by the arrival in Vienna of Cardinal Bessarion, who, as part of his campaign to bring ancient Greek authors to the attention of intellectuals in the Latin west, persuaded Peuerbach to translate Ptolemy's *Almagest* from Greek into Latin. But Peuerbach failed to finish this mammoth task and on his deathbed, in April 1461, he pledged Regiomontanus to complete the project. Regiomontanus complied with this last wish and, in addition to translating the work, he added more recent observations, revised some computations and added his own criticisms. Regiomontanus named the complete translation *Epitome*, but it was not printed until 20 years after his death. Copernicus had been aware of many of the inaccuracies in Ptolemy's system (which had prevailed for more than 1,300 years) and it was the critical reflections in the *Epitome* that led him to overthrow the Ptolemaic system and so lay the foundations of modern astronomy.

In 1467 Regiomontanus started compiling trigonometric and astronomical tables. He began computing his *Tables of Directions*, which gave the longitudes of celestial objects in relation to the apparent daily rotation of the heavens and was relevant to observers as far north as 60 degrees (although the finished work was not published until 1490). In 1468 he completed his sine tables, which facilitated the making of astronomical observations prior to the advent of logarithms, but these too were not published until more than 50 years after his death.

In 1471 Regiomontanus moved to Nuremberg, where he installed a printing press in his own house and so became one of the first publishers of astronomical and scientific literature. Among his first publications were Peuerbach's *New Theory of the Planets* and his own *Ephemerides*, which was issued in 1474. This was the first publication of its kind to be printed; it gave the positions of the heavenly bodies for every day from the year 1475 to 1506. It acquired some historical interest when it was used by Christopher Columbus in Jamaica to predict a lunar eclipse that frightened the hostile Indians into submission.

According to the *Nuremberg Chronicle*, Regiomontanus went to Rome in 1475 in response to a papal invitation to assist in amending the notoriously incorrect ecclesiastical calendar. Unfortunately, he died within a year of leaving Nuremberg, probably falling victim to the plague that swept through Rome after the Tiber overflowed in 1476.

After Regiomontanus' death, the statement "the motion of the stars must vary a tiny bit on account of the motion of the Earth" was found to be written in his handwriting. This fact has led some people to believe that Regiomontanus was a Copernican before Copernicus. It has also been suggested that Regiomontanus sent the letter containing this statement to Novara (who was Copernicus' teacher), who in turn communicated it to Copernicus. Thus some people infer that the revolutionary geocentric doctrine was first conceived by Regiomontanus.

N

Neugebauer, Gerald (*1932–*), is an American astronomer whose work has been crucial in establishing infrared astronomy.

Neugebauer was born on 3 September 1932 and was educated at Cornell University. He received his PhD from the California Institute of Technology in 1960.

Having completed his education, he served in the US army, from 1960 to 1962 and was stationed at the Jet Propulsion Laboratory. In 1962 he accepted a post as Assistant Professor of Physics at the California Institute of Technology, being promoted to Associate Professor in 1965. In 1965 he was also appointed a Staff Associate of Mount Wilson and Palomar Observatories. Since 1970 he has been Professor of Physics at the California Institute of Technology and since 1981 he has been Director of the Palomar Observatory.

During his professional career, Neugebauer has been closely involved with NASA's interplanetary missions and the design of new infra-red telescopes. From April 1969 to July 1970 he was a member of the NASA Astronomy Missions Board and from 1970 to 1973 he was appointed as the Principal Investigator of the infra-red radiometers carried aboard the Mariner missions to Mars and the Infrared Explorer Satellite. He was also the team leader of the Infrared radiometer for the Large Space Telescope Definition Study. Since 1976 he has been the US Principal Scientist on the Infrared Astronomical Satellite.

During the mid-1960s Neugebauer and his colleagues began to establish the first infrared map of the sky. As their telescope was designed to pick up radiation of in the region of 2.2 microns, this project became known as the "Two Micron Survey". The results of this survey were astounding; from the part of the sky that can be mapped from the top of Mount Wilson, some 20,000 new infra-red sources were detected and most of these did not coincide with known optical sources. The survey also highlighted a large number of curious objects that demanded further study, among the most interesting of which are cool objects that are immersed in thick warm dust. These are thought to be stars that are in the process of formation. Among the brightest and strangest of these sources is an object known as the Becklin–Neugebauer object, named after its discoverers. It is located in the Orion Nebula, but it cannot be seen in photographs taken in visible light. Carbon monoxide, detected as being associated with this object, is blowing outward from it at a high velocity. This phenomenon is being interpreted as a strong stellar wind blowing from a young star that only began the process of nuclear fusion as recently as 10,000 or 20,000 years ago.

Newcomb, Simon (*1835–1909*), was a Canadian-born American mathematician and astronomer who compiled charts and tables of astronomical data with phenomenal accuracy. His calculations of the motions of the bodies in the Solar System were in use as daily reference all over the world for more than 50 years, and the system of astronomical constants for which he was most responsible is still the standard.

Newcomb was born in Wallace, Nova Scotia, on 12 March 1835. He had little or no formal education, although his father later claimed he was a mathematical prodigy. At the age of 16 he was apprenticed to a quack doctor in Salisbury, New Brunswick, but after two or three years he ran away and settled in Maryland, in the United States, as a country schoolmaster. Deciding that his talents lay in mathematics, he became a "computer" at Cambridge, Massachusetts, in 1857. He enrolled in the Lawrence scientific school of Harvard University and received a degree in 1858. In 1861 he applied for, and received, a commission in the corps of Professors of Mathematics in the United States Navy, where he was assigned to the United States Naval Observatory at Washington DC. Sixteen years later he was put in charge of the American Nautical Almanac office, then also in Washington. In 1884 he obtained the additional appointment of Professor of Mathematics and Astronomy at the Johns Hopkins University, Baltimore, but continued to live in Washington. When he reached the compulsory retiring age for captains in 1897, he received the unusual distinction of retirement with the rank of rear admiral.

For many years the editor of the *American Journal of Mathematics*, Newcomb was also one of the founders of the American Astronomical Society and its first President (1899–1905). He received honorary degrees from 17 universities and was a member of 45 foreign societies; he was awarded the Gold Medal of the Royal Astronomical Society in 1874, the Copley Medal of the Royal Society in 1890, and the Schubert Prize of the Imperial Academy of Sciences, St Petersburg (now Leningrad), in 1897. He wrote several popular books on astronomy, one or two on finance and economics, and even published some fiction. Altogether his books and papers totalled an amazing 541 titles.

Newcomb died on 11 July 1909 and was buried in Arlington National Cemetery.

Assigned to the US Naval Observatory in Washington in 1861, Newcomb worked for more than ten years determining the positions of celestial bodies with the meridian instruments, and for two years with the new 26-inch (66 cm) refractor. When he was put in charge of the American Nautical Almanac office, he started the great work that was to occupy most of his time for the rest of his life: the calculation of the motions of the bodies in the Solar System. His most important work appeared in *Astronomical Papers Prepared for the Use of the American Ephemeris and Nautical Almanac*, a series of memoirs which he founded in 1879. Newcomb was the principal author of 25 of 37 articles in the first 9 volumes. Among them were his tables of data concerning the Sun, Mercury, Venus, Mars, Uranus and Neptune, together with Hill's tables concerning Jupiter and Saturn. This series of papers is of virtually unsurpassable standard; hardly a figure or statement in them has been found to be incorrect, and they are still widely used to calculate daily positions of celestial objects.

Newcomb's most far-reaching contribution, however, was his establishment, jointly with Arthur Matthew Weld Downing (1850–1917), Superintendent of the British Nautical Almanac office, of a universal standard system of astronomical constants. Until then there had been a considerable diversity in the fundamental data used by astronomers of different countries and institutions. In May 1896 a conference was held in Paris for the directors of the astronomical almanacs of the United States, Great Britain, France and Germany. They came to the resolution that after 1901 a single set of constants, mainly Newcomb's, should be used by each country. Although some of Newcomb's work was not complete then, time has proved the decision to have been a wise one. A similar conference held in 1950 decided that the system of constants that had been adopted in 1896 was still preferable to any other for practical use.

Newton, Isaac (*1642–1727*), was a brilliant English physicist, mathematician, astronomer and theoretician whose work was fundamental to the development of several scientific disciplines. A true scientist, interested in everything and practical enough to make some of his own equipment, he became a celebrity in his time, held public posts and enjoyed the life of high society. He could also be petty and, especially in his bouts of depression, uncharitable; he was perhaps fortunate for much of his later adult life to have the friendship, and occasionally the steadying influence, of Edmond Halley (1656–1742).

Newton was born in Woolsthorpe, near Grantham, Lincolnshire, on Christmas Day 1642 by the old Julian calendar, but on 4 January 1643 by modern reckoning. A premature, sickly baby born after his father's death, he was not expected to survive. When he was three, his mother remarried and for eight years the young Isaac was left in his grandmother's care. He soon began to take an interest in things mechanical, reputedly making water-clocks, "fiery kites" and a model mill powered by a mouse, as well as innumerable drawings and diagrams. For a time, he attended King's School, Grantham, until his mother, widowed for the second time, withdrew him, with the intention of making him a farmer. Luckily his uncle recognized Newton's ability and encouraged his admission, in June 1661, to Trinity College, Cambridge. In 1665, the year in which he obtained his bachelor's degree, the University was closed because of the plague, and Newton returned to spend 18 months at Woolsthorpe, with only an occasional visit to Cambridge. Seclusion was an important feature of Newton's creative life and during this period he laid the foundations of his work in mathematics, optics and astronomy, performing his first experiments with prisms and reflecting on gravitation.

Two years after his return to the University, still aged only 26, Newton, by now a Fellow of Trinity College, was elected Professor of Mathematics. He held the Chair for more than 30 years, studying alone for the most part, although in frequent contact with other leading scientists by letter and through the Royal Society in London, which elected him a Fellow in 1672. These were Newton's most fertile years. He laboured day and night in his chemical laboratory, at his calculations, or in theological and mystical speculation. With the encouragement and financial backing of Edmund Halley, he completed what may be described as his greatest single work, the *Principia Mathematica*, published in 1687. In this monumental work, building logically and analytically from given mathematical premises, Newton developed a scientific model of the Universe which finally discredited the traditionally accepted doctrines of Aristotle and completed the scientific revolution begun by Nicolaus Copernicus 150 years earlier.

Perhaps with the appearance of the *Principia* Newton considered he had carried out his life's work. In any case, he seems to have then become bored with Cambridge and his scientific professorship. In 1689 he was elected Member of Parliament for the University, and in London he encountered many other eminent minds, including those of Christiaan Huygens, Samuel Pepys and the philosopher John Locke. But the strain of Newton's studies, and the disputes which arose from them, caused him to suffer a severe depression in 1692 when, at one stage, he was described

This print published in the 1890s shows a Newtonian reflecting telescope at the Paris Observatory. The astronomer is looking into the eyepiece at the top of the instrument. (Ann Ronan Picture Library)

as having "lost his reason". Four years later, he accepted the appointment as Warden (and later Master) of the London Mint. He took these new, well-paid duties very seriously and, although his scientific work continued, it was greatly diminished. Newton was elected President of the Royal Society in 1703, an office he held until his death, and in 1705 he was knighted by Queen Anne. Although he had turned grey at 30, his constitution remained strong, and it is said that he had sharp sight and hearing, as well as his full complement of teeth, at the age of 80. He died on 20 March 1727, and was buried in Westminster Abbey.

Newton's work has many parts: he was a brilliant mathematician and an equally exceptional optical physicist; he revolutionized the contemporary understanding of gravity; and, throughout his life, he studied chemistry, alchemy, and wrote millions of words on theological speculation and mysticism.

The core of his mathematics appeared in the *Principia Mathematica*. Newton's plan for this work in three volumes was first to develop the subject of general dynamics from a mathematical standpoint, and then to apply the results in the solution of important astronomical and physical problems. It included a synthesis of the laws of planetary motion recently published by Johannes Kepler (1571–1630) and Galileo's laws of falling bodies, and thereby developed the modern system of mechanics, incorporating his own three famous Laws of Motion. Although he had already developed the calculus, Newton did not use it in the *Principia*, preferring to prove all his results geometrically. (This led to a bitter and protracted argument later with the German mathematician and philosopher Gottfried Leibniz – or Leibnitz – (1646–1716) over who had first devised the method.)

Newton developed his general theory of gravitation as a universal attraction between any two objects, obeying an inverse square law – i.e. the force decreases in proportion to the square of the distance between the two bodies. According to his notes, Newton began to think of gravity "extending to the orb of the Moon" in 1666. Much of Book 3 of the *Principia* deals with the satellites of Jupiter, recently observed by the Astronomer Royal, John Flamsteed (1646–1719), and Edmond Halley, and shows that their orbits are governed by the inverse square law; it then does the same for the satellites of Saturn, discovered as the *Principia* was being written.

Newton investigated several other topics in celestial mechanics. He corresponded at length with Flamsteed about comets and their orbits; other sections of Book 3 of the *Principia* are taken up with the working out of a parabolic path for the great comet of 1680. In the 1690s Newton studied the effect of solar perturbations on the motion of the Moon; he examined how the Moon and the Sun combine to produce tides; and he explained the precession of the Moon's elliptical path around the Earth.

The other major contribution Newton made to astronomy is a strange byproduct of his brilliant and fundamental work in optics, begun in 1665,

the *annus mirabilis* he spent at Woolsthorpe. Although he discovered so much, Newton held the quite erroneous view that the optical dispersion of light was independent of the medium through which the light was refracted and that nothing, therefore, could be done to improve refracting telescopes by correcting chromatic aberration. This led him to design the first reflecting telescope, which gained him a Fellowship of the Royal Society when he demonstrated it in 1671.

Newton fundamentally influenced the growth of astronomy in a practical way, as much as by his theoretical work. In a more general fashion, his notions of the nature of space and the action of force at a distance contributed greatly to the modern understanding of the Universe.

Olbers, Heinrich Wilhelm Matthäus (*1758–1840*), was a German doctor, mathematician and astronomer who is now chiefly remembered for his work on the discovery of asteroids and the formulation of Olbers' method for calculating the orbits of comets. He also caused considerable scientific controversy by asking the basic question, why is the night dark?

Olbers was born near Bremen on 11 October 1758. He attended the local school where, at the age of 16, his mathematical and astronomical interests were so advanced that he computed the time of a solar eclipse. In 1777 he went to Göttingen to study medicine, but attended lectures also in physics and mathematics, coming under the influence of Kästner, the Director of the small Observatory there. Olbers' lifelong concern with comets began two years later, when he used his observations of Bode's comet to calculate its orbit according to a method devised by Euclid. In 1781 he received his degree in medicine, settled in Bremen, and soon acquired an extensive medical practice from which he retired only at the age of 64, in 1823. Astronomy had in the meantime become a consuming hobby, to satisfy which he had early on installed all the equipment for a full observatory on the second floor of his house – refractors, a reflector, a heliometer and three comet-seekers. He collected the finest private library of literature on comets (now part of the Pulkovo collection). Olbers died in Bremen on 2 March 1840.

In 1796 Olbers discovered a comet and calculated its parabolic orbit with a new method, simpler than that used earlier by Pierre Laplace

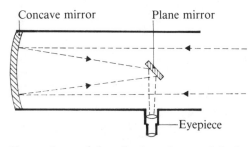

Concave mirror   Plane mirror

Eyepiece

Newton invented the reflecting telescope; it had a concave main mirror and a plane secondary mirror.

(1749-1827). Laplace had given formulae for the computation of a parabola through successive approximations, but the procedure was cumbersome and unsatisfactory. It has been assumed that when three observations of a comet had been obtained within a short period of time, the radius vector of the middle observation would divide the chord of the orbit of the comet from the first to the last observation in relation to the traversed time. Olbers' contribution was to establish that this assumption could be applied with equal advantage to the three positions of the Earth in its orbit. After reading his treatise on this, Baron von Zach used it to compute the orbit of the comet of 1779. In publishing his work the Baron thus established Olbers among the foremost astronomers of his time; his method was used throughout the nineteenth century.

For some years astronomers had searched the apparent "gap" in the solar system between the planets Mars and Jupiter – a gap emphasized by the formulation of Bode's Law. Then the first asteroid was discovered in 1801 by Giuseppe Piazzi (1746-1826), who noticed a star-like object that moved during successive days. He communicated this news to other astronomers, but although it was soon realized that this must be a new planet, which Piazzi named Ceres, it disappeared before further observations could be made. (At that time it was still impossible to compute an orbit from such a small arc without having to make assumptions about the eccentricity.) However, the young astronomer Karl Gauss (1777-1855) determined the orbit and Olbers, in January 1802, re-found the new planet, very near where Gauss had calculated it would be. This was the beginning of lifelong friendship and collaboration between the two men.

While following Ceres, Olbers discovered a second asteroid, Pallas, in 1802; a third, Juno, was discovered by Karl Harding (1765-1834) at Lilienthal in 1804. The orbits of these small planets suggested to Olbers that they had a common point of origin and might have originated from one large planet. For years Olbers searched the sky, where the orbits of Ceres, Pallas and Juno approached each other; this resulted in his discovery of Vesta in March 1807.

Olbers' main interest remained the search for comets, however, and his efforts were rewarded with the discovery of four more. Of particular interest is the comet which he discovered in March 1815, which has an orbit of 72 years, similar to Halley's. Olbers calculated the orbits of 18 other comets. Noticing that comets consist of a star-like nucleus and a parabolic cloud of matter, he suggested that this matter was expelled by the nucleus and repelled by the Sun.

In a publication of 1823 Olbers discussed the paradox that now bears his name, that if we accept an infinite, uniform Universe, the whole sky would be covered by stars shining as brightly as our Sun. Olbers explained the darkness of the night sky by assuming that space is not absolutely transparent and that some interstellar matter absorbs a very minute percentage of starlight. This effect is sufficient to dim the light of the stars, so that they are seen as points against the dark sky. (In fact darkness is now generally accepted as a byproduct of the red-shift caused by stellar recession.)

Although interested in the study of comets, Olbers was also interested in the influence of the Moon on the weather, the origin of meteorite showers and the history of astronomy. A very modest man, he encouraged many young astronomers and claimed that his greatest contribution to astronomy had been to lead Friedrich Bessel (1784-1846) to become a professional astronomer after Bessel had approached him in 1804 with his calculation of the orbit of Halley's comet.

Oort, Jan Hendrik (*1900-*), is a Dutch astrophysicist whose main area of research has been the composition of galaxies. In his investigation of our own, he used data provided by other scientists to demonstrate the position of the Sun within the rotating Galaxy, and through the use of the radio telescope, he traced our Galaxy's spiral arms by the detection of interstellar residual hydrogen.

Oort was born in Franeker, The Netherlands, on 28 April 1900, the son of a doctor. Completing his education at the University of Groningen, he studied under Jacobus Kapteyn (1851-1922), from whom, perhaps, he derived his great interest in galactic structure and movement. In 1926 he received his PhD at Groningen and went immediately (for a short time) to work at Yale University in the United States. He then returned to join the staff of Leiden University, in The Netherlands, where he became Professor of Astronomy in 1935. Ten years later he was made Director of the Leiden Observatory, retiring finally in 1970.

Oort's teacher, Jacobus Kapteyn, only four years after Oort was born, published in 1904 the results of an investigation to find the centre of our Galaxy. He preferred to believe that the Sun itself was at or very near the middle, but he was puzzled by two definite "streams" of galactic stars apparently moving in a linear sequence in two opposing directions; moreover, a line connecting the streams would follow the Milky Way. The Swedish astronomer Bertil Lindblad (1895-1965), using these data in the year that Oort was receiving his PhD, suggested that if the Sun were not at the centre, the two streams could represent stars going to the centre and stars returning, and on this basis he worked out that the centre of the Galaxy was somewhere in the direction of the constellation Sagittarius – incidentally agreeing with independent calculations by the American Harlow Shapley (1885–1972). Oort's major success was to provide confirmation for Lindblad and Shapley, although he located the centre of the Galaxy at a distance of 30,000 light-years rather than at Shapley's 50,000.

Oort went on to show that the streams of stars were not in fact linear, but very much like the planets revolving round a sun, in that the stars nearer the centre of the Galaxy revolved faster round the centre than those farther out. Noting the Sun's position in the Galaxy, and calculating its period of revolution as slightly more than 200 million years, Oort derived a calculation also of the mass of the Galaxy: about 100,000 million (10^{11}) times that of the Sun.

The beginning of radio astronomy during and just after World War II was of great assistance to Oort's investigations. After considerable theoretical work on the structure of the hydrogen atom, over the passage of time and under different circumstances, he and Hendrik van de Hulst (1918–) discovered in 1951 the radio emission at a wavelength of 21cm of interstellar neutral hydrogen. The fact that hydrogen occurs between galactic stars, not in open space (so to speak), meant that the shape of the Galaxy could now be traced by the shape of the hydrogen between the stars. For the first time it was possible accurately to chart the spiral arms of our Galaxy. It was also possible to study the centre of the Galaxy in detail, by monitoring its radio waves.

At about the same time, Oort put forward an ingenious theory concerning the origin of comets. He suggested that at a great distance from the Sun – a light-year, say – there was an enormous "reservoir" of comets in the form of a cloud of particles. Gravitational perturbations by passing stars could, he suggested, every now and then cause one of them to be hurled into the Solar System and become a comet.

In 1956, Oort and Theodore Walraven studied the radiation emitted from the Crab Nebula and found it to be polarized, indicating synchrotron radiation produced by high-speed electrons in a magnetic field.

Öpik, Ernst Julius (*1893–*), is an Estonian astronomer whose work on the nature of meteors and comets has been instrumental in the development of heat-deflective surfaces for spacecraft on their re-entry into the Earth's atmosphere.

Öpik was born in Kunda, a coastal village 15 km north of Rakvere in Estonia (now the Estonian Soviet Socialist Republic), on 23 October 1893. He completed his education at the Tartu State University, and in 1916 began working at the Tashkent Observatory in Uzbekistan (now called Uzebekskaja); he then moved in 1918 to the Observatory at the University of Moscow, where he worked as an Assistant and Instructor. From 1920 to 1921 he served as a Lecturer at Turkistan University, before returning to Tartu University as a Lecturer in Astronomy. Apart from four years as a Research Associate and visiting Lecturer at the Harvard College Observatory, in the United States, Öpik remained at Tartu University until 1944. He was then appointed Research Associate at the University of Hamburg; he became Professor and Estonian Rector at the German Baltic University in 1945. Three years later, Öpik moved to Northern Ireland where, initially appointed as a Research Associate, he eventually became Director of the Armagh Observatory. From 1956 onwards he held a concurrent post as a visiting Professor (and later Associate Professor) at the University of Maryland, in the United States, where in 1968 he was appointed to the Chair of Physics and Astronomy. Öpik has since divided his time between Northern Ireland and the United States. Öpik has received several awards, including the Gold Medal of the Royal Astronomical Society (1975).

Öpik's early research was devoted to the study of meteors; he is the originator of the "double-count" method for counting meteors, a method which requires two astronomers to scan simultaneously. His theories on surface events in meteors upon entering the Earth's atmosphere at high speed (the ablation, or progressive erosion, of the outer layers) have proved to be extremely important in the development of heat shields and other protective devices to enable a spacecraft to withstand the friction and the resulting intense heat upon re-entry.

Much of Öpik's other work has been directed at the analysis of comets that orbit our Sun. He postulated that the orbit of some of these comets may take them as far away as one light-year. He has also made studies of double stars, cosmic radiation and stellar photometry. His interests and contributions have thus covered a broad range of astronomical disciplines.

Oppolzer, Theodor Egon Ritter von (*1841–1886*), was an Austrian mathematician and astronomer whose interest in asteroids and comets and eclipses led to his compiling meticulous lists of such bodies and events for the use of other astronomers.

Oppolzer was born in Prague (then in the Austrian Empire now in Czechoslovakia) on 26 October 1841. He displayed keen mathematical abilities from an early age and was a top student at the Piaristen Gymnasium in Vienna (1851–1859). Although he followed his father's wishes and studied to qualify as a doctor – he was awarded his medical degree in 1865 – Oppolzer devoted most of his spare time to carrying out astronomical observations. In 1866 he became Lecturer in Astronomy at the University of Vienna. He was promoted to Associate Professor in 1870, made Director of the Austrian Geodetic Survey in 1873, and in 1875 became Professor of Geodesy and Astronomy at Vienna. In addition to his teaching and research activities, Oppolzer was active in many European scientific societies. He was elected to the Presidency of the International Geodetic Association in 1886, shortly before his death in Vienna on 26 December 1886.

Oppolzer was fortunate to possess a private observatory, which permitted him to make accurate and thorough investigations of the behaviour of comets and asteroids. (Asteroids were in fact only discovered by Giuseppe Piazzi in 1801, and the details of their orbits were of considerable interest to the astronomical community.) Oppolzer methodically sought, by observation and calculation, to confirm and amend, where necessary, the putative orbits of these bodies. He was the originator of a novel technique for correcting orbits he found to be inaccurate. His two-volume text on the subject (1870–1880) provides a clear description of this work.

In 1868 Oppolzer participated in an expedition to study a total eclipse of the Sun and his interest in eclipses dates from that time. He decided to calculate the time and path of every eclipse of the Sun and every eclipse of the Moon for as long a period as possible. The resulting *Canon der Finsternisse* was published posthumously in 1887. It covered the period from 1207 BC to AD 2163, an astonishing total of 3,370 years.

Oppolzer's contributions to astronomy were characterized by their great thoroughness and by the accuracy of his mathematical procedures.

P

Parsons, William, Third Earl of Rosse (*1800–1867*), was an Irish politician, engineer and astronomer, whose main interest was in rediscovering the techniques used by William Herschel (1738–1822) to build bigger and better telescopes. After considerable expense and dedicated effort

he succeeded, and with his new instruments made some important observations, particularly of nebulae.

Parsons was born in York on 17 June 1800. But it was at his ancestral home – Birr Castle in County Offaly – that he received his early education. He then attended Trinity College, Dublin, for a year before going up to Magdalen College, Oxford, in 1819, and graduating with a First in mathematics at the age of 22. A political career commensurate with his family's land ownership and title was virtually obligatory for Parsons, as the eldest son, and even while still an undergraduate he was elected to the House of Commons to represent King's County, a seat he then held at Westminster for 13 years. In 1831 he became Lord Lieutenant of County Offaly, and although he retired from parliamentary life in 1834, seven years later he was back, at the House of Lords, an elected Irish representative peer, having succeeded to the title of Rosse on his father's death. During and after the potato famine of 1846, Parsons worked to alleviate the living conditions of his tenants. It was work that Irish landowners were more or less forced to undertake when the Government in London delayed aid; but his tenants were grateful to Parsons, and when he died in Monkstown on 31 October 1867, thousands of them attended his funeral.

The work of William Herschel was a source of fascination to Parsons. Early on he decided that he too would construct enormous telescopes and make great astronomical discoveries. Accordingly, he learned to grind mirrors, made a few small ones, and then began to seek a material capable of being cast as a large mirror. An alloy using copper and tin was considered but found difficult to cast directly. An attempt at another solution, using sectional mirrors surrounding a central disc soldered on to a brass disc, proved unsatisfactory for instruments with an aperture larger than 18 inches (46 cm). Subsequently, Parsons developed a way of casting solid discs, designing a mould ventilator that permitted the even cooling of the metal forming the mirror, in an annealing oven. Thirteen years after his experiments began, Parsons was able to construct a 36-inch (92 cm) mirror in sections; a solid mirror of the same size was completed a year later. And in 1842 Parsons cast the first 72-inch (1.8 m) disc, the "Leviathan of Parsonstown", which weighed nearly 4 tonnes and was incorporated into a telescope with a focal length of 54 feet (16.2 m). It took three years to put together, including setting it up on two masonry piers.

At last Parsons was ready for the observational side of his work. And during the next 13 years, when the Irish weather allowed, he made a number of important observations. His telescope was, after all, the largest in contemporary use, and with it he researched particularly into nebulae. He was the first to remark that some were shaped in a spiral – in fact he went on to find 15 spiral nebulae – and resolved others into clusters of stars. It was he who named the famous Crab Nebula.

In constructing his "Leviathan", Parsons designed a mechanism (since copied by many others) for grinding and polishing metal mirrors. He also invented a clockwork drive for the large equatorial mounting of an observatory. He was even among the first to take photographs of the Moon.

His other interests included a study of problems in constructing iron-armoured ships.

Payne-Gaposchkin, Cecilia Helena (*1900–1979*), was a British-born American astronomer and author whose interest in stellar evolution and galactic structure led to important research in the study of variable, binary and eclipsing stars.

Payne-Gaposchkin was born Cecilia Helena Payne in Wendover, Buckinghamshire, on 10 May 1900. She attended schools in Wendover and London before entering Newnham College at Cambridge University in 1919. Although her scientific interests were not at first clearly defined, contact with much eminent astronomers as Arthur Eddington (1882–1944) quickly induced her to choose astronomy as her main interest and career. After graduation in 1923, Payne-Gaposchkin went to the Harvard College Observatory in Cambridge, Massachusetts, to continue her

The Crab Nebula was named by William Parsons (the Earl of Rosse), who studied it using his huge 72-inch (1.8 m) metal-mirrored telescope. (Royal Astronomical Society)

studies under Harlow Shapley (1885–1972). For her research into stellar atmospheres she was awarded her PhD in 1925, and in 1927 was appointed an Astronomer at the Observatory. In 1938 she was made Phillips Astronomer at Harvard, before being awarded the Chair in Astronomy there in 1956 (the first woman to receive such an appointment at Harvard).

The author of many scientific papers, Payne-Gaposchkin also wrote a number of successful books on astronomical topics, ranging from introductory texts for the layman to erudite academic monographs on specialized subjects. Her introductory textbook, first published in 1953, was revised with the help of her daughter in 1970. She died on 7 December 1979.

Stellar astronomy held a prominent place in Payne-Gaposchkin's research from an early stage in her career. One of her earliest significant findings, published in 1925, was the discovery of the relationship between the temperature and spectral class of a star. She continued to employ a variety of spectroscopic techniques in the investigation of stellar properties and composition, and her further investigation of stellar atmospheres during the 1920s led her to encounter some of the first indications of the overwhelming abundance of the lightest elements (hydrogen and helium) in the Galaxy.

During the 1930s Payne-Gaposchkin concentrated increasingly on the study of variable stars; she was particularly concerned to use the information she obtained towards an improvement in the understanding of galactic structure. Much of this work, especially the studies of the Large and Small Magellanic Clouds, was carried out in collaboration with her husband, S. Gaposchkin.

Other major areas of her interest included the devising of methods to determine stellar magnitudes, the position of variable stars on the Hertzsprung–Russell diagram, and novae.

Penrose, Roger (*1931–*), is a British mathematician who, through his theoretical work, has made important contributions to the understanding of astrophysical phenomena. He has examined especially those anomalies in space-time, the singularities known as black holes, which occur when a sufficiently large mass is contained within a sufficiently small volume so that its gravitational pull prevents the escape of any radiation.

Penrose was born the son of an eminent British human geneticist in Colchester, Essex, on 8 August 1931. He grew up amid a family tradition of scholarship and creativity, and completed his education at University College, London. Even as he worked for his doctorate at Cambridge in 1957, Penrose and his father were devising geo-metrical figures of which the construction is three-dimensionally impossible. (Published the following year in the *British Journal of Psychology*, they became well known when incorporated by the Dutch artist H.C. Escher into a couple of his disturbing lithographs.) A series of lecturing and research posts followed, both in Britain (London and Cambridge) and the United States (Princeton, Syracuse (New York) and Texas). In 1966 Penrose was made Professor of Applied Mathematics at Birkbeck College, London. Since 1973 he has been Rouse Ball Professor of Mathematics at Oxford University, where he is engaged in theoretical work on the nature of space and time.

Penrose's early work in mathematics included the formulation of some of the fundamental theorems that describe black holes. The explanation of the occurrence of black holes in terms of gravitational collapse is now usually given in a form which owes a great deal to Penrose's work in stressing the importance of space-time geometry. A model of the behaviour of stars that collapse upon themselves had first been proposed by Oppenheimer and Snyder in 1939 and their results have been proved valid to a remarkable degree by later work. Their model of spherical collapse, together with an interest in gravitational collapse stemming from study of black holes, led to vigorous research on the dynamics and the inevitability of collapse to a singularity. The most important result of such research was a set of theorems formulated by Penrose and Stephen Hawking (1942–) in 1964, which extend the dynamics of simple spherical collapse to the much more complex situation of gravitational collapse. Singularities in any physical theory might naturally be taken to indicate the breakdown of the theory, but using techniques developed jointly with Hawking and Geroch, Penrose has established that once gravitational collapse has proceeded to a certain degree, assuming the truth of General Relativity Theory that gravitation is always attractive, singularities are inevitable. These techniques are now famous as the singularity theorems.

The existence of a trapped surface within an "event horizon" (the interface between the black hole and space-time), from which little or no radiation or information can escape, implies that some events remain hidden to observers outside the black hole. But it remains unknown whether all singularities must be hidden in this way. Penrose has put forward the hypothesis of "cosmic censorship" – that they are all so hidden – which is now widely accepted.

Since he moved to Oxford University, Penrose has been developing an intuition that first occurred to him in Texas in 1964. This is a model of the Universe whose basic building blocks are what he calls "twistors". The model arises in response to a dichotomy in physics, in that calculations in the macroscopic world of ordinary objects (including Einstein's theory of gravity and the General Theory of Relativity) use real numbers, whereas the microscopic world of atoms and quantum theory often requires a system using complex numbers, containing imaginary components that are multiples of the square-root of -1. Penrose holds that, as everything is made up of atoms, and as energy exists as discrete quanta bundles, all calculations about both the macroscopic and microscopic worlds should use complex numbers. Logically to maintain such a hypothesis would require reformulation of the major laws of physics and of space-time.

In developing these ideas, Penrose invented a new way of conceptualizing the Universe, called "twistor theory", using complex numbers. The theory tries to take account of empty space, of the sort that ordinary atomic physics takes to subsist around neutrons, electrons and other particles, rather than considering only the "solid" matter with which physics is usually concerned. Space and time are usually assumed to be a homogenous and indivisible matrix in which matter and energy occur. Twistor theory questions this assumption, attempting to replace the Einsteinian view (which describes the Universe in terms of four real numbers: three spatial dimensions and a fourth temporal dimension) with a description of the universe that uses four complex numbers. Because each complex number (a multiple of $\sqrt{-1}$) is made up of a real and an imaginary part, a total of eight numbers is used to describe reality: three dimensions of position in space, two angular directions of motion through space–time, and the energy, spin and polarization of that motion. The theory yields a much more complicated but in many ways a more logical picture of the constitution of the Universe.

In addition to being able to generate observed time and space, twistor theory also implies a complex gravity theory. Einsteinian theory accounted for "the force of gravity" in terms of a warping of space and time resulting from the presence of matter. Likewise, in twistor theory gravity is caused by mass effecting a curvature in space; instead of a warping of space–time, however, it is now a warping of twistor space, involving all the more complex ways in which twistor theory views reality. Ultimately, by this theory, different deformations in twistor space will be seen to produce natural physical forces like gravitation, nuclear power, electricity, radio and magnetism.

A great deal of work remains to be done; but, if successful, twistor theory will cause a fundamental shift in the understanding of physical reality and, therefore, in the conception of astrophysics.

Penzias, Arno Allan (*1933–*   ), is a German-born American radio engineer who, with Robert Wilson (1936–   ), was the first to detect isotropic cosmic microwave background radiation. This radiation had been predicted on the basis of the "hot big bang" model of the origin of the Universe, and it represents some of the strongest evidence in favour of this model.

Penzias was born in Munich, Germany, on 26 April 1933. For political reasons his parents emigrated to the United States, taking their young son with them; all were later naturalized. Studying at the City College of New York (CCNY), Penzias earned his bachelor's degree in physics in 1954. He then continued his studies at Columbia University in New York, where he was awarded his master's degree in 1958 and his doctorate in 1962. Since 1961 Penzias has been associated with the Radio Research Laboratories of the Bell Telephone Company. From then to 1972 he was a staff member of the radio research department, and from 1972 to 1974 he was head of the technical research department. He then became head of the radiophysics research department before, in 1976, becoming Director of the Radio Research Laboratory. Since 1979 he has been Executive Director of Research and Communication Sciences at Bell Telephone Laboratories.

In addition to his posts in the telecommunications industry, Penzias has also concurrently held a series of academic positions. The first of these was as Lecturer in the Department of Astrophysical Science of Princeton University (1967–1982). He was appointed an Associate of the Harvard College Observatory in 1968, visiting Professor at Princeton University in 1972, adjunct Professor at the State University of New York (SUNY) at Stony Brook in 1975, and made Trustee of Trenton State College in New Jersey in 1976.

Penzias' many important contributions to radio-astronomy have brought him widespread acclaim. He received the Henry Draper Medal of the National Academy of Sciences in 1977, the Herschel Medal of the Royal Astronomical Society in 1977, and in 1978, with Robert Wilson and Pyotr Kapitsa (1894–   ), the Nobel Prize in physics.

In 1963 Penzias and Wilson were assigned by the Bell Telephone Company to the tracing of radio "noise" that was interfering with the development of a communications programme involving satellites. By May 1964 the two had detected a surprisingly high level of radiation at a wavelength of 7.3 cm, which had no apparent source (i.e. it was uniform in all directions, or isotropic). They excluded all known terrestrial sources of such radiation and still found that the noise they were detecting was one hundred times more powerful than could be accounted for. They also found that the temperature of this background radiation was 3.5K (although they later revised this value to 3.1K).

They took this enigmatic result to Robert Dicke, Professor of Physics at Princeton University. Dicke was interested in microwave radiation and had predicted that this sort of radiation should be present in the universe as a residual relic of the intense heat associated with the birth of the Universe following the "hot big bang". His department was then in the process of constructing a radio telescope designed to detect precisely this radiation, at a wavelength of 3.2 cm, when Penzias and Wilson presented their data.

Since then, background radiation has been subjected to intense study. Its spectrum conforms closely to a black-body pattern and its temperature is now known to be just under 3K. For cosmologists this constitutes the most convincing evidence in favour of the "hot big bang" model for the origin of the Universe, although it also raises some fundamental questions, such as the possible "oscillation" of the Universe between total contractions and total expansions.

Penzias' later work has been concerned with developments in radio-astronomy, instrumentation, satellite communications, atmospheric physics and related matters. It was, however, for his work on the black-body background radiation that he received the Nobel Prize.

Piazzi, Giuseppe (*1749-1826*), was an Italian monk originally trained in theology, philosophy and mathematics, who nevertheless was put in charge of an observatory, where he carried out astronomical studies of considerable importance. He is, for example, credited with the discovery of the first asteroid, or "planetoid", as he more logically termed it.

Piazzi was born in Ponte di Valtellina (then part of Italy, now in Switzerland) on 16 July 1746. He studied in various Italian cities and in 1764 entered the Theatine Order in Milan, where he lived as a monk for several years. He continued his studies of philosophy and mathematics in Milan and Rome and was awarded a doctorate in both subjects. For ten years after 1769 he worked as a teacher in Genoa and in Malta, before he became Professor of Higher Mathematics at the Palermo Academy in Sicily. During the latter part of the 1780s the Bourbons, then the rulers of the independent Kingdom of Naples, decided to establish observatories in Palermo and Naples. Put in charge of the one at Palermo, Piazzi travelled to observatories in England and France to obtain advice and equipment, and met such great astronomers as William Herschel, Jesse Ramsden and Nevil Maskelyne. He examined their equipment and commissioned from Ramsden a 5-foot (1.5 m) vertical circle that he intended to use to determine star positions. (The device was installed in Palermo in 1789 and still exists.)

The Palermo Observatory opened in 1790 and Piazzi served as its Director until his death. He conducted many astronomical studies and became a Fellow of the Royal Society of London (1804). He also took on additional responsibilities, including the reformation of the Sicilian system of weights and measures (1812), and finally in 1817 he was put in charge of the other observatory at Naples. For a time Piazzi split his time between the two observatories, but eventually he moved to Naples in 1824 because his health was failing. He died in Naples on 22 July 1826.

Piazzi's first astronomical publication appeared in 1789, but his great project on mapping the positions of the fixed stars did not begin until the 1790s. He was fortunate in working at the southernmost observatory in Europe in a favourable climate. These conditions, together with the quality of his equipment, enabled him to produce new and accurate measurements.

Piazzi was examining the apparent "gap" in the Solar System between Mars and Jupiter, long a source of speculation for astronomers, when, on 1 January 1801, he detected a faint body that had not previously been noted. He followed it for six weeks, until it could no longer be detected because of its position relative to the Sun. Using Piazzi's data, the German Karl Gauss (1777-1855) managed to calculate the orbit of the body, and sent his prediction to Baron von Zach of the Gotha Observatory. The body was rediscovered by Heinrich Olbers (1758-1840), just where Gauss had predicted it would be found; its dimness, considering its distance from the Earth, indicated that it was very small. (Herschel calculated that it was only 320 km in diameter and did not therefore warrant being called a planet. He proposed the name "asteroid", a term that became popular, although it is now no longer quite so accepted a term.) The body that Piazzi discovered was named Ceres, and is now known to have a diameter of 780 km. Three more "asteroids" were discovered before Piazzi's death, and there are probably in all more than 40,000 of them.

In 1803 Piazzi published his first catalogue of fixed stars, which located 6,748 stars with unprecedented accuracy. His second catalogue, produced in collaboration with N. Cacciatore, appeared in 1813. It described 7,646 stars. Both publications won prizes.

Pickering, Edward Charles (*1846-1919*), was an American astronomer, one of the most famous and hard-working of his time, who was a pioneer in three practical areas of astronomical research: visual photometry, stellar spectroscopy and stellar photography. As Director of the Harvard College Observatory for more than 40 years, he was instrumental in educating and inspiring an entire generation of young astronomers; unusually for his generation, he was also keen to encourage women to take up astronomy as a career.

Pickering was born on 19 July 1846 in Boston, Massachusetts. He began his academic career as an Assistant Instructor of Mathematics at the Lawrence scientific school at Harvard, but after two years he was appointed Assistant Professor of Physics at the newly founded Massachusetts Institute of Technology. During his subsequent ten years in this post he revolutionized the teaching of physics. Then, in 1876, he was appointed Director of the Harvard College Observatory, a post he was to hold for 42 years. In that time he received honorary doctorates from six American and two European universities; in addition he was awarded the Rumford Gold Medal of the American Academy of Arts and Sciences and was twice a recipient of the Gold Medal of the Royal Astronomical Society. He died in Cambridge, Massachusetts, on 3 February 1919.

As a basis for the photometric work he carried out, Pickering made two critical decisions. First, he adopted the magnitude scale suggested by Norman Pogson (1829-1891) in 1854, on which a change of one magnitude represented a change of a factor of 2.512 in brightness. Second, choosing the Pole Star (Polaris), then thought to be of constant brightness, as the standard magnitude and arbitrarily assigning a value of 2.1 to it, he redesigned the photometer to reflect a number of stars round the meridian at the same time so that comparisons were immediately visible. The photometric work that followed continued for nearly a quarter of a century. (Unfortunately Polaris has since been found to vary in brightness to a small degree.)

The first great catalogue of magnitudes, containing 4,260 stars, was published in 1884. It was known as the *Harvard Photometry*. Pickering never wearied of the routine work this procedure involved; he is estimated to have made more than 1.5 million photometric readings. The brightness of every visible star was measured, then taken again to be sure of the greatest possible accuracy. The photometric studies culminated in 1908 with the publication of the *Revised Harvard Photometry*. Printed as Volumes 50 and 54 of the *Annals* of Harvard College Observatory, it tabulates the magnitudes of more than 45,000 stars brighter than the seventh magnitude. It remained the standard reference until photometric methods had largely supplanted visual ones.

A further production of the Harvard College Observatory was the *Henry Draper Catalogue*, a classification of stellar spectra. Pickering's researches into stellar spectroscopy were made possible by a practical invention of his whereby the spectra of a number of stars could be surveyed simultaneously and by the establishment of the Henry Draper fund in 1886. Draper's widow supplied the financial backing for Pickering and his assistants to photograph, classify and measure the spectra of the stars and publish the resulting catalogue in the *Annals* as a memorial volume to her husband. Finally issued in 1918, the complete *Draper Catalogue* contained the spectra of no fewer than 225,000 stars, classified according to the new, improved alphabetical system devised by Pickering's pupil and colleague, Annie Cannon (1863-1941).

Pickering's interest in stellar photography was responsible for the first *Photographic Map of the Entire Sky*, published in 1903. It comprised 55 plates of stars down to the twelfth magnitude, taken both at Harvard and at its sister station in the Southern hemisphere, at Arequipa in Peru, where Pickering's younger brother, William (1858-1938), was Director. In addition, Pickering photographed large areas of the sky on clear nights, building up a 300,000-plate Harvard photographic library that has since proved invaluable to astronomers searching for changes in the brightness and position of celestial objects.

One of the most important products of Pickering's researches was the creation of the astronomical colour index: a measure of the apparent colour of a star and thus of its temperature. Cooler stars emit more light at longer wavelengths and so appear redder than hot stars. The colour index is expressed as the difference in a star's brightness when measured on two selected wavelengths. The international colour index, defined by Pickering in about 1890, is the difference between the photographic magnitude (blue light) and the photovisual magnitude (yellow light); it is zero for white stars, positive for red stars, and negative for blue stars. Magnitudes are now seldom measured photographically; instead, colour filters on photoelectric cells measure the colour index between the two wavelengths. The widely used UBV system utilizes the ultra-violet blue and yellow (visual) images.

Plaskett, John Stanley (*1865-1941*), was a Canadian engineer whose work in instrument design and telescope construction led to his becoming Director of the Observatory in Victoria, British Columbia. There, he used the large reflecting telescope that he designed to carry out important research into binary stars and stellar radial velocities.

Plaskett was born at Hickson, near Woodstock, Ontario, on 17 November 1865. After completing his schooling locally, he was employed as a mechanic in various parts of North America. In 1889, however, he became a mechanic in the Department of Physics at Toronto University, where he decided to take up undergraduate studies; he eventually became a Lecturer there. From 1903 Plaskett was in charge of astrophysical work at the new Dominion Observatory in Ottawa and he initiated comprehensive programmes of research into stellar radial velocities using the observatory's 15-inch (38 cm) reflector. The spectroscope he produced for the reflector so improved the instrument that it was comparable with the best in North America. Having repeatedly urged the Canadian Parliament to sanction the construction of a 72-inch (1.8 m) reflector, Plaskett was finally appointed to supervise its creation for the Dominion Astrophysical Observatory in Victoria; he was also appointed the observatory's first Director in 1917, and remained there until he retired in 1935, at which time he was elected a Fellow of the Royal Society and President of the Royal Astronomical Society of Canada. He then supervised the construction of the 82-inch (2.05 m) mirror for the MacDonald Observatory at the University of Texas. He died at Esquimalt, near Victoria, on 17 October 1941.

Using his new telescope at Victoria in conjunction with a spectrograph of high sensitivity, Plaskett discovered many new binary stars, including "Plaskett's Twins", previously thought to be a single, massive star (B.D. + 6° 1309, for many years considered the most massive star known). His work on the radial velocities of galactic stars enabled him to confirm the contemporary discovery of the rotation of the Galaxy and to indicate the most probable location of the gravitational centre of the Galaxy. In turn, this led to a study of the motion and distribution of galactic interstellar matter, particularly involving the detection of spatial calcium.

Plato (*c. 420* BC*-340* BC) was a Greek mathematician and philosopher who founded an influential school of learning in which the basic precept was not so much one of practical experimentation, as of striving to find mathematical and intellectual harmony. In consequence, most of Plato's astronomical theories involved the most idealistic forms of mathematical wishful thinking, the most fundamental premise being that the Earth, a perfect sphere, was at the centre of a Universe in which all other celestial bodies described perfectly circular orbits.

Plato's real name was Aristocles; he was called Plato, "broad-shouldered", from an early age, however. Born into a patrician Athenian family, he was naturally expected to take up a political career, but as a pupil of Socrates he came to regard politicians with ever-increasing scepticism, and following the trial and death of his mentor in 399 BC, he resolved to become a philosopher and teacher. He travelled for some years, probably to Cyrene, certainly to Sicily, perhaps also to Egypt, before returning at last to Athens in 388 BC where he set up a school that became known as the Academy on part of the premises of a gymnasium. (In one form or another, the Academy continued to exist for about 900 years.) In about 367 BC, Plato returned to Sicily as tutor to King Dionysus II, but after a few years he became disgusted with the sybaritic life-style of the court and (it is thought) went back again to Athens; nothing more is known of his life.

The extant works of Plato, believed on good authority to be genuine, consist of philosophical dialogues among which are *Timaeus*, the *Symposium*, the *Republic* and the *Laws*. In all of them an idealized form of Socrates appears as one of the speakers. Plato divided philosophy into three branches: ethics, physics and dialectics. The basic tenet behind all his arguments is the doctrine of ideas. True science, he reasoned, investigates the nature of those purer and more perfect patterns which were the models after which all created things were formed by the great original intelligence.

Accordingly, it was in particular the science of geometry - with its premise of symmetry and the irrefutable logic of its axioms - that had the most appeal to Plato. In several of his works he therefore presents a picture of the world that is purely conceptual in form. Little thought was given to the idea observing phenomena before putting forward a theory to explain them. In this legend Plato had been strongly influenced by the ideas of Pythagoras of Samos (*c.*572 BC-500 BC), the most famous of Greek geometricians. For both Pythagoras and Plato, the ideal of mathematical harmony in the attainment of the perfection of the Creator's original intentions simply meant that the Universe had to be spherical because the sphere was the perfect volume; for the same reason the movements of the heavenly bodies had to be circular and uniform. Moreover, the Earth, which lay at the exact centre of the cosmos, was a sphere and was surrounded by a band of crystalline spheres which held in place the Sun, the Moon and the planets.

At one stage, Plato asked one of his pupils, Eudoxus of Cnidus, to make a model showing the circular movements of all celestial bodies. Eudoxus, a skilled mathematician, managed to construct one that demonstrated the movements of Mercury and Venus as epicycles round the Sun, thereby taking the first step towards a heliocentric system.

Despite the high degree of interest shown in such revolutionary concepts, Plato never accepted any concept but that the Earth was at the centre of the Universe. This strongly conservative outlook and the unequalled authority which Plato's name gave to it resulted in the acceptance of a geocentric Universe until it was invalidated by the findings of Nicolaus Copernicus 19 centuries later.

Pliny (Gaius Plinius Secundus) (AD 23-79), was a Roman military officer of wide interests. Prudently retiring from his commission during the troubled times of the Emperor Nero (54-68), Pliny devoted his energy to a massive compilation of all the known sciences of his day. He is usually now called Pliny the Elder to distinguish him from his nephew and biographer, Pliny the Younger.

Born into a wealthy provincial family at Como in the year 23, Pliny completed his studies in Rome and, in his early twenties, took up a military career in Germany, where he became a cavalry commander and friend of Vespasian. He kept out of harm's way while Nero was on the imperial throne, and (it is assumed) spent much of his time in writing. But when in 69 his old comrade Vespasian was made Emperor, Pliny returned to Rome - where his routine included a daily visit to the Emperor to talk of this and that - and took up various public offices. It was in the course of his duties that Pliny's life came to a tragic and untimely end. In the year 79 Pliny was in command of the fleet at Misenum, in the bay of Naples, when the famous eruption of Vesuvius that destroyed the towns of Pompeii and Herculaneum took place. Observing a strange cloud formation, subsequently found to have resulted from the eruption of the volcano, Pliny made for Stabiae where he landed. Here, however, he was fatally overcome by a cloud of poisonous fumes. It is possible that he saw himself as doing his duty, but it is equally possible that he died a martyr to science, his curiosity at this critical moment having been greater than his fears.

Virtually all pursuits, human or scientific, interested Pliny and in his early years he produced a grammar, a history of Rome, a biography of Pomponius Secundus, a report on the Roman military campaign in Germany and a manual on the use of the lance in warfare. All these texts have long since diappeared, but there remains intact what is by far his most ambitious and large scale work, the *Historia Naturalis* or "Natural History", in which he surveys all the known sciences of his day, notably astronomy, meteorology, geography, mineralogy, zoology and botany. At the commencement of the work he states that he has covered 20,000 subjects of importance drawn from 100 selected writers to whose observations he has added many of his own.

All the important assumptions of classical astronomy are described in Book II of the *Natural History*. It is of special interest in that it presents not only the author's opinions, but also those of Hipparchus (c.146 BC–c.27 BC) and Eratosthenes (276 BC–95 BC), major figures in the early history of the science. According to Pliny the Earth lay on the pivot of the heavens and was surrounded by the seven stars: the Sun, the Moon, Mercury, Venus, Mars, Jupiter and Saturn. Nevertheless, he saw the Sun as the ruler of the heavens, providing the Earth with light and with the changing pattern of the seasons. Ascribing to the Sun a zodiacal orbit round the Earth, divided into twelve equal parts then occupied by the zodiacal constellations, Pliny goes on to describe in turn the different orbits of the seven stars, correctly adjudging Saturn to be farthest from the Earth and therefore taking 30 years to complete its circuit. Jupiter being much nearer is able to finish its journey in only 12 years, and Mars in about 2. After the remaining planets have been described, Pliny again discusses the Sun which, in order that it may concur with a mathematically desirable end, is represented as taking 360 days to complete its circuit, to which a surplus of $5\frac{1}{4}$ days has to be added to ensure that this great star is seen to rise at the identical point each successive year. Such were the specifications of the Julian calendar, established by Julius Caesar in 46 BC. (It was to result in the error of overestimating the time of the Sun's journey by 11 minutes, 14 seconds, but in Pliny's time this was too small a miscalculation to have had time to become apparent.) The Moon is the last of the seven stars to be described, her puzzling progress of waning being explained as a result of the slant of the zodiacal sky and highly sinuous nature of her course.

Pliny, having no knowledge of distances in the Universe, assumed that the Moon is larger than the Earth, for otherwise he could not see how the entire Sun could be obscured from the Earth during an eclipse by the coming of the Moon between them. The Sun, however, he judged to be of far greater size than the Earth for the reasons, among others, that "the shadow that it throws of rows of trees along the edges of fields are at equal distances apart for very many miles, just as if over the whole of space the Sun lay in the centre" and that "during the equinoxes it reaches the vertical simultaneously for all the inhabitants of the southern region". By his knowledge of the night sky at various latitudes, observed during his military journeys, Pliny even reasoned that the Earth must be a globe. In this connection, he cites the experience of Eratosthenes, who reported that in summer the days are considerably longer the farther north the observer travels. He then gives Eratosthenes's famous calculation of the overall circumference of the Earth. As for gravitation, to Pliny the world consisted of four elements - earth, air, fire and water. Of this number the "light" substances were prevented from rising by the weight of the "heavy" ones, while the latter were prevented from falling by the countervailing pressures from the more buoyant elements. Such was the earliest hypothesis on the nature of gravity.

In a discussion of comets, Pliny dismisses the popular belief that their arrival portended dramatic events in the fortunes of the Roman world. He alludes to the great impact the appearance of a comet had on Hipparchus and how in order that the appearance of a new star in the heavens could more surely be assessed he made a catalogue of all the stars visible to the naked eye, in the process systematizing a classification that lasted for more than seventeen centuries.

The other books of the *Natural History* are just as detailed. Books 3 to 6 record the geography and ethnography of the then known world, in which frequent references are made to great cities which have since disappeared. Book 7 is concerned with the physiology of man; Books 8 to 9 with that of fishes and other marine animals; Book 10 of birds, and Book 11 of insects. Books 12 to 19 are concerned with botany, agriculture and horticulture, the subjects that appear to have awakened Pliny's keenest interest (he is one of our chief sources of information on early Roman gardens and ancient botanical writings). Books 20 to 27 cover medicine and drugs, Books 28 to 32 medical zoology, and Books 32 to 37 minerals, precious stones and metals, especially those used by Roman jewellers and craftsmen.

The scientific value of this great undertaking varies. The further the subjects covered are removed from Pliny's own experiences and observations, the more credulous and even silly he becomes, particularly in reporting the existence of strange animals with patently fabulous qualities. His fluency with the Greek language also induced him to translate from it into Latin too freely, often thereby blurring a critical distinction in mathematical or technical passages. The *Natural History* is, however, invaluable in many instances as the only surviving record of man's early reactions to the physical world and the gradual advance of careful observation and systematic classification of natural orders. This great undertaking appears to have been completed in the year 77, only two years before Pliny's death.

Pond, John (*1767-1836*), was a British astronomer whose meticulous observations at his private observatory led to his discovering errors in data published by the Royal Observatory in Greenwich. When he himself became Astronomer Royal, he therefore implemented a vigorous programme of renovation and reorganization at Greenwich that restored the Observatory to its former standards of excellence.

Pond was born in London in 1767 - no more exact date is known. His scientific talents were apparent from an early age and he entered Trinity College, Cambridge, in 1783 to study chemistry. Forced by poor health to leave the university before he could take his degree, he travelled in warmer climates to recover his strength. He went to several Mediterranean and Middle Eastern countries, making astronomical observations wherever possible. When he returned to England in 1798, he established a small private observatory in Westbury, near Bristol. From there he published observations of considerable astronomical interest, and in 1807 he was elected a Fellow of the Royal Society. This prompted him to return to London, and in 1811 he was appointed Astronomer Royal. He immediately set about reorganizing and modernizing the Greenwich Observatory, which until that time had only one assistant and a collection of equipment that was sadly in need of repair. In 1835, however, he was forced to retire from all professional duties because of ill health. He was awarded the Lalande Prize of the French Academy of Sciences in 1817, and the Copley Medal of the Royal Society in 1823. He died in Blackheath on 7 September 1836.

Pond first demonstrated his skills as an astronomer at the age of 15. He noticed errors in the observations being made at the Greenwich Observatory and made a thorough investigation of the declination of a number of fixed stars. By 1806 he had clearly and publicly demonstrated that the quadrant at Greenwich, designed by Bird, had become deformed with age and needed replacing. It was this in particular that prompted his programme to modernize the whole observatory.

One of the first results of the revitalization programme was his 1813 catalogue of the north polar distances of 84 stars. These data were obtained with the new mural circle designed by Edward Troughton and were highly esteemed by Pond's contemporaries. Pond was able to dispute, in 1817, the validity of J. Brinkley's observations which were ostensibly on the parallax of a number of fixed stars. Pond held that Brinkley had not in fact detected stellar parallax, which was being sought by numerous astronomers as a proof of Copernican cosmology, and he was later proved to be right. The interest that the controversy generated contributed to Friedrich Bessel's later successful efforts in this field.

Another controversy, of an unpleasant kind, surrounded Pond's work a few years later – surprisingly, considering how meticulous (even pedantic) he was known to be. A committee of enquiry, set up by the Royal Society, found that two of Pond's assistants were responsible for work that was less than accurate or conscientious, and reprimanded them; Pond was cleared.

Instituting new methods of observation, Pond went on to produce a catalogue of more than 1,000 stars in 1833. His work continued to be admired by many of his fellow astronomers in Britain and in Europe. Nevertheless, he remains remembered most for his modernization of the Greenwich Observatory.

Pons, Jean-Louis (*1761–1831*), was a French astronomer who, in a career that began at a comparatively late age, nevertheless discovered more than 35 comets and became Director of the Florence Observatory.

Pons was born on Christmas Eve in 1761 at Peyre, near Dauphine. The son of a poor family, he was not well educated and held several labouring jobs until the age of 28, when he became a porter and door-keeper at the Marseilles Observatory. Noting his interest in astronomy, the directors of the Observatory gave him instruction in the subject, paying particular attention to Pons's training in practical observation. Pons learned quickly; knowledge of the sky together with excellent eyesight and considerable patience stood him in good stead. And as a result of his diligence and achievement, Pons was named *astronome adjoint* at the Marseilles Observatory in 1813. Five years later he became its Assistant Director. His achievements were recognized outside the Marseilles Observatory when, in 1819, on the recommendation of Baron Frederick von Zach, Pons became Director of a newly constructed observatory at Luca, in northern Italy. Three years later, when the observatory was closed, Pons was invited by the Grand Duke Leopold of Tuscany to become Director of the Florence Observatory. Before failing eyesight finally forced him to give up much of his observational work, he received many honours and awards (including no fewer than three Lalande Prizes). He retired from the Observatory a few months before his death on 14 October 1831.

The first Lalande Prize that Pons was awarded by the French Academy of Sciences was for his discovery in 1818 of three small, tailless comets, among which was one that Pons claimed had first been seen in 1805 by Johann Encke of the Berlin Observatory. Alerted to this possibility, Encke carried out further observations and calculations, and finally ascribed to it a period of 1,208 days – which meant that it would return in 1822. Its return was duly observed, in Australia, only the second instance ever of the known return of an identified comet. Encke wanted the comet to be named after Pons, but it continued to be called after its discoverer. Encke received the Gold Medal of the Royal Astronomical Society of London and Pons the Silver.

At Luca Pons discovered a number of new comets, for one of which he received his second Lalande Prize. His third Lalande Prize followed his discovery of more comets at the Florence Observatory, raising the total number of his discoveries to 37.

Ptolemy (Claudius Ptolemaeus) (*fl.* AD *2nd century*) was an astronomer, astrologer, geographer and philosopher, probably of Egyptian extraction, working in a centre of Greek culture technically under Roman domination. His collected works on astronomical themes – known generally as the *Almagest* (although he called it *Syntaxis*) – influenced astronomical and religious conceptions for at least 13 centuries after his death.

Almost nothing is known of Ptolemy's life. His name suggests to some commentators that he was born in the city of Ptolemais Hermii, on the banks of the Nile. Certainly it was at Alexandria, in the Nile Delta, that he mostly lived and worked, setting up his observatory on the top floor of a temple in order to view the heavens with greater clarity. Again, the exact date of his death is unknown, although there is some evidence that he may have lived to around the age of 78, and died in either AD 141 or 151.

Ptolemy had often been accused of plagiarizing the theories of Hipparchus, the Greek astronomer and philosopher of two centuries earlier, and of using Plato as his authority for adapting Hipparchus where necessary to maintain his own

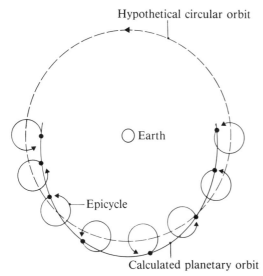

Hypothetical circular orbit

Earth

Epicycle

Calculated planetary orbit

Ptolemy developed the idea of epicycles, first proposed by Aristarchos, to explain the observed departure of planetary orbits from perfect circles.

point of view. It is sometimes forgotten, however, how many sources Ptolemy had at his disposal. Living in Alexandria, whose library was the repository of the greatest store of knowledge in the world, Ptolemy had to hand the entire accumulated wealth of information compiled by Greek and other scholars of the civilized world during the previous four centuries. Some of those scholars, particularly Greek ones (such as Aristarchos), had proposed a Sun-created (heliocentric) solar system. Even Hipparchus favoured a heliocentric Universe. Yet Ptolemy managed to put together a cosmology that it would be difficult to make less accurate – and for various reasons (at least as far as Western Europe was concerned) the science of astronomy stuck fast at that point.

It was Plato (*c*.420 BC–340 BC) who loved symmetry and sought mathematical perfection in the workings of nature, who probably inspired Ptolemy as much as Hipparchus did. Ptolemy began with the premise that the Earth was a perfect sphere. Because gravity brought things demonstrably towards the centre of the Earth, all celestial bodies must likewise conform to it. Thus the Earth was at the centre of the Cosmos, and the Moon, Mercury, Venus, the Sun, Mars, Jupiter, Saturn, and the stars (in that order), in their various spheres, orbited the Earth. All orbits were circular, but Earth was not always at the centre, and indeed of Mercury and Venus, and possibly Mars (Ptolemy was not sure), the orbits were epicyclic (the planets orbited a point which itself

was orbiting the Earth). The sphere of the stars comprised a dome with points of light attached or pricked through.

Apart from Ptolemy's interest in astronomy and his desire to find mathematical answers to natural problems, he also studied geography in great detail, producing vivid maps of Asia and large areas of Africa. These, together with his notes on longitude and latitude, were combined into a collection known as his *Geography*, and it was from these maps that Christopher Columbus many centuries later decided that it ought to be possible to reach India by sailing west across the Atlantic.

The work of Ptolemy that is most available today is his thesis on astrology, the *Tetrabiblios*, in which he suggests that some force from the stars may have considerable influence over the lives and events in the human experience.

Ptolemy's legacy to the world was an attempt at a complete understanding of all he could observe. It has not proved accurate, but it was popular and it endured for hundreds of years.

R

Rayet, George Antoine Pons (*1839–1906*), was a French astronomer who, in collaboration with Charles Wolf, detected a new class of peculiar white or yellowish stars whose spectra contain broad hydrogen and helium emission lines. These stars were subsequently named Wolf-Rayet stars, after their discoverers.

Rayet was born near Bordeaux on 12 December 1839. He did not attend school until the age of 14, when his family moved to Paris. In 1859 he was admitted to the École Normale Supérieure and graduated with a degree in physics three years later. After teaching for a year he obtained a post as a physicist in the new weather forecasting service created by Urbain Le Verrier (1811–1877) at the Paris Observatory. In 1873 Le Verrier entrusted the running of the meteorological service to Rayet, but within a year the two men disagreed over the practical forecasting of storms and this led to Rayet's dismissal. Rayet then became a lecturer in Physics at the Faculty of Sciences of Marseilles and in 1876 he was appointed as Professor of Astronomy at Bordeaux.

As a result of a government proposal to construct several new observatories in France, Rayet was asked to organize a collective survey of the history and equipment of the world's observatories. Subsequently, he was offered the appointment of Director of the new observatory to be built at Floirac, near Bordeaux, and from 1879 he held this post along with his appointment at Bordeaux. During his last years Rayet was troubled by a serious lung complaint, and died in Floirac on 14 June 1906.

At the Paris Observatory, Rayet collaborated with Charles Wolf and their first joint success came in 1865 when they photographed the penumbra of the Moon during an eclipse. On 4 May 1866 a nova appeared, and while observing it on 20 May, after its brilliance had significantly diminished, Rayet and Wolf discovered bright bands in its spectrum – a phenomenon that had never been noticed in a stellar spectra before. The bands were the result of a phase that can occur in the later stages of evolution of a nova. The two astronomers went on to investigate whether permanently bright stars exhibit this phenomenon and in 1867 they discovered three such stars in the constellation of Cygnus. These stars, with characteristically broad and intense emission lines, are now known to be relatively rare and are called Wolf-Rayet stars. They are about twice the size of the Sun, very hot, with an expanding outer shell, and a disparity between the energy produced in the interior and the radiated energy.

In 1868 Rayet took part in an expedition to the Malay Peninsula to observe a solar eclipse and was given the responsibility for the spectroscopic work of the expedition. His observations of solar prominences provided valuable information and in conjunction with other observations made during the same eclipse, notably those of Pierre Janssen, they contributed to the establishment of the first precise data on the Sun.

As Director, Rayet equipped the new observatory in Floirac with the most modern astrometric equipment and began a programme of accurately measuring the co-ordinates of stars, the positions of comets and nebulae, and the components of double stars. He was one of the first supporters of the *Carte internationale photographique du ciel* which was established in order to map the entire sky using identical telescopes around the world, simultaneously. He also had the satisfaction of being able to publish the first volume of the Bordeaux Observatory's *Catalogue photographique*, a year before his death. Despite his poor state of health, Rayet took part in a 1905 expedition to Spain to study a solar eclipse.

Reber, Grote (*1911–*), is an American radio-astronomer – indeed, at one time he was probably the world's only radio-astronomer – who may truly be said to have pioneered the new aspect of astronomical science from its inception. His major project has been to map all the extraterrestrial sources of radio emission that can be traced.

Reber was born in Wheaton, Illinois, on 22 December 1911. Completing his education at the Illinois Institute of Technology, he became a radio engineer. After Karl Jansky (1905–1950) stumbled on the existence of cosmic radio waves, Reber was among the first to explore this new field. Since then his research has taken him all over the world. From Illinois, Reber moved his telescope to Virginia in 1947, where he was appointed chief of the University's Experimental Microwave Radio Section. Four years later he moved to Hawaii, where a new telescope, sensitive to lower frequencies than he had been able to detect previously, was constructed. In 1954 he moved yet again, this time to Australia, where he joined the Commonwealth Scientific and Industrial Research Organization in Tasmania. Although he then went to the National Radio Astronomy Observatory at Green Back, in West Virginia, in 1957 to work with the 43 m radio telescope installed there, he returned to Tasmania in 1961 to help complete the mapping project he had helped to begin.

After a first, unsuccessful, attempt, Reber finally completed the construction of a bowl-shaped reflector 9 m in diameter, with an antenna at its focus, in the back garden of his Illinois home in 1957. He immediately began to map radio sources in the sky, noting particularly that many seemed to come from the direction of the Milky Way. He took his first results to the Yerkes Observatory for discussion with the astronomers there. Satisfactory explanations of radio emission and radio sources were to come later, with the further development of radio-astronomy, but at the time, and for a number of years, Reber's was probably the only radio telescope in existence.

Despite the fact that the resolution of his home-made apparatus was no better than 12°, which meant that he could identify only a general direction from which radio waves were coming, he compiled a map of the sky, noting as he did so how many radio sources seemed to have no optically identifiable presence. The most intense radiation he recorded emanated from the direction of Sagittarius, near the centre of the Galaxy.

The radio telescope in Hawaii represented a great improvement in facilities for him, since it was sensitive to lower frequencies. But it is the equipment in Tasmania that has really held Reber's attention. The project there is to complete a map of radio sources emitting waves around 144 m in length, and it is to this work that he has devoted most of the rest of his professional career.

Redman, Roderick Oliver (*1905–1975*), was a

British astronomer who was chiefly interested in stellar spectroscopy and solar physics. A practical man, he also established a thriving solar observatory in Malta and organized the re-equipping of the Cambridge Observatories after World War II.

Redman was born on 17 July 1905 in Rodborough, Gloucestershire. At the age of 18 he won an Exhibition scholarship from Marling School in Stroud to St John's College at Cambridge University, where he studied until 1929. By that time he was working under Sir Arthur Eddington (1882-1944) at the University Observatory for his PhD in astronomy. The doctorate was awarded in 1930, while Redman was serving as Assistant Astronomer at the Dominion Astrophysics Observatory in Victoria, British Columbia. The following year, Redman returned to Cambridge to become Assistant Director under F. Stratton at the Solar Physics Observatory. He became Chief Assistant of the Radcliffe Observatory in 1937 and moved to the new Observatory site in Pretoria in 1939. World War II prevented the Observatory from being fully equipped so, after being elected Fellow of the Royal Society in 1946, Redman returned again to Cambridge in 1947 and was appointed Professor of Astrophysics and Director of the Observatory. He retained these positions until 1972, when he was made Director of the newly amalgamated Observatories and Institute of Theoretical Physics. He retired later that same year, and died not long after, on 6 March 1975.

From the beginning of his career as an astronomer, Redman was interested in spectroscopic analysis. During his years as a research student under Sir Arthur Eddington, Redman contributed to the early analysis of the Hertzsprung-Russell diagram by studying absolute stellar magnitudes. Upon his return to Cambridge in 1931, Redman concentrated his efforts in stellar spectroscopy, and in the development of spectroscopic techniques.

He applied the method of photographic photometry to the study of elliptical galaxies and later, in South Africa, also to the study of bright stars, for which he developed the "narrow band technique" which was of great value in stellar photometry.

The Sun was a source of fascination for Redman. He devoted considerable time and energy to studies and analyses of the solar spectrum, and went all over the world in order to observe total eclipses, during which he was able to identify thousands of the emission lines in the chromospheric spectrum and to investigate the question of chromospheric temperature.

Redman's final contribution to astronomy was his initiation of a large stellar photometry programme.

Römer, Ole (or Olaus) Christensen (*1644-1710*), was a Danish astronomer and civil servant who, through the precision of both his observations and his calculations, first derived a rate for the speed of light. This was all the more remarkable in that most scientists of his time considered light to be instantaneous in propagation. A practical man, Römer was also talented at designing scientific instruments.

He was born at Århus, in Jutland, on 25 September 1644. Educated in Copenhagen, he attended the university there, where he studied under the Bartholin brothers - Thomas (1616-1680, Professor of Mathematics and Anatomy) and Erasmus (1625-1698, physicist and astronomer). First as a student of mathematics and astronomy, then as personal assistant, Römer lived at the house of Erasmus Bartholin and finally became his son-in-law. In 1671 he collaborated with Jean Picard (1620-1682), who had been sent by the French Academy to verify the exact position of Tycho Brahe's observatory. Evidently impressed by Römer's work, Picard invited him to come back to Paris with him once the investigations were over; Römer gladly accepted. At the Academy in Paris, Römer worked initially as an assistant, but within a year was made a member in his own right. He was also appointed tutor to the Crown Prince. There then followed several years in which he conducted observations, designed and improved instruments, and submitted various papers to the Academy, all culminating, in 1679, in the exposition of his calculation of the speed of light. With his new-found fame, Römer then visited England and met some of the greatest astronomers of his age - Sir Isaac Newton, Sir Edmond Halley and the Astronomer Royal, John Flamsteed. He returned to Denmark in 1681 to take up the dual post of Astronomer Royal to King Christian V and Director of the Royal Observatory in Copenhagen. He also accepted a number of civic duties. He died in Copenhagen on 23 September 1710.

It was while he was in Paris that Römer carried out his famous research which not only demonstrated that light travels at a finite speed but also put a rate to it. His observations of the satellites around Jupiter, especially of the innermost one, Io, led him to notice that the length of time between eclipses of Io by Jupiter was not constant. He found that when the distance between the Earth and Jupiter was least, the interval between eclipses was also smallest. He therefore measured the inter-eclipse period when the two planets were closest and then announced in September 1679 that the eclipse of Io by Jupiter predicted for 9

November would occur 10 minutes later than expected on the basis of all previous calculations.

Römer's prediction was borne out; his interpretation of the delay provoked a sensation. He said that the delay was caused by the time it took for the light to traverse the extra distance across the Earth's orbit when the positions of Jupiter and the Earth were such that they were not as close to each other as they sometimes were. This meant that light did not traverse space instantaneously, but travelled at a finite speed. Römer estimated that speed to be 225,000 km per second – which is remarkably close (considering that it was the first estimate ever) to the modern value of 299,792 km per second. Römer's interpretation of his observations was not accepted by all of his contemporary astronomers, particularly not in France, but was confirmed sixty years later – after Römer's death – by James Bradley (who was also able to improve upon Römer's estimate, obtaining a value of 294,995 km per second).

Römer's later work was on optics, instrument design and the systematization of weights and measures. Unsatisfied by the Copenhagen Observatory, he established his own private observatory, which he named the Tuscalaneum and which possessed the first telescope attached to a transit circle, a device of his own invention.

Russell, Henry Norris (*1877-1957*), was an American astronomer who was chiefly interested in the nature of binary stars, but who is best remembered for his publication in 1913 of a diagram charting the absolute magnitude of stars plotted against their spectral type. Ejnar Hertzsprung (1873-1967) had in fact published similar results previously in a photographic journal that was seen by few astronomers (and noted by none), but Russell was the first to put in graphic form what became known as the Hertzsprung-Russell diagram. Its impact on the scientific world was enormous and the diagram remains of great importance for research into stellar evolution, although some of Russell's initial extrapolations have since been superseded.

Born in Oyster Bay, New York, on 25 October 1877, Russell was five years old when his parents pointed out to him the transit of Venus that inspired him to become an astronomer. He received his early education at home, and then went on to Princeton University, from which he graduated, with distinction, in 1897. He remained at the University, working in the Astronomy Department, until he received his PhD in 1899 for devising a new way of determining the orbits of binary stars. Russell then travelled to England, and joined Arthur Hinks at the Cambridge University Observatories. He worked with Hinks on stellar

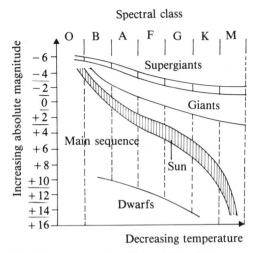

The Hertzsprung–Russell, or H–R, diagram relates the absolute magnitudes of stars to their spectral class or temperature. The Sun is a typical main-sequence star.

photography and evolved a technique for the measurement of stellar parallax. Further research into binary stars followed before, in 1905, Russell returned to Princeton, where he was made Professor and Director of the University Observatory. In 1921 he was appointed Research Associate of the Mount Wilson Observatory, and in 1927 he received the appointment of C.A. Young Research Professorship. Russell was awarded many honours from academies and universities. Described as the Dean of American Astronomers by a contemporary, he died at Princeton in 1957.

Like Hertzsprung, Russell concluded from his early works on stellar distances that stars could be grouped in two main classes, one much brighter than the other. By plotting the luminosities against the spectra of hundreds of stars in a diagram, Russell managed to show a definite relationship between true brightness and type of spectrum. (He used Annie Cannon's system of spectral classification, which also indicated surface temperature.) Most of the stars were grouped together in what became known as the "main sequence" that appeared to run from the top left of the diagram to the bottom right. But there was a group of very bright stars plotted above the main sequence – indicating that stars of similar spectral type could have very different magnitudes. This was a significant discovery, yet the fact that there was a "main sequence" at all was profoundly stimulating to Russell, who immediately founded a theory of stellar evolution upon it. He proposed that all stars progress at one time or another either up or down the "main sequence", depending on whether they are contracting (and therefore becoming hotter) or expanding (thus cooling), and he tried to derive a logical progression. The progression he finally proposed, however, was discredited within a decade – although it provoked considerable scientific research. Stellar evolution is now known to be far more complex than a simple progression.

Russell's lifelong study of binary stars resulted in a method for calculating the mass of each star from a study of its orbital behaviour. He pioneered a system using both orbits and masses in order to compute distance from Earth, and his research into eclipsing binary stars (one of which moves in front of the other, from the viewpoint of Earth) led to the amassing of valuable data on variations in light emission.

Finally, his investigation of the solar spectrum and his analysis of the composition of the solar atmosphere led him to a general speculation on the composition of stars. For the first time he suggested that there was a considerable abundance of hydrogen present, and hesitantly put forward a fairly high percentage figure. The "Russell mixture" turned out in fact to have *under*estimated the abundance of hydrogen (more than 80 per cent of the Sun's volume).

Rutherfurd, Lewis Morris (*1816–1892*), was an American spectroscopist and celestial photographer.

Rutherfurd was born in Morrisania, New York, on 25 November 1816, into a well-established family of Scottish descent. He showed an early interest in science, and during his student days at Williams College, Massachusetts, he was made an assistant to the Professor of Physics and Chemistry. After graduating, however, he went on to study law. His independent means was augmented by his marriage to Margaret Stuyvesant Chanler, which freed him from the need to practice law and allowed him to travel abroad for seven years. When he returned to the United States in 1856, he had his own observatory built and he spent the rest of his life working on astronomical photography and spectroscopy. He died in Tranquility, New Jersey, on 30 May 1892.

From 1858 Rutherfurd produced many photographs that were widely admired of the Moon, Jupiter, Saturn, the Sun and stars down to the fifth magnitude, using an $11\frac{1}{2}$-inch (29cm) achromatic refracting telescope built by Henry Fitz. He went on to map the heavens by photographing star clusters and to enable him to analyse the information of his stellar photographs he devised a new micrometer that could measure the distances between stars more accurately. After 1861 he became more and more interested in the spec-

troscopic work of Robert Bunsen and Gustav Kirchoff and from 1862 he began to make spectroscopic studies of the Sun, Moon, Jupiter, Mars and 16 fixed stars. From his stellar studies, he independently produced a classification scheme of stars based on their spectra that turned out to be remarkably similar to Angelo Secchi's star classification. Apparently, at the January 1864 meeting of the National Adademy of Sciences, he displayed an unpublished photograph of the solar spectrum that had three times the number of lines that had been noted by Kirchoff and Bunsen. To help his spectroscopic work he began devising more sophisticated diffraction gratings and his innovative skill in producing these became generally well known to other contemporary astronomers, providing them with diffraction gratings with up to 17,000 lines to the inch (6,700 lines per cm).

Rutherfurd made his last observations in 1878. In 1883 he donated his equipment and large collection of photographic plates to the Observatory of the University of Columbia.

Ryle, Martin (*1918–*), is a British astronomer whose main work has been the organization, construction, development and use of the radio telescopes at the famous establishment in Cambridge. For this work he received the 1974 Nobel Prize in physics (jointly with his friend and colleague Anthony Hewish, the discoverer of pulsars).

Ryle was born on 27 September 1918. He attended a public school, then studied at Oxford University, graduating in 1939. His interest in radio was already pronounced, and on the outbreak of war he joined the Telecommunications Research Establishment in Malvern, where he was involved in the development of radar and other systems. After the war he was invited by John Ratcliffe (1902–), a former colleague at Malvern, to join him at the Cavendish Laboratory in Cambridge, working on the study of solar radio frequency emissions. As a result of his research, Ryle was appointed to a Lectureship in physics in 1948 and, the following year, to a Fellowship at Trinity College. Election to a Fellowship at the Royal Society came in 1952, and seven years later Ryle became the first Cambridge University Professor of Radio Astronomy. A knighthood conferred in 1966 was followed by his appointment as Astronomer Royal in 1972.

At the Cavendish Laboratory, Ryle's first task as one of the first radio-astronomers was to study solar emission at 1m wavelengths. This necessitated the building of a suitable instrument. His choice lay between a steerable parabolic dish (like the one in use at Jodrell Bank) and an interferometer-type instrument (which consists, in essence, of two separated aerials, each receiving the same signal from the same source, coupled to a receiver). Ryle chose the interferometer variety that the Cambridge site is now famous for. This type of telescope was first constructed merely to distinguish and measure sources of different angular size, identifying "compact" emitters and distinguishing them from diffuse sources, but it was then seen also to allow positions to be measured with much greater accuracy than was possible with a single parabolic reflector. The earliest instruments, built at Grange Road on the outskirts of the city, used a spacing of about half a mile between the two parabolic dishes used as aerials.

One of the interferometers was built specifically to study the compact source of radio emission in the constellation Cygnus noted by James Hey (1909-   ) during the war. On the first night of its operation Cassiopeia-A, the most intense compact source in the sky, was also found - a great discovery. Optical astronomers at Mount Palomar were able to identify both these sources only because of the extreme accuracy (to within one minute of arc) of the later radio measurements: Cygnus as a very distant galaxy and Cassiopeia as a supernova within our own Galaxy.

In 1949 the use of this type of aerial led to a breakthrough in radio telescope design. By making observations from a number of different spacings to construct a radio map of the Sun, the forerunner of the "synthesis" aerials was produced. This work was extended in 1954 to provide the first radio map of the sky. In the earlier sun-mapping a certain symmetry of the source had been assumed so as to simplify the complex mathematical treatment of the signal data. Now, with an arbitrary distribution of sources, the accurate Fourier inversion required involved a precise locating of the sites of the aerial components and enough computer capacity - which was just becoming available - to interpret the signal information. In 1956 the group (generously assisted by Mullard Ltd) extended their activities to the Lord's Bridge site as more and larger instruments demanded increasing ground space and freedom from electrical interference with the weak signals.

With such equipment it was now possible to begin the First Cambridge Catalogue Survey (1C): a map of the most powerful known radio sources in the northern sky. By increasing yet further the collecting area of the detectors, the resolution and sensitivity of the instrument is also increased - as are also, unfortunately, the problems of alignment and scale of construction. So for the Second Survey, 2C - the first really com-

prehensive radio mapping of the sky, completed in 1955 - a collecting area of one acre was used. The definitive 3C survey, published in 1959 and now used as reference by all radio astronomers, was made with a similar arrangement of parabolic reflectors, but working at a shorter wavelength (1.7 m) which gave better resolution.

As this work went on, the first large-aperture synthesis aerial was being built, and it was that which was used to complete the 4C survey. This survey catalogued no fewer than 5,000 sources.

It was in turn superseded by an extension in concept to "supersynthesis", in which a fixed aerial maps a band of the sky using solely the rotation of the Earth, and another aerial maps successive rings out from it concentrically. The "One Mile" telescope was built in 1963 on this principle, and was designed both for the 5C survey - a programme to scan only part of the sky, but in considerable depth and detail - and for the compilation of radio maps of individual sources.

A 5-kilometre instrument was completed in 1971, incorporating further advances in design. It can provide a resolution of up to one third of a second of arc - 0.001 of a degree - to give very detailed maps of known sources. The variety of programmes for which it is now in use includes, most importantly, the mapping of extragalactic sources - radio galaxies and quasars - and the study of supernovae and newly born stars. It can provide as sharp a picture as the best ground-based optical telescopes.

Ryle has personally been responsible for most of these developments. The site at Cambridge has gained its renown in large measure through his efforts and the results that his team has obtained.

S

Sagan, Carl Edward (*1934-*   ), is an American astronomer and popularizer of astronomy whose main research has been on planetary atmospheres, including that of the primordial Earth. His most remarkable achievement has been to provide valuable insights into the origin of life on our planet.

Sagan was born on 19 November 1934 in New York City. Completing his education at the University of Chicago, he obtained his bachelor's degree in 1955 and his doctorate in 1960. Then, for two years, he was a Research Fellow at the University of California in Berkeley, before he transferred to the Smithsonian Astrophysical Observatory in Cambridge, Massachusetts, lecturing also at Harvard, where he became Assistant Professor. Finally, in 1968 Sagan moved to Cornell University, in Ithaca (New York), and took up a position as Director of the Laboratory for Planetary Studies; since 1970 he has been Professor of Astronomy and Space Science there.

The editor of the astronomical journal *Icarus*, Sagan has published a number of popular books on planetary science and the evolution of life; he has also dabbled in UFOlogy and presented a very successful series of astronomical television programmes.

In the early 1960s Sagan's first major research was into the planetary surface and atmosphere of Venus. At the time, although intense emission of radiation had shown that the dark-side temperature of Venus was nearly 600K, it was thought that the surface itself remained relatively cool – leaving open the possibility that there was some form of life on the planet. Various hypotheses were put forward to account for the strong emission actually observed: perhaps it was due to interactions between charged particles in Venus's dense upper atmosphere; perhaps it was glow discharge between positive and negative charges in the atmosphere; or perhaps emission was due to a particular radiation from charged particles trapped in the Venusian equivalent of a Van Allen Belt. Sagan showed that each of these hypotheses was incompatible with other observed characteristics or with implications of these characteristics. The positive part of Sagan's proposal was to show that all the observed characteristics were compatible with the straightforward hypothesis that the surface of Venus was very hot. On the basis of radar and optical observations the distance between surface and clouds was calculated to be between 44km and 65km; given the cloud-top temperature and Sagan's expectation of a "greenhouse effect" in the atmosphere, surface temperature on Venus was computed to be between 500K and 800K – the range that would also be expected on the basis of emission rate.

Sagan then turned his attention to the early planetary atmosphere of the Earth, with regard to the origins of life. One way of understanding how life began is to try to form the compounds essential to life in conditions analogous to those of the primeval atmosphere. Before Sagan, Stanley Miller (1930–) and Harold Urey (1893–1981) had used a mixture of methane, ammonia, water vapour and hydrogen, sparked by a corona discharge which simulated the effect of lightning, to produce amino and hydroxy acids of the sort found in life forms. Later experiments used ultraviolet light or heat as sources of energy, and even these had less energy than would have been available in Earth's primordial state. Sagan followed

a similar method and, by irradiating a mixture of methane, ammonia, water and hydrogen sulphide, was able to produce amino acids – and, in addition, glucose, fructose and nucleic acids. Sugars can be made from formaldehyde under alkaline conditions and in the presence of inorganic catalysts. These sugars include five carbon sugars which are essential to the formation of nucleic acids, glucose and fructose – all common metabolites found as constituents of present-day life forms. Sagan's simulated primordial atmosphere not only showed the presence of those metabolites, it also contained traces of adenosine triphosphate (ATP) – the foremost agent used by living cells to store energy.

In 1966, in work done jointly with Pollack and Goldstein, Sagan was able to provide evidence supporting a hypothesis about Mars put forward by Wells, who observed that in regions on Mars where there were both dark and light areas, the clouds formed over the lighter areas aligned with boundaries of adjacent dark areas. Wells suggested that they were lee clouds formed by the Martian wind as it crossed dark areas. The implication, that dark areas mark the presence of ridges, was given support by Sagan's finding that dark areas had a high radar reflectivity that was slightly displaced in longitude. Sagan concluded that these dark areas were elevated areas with ridges of about 10km and low slopes extending over long distances.

During the 1970s Sagan studied the present atmosphere of the Earth; with Toon and Pollack he has been examining how volcanic activity affects atmospheric temperature.

Scheiner, Christoph (*1573–1650*), was a German astronomer who carried out one of the earliest and most meticulous studies of sunspots and who made significant improvements to the helioscope and the telescope.

Scheiner was born in Wald, near Mindelheim, on 25 July 1573. He attended the Jesuit Latin School at Augsburg and then the Jesuit College at Landsberg, In 1600 he was sent to Ingolstadt, where he studied philosophy and mathematics, and from 1603 to 1605 he taught humanities in Dillingen. It was during this period that he invented the pantograph – an instrument that can be used for copying plans and drawings to any scale. He returned to Ingolstadt to study theology and after completing his studies, in 1610, he was appointed as Professor of Mathematics and Hebrew at Ingolstadt University. It was there that he began to make his astronomical observations and, as well as carrying out his own research, he also organized public debates on current issues in astronomy. In 1616 Scheiner accepted an invitation to take up residence at the court in Innsbruck and the following year he was ordained to the priesthood. From 1633 to 1639 he lived in Vienna and from then until his death on 18 June 1650 he lived in Neisse (now Nysa in Poland).

Scheiner built his first telescope in 1611 and began making astronomical observations of the Sun. He was among the earliest observers of the Sun and, using one of the first properly mounted telescopes, he was sensible enough to project the image of the Sun onto a white screen so that it would not damage his eyes. Within a matter of weeks of observation, he detected spots on the Sun, but his religious superiors did not wish him to publish his observations under his own name in case he was mistaken and might thus bring discredit on the Society of Jesus. He communicated his discovery to his friend, Marc Wesler, in Augsburg, who had Scheiner's letters printed under a pseudonym and sent copies to Galileo and Kepler. Scheiner believed that the spots were small planets circling the Sun and in a second series of letters, published in the same year under the same false name, Scheiner discussed the individual motion of the spots, their period of revolution and the appearance of brighter patches, or "faculae", on the surface of the Sun. Having observed the lower conjunction of Venus with the Sun, he concluded that Venus and Mercury revolve around the Sun. But because of his religious beliefs he upheld the traditional view that the Earth is at rest at the centre of the Universe.

Although Scheiner had tried to conceal his identity, Galileo identified him and claimed priority for the discovery of sunspots, hinting that Scheiner was guilty of plagiarism. It seems that this criticism was unfair, however, because the sunspots were observed independently, not only by Galileo in Florence and Scheiner in Ingolstadt, but also by Thomas Harriot in Oxford and Johann Fabricius in Wittenberg. In his *Solellipticus*, published in 1615, and *Refractiones Caelestes*, published in 1617, which were both dedicated to Maximillian, the Archduke of Tirol, Scheiner drew attention to his observations of the elliptical form of the Sun near the horizon, which he explained as being due to the effects of refraction. In his major work, *Rosa ursina sive sol*, which was published between 1626 and 1630, Scheiner described the inclination of the axis of rotation of the sunspots to the plane of the ecliptic, which he accurately determined as having a value of $7°30'$, the modern value being $7°15'$.

Unfortunately, Scheiner lived in an age when observational astronomy posed grave confrontations to his theological principles and this not only affected Scheiner's scientific career, but also hindered the progress of science as a whole.

Schiaparelli, Giovanni Virginio (*1835–1910*), was an Italian astronomer whose long experience of rather ancient equipment led to considerable caution in making his discoveries known, but who nevertheless carried out significant research into the nature of comets and the inner planets of the Solar System. He is best known – and most misunderstood – for allegedly discovering "canals" on Mars.

Schiaparelli was born in Savigliano, a village in Cueno Province, on 14 March 1835. After leaving school, he first trained as a civil engineer. Only after he had graduated from the University of Turin and was teaching mathematics at the University did Schiaparelli begin a study of modern languages and astronomy. Support from the Piedmont government permitted him to engage in advanced studies at the Observatories of Berlin and Pulkovo. On his return in 1860, Schiaparelli was appointed Astronomer at the Brera Observatory in Milan; he remained there until his retirement in 1900. His first observations, using only the primitive instruments then available to him, resulted in the discovery of the asteroid Hesperia. For most of the next 15 years, Schiaparelli's major interest was in comets. In later years, when more sophisticated instruments became available at Milan, Schiaparelli turned his attention to the planets. Towards the end of his working life, he made use of his linguistic skills by assisting in the translation from the Arabic or a historic work on astronomy; it was published after his death, which occurred on 4 July 1910 in Milan.

Schiaparelli's study of comets began with theoretical research into the nature of a comet's tail. Two years later his work on the tails was extended to a consideration of other features of a comet, including the histories of comets recorded in years previously. From these, and from his own notes on the bright comet of 1862, Schiaparelli was led to conjecture that all meteor showers are the result of the disintegration of comets. Such a hypothesis had been put forward before, but Schiaparelli could point to his compilation of extensive observational evidence to show that all meteors moved in elliptical or parabolic orbits around the Sun, orbits which (as would have to be the case for Schiaparelli's hypothesis to be true) were identical with or similar to those of comets. Schiaparelli also argued that meteors became visible as luminous showers falling from a determinable position in the celestial sphere. Pietro Secchi's observations of the 1862 comet were to confirm this hypothesis; and, in the years following, observations by Peters, Galle, Weiss, von Biela and d'Arrest (among others) served to confirm Schiaparelli's theory.

In 1877, using new equipment far superior to

the instruments he had used before, Schiaparelli began detailed observation of Mars, preparatory to drawing a map of the fundamental features of its surface. In noting what Pietro Secchi had previously called "channels" (*canali*), and while introducing further nomenclature involving "seas" and "continents", Schiaparelli made it quite clear, in publishing his results, that such terms were for convenience only and did not represent terrestrial actuality. Nevertheless, possibly through mistranslation – and certainly through wishful thinking – fanciful stories of advanced life on Mars proliferated, especially in France, the United States and England, for the next 40 years or more.

Schiaparelli's observations of Mars continued through the next few years, being more frequent during the seven oppositions between 1879 and 1890. All manner of variations, of inclination to axis, of the apparent diameter, of geometric declination, of observational conditions and so on, allowed Schiaparelli to build up a complex picture of Mars. During the 1877 opposition Schiaparelli noted that when Mars moved away from the Earth, its diameter appeared to decrease. He also observed that certain canals seemed to be splitting into two parts and he suggested that this "gemination" had serious implications for the understanding of the physical constitution of Mars. His observations of 1888 occurred under such good atmospheric conditions that Schiaparelli found it impossible to represent all the features of Mars in adequate detail or colour. New geminations, absent from the last observation, led him to propose that they were the effect of a periodic phenomenon related to the solar year on Mars. Schiaparelli also observed that split canals were visible for a few days or weeks before becoming single canals or disappearing entirely. He continued his observations until 1890, and their detail and accuracy far surpassed observations made by others using similar instruments.

Schiaparelli also observed Mercury, studying the dark spots that form shadowy bands on the surface of the planet. He concluded that Mercury revolved around the Sun in such a way as always to present the same side to the Sun. He came to exactly the same conclusion about the rotation of Venus. Other observation included a study of binary stars in order to deduce their orbital systems.

Schiaparelli's role in the history of astronomy extends beyond the part he played through his observations. He also made a noteworthy contribution in helping Nallino to translate the only existing arabic text of al-Battani's *Opus Astronomicum* into Latin and in writing explanatory notes to many chapters. The translation is a major landmark in understanding the development of astronomy in the Arabic world. Schiaparelli intended to compile a major work on the history of ancient astronomy and he published a number of monographs on the subject.

Schmidt, Bernhard Voldemar (*1879–1935*), was an Estonian lens- and mirror-maker who devised a special sort of lens to work in conjunction with a spherical mirror in a reflecting telescope. The effect of this was to nullify "coma", the optical distortion of focus away from the centre of the image inherent in such telescopes, and thus to bring the entire image into a single focus, useful for general surveys of the night sky or for photography.

Schmidt was born on the island of Naissaar in Estonia (now the Estonian Soviet Socialist Republic) on 30 March 1879, the child of poor parents. Inclined to scientific pursuits, one of his earliest successes was to make a convex lens by grinding the bottom of a bottle using fine sand. Another experiment had disastrous consequences, however: he made some gunpowder, packed it tightly into a metal tube and ignited it. The explosion caused him to lose most of his right arm. At the age of 21 he began to study engineering at the Institute of Technology at Gothenburg (Göteborg). After one year he went on to the Institute at Mittweida in Germany. After graduating in 1904 he stayed in Mittweida making lenses and mirrors for astronomers. One of his early accomplishments, in 1905, was a 40 cm f 2.26 mirror for the Potsdam Astrophysical Observatory. Schmidt worked independently, producing optical equipment of very high quality until 1926, when Schorr, the Director of the Hamburg Observatory, asked him to move into the Observatory and work there. Schmidt accepted the invitation. He worked on the mountings and drives of the telescopes, as well as on their optics. It was in Hamburg that he perfected his lens and built it into the Observatory telescope, specifically for use in photography.

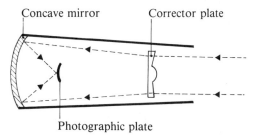

In a Schmidt camera, a corrector plate allows a distortion-free image to be formed on a curved photographic plate or film.

He died in Hamburg, at an asylum for the insane, on 1 December 1935.

It is usual for reflecting telescopes to have parabolic mirrors, rather than spherical ones; spherical ones are subject to an optical distortion known as spherical aberration. Parabolic mirrors too, however, suffer from their own optically distortive effect, "coma"; but they provide an image that is at least centrally clear and focused. What Schmidt devised was a means of correcting the image formed by a spherical mirror - a disc-shaped lens thicker at the centre and edges than at half-radius. By replacing the parabolic mirror of a telescope with a spherical one plus his lens - his "corrector plate" he called it - he could produce an image that was sharply focused at every point (generally on a curved photographic plate, although on later models Schmidt used a second lens to compensate for the use of a flat photographic plate).

Later astronomers, opticians and engineers improved on Schmidt's basic designs to produce such instruments as the super-Schmidt meteor camera which has been used to great effect at Las Cruces, New Mexico and the large 48-inch (1.2 m) Schmidt on the same site as the 200-inch (5 m) Mount Palomar reflecting telescope, and used in the Palomar Sky Survey.

The Schmidt telescope at the Royal Observatory, Edinburgh, is used to photograph large areas of the night sky. (Royal Observatory Edinburgh)

Schwabe, Samuel Heinrich (*1789-1875*), was a German chemist and astronomer who was the first man to measure the periodicity of the sunspot cycle.

Schwabe was born in Dessau (now in East Germany) on 25 October 1789; his father was a doctor and his mother ran a pharmacy. Educated in Berlin, he entered his mother's business as a pharmacist at the age of 17. Three years later he returned to Berlin and took up pharmaceutical studies at the University there, under Martin Klaproth. It was at the University that he became absorbed in both astronomy and botany. His two years' course over, Schwabe went back to the pharmacy in 1812. Seventeen years later his amateur astronomical research - particularly his study of sunspots - became engrossing. He sold his pharmacy business and became an astronomer. As a result of his work he was presented with the Royal Astronomical Society's Gold Medal in 1857 and was elected to the Royal Society in 1868. During his lifetime he published no fewer than 109 scientific papers, and after his death - which occurred on 11 April 1875 - 31 volumes of his astronomical data were presented to the Royal Astronomical Society. They are stored in its archives.

Wanting to commence his astronomical research while still a pharmacist, Schwabe looked for some branch of astronomy that would occupy him during the daytime. His first thought was that he might find a new planet close to the Sun - inside the orbit of Mercury - spotting it as it passed in front of the Sun's disc. He began to watch the Sun in 1825 with a small 2-inch (5 cm) telescope and could not help but notice sunspots. After a while he forgot his hopes of discovering an intramercurial planet and concentrated on the sunspots, making daily counts of them for most of the rest of his life. Day after day, year after year he tabulated his results under four headings: the year, the number of sunspots, the number of days free from sunspots, and the number of days when observations were made. Schwabe realized that with his modest apparatus, in a private observatory, numerical determinations were problematical. He acknowledged that on days when there were large numbers of sunspots, it was more than probable that he underestimated the total. Nevertheless, after carefully collating his results, his patience was rewarded when, in 1843, he was able to announce a periodicity. He declared that the sunspots waxed and waned in number according to a ten-year cycle.

His discovery was ignored at the time, but in 1851 it was republished by the explorer and naturalist, Alexander von Humboldt, in his book *Kosmos* and given the recognition it deserved.

Immediately afterwards, Rudolf Wolf of Berne collated all existing support data in other astronomical records, recalculated the value of the periodicity more accurately, and fixed it at 11.1 years.

Schwabe's revelation of the periodicity – which may be considered as marking the precise beginning of solar physics – was all the more remarkable because Joseph Lalande (1732-1807) and Jean-Baptiste Delambre (1749-1822) had previously considered such an investigation and decided it would not be profitable. In 1851, the year the more accurate value for the periodicity was set, the period was first linked with the occurrence of magnetic storms. It was not long before Johann von Lamont showed that the sunspot cycle had further effects upon the Earth in terms of magnetic disturbances, weather conditions, and plant and animal growth rates. Nor was it long before astronomers began using the photo-heliograph in order to keep daily counts of sunspots.

Although Schwabe was preoccupied with his sunspot counts on every sunny day, he nevertheless found the time for other astronomical research. In December 1827 he rediscovered the eccentricity of Saturn's rings. Four years later he drew a picture of the planet Jupiter on which the Great Red Spot was shown for the first time. And he also found time to write scientific papers on the phenomena of frost patterns, haze and rock sources.

Schwarzschild, Karl (*1873-1916*), was a German astronomer and theoretician who achieved great things despite a short life span. In addition to the conceptual work he carried out, he was a practical man who designed and constructed some of his own instruments and devised considerable improvements in the use of photography for astronomical purposes.

Schwarzschild was born in Frankfurt on 9 October 1873, the eldest of a family of five sons and one daughter. His father was a prosperous member of the Jewish business community in Frankfurt, and Schwarzschild spent a happy childhood surrounded by relatives who were talented in art and music. The first in his family to be scientific, he was educated at the local municipal school; in 1891 he went to Strasbourg Univeristy and spent two years there. He then continued his studies at Munich University. After graduating, he became an Assistant at the Kuffner Observatory in Ottakring, Vienna, and in 1901 he was appointed Associate Professor at the University of Göttingen, where the Observatory had been equipped by Karl Gauss (80 years previously). In the following year he was appointed full Professor at the age of only 28, and he was

also made Director of the Observatory. He left Göttingen in 1909 to succeed Hermann Vogel (1842-1907) as Director of the Astrophysical Observatory at Potsdam. At the outbreak of World War I he volunteered for service and was sent to Belgium to man a weather station. He was then transferred to France to calculate trajectories for long-range shells, and to the Eastern Front, in Russia, where he contracted pemphigus, a metabolic disease of the skin that was then incurable. He died in Potsdam, Germany, on 11 May 1916. By his own request he was buried in Göttingen. For his war work he was awarded a posthumous Iron Cross, and in 1960 the Berlin Academy honoured him as the greatest German astronomer of the preceding century.

At secondary school, Schwarzschild bought himself some lenses in order to make a telescope. Seeing his interest, his father introduced him to J. Epstein, a mathematician who owned a private observatory, and it was with Epstein's son - later to become Professor of Mathematics at the University of Strasbourg - that Schwarzschild learned to use the telescope and studied advanced mathematics and celestial mechanics. His first published work was a paper on celestial orbits, written at the age of 16. His thesis for his PhD was on the applications of Poincaré's theory of stable configurations in rotating bodies to some astronomical problems. He investigated the tidal deformation in satellites and the validity of Pierre Laplace's theory on the origin of the Solar System. Even before he graduated, he devised a multi-slit interferometer and used it to measure the separation of close double stars. Between 1896 and 1899 he gave lectures that conveyed an infectious natural enthusiasm to non-astronomers and were to become famous.

In observational astronomy Schwarzschild was the first to apply precise methods using photographic photometry, substituting a photographic plate at the telescope in place of the eye and measuring densities with a photometer. He photographed an aggregate of 367 stars and presented the results to the University of Munich as credentials to entitle him to teach there.

In 1900, he suggested that the geometry of space was possibly not in conformity with Euclidean principles. (This was 16 years before the publication of Einstein's General Theory of Relativity.)

He introduced the concept of radiative equilibrium in astrophysics and was probably the first to see how radiative processes were important in conveying heat in stellar atmospheres. In 1906 he published work on the transfer of energy at and near the surface of the Sun. He observed the total solar eclipse on 30 August 1905, and obtained spectrograms, using a camera fitted with an objective prism, which gave information on the chemical composition of regions at various heights on the Sun. He also developed methods and techniques later to become standard in the preparation of stellar statistics.

In 1910 he measured photographs of Halley's comet taken by the Potsdam expedition to Tenerife, and suggested that fluorescent radiation occurs in the tails of comets. In spectroscopy, he designed a spectrographic objective that provided a quick, reliable way to determine the radial velocities of stars. He then made further important contributions to geometric optics and to the theory behind the design of optical instruments.

Although primarily an astronomer, he was also a theoretical physicist and was one of the great promoters of Niels Bohr's theory of atomic spectra (1913). As he lay dying, he completed a famous paper, in which he developed the "rules of quantization". (Work carried out independently by Arnold Sommerfeld gave the theory of the Stark effect and the quantum theory of molecular structure.) These last papers also dealt with the gravitational field of a point mass in empty space and gave the first exact solution of Einstein's field equations.

Schwarzschild, Martin (*1912-*   ), is a German-born American astronomer whose most important work has been in the field of stellar structure and evolution.

Schwarzschild was born in Potsdam on 31 May 1912, the son of the astronomer and mathematician, Karl Schwarzschild. Schwarzschild the younger was educated at the University of Göttingen, where he obtained a PhD in astronomy in 1935. He then emigrated to the United States, eventually becoming a naturalized American citizen. He was Nansen Fellow at the University of Oslo (1936–37) and a Littauer Fellow at Harvard University (1937–40). In 1940 he was made a Lecturer in Astronomy at Columbia University, later becoming Assistant Professor (1944) and Professor (1947). Since 1951 Schwarzschild has held the position of Huggins Professor of Astronomy at Princeton University. He is a member of the National Academy of Sciences and the American Astronomical Society, of which he was President from 1970 to 1972.

Schwarzschild's research has been primarily concerned with the theory of stellar structure and evolution. He has written numerous articles on the internal constitution of stars and has made astronomical observations with telescopes carried by balloons into the stratosphere. In 1959 he obtained structural details of the surface of the Sun and photographs of sunspot penumbrae by using a balloon-supported solar telescope at 24,385 m.

Arthur Eddington was interested in the fact that whereas stars differ greatly in brightness, density and in some physical properties, they differ relatively little in mass. By 1926 the range of known stellar masses lay from 1/6 to 100 times that of the Sun. Since then the upper limit has been reduced and much of the work on assessing these limits has been done by Schwarzschild. It is now thought that the upper limit may be only 65 solar masses. The smallest stellar masses known are about 1/100 that of the Sun or about 10 times the mass of Jupiter.

Schwarzschild has also worked out a quantity (Z_{He}) for the total mass density of the elements heavier than helium, using the density of hydrogen as one unit. The values of Z_{He} are smallest for old stars (0.003) and largest for young stars (0.04), implying that the most recently formed stellar objects were formed out of a medium of interstellar gas and dust that was already enriched with heavy elements. These elements were probably produced in stellar interiors and expelled by the oldest stars.

Schwarzschild has been involved with what is known as pulsation theory. In 1879, even before variations in radial velocities were known, Arthur Ritter had considered the periodic expansions and contractions of a star which are termed radial pulsations. In 1938 Schwarzschild suggested that the star's deepest interior pulsates, but that in the outermost regions the elements of gas do not all vibrate in unison, causing a lag in the light curve by the observed amount.

Throughout his distinguished career, Schwarzschild has made an enormous contribution to our understanding of the dynamics and structure of stellar objects.

Secchi, Angelo (Pietro) (*1818–1878*), was an Italian astronomer and physicist famous for his work on solar phenomena, stellar spectroscopy and spectral classification.

Secchi was born on 18 June 1818 in Reggio. At the age of 25 he joined the Society of Jesus and trained to become a Jesuit priest before becoming lecturer in physics and mathematics at the Collegio Romano in 1839. In 1848 he was driven into exile for being a Jesuit and went first to Stonyhurst College, England, then to Georgetown University in Washington DC, where he continued his mathematical and scientific work. In 1849 he was appointed Director of the Gregonia University Observatory at the Collegio Romano and Professor of Astronomy. He was made a member of the Royal Society in 1856. He died on 26 February 1878 in Rome.

While the Collegio Romano was in papal hands there was no lack of funds for the Observatory. There were plenty of assistants and good equipment. Secchi's memoirs testify to the variety of fields in which he researched, and his position gave him the facilities for gaining the widest publicity for his work. He wrote many papers in astronomy, magnetism and meteorology.

Secchi's interest in solar physics was aroused in America, where he assisted in the first experiments on the heat radiated at different locations on the Sun's disc. His interest in spectroscopy dates from a visit of Pierre Janssen (1824–1907) to Rome.

When Secchi returned to Rome in 1849 he equipped his new observatory with a Merz refractor and with this he carried out research into stellar spectroscopy, terrestrial magnetism and meteorology. With William Huggins (1824–1910), Secchi was the first man to adapt spectroscopy to astronomy in a systematic manner and he made the first spectroscopic survey of the heavens. He pointed out that stellar spectra differ from one another and that stars differ in other respects than brightness, position and colour. He proposed that the differences in stellar spectra reflected differences in chemical composition.

In 1867 Secchi suggested the establishment of spectral classes of stars and he divided the spectra he had studied into four groups. Data accumulated since Secchi's day have necessitated a considerably more complex division, but his classification led to schemes of stellar evolution. His groups were based on stars like Sirius, with strong hydrogen lines; stars similar to the Sun, with numerous fine spectral lines; stars of the Herculis type, with nebulous bands towards the red end of the spectrum; and carbon stars with bands in the violet end of the spectrum. The modern system of spectral classification was based on these four groups.

Secchi's other work included photographing the solar eclipse of 1860 in Spain and observing one in Sicily in 1870. In 1867 he demonstrated his universal meteorograph in the Paris Exhibition and gave lectures, some of which eventually formed the basis of his book on the Sun. He also proved that prominences are appendages of the Sun and he determined many features of their behaviour. He was an active observer of double stars and, with Warren De La Rue and William Cranch Bond, was among the first to use the new technique of photography for astronomical purposes. By 1859 he had a complete set of photographs of the Moon. Towards the end of his life, Secchi founded the Società degli Spettroscopisti Italiani, a society formed for the recording of

daily spectroscopic observations of the Sun, mainly from various observatories in Italy.

Secchi achieved a great deal during his lifetime. Before outlining his stellar classification he examined 4,000 stars. He observed comets, meteors and planets, in particular Jupiter, Saturn and Mars. He published his findings in many volumes and he belonged to most scientific societies of the day. Much of our modern knowledge of astronomy has its roots in Secchi's findings.

Seyfert, Carl Keenan (*1911–1960*), was an American astronomer and astrophysicist whose interests in photometry, the spectra of stars and galaxies, and the structure of the Milky Way resulted in the identification and study of the type of galaxy that now bears his name.

Seyfert was born on 11 February 1911 in Cleveland, Ohio. He graduated from Harvard with a BSc in 1933, gaining an MA two years later. His PhD in astronomy was awarded in 1936 while he was Parker Fellow at Harvard. Before joining the Mount Wilson Observatory as National Research Fellow in 1940, Seyfert worked at the McDonald Observatory in Chicago for four years, carrying out research on the spectra of stars in the Milky Way. He was Director of Barnard Observatory (1946–1951) and then he was appointed Professor of Astronomy at Vanderbilt University, where he became Director of the Arthur S. Dyer Observatory.

Apart from his research work in astronomy, Seyfert held a number of administrative posts, the most important of which was the civilian member of the National Defence Research Committee. He was a member of the International Astronomical Union and the American Astronomical Society and was a Fellow of the Royal Astronomical Society. He died in 1960.

In 1943 Seyfert was studying a series of 12 active spiral galaxies which possess barely perceivable arms and exceptionally bright nuclei. His investigations showed that these galaxies contain small, unusually bright nuclei, often bluish in colour, and have distinctive spectral lines denoting the emission of radio waves and infra-red energy. The highly excited spectra of these galaxies showed that they contain hydrogen as well as ionized oxygen, nitrogen and neon. Sulphur, iron and argon were also common to such galaxies. On the basis of their spectra, Seyfert divided the galaxies into two types, I and II.

Radiation from the nuclei of the galaxies is due to the very hot gases that they contain at their centres. The gases are subject to explosions which cause them to move violently, with speeds of many thousands of kilometres per second relative to the centre of the galaxy in the case of Type I, and of several hundreds of kilometres per second in the case of Type II galaxies. Seyfert galaxies also emit a fairly large quantity of X-rays and differ from other active galaxies in that they exhibit substantial amounts of non-thermal emission.

Only a small percentage of galaxies show these and related phenomena. Seyfert's original list has been extended and these galaxies are still the subject of research. The most intensively studied are NGC 1068, 1275 and 4151. Their spectra are so rich, however, that it is not possible to construct any single model that will satisfactorily account for all the known characteristics.

In 1951 Seyfert began a study of the objects now known as Seyfert's Sextet - a group of diverse extra-galactic objects, of which five are spiral nebulae and one an irregular cloud. One member of the group is moving away from the others at a velocity nearly five times that at which the others are receding from each other. Seyfert's original proposal, however, that the six were grouped together because of a chance meeting between objects at different distances is not now the accepted explanation.

Shapley, Harlow (*1885-1972*), was an American astronomer who made what Otto von Struve called "the most significant single contribution toward our understanding of the physical characteristics of the very close double stars".

Shapley was born on 2 November 1885 in Missouri, the son of a farmer. By the age of 16 he was working as a reporter on a newspaper in Kansas, having received a limited education. He then attended Carthage Presbyterian Collegiate Institute, graduating after two years with the intention of enrolling in the University of Missouri's School of Journalism. The School did not open for another year and Shapley, not wanting to waste time, took up astronomy. After graduating from a three-year course at Laws Observatory, he became a teaching assistant there and gained an MA a year later.

In 1911 Shapley moved to Princeton where he worked with Henry Russell (1877-1957) on eclipsing binary stars. Using a new method of computing and a polarizing photometer with a 58 cm refractor, Shapley obtained nearly 10,000 measurements of the sizes of stars in order to analyse some 90 eclipsing binaries. He also showed that Cepheid variable stars were pulsating single stars, not double stars.

In 1914, having completed his PhD thesis, Shapley moved to Mount Wilson Observatory. In 1921 he was appointed Director of the Hale Observatory at Harvard. Under Shapley the Obser-

vatory became an important centre for astronomical research. He introduced a graduate programme whose alumni included Carl Seyfert (1911-1960), Jesse Greenstein (1909-   ) and Leo Goldberg (1913-   ).

Shapley continued as Director until 1952. He was active in retirement, being involved in the grants committee of the American Philosophical Association and undertaking a number of lecture tours. He was subpoenaed by the House of Representatives Committee on Unamerican Activities, having been named by Senator Joseph McCarthy in 1950 as one of five alleged Communists associated with the State Department. Shapley was exonerated, however, by the Senate Foreign Relations Committee.

Shapley received a number of honours during his career, including the Draper Medal, the Rumford Medal of the American Academy of Art and Science, the Gold Medal of the Royal Astronomical Society and the Pope Pius XI Prize. He played a part in the setting up of UNESCO and was one of the American representatives who participated in drafting its charter. He died on 20 October 1972 in Boulder, Colorado.

While he was at the Mount Wilson Observatory, Shapley began observations of light changes from the variable stars in globular clusters. His studies required a great deal of detailed work, gaining and collating information from these very remote stellar systems. The systems were spherical, containing a concentration of tens of thousands of stars. Shapley discovered many previously unknown Cepheid variables and he devised a method, based on the fact that brighter stars have longer cycles of light variation, to measure distances across space. For this relationship between cycle, period and luminosity to be useful, it was first necessary to determine the luminosity of one Cepheid. The great distances involved prevented Cepheids from being measured by direct trigonometric methods. Shapley devised a statistical procedure to establish the distance and luminosity of a Cepheid variable.

Shapley's research served to overthrow previous conceptions about the shape and size of the Milky Way. Jacobus Kapteyn (1851-1922) had argued that the Sun was at the centre of a flat stellar assemblage in which a high proportion of stars were within a boundary some 10,000 light-years in diameter. Shapley proposed that Kapteyn's stellar assemblage was only a small part of a much larger galactic system, extending far beyond the visible stars to which Kapteyn had limited it. The centre of Shapley's system was a congregation of globular clusters some 60,000 light-years away in the direction of the constellation of Sagittarius, and the whole system was said to have an equatorial diameter of about 300,000 light-years.

Next, Shapley turned his attention to the debate about whether spiral nebulae were satellites of our Galaxy or independent stellar systems, similar to the Milky Way, but located well outside our galactic system. The luminosity of novae discovered in spiral nebulae could be used to measure their distances. The distance of 1,000,000 light-years that Shapley proposed for the Andromeda Galaxy is close to the figure now accepted, although Shapley withdrew his results soon after publishing them.

In 1919, on Edward Pickering's death, Shapley was offered, but declined, the position of Director of the Hale Observatory at Harvard; he did, however, take up the position two years later. He encouraged completion of the Draper Catalogue, preferring its extension by Annie Cannon to the new, more sophisticated spectral catalogue constructed by Antonia Maury (1866-1952). Shapley's study of the Magellanic Clouds was also begun at Harvard. The Observatory had maintained a southern station in Peru, keeping photographic records that went back many years. Shapley was able to use these to revise his estimate of the distance of the Clouds to 100,000 light-years. He also conducted a study of the giant emission nebula 30 Doraches and published the first photographs of the obscured cluster.

Shapley increasingly turned his attention to galaxies, carrying out surveys that recorded the presence of tens of thousands of them in both hemispheres. The surveys showed the irregular distribution of galaxies, a point Shapley used to refute the homogeneity necessary in Edwin Hubble's cosmological model. As a result of these surveys, Shapley also identified two dwarf systems in the constellations of Sculptor and Fornax.

Shapley's contributions to early 20th-century astronomy are indisputable, especially with regard to galaxies and the structure of the Universe. He can be considered one of the founding fathers of modern cosmology.

Slipher, Vesto Melvin (*1875-1969*), was an American astronomer whose important work in spectroscopy increased our knowledge of the Universe and paved the way for some of the most important results obtained in more recent astrophysics.

Slipher was born on 11 November 1875 in Mulberry, Indiana. He attended Indiana University and then in 1902, shortly after graduating, joined the Lowell Observatory in Arizona at the request of Percival Lowell (1855-1916). There he began the spectroscopic analyses that led to important conclusions about planetary and nebular rota-

tion, planetary and stellar atmospheres, and diffuse and spiral nebulae.

Slipher's academic and administrative positions show the range of his achievements. He received an MA in 1903 and a PhD in 1909 from the University of Indiana, and he was awarded honorary degrees from a number of universities. He became acting Director of Lowell Observatory in 1916 and was Director from 1926 until his retirement in 1952. He instigated the search that resulted in the discovery of the planet Pluto by Clyde Tombaugh (1906-   ) in 1930. Slipher was active in the International Astronomical Union and the American Association for the Advancement of Science, and he was a member of a number of other astronomical and scientific societies. He died in Flagstaff, Arizona, on 8 November 1969.

Slipher studied Venus, Mars and Jupiter. The lack of surface detail on Venus made calculation of the rotation period difficult. Slipher's method was to measure changes in the inclination of the spectral lines while keeping a spectrograph perpendicular to the terminator. The 26 photographs that he took gave a result that was close to the figure now generally accepted on the basis of more modern methods of computation. In the years following Slipher also published measurements of the period of rotation for Mars, Jupiter, Saturn and Uranus, and in 1933 he was awarded the Royal Astronomical Society's Gold Medal for his work on planetary spectroscopy.

Slipher was responsible for a number of planetary discoveries. His work on Jupiter first showed the existence of bands in the planet's spectrum, and he and his colleagues were able to identify the bands as belonging to metallic elements, including iron and copper. He also showed that the diffuse nebula of the Pleiades had a spectrum similar to that of the stars surrounding it and concluded that the nebula's brightness was the result of light reflected from the stars.

Another of Slipher's discoveries was instrumental to work done by Edwin Hubble (1889-1953), Ejnar Hertzsprung (1893-1967) and others on emission and absorption nebulae. This work depended on Slipher's recognition of the existence of particles of matter in interstellar space. His discovery of a non-oscillating calcium line in the spectra of various celestial objects showed that there was gas between the stars and the Earth.

Slipher's most significant contribution to astronomy concerned spiral nebulae. His investigations paved the way for an understanding of the motion of galaxies and for cosmological theories that explained the expansion of the Universe. While Hubble must be given the credit for formulating the relationship between velocity and distance in interstellar space, his work used results gained by Slipher in his research into spiral nebulae. In 1912 Slipher gained a set of spectrographs that showed that the Andromeda spiral nebula was approaching the Sun at a velocity of 300 km/sec. He continued his observations of this and other nebulae, looking at the Doppler shifts for 14 spirals. By 1925 Slipher's catalogue included measurements of the radial velocities of nearly all the 44 known spirals. His results suggested that spirals were external to our Galaxy as their radial velocities could not be contained within the Milky Way system. His work influenced not only Heber Curtis (1872-1942) and Hubble, who each put forward an account of the nature of the phenomenon, but also other astronomers who were interested in discovering the relationship between velocity and distance in interstellar space. Slipher's contribution to this field of study was outstanding and fundamental.

Smith, Francis Graham (*1923-*), is a British astronomer, one of the leaders in radio-astronomy, since its earliest post-war days.

Smith was born in Roehampton, Surrey, on 25 April 1923. He studied at Epsom College before entering Downing College, Cambridge, in 1941 to read natural sciences. His undergraduate studies were interrupted in 1943, when he was assigned to the Telecommunications Research Establishment at Malvern as a Scientific Officer. In 1946 Smith returned to Cambridge to complete his degree, and he then became a research student in the radio research department at the Cavendish Laboratories. He was awarded the 1851 Exhibition Scholarship in 1951 and received a PhD the following year.

In 1952 Smith went to the Carnegie Institute in Washington DC, where he spent a year as a research fellow before returning to Cambridge. He was appointed Professor of Astronomy at the University of Manchester in 1964 and then moved to Jodrell Bank, where he worked under Bernard Lovell for the next 10 years. In 1974 Smith was made Director-designate of the Royal Greenwich Observatory, and in 1975 he was appointed Visiting Professor of Astronomy at the University of Sussex. He became full Director of the Royal Greenwich Observatory in 1976. In 1981 he moved back to Jodrell Bank to become Director there. In 1982 Smith was appointed Astronomer Royal.

As Director of the Royal Greenwich Observatory, Smith's interests were divided between the running of the Observatory itself and the supervision of the early stages of the Northern Hemisphere Observatory. He was active in the choice of site (Las Palmas in the Canary Islands), the specificiations of the new observatory and in setting up the team to run it. He also organized the equipping of the site with new telescopes, the last of which will be operational by 1986. The Observatory is a genuinely international venture and is dedicated to both optical and radio research.

In addition to his many academic papers, Smith has written successful books on radioastronomy. He is a Fellow of the Royal Society and a Fellow of the Royal Astronomical Society. He has served the latter body as Secretary (1964-1970) and as President (1975-1977).

The disruptive effect on Smith's education of his assignment to the Telecommunications Research Establishment in 1943 was more than compensated for by the valuable opportunity it afforded him of learning the sophisticated techniques used in radar research. These methods were to be most useful in his later work in radio astronomy. His earliest experiments at the Cavendish Laboratories were conducted with a small group of scientists that included Martin Ryle (1918-). Their initial interest lay in studying radio waves emanating from the Sun, using the radio interferometer that had been designed by Ryle. Methods that evolved during this and other projects were soon applied to the study of other celestial sources of radio waves.

Other early radio-astronomers – most notably Karl Jansky (1905-1950), Grote Reber (1911-), and James Hey (1909-) – had established that there were powerful localized sources of radio waves in the sky. In 1948 Smith and Ryle set out to investigate the source that had been found in the constellation of Cygnus. They set up a radio interferometer and recorded oscillations in receiver output that indicated that they had found two sources of radio waves. One of these was the Cygnus source. Smith analysed the timing and duration of the second signal in order to work out its position. This source lay in the constellation Cassiopeia.

The interferometer that Smith and Ryle used to obtain this important result had not been aligned with great accuracy; so Smith set himself the task of determining the precise location of both sources. He used interferometers that were more correctly aligned and devised methods of calibrating the interferometers more accurately. It was not until 1951 that he began to seek the assistance of an experienced optical astronomer. He approached D. Dewhirst at the Cambridge Observatory and asked him to attempt to correlate the radio location with an observable optical feature. Dewhirst gave, as a tentative identification, a faint nebulous structure in Cassiopeia. He was not able to provide any details about the nebula.

Smith then wrote to Jan Oort (1900-   ), who put him in touch with Walter Baade (1893-1960) and Rudolph Minkowski (1898-1976) at Mount Palomar. These two astronomers had at their disposal the most powerful optical instrument in the world, the Hale telescope, and they were able to pinpoint optical counterparts. Cassiopeia A, as the source is now known, was shown to derive from a Type II supernova explosion within our Galaxy; and the Cygnus A is a double radio galaxy.

These discoveries provided a powerful impetus to the development of radio-astronomy. They presented a valuable new method for observing strong signals from sources that would otherwise have been invisible and inaccessible to study. In essence, this opened up a whole new dimension to the Universe.

During the 1950s Smith participated in a systematic search for radio sources, which culminated in 1959 in the publication of the 3C catalogue. This still provides the standard system of nomenclature for the field. Smith and Ryle were the first to publish (in 1957) a paper on the possibility of devising an accurate navigational system that depended on the use of radio signals from an orbiting satellite. This was proposed in the wake of the first Sputnik satellite.

During the early 1960s Smith was active in early scientific experiments that used artificial satellites. In 1962 he installed a radio receiver in *Aeriel II*, one of a series of joint US-UK satellites. It was able to make the first investigation of radio noise above the ionosphere.

At Jodrell Bank from 1964 to 1974 Smith studied radio waves from our Galaxy and from pulsars. His most important discoveries were the strongly polarized nature of radiation from pulsars (1968), an estimate of the strength of the magnetic field in interstellar space, and a theory of the mechanism of radiation in pulsars (1970). This theory is known as the theory of "relativistic beaming". Current opinion in the field of pulsar research is divided between supporting this theory and the "polar cap" theory.

Smith's contributions to radio astronomy have been to the experimental, theoretical and administrative aspects of the field. He has seen the subject grow from a hardly recognized discipline to an integral part of modern astronomy.

South, James (*1785-1867*), was a British astronomer noted for the observatory that he founded and his observations of double stars.

South was born in London in October 1785. He first studied medicine and surgery and became a member of the Royal College of Surgeons before renouncing medicine at the age of 31 in order to devote himself to astronomy. His marriage in 1816 made him wealthy enough to establish observatories in London and in Paris and to equip them with the best telescopes then available.

South became a member of the Royal Society of London in 1821 and he held a variety of positions in the Astronomical Society of London. When the latter body gained a royal charter in 1831, a technicality barred South from serving as its first president and he resigned from the Society. He was knighted in that year and two years later was awarded an honorary LLD by Cambridge University. He was also a member of a number of scientific organizations in Scotland, Ireland, France, Belgium and Italy. He died on 19 October 1867 in London.

South's contribution to astronomy and the development of scientific work in England has been obscured by his argumentative temperament. His public criticism of the Royal Society for participating in the decline of the sciences in Britain offended other members. He published criticisms of other works, including the *Nautical Almanac*, finding it inferior to continental work. None of this endeared him to his peers. South's quarrel with Troughton about the quality of the latter's workmanship was consistent with South's apprehension about declining standards, but it led to a law suit which South lost. He then publicly destroyed the equipment that Troughton had made for him.

Despite such quarrels, South continued to work until his retirement. He is perhaps best remembered for his work with John Herschel (1792-1871) in observing double stars. They charted and catalogued changes in the positions of some 380 such stars. Their work was presented to the Royal Society in 1824 and rewarded with the Gold Medal of the Astronomical Society and the first prize of the Institut de France. In 1826 South completed another catalogue of double stars and for this he was awarded the Copley Medal of the Royal Society.

Spitzer, Lyman (*1914-   *), is an American astrophysicist who has made important contributions to cosmogony.

Spitzer was born on 26 June 1914 in Toledo. He graduated from Yale in 1935 and then went to Cambridge University to work with Arthur Eddington. In 1936 he returned to Yale, where he gained a PhD two years later. Spitzer stayed at Yale until 1947, when he moved to Princeton as head of the Astronomy Department. He is a member of a number of scientific organizations.

Spitzer's initial interest was in star formation.

One hypothesis proposed that stars were formed when gases and dust in interstellar space fused together under the influence of weak magnetic forces. A satisfactory understanding of this hypothesis required an appreciation of the fusion power of gases at temperatures as high as 100 million degrees, by which point hydrogen gas fuses to form helium. Spitzer proposed that only a magnetic field could contain gases at these temperatures, and he devised a figure-of-eight design to describe this field. His model remained important to later attempts to bring about the controlled fusion of hydrogen.

Spitzer's interest in the origin of planetary systems led him to criticize the tidal theory, proposed by James Jeans (1877-1946) amongst others. This was the idea that our planetary system is the result of an encounter between the Sun and a passing star: the star's closeness set up a tidal effect on the Sun, causing it to give off gaseous filaments that subsequently broke off from the main body to become planetary fragments. Spitzer showed that such a theory overlooked the fact that a gas would be dispersed into interstellar space long before it had cooled sufficiently to condense into planets. This objection also applied to Fred Hoyle's hypothesis that the Sun was a binary star whose companion long ago exploded as a supernova, leaving a gas cloud that condensed into planets.

Stebbins, Joel (*1878-1966*), was an American astronomer, the first to develop the technique of electric photometry in the study of stars.

Stebbins was born on 30 July 1878 in Omaha. He was interested in astronomy from an early age, and pursued his studies in the subject at the Universities of Nebraska, where he received a BA in 1899, Wisconsin and California. He worked at the Lick Observatory from 1901 until 1903, when he earned a PhD. He was then appointed instructor in astronomy at the University of Illinois and was made Assistant Professor in 1904. After a sabbatical year at the University of Munich (1912-1913), he became Professor of Astronomy at the University of Illinois and was made Director of the University Observatory.

In 1922 Stebbins became Director of the Washburn Observatory and Professor of Astronomy at the University of Wisconsin. He retired as Professor Emeritus in 1948, but continued active research at the Lick Observatory until 1958. Stebbins was a member of the National Academy of Sciences, the American Association for the Advancement of Science and other prominent scientific organizations. He was the recipient of the Draper Medal of the National Academy of Sciences (1915), the Gold Medal of the Royal Astronomical Society (1950) and other honours. He died in Palo Alto on 16 March 1966.

Stebbins' earliest astronomical research was in spectroscopy and photometry. In 1906 he began attempting to use electronic methods in photometry. The results were encouraging, although at first only the brightest objects in the sky (such as the Moon) could be studied in this manner. From 1909 to 1925 he devoted much of his time to improving the photoelectric cell and using it to study the light curves of eclipsing binary stars. As the sensitivity of the device was increased, it could be used to measure the light of the solar corona during total eclipses. Stebbins discovered that although there was no detectable variations in the light output of the Sun, he could observe variations in the light of cooler stars.

During the 1930s Stebbins applied photoelectric research to the problem of the nature and distribution of interstellar dust and its effects on the transmission of stellar light. He analysed the degree of reddening of the light of hot stars and of globular clusters. His discoveries contributed to an understanding of the structure and size of our Galaxy. He investigated whether interstellar material absorbed light of all wavelengths equally, and found that over a range from the infra-red as far as the ultraviolet absorption was constant, but that absorption of ultraviolet light itself was less strong.

Stebbins' other work included studies using photoelectric equipment of the magnitudes and colours of other galaxies. He demonstrated that his method was more accurate than those that relied on the eye or photography, and the advent of the photomultiplier extended the usefulness of his technique even further.

Strömgren, Bengt Georg Daniel (*1908-*), is a Swedish astronomer who is best known for his hypothesis about the so-called "Strömgren spheres" - zones of ionized hydrogen gas surrounding hot stars embedded in interstellar gas clouds.

Strömgren was born on 21 January 1908 in Göteborg, the son of Elis Strömgren, who was also an astronomer of distinction. In 1927 he received an MA from the University of Copenhagen and he was awarded a PhD from the same university in 1929. He was appointed a lecturer there, but in 1936 he moved to the University of Chicago as an Assistant (and later Associate) Professor. In 1938 he became Professor of Astronomy at the University of Copenhagen and in 1940 he succeeded his father as Director of the Observatory there.

In 1946 Strömgren served as Visiting Professor to the University of Chicago. He was appointed a special lecturer in astronomy at the University of London in 1949 and was Visiting Professor to both the California Institute of Technology and to Princeton University in 1950. From 1951 to 1957 he was Professor at the University of Chicago and Director of both the Yerkes and McDonald observatories. From 1957 to 1967 he was a member of the Institute of Advanced Study at Princeton. He is a member of many scientific associations in Europe and the United States and was awarded the Bruce Medal of the Astronomical Society of the Pacific in 1959. Strömgren retired in 1967.

Some gaseous nebulae that can be observed within our Galaxy are luminous. In 1940 Strömgren proposed that this light was caused by hot stars embedded within obscuring layers of gas in the nebulae. He suggested that extremely hot stars ionize hydrogen gas and that the dimensions of the ionized zone (the H II zone) depend on both the density of the surrounding gas and the temperature of the star.

Strömgren's calculations of the sizes of these H II zones or "Strömgren spheres" have been shown by observations to be largely correct. This concept was fundamental to our understanding of the structure of interstellar material. Strömgren's other work has included an analysis of the spectral classification of stars by means of photoelectric photometry, and research into the internal make-up of stars, all these areas being fundamental to the development of modern astronomy.

Struve, Frederich Georg Wilhelm (Vasily Yakovlevich) von (*1793–1864*), was a German astronomer who was an expert on double stars and one of the first astronomers to measure stellar parallax. He was also the founder of a dynasty of famous astronomers that spanned four generations.

Struve was born in Altona, in Schleswig-Holstein, on 15 April 1793. To avoid conscription into the German army, he fled to Dorpat (now Tartu) in Estonia in 1808. He entered the University of Dorpat and graduated in 1810. His interest in astronomy led to his appointment as an observer at the Dorpat Observatory in 1813. In the same year he was awarded his PhD and became Extraordinary Professor of Mathematics and Astronomy at the University of Dorpat.

From 1817 onwards Struve served as Director of the Dorpat Observatory, but after 1834 he was primarily concerned with the construction and equipping of an observatory at Pulkovo near St Petersburg, which was opened in 1839. He retired in 1862 and was succeeded as Director of the Pulkovo Observatory by his son. Struve died in Pulkovo on 23 November 1864. At the time of his

death he was a member of virtually every European scientific academy.

Struve's earliest research dealt with questions of geodesy and stellar motion. His primary interest, however, was in the discovery and measurement of double stars. In 1822 he published a catalogue of about 800 known double stars, and he instigated an extensive observational programme. The number of such stars known had increased to more than 3,000 by 1827. Struve published a paper in 1843 in which he described more than 500 multiple stars in addition to his earlier work on double stars.

Struve was one of the first astronomers to detect stellar parallax successfully. His interest in that subject dated from 1822, and in 1830 he measured the parallax of Alpha Lyrae. Other work of particular note included his observations, published in 1846, of the absorption of stellar light in the galactic plane, which he correctly deduced to be caused by the presence of interstellar material. He also investigated the distribution of stars in space. In addition to his work in astronomy, Struve made significant contributions to geodesy with his survey of Livonia (1816–19) and his measurements of the arc of meridian (1822–27).

Struve, Gustav Ludwig Wilhelm (Ludwig Ottovich) von (*1858–1920*), the younger brother of Karl Hermann von Struve and son of Otto Wilhelm von Struve, was an expert on the occultation of stars and stellar motion.

Struve was born on 1 November 1858 at Pulkovo, near St Petersburg. He attended school at Vyborg and followed the family tradition by studying astronomy at the University of Dorpat (now Tartu, Estonia). After his graduation in 1880 he began research at the Pulkovo Observatory. From 1883 to 1886 Struve travelled through Europe, visiting observatories in many countries.

When he returned to Pulkovo in 1886 Struve continued his work at the Observatory. He wrote a thesis on the constant of precession and was awarded his doctorate in 1887. In 1894 he moved to the University of Kharkov, where he was made Extraordinary Professor of Astronomy. In 1897 he became a full Professor and Director of the University Observatory. In 1919 he left Kharkov for Simferopol, where he was appointed Professor at the Tauris University. He died in Simferopol on 4 November 1920.

Struve's father had done excellent work on determining the constant of precession. Struve was also interested in this subject and he investigated the whole question of motion within the Solar System. This led him on to work on the positions and motions of stars, and to an estimation of the rate of rotation of the Galaxy.

Struve was best known for his expert knowledge about the occultation of stars during a total lunar eclipse. Much of his early work on this subject was done in the 1880s, but his interest in it continued until the end of his career.

Struve, Karl Hermann (Hermann Ottovich) von (*1854–1920*), third in the line of famous astronomers, was an expert on Saturn. His other work was largely concerned with features of the Solar System, although he also shared the family interest in stellar astronomy.

Struve was born on 30 October 1854 at Pulkovo. He studied at Karlsruhe, Vyborg and Reval (Tallinn), before enrolling at the University of Dorpat (Tartu) in 1872. On completing his undergraduate studies in 1877, Struve travelled in Europe and visited major centres of astronomical research. He was awarded his PhD from Dorpat in 1882.

A year later Struve was appointed Astronomer at Pulkovo and he became Director there in 1890. In 1895 he left to become Professor of Astronomy at the University of Königsberg. He was later appointed Director of the Observatory of Berlin-Babalsberg (1904), and in 1913 he became the founder-Director of the Neubabalsberg Observatory. He was a member of numerous scientific societies and the recipient of the 1903 Gold Medal of the Royal Astronomical Society. He died in Herrenalb, Germany, on 12 August 1920.

Among the many features of the Solar System studied by Struve were the transit of Venus, the orbits of Mars and Saturn, the satellites (especially Iapetus and Titan) of Saturn, and Jupiter and Neptune. Struve's best work was his 1898 paper on the ring system of Saturn. Data in this publication formed the basis of much of his later research.

Struve, Otto von (*1897–1963*), was the last of four generations of a family of eminent astronomers. He contributed to many areas of stellar astronomy, but was best known for his work on interstellar matter and stellar and nebular spectroscopy.

Struve was born on 12 August 1897 at Kharkov in Russia. He studied at the Gymnasium at Kharkov before entering a school for artillery training in Petrograd (now Leningrad) in 1915. He served in the Imperial Russian Army on the Turkish front during World War I. After the war he studied at the University of Kharkov, where he was awarded a degree with top honours in 1919. He was conscripted into the counter-revolutionary

White Army during the Civil War in 1919, but he fled to Turkey in 1920.

With the aid of E.B. Frost, Director of the Yerkes Observatory, Struve went to the United States in 1921. He became an assistant at the Observatory and studied for his doctorate, which was awarded in 1923. He then rose to the ranks of Instructor (1924), Assistant (1927) and Associate (1930) Professor, and Assistant Director of the Observatory (1931). He became Professor of Astrophysics at the University of Chicago in 1932. When Frost retired in 1932, Struve was made Director of the Yerkes Observatory. He was also the founder-Director of the McDonald Observatory in Texas.

Struve taught at the University of Chicago until 1950, when he became Professor of Astrophysics and Director of the Leuschner Observatory at the University of California at Berkeley. He left in 1959 to become Director of the newly established National Radioastronomy Observatory at Green Bank, West Virginia. He retired because of ill-health in 1962, but was appointed joint professor of the Institute of Advanced Studies and California Institute of Technology.

Struve was a member of the National Academy of Sciences, the Royal Society and the Royal Astronomical Society. He was the recipient of numerous honours including the Gold Medal of the Royal Astronomical Society (1944) and the Draper Medal of the National Academy of Sciences (1950). He died on 6 April 1963 in Berkeley.

Struve's early work was on stellar spectroscopy and the positions of comets and asteroids. Spectroscopic analysis of interstellar space had fascinated him from early in his career, as had double stars. He did early work on stellar rotation and demonstrated the rotation of blue giant stars and the relationship between stellar temperature (and hence spectral type) and speed of rotation. In 1931 he found, as he had anticipated, that stars that spun at a high rate deposited gaseous material around their equators.

In 1936, together with C.T. Elvey, Struve developed a nebular spectrograph that was used to study interstellar gas clouds. In 1938 they were able to demonstrate for the first time that ionized hydrogen is present in interstellar matter. They also determined that interstellar hydrogen is concentrated in the galactic plane. These observations had important implications for later work on the structure of our Galaxy and for radio-astronomy.

Struve was also interested in theories of the evolution of stars, planetary systems and the Universe as a whole. He believed that the establishment of a planetary system should be thought of as the normal course of events in stellar evolution and not a freak occurrence. Struve's contributions to astronomy were of fundamental importance to the fast-growing science of the present century, just as his forefathers' work had been in their time.

Struve, Otto Wilhelm (Otton Vasilievich) von (*1819-1905*), was an active collaborator with his father, Frederick von Struve, in many astronomical and geodetic investigations. He is best known for his accurate determination of the constant of precession.

Struve was born in Dorpat (now Tartu), Estonia, on 7 May 1819. He took his degree at the University of Dorpat in 1839, although he had begun work as an astronomer two years earlier. From 1839 to 1848 he worked at the Pulkovo Observatory, becoming its deputy Director in 1848, and its Director in 1862. From 1847 to 1862 he held a concurrent post as a military adviser in St Petersburg (now Leningrad). In 1889 he retired from the Pulkovo Observatory and moved to Karlsruhe. He was a member of numerous scientific academies and was the recipient of the Gold Medal of the Royal Astronomical Society. He died in Karlsruhe on 16 April 1905.

One of the most ambitious observational programmes initiated at the Pulkovo Observatory in its early days was a systematic survey of the northern skies for the purpose of discovering and observing double stars. Struve was one of the most active participants in this programme and he has been credited with the discovery of about 500 double stars. He also made detailed measurements of binary systems.

Struve was interested in the Solar System and he made a careful study of Saturn's rings. He discovered a satellite of Uranus and calculated the mass of Neptune. He also concerned himself with the measurement of stellar parallax, the movement of the Sun through space and the structure of the Universe, although he was among those astronomers who erroneously believed our Galaxy to be the extent of the whole Universe. His determination of the constant of precession, which served as the best estimate for nearly half a century, served to seal his reputation as an astronomer of distinction.

Swings, Pol F. (*1906-*), is a Belgian astrophysicist with a particular interest in cometary spectroscopy.

Swings was born in Ransart on 24 September 1906. He studied mathematics and physics at the University of Liège, where he earned his doctorate in mathematics in 1927. He served as an assistant at the University from 1927 to 1932, although he

spent much of his time abroad conducting his post-doctoral research. In 1930 he was awarded a special DSc in physics and he was appointed Professor of Astrophysics at the University of Liège in 1932.

During the 1930s and 1940s, Swings spent several years in the United States as Visiting Professor at a number of universities, including Chicago and California. He has been a member of numerous professional bodies including the International Astronomical Union, which he served both as vice-president and president, the National Academy of Sciences in the United States, the Royal Astronomical Society in London and the Royal Belgian Academy of Sciences. He received the Francqui Prize in 1947 and the Decennial Prize in 1958, the highest Belgian honours. Swings was co-author of an atlas of cometary spectra, published in 1956, and the recipient of several honorary degrees. He is now associated with the Institut d'Astrophysique in Sclessin in Belgium.

Swings' early astronomical studies concentrated on celestial mechanics, but he soon displayed an interest in the more modern discipline of spectroscopy. At first he approached the subject in an experimental laboratory fashion, but later he applied his expertise in spectral analysis to an investigation of the constitution of a number of types of celestial bodies. His most influential work dealt with the study of cometary atmospheres, and he is credited with the discovery of the Swings bands and the Swings effect. Swings bands are emission lines resulting from the presence of certain atoms of carbon; the Swings effect was discovered with the aid of a slit spectrograph and is attributed to fluorescence resulting partly from solar radiation.

Swings has also made spectroscopic studies of interstellar space and has investigated stellar rotation, as well as nebulae, novae and variable stars.

T

Thales of Miletus (*c.624-c.547* BC), was a Greek philosopher who was among the first early Greek philosophers to reject mythopoetic forms of thought for a basically scientific approach to the world.

Thales was born in Miletus, the son of Examyas and Cleobuline, both of whom were members of distinguished Miletan families. Thales' precise date of birth is unknown, but his peak of activity is traditionally dated as 585 BC, the year in which he predicted an eclipse of the Sun. It is his prediction of this eclipse that is the basis of his reputation as a scientist.

Claims are made also for his ingenuity and practicality as an astronomer, mathematician, statesman and businessman. Aristotle records that, when he was reproached for being impractical, Thales, having predicted that weather conditions the next year would be conducive to a large olive harvest, bought up all the olive presses in Miletus and exploited his monopoly to make a large profit. Herodotus gives another example of Thales' belief in the control of physical nature when he recounts that Thales diverted the River Halys to enable Croesus' army to cross. Such engineering required that any divine connotations attaching to the flow of rivers be ignored and objects and events in the world treated much as they are in present-day scientific research.

Thales sought unifying and general hypotheses that relied on the relationships between natural phenomena to explain natural events. The order he believed to be inherent in the world was not to be explained by reference to divine or mystical forces, but was to be discovered and articulated in terms of natural causes.

In astronomy Thales is credited with defining the constellation of Ursa Minor (Little Bear) and with writing a work on navigation in which the Little Bear is commended for its usefulness in this regard. But his reputation as an astronomer rests on a number of doubtful sources which, among others, ascribe to him the introduction of Egyptian mathematics to Greece and the use of a "Babylonian saros" (a cycle of 223 lunar months) to calculate the solar eclipse. It has been argued that the Babylonian saros was the invention of Edmund Halley (1656–1742) and could not have been the basis of Thales' calculation.

It has also been argued that Egyptian mathematics and geometry were quite primitive, consisting of a set of rules covering practical measurement only. The discoveries with which Thales is credited may represent no more than the most efficient solutions, probably formulated by Thales, to particular problems.

Cosmological views attributed to Thales are known almost entirely from the writings of Aristotle. Thales is said to have proposed that water was the material constituent of all things and that the Earth floats on water. He explained the occurrence of earthquakes by reference to this idea of a floating Earth. Thales' explanation of events is couched in terms of natural phenomena and objects, not in the usual terms of activity by the god Poseidon. His cosmology may be reminiscent of Near Eastern mythology, but the Greek thinkers

who followed the path he established by seeking explanations of natural events in terms of natural agencies were the precursors of modern scientists and astronomers.

Theon of Smyrna (*fl.* AD *130*), was a mathematician and astronomer who is remembered chiefly for his *Expositio rerum mathematicarum ad legendum Platoneum utilium*. Most of the text of this work, at present in Venice, is in two manuscripts, one on mathematics and one on astronomy and astrology.

Little is known of Theon's birth or life. The latest thinkers he names in the *Expositio* are Thrasyllus and Adrastus. Assuming that Theon tried to take account of the most modern contemporary writers, and as Thrasyllus was active when Tiberius was Emperor of Rome and Adrastus died in the late 100s, Theon is generally taken to have been active in the early second century AD. He is also referred to by other writers: Ptolemy's work includes Theon's observations of Venus and Mercury between 127 and 132.

Theon's *Expositio* is useful as a source of quotations from other writers. Its main task, in keeping with the suppositions of Platonic philosophy, is to articulate the interrelationships between arithmetic, geometry, music and astronomy. The section on mathematics deals with prime, geometrical and other numbers in the Pythagorean pantheon, while the section on music considers instrumental music, mathematical relations between musical intervals and the harmony of the Universe. Neither the mathematical nor the musical sections exhibit any great originality. Theon was concerned to collate and organize discoveries made by his predecessors. His own contribution seems at times to consist of a mysticism about numbers and mathematical calculations.

The astronomical section is by far the most important. Music is included: the planets, Sun, Moon and the sphere of fixed stars are all set at intervals congruent with an octave. The Earth is a sphere standing at the centre of the Universe, surrounded by several circles of the heavens. The text sets out the different explanations of the order of heavenly bodies and of deviations in latitude of the Sun, Moon and planets. Theon also shows how different writers, including Aristotle (384–322 BC), Callipus (*c.*370–*c.*330 BC) and Eudoxus (408–355 BC), accounted for the workings of the system of rotating spheres, and he puts forward what was then known about conjunctions, eclipses, occultations and transits. Other subjects covered include descriptions of eccentic and epicyclic orbits, and estimates of the greatest arcs of Mercury and Venus from the Sun.

No other works of Theon have survived,

although he is known to have written a commentary on Plato's *Republic*.

Tombaugh, Clyde (*1906–*), is an American astronomer whose painstaking work led to the discovery of Pluto.

Tombaugh was born on 4 February 1906 in Streator, Illinois. He had a deep fascination for astronomy and constructed a 23 cm telescope out of parts of old machinery on his father's farm. His family could not afford to send him to college and he joined the Lowell Observatory in 1929 in the hope that he would learn about the subject while working there as an assistant. In 1933, after his discovery of Pluto, Tombaugh won a scholarship to the University of Kansas, from where he obtained an MA in 1936.

Several astronomers had shown that the orbital motions of Uranus and Neptune exhibited gravitational perturbations suggestive of the existence of a planet beyond them. Percival Lowell (1855–1916) made the first generally accepted calculation of the new planet's likely position and, as Director of the Lowell Observatory, he set up a team to look for the planet. This work continued when Vesto Slipher (1875–1969) became Director in 1926.

On joining the Observatory, Tombaugh worked on Slipher's team. There were various problems. The new planet would be too dim for a telescope to reveal without bringing thousands of dim stars into view also and, because of its distance from the Earth, any visible motion would be very slight. Tombaugh devised a technique by means of which he compared two photographs of the same part of the sky taken on different days. Each photograph could be expected to show anything between 50,000 and 500,000 stars. Tombaugh looked to see if any of the spots of light had moved in a way not expected of stars or the then known planets. Any movement would be noticeable if the different photographic plates were focused at a single point and alternately flashed rapidly on to a screen. A planet moving against the background of stars would appear to move back and forth on the screen.

It was a painstaking process. On 18 February 1930 Tombaugh discovered a moving light in the constellation of Gemini. On 13 March (the late Lowell's birthday) the discovery of the new planet was announced and it was named after the god of the nether darkness, which seemed appropriate for the most distant planet.

There was some doubt that this could be the planet that Lowell had predicted, since it was only one-tenth as bright and too small to account for all the gravitational perturbations, but the doubt was soon dispelled and Tombaugh was

recognized for his great contribution to the furthering of our knowledge of the Solar System.

Trumpler, Robert Julius (*1886–1956*), was a Swiss astronomer who is known for his studies and classification of star clusters found in our Galaxy. He also carried out observational tests of the general theory of relativity.

Trumpler was born in Zurich on 2 October 1886, the third son of a family of ten children of the Swiss industrialist, Wilhelm Trumpler. He attended the University of Zurich for two years and then transferred to the University of Göttingen, where he gained his PhD in 1910. For the following four years, Trumpler work on the Swiss Geodetic Survey determining longitudes and latitudes, and it was during this time that he developed a personal interest in the annual proper motion of the stars in the Pleiades cluster. The latter interest coincided with that of Frank Schlesinger (1871–1943), Director of the Allegheny Observatory, near Pittsburgh, Pennsylvania. A meeting between the two men led Trumpler in 1915 to accept an invitation by Schlesinger to work at the Allegheny Observatory on comparative studies of galactic star clusters. In 1919 Trumpler was invited to work with William Campbell (1862–1938) at the Lick Observatory, near Chicago, to assist with tests of the general theory of relativity. Trumpler was appointed as Professor of Astronomy at the University of California in 1930. He was elected to the National Academy of Sciences in 1932 and in the same year he became President of the Astronomical Society of the Pacific, being re-elected to the Presidency in 1939. He retired in 1951 and died five years later in Oakland, California, on 10 September 1956.

At the Allegheny Observatory Trumpler showed that galactic star clusters contain different classes of stars, with no observable regularity in the occurrence of blue stars, yellow stars or red giants, and these observations paved the way for later theories about stellar evolution. In 1930 he showed that interstellar material was responsible for obscuring some light from galaxies, which had led to over-estimations of their distances from Earth; this work supported Harlow Shapley's research on the size of our Galaxy.

Three years after joining Campbell at the Lick Observatory, Trumpler took part in a test of the theory of relativity in which stars near the totally eclipsed Sun were photographed from Australia and compared with photographs taken simultaneously from Tahiti. Readings showed that light suffered an outward deflection of 4.45010.02270 cm at the edge of the Sun, compared with Einstein's prediction that the amount of deflection would be 4.4323 cm.

Trumpler also used the refractor at the Lick Observatory to study the planet Mars, concluding that, while most of Giovanni Schiaparelli's observations were incorrect, there was still a possibility that some of the supposed observations of "canals" could be volcanic faults. This conclusion exemplifies the accuracy of Trumpler's observational astronomy because his hypothesis was made in 1924 and it only gained real support on the return of the photographs taken by the Mariner 9 space probe to Mars, more than 50 years later.

V

Van Allen, James Alfred (*1914-*), is an American physicist whose particular fields of interest are terrestrial magnetism and cosmic radiation. He was closely involved with the early development of the United States space programme and in connection with it discovered the Earth's magnetosphere.

Van Allen was born in Mount Pleasant, Iowa, on 7 September 1914. He earned his BA in 1935 from Iowa Wesleyan College and his PhD in 1939 from the University of Iowa. From 1939 to 1942 he worked as a Research Fellow at the Carnegie Institution in Washington and from 1942 to 1946 he served as an Ordnance and Gunnery Officer in the US Navy. He went on to become Supervisor of the High Altitude Research Group and the Proximity Fuse Unit in the Applied Physics Department of Johns Hopkins University. In 1951 Van Allen was appointed as Professor of Physics at the University of Iowa and in 1959 this post was extended to incorporate him as Professor of both Astronomy and Physics. Since 1972 Van Allen has been Carver Professor of Physics at the University of Iowa. From 1953 to 1954 he was active in Project Matterhorn, which was aimed at the study of thermonuclear reactions, and he was also closely involved in the organization of the International Geophysical Year from 1957 to 1958.

After World War II Van Allen's early research was devoted to the study of cosmic radiation. He used the undeployed stock of captured German V-2 and US Aerobee rockets to carry instruments into the outer atmosphere to measure the amount of cosmic radiation there. Van Allen also designed the "rockoon", or rocket balloon, technique in 1949. By using a balloon to lift a small rocket into the stratosphere so that the rocket

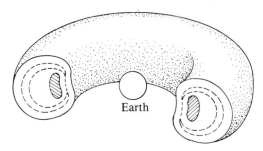

Van Allen radiation belts, an early discovery of the American space programme, form a torus girdling the Earth.

could be fired from high altitude, he avoided the drag experienced by a rocket that is fired from the ground. This technique enabled rockets to reach much greater heights than would otherwise have been possible. During the years between 1949 and 1957, he organized a total of five scientific expeditions to study cosmic radiation.

In 1955 Van Allen was given responsibility for the instrumentation of the first American artificial satellites, whose launch was scheduled to coincide with both the International Geophysical Year and peak solar activity. *Explorer I* was launched on 31 January 1958, carrying a Geiger counter with which Van Allen intended to measure levels of cosmic radiation. To his astonishment the counter registered a radiation level of zero at a height of 800 km. This was an impossible result and at first he suspected that the instrument had failed. But when he obtained the same reading for the device launched with *Explorer III*, he realized that the counters must have been swamped with enormously high levels of radiation, since on returning to lower altitudes they resumed normal operation. To test his theory, the radiation counter carried aboard *Explorer IV* was shielded with lead to permit less radiation to penetrate. It functioned normally. From these results it was quite apparent that certain zones of the space around the Earth contained much higher radiation levels than had hitherto been suspected.

Van Allen investigated the size and distribution of these radiation zones and found two torroidal belts around the Earth, above the equator. These high radiation zones were proposed to have arisen by the trapping of charged particles in the Earth's magnetic field. Their intensity was found to vary in relation to solar activity and they were named the "Van Allen belts". Their discovery revealed a potential hazard to astronauts and to reduce the risk flight paths were carefully planned to avoid traversing the Van Allen belts (although the health hazard to astronauts who do pass through the belts is less than the potential risk from solar flares).

Van Allen is a pioneer of high-altitude research by means of rockets, satellites and space-probes. He is particularly renowned for initiating the rockoon technique and for discovering the intense zones of high-level radiation, caused by trapped charge particles around the Earth. His other interests include the study of aurorae and high-energy particles in interplanetary space.

Van Maanen, Adriaan (*1884–1946*), was a Dutch-born American astronomer who carried out a full programme of research, observation and photography during his career and where meticulous measurements formed the basis for later investigation by astronomers.

Van Maanen was born in Sneek, The Netherlands, on 31 March 1884. He was of aristocratic parentage, his father being John William Gerbrand and his mother Catharina Adriana Visser van Maanen. He attended the University of Utrecht, where he gained his BA in 1906, his MA in 1909 and his PhD two years later. His first appointment was at the University of Groningen, but in 1911 he left the Netherlands for the United States to join the staff of the Yerkes Observatory, near Chicago, in an unpaid capacity to gain experience in astronomy. By 1912 he had secured himself a position at the Mount Wilson Observatory, where he was mostly involved with the measurement of the proper motions and parallaxes of stars. He went on to spend much of his working life studying the motion of planetary nebulae and faint stars. At one stage he was also involved with measuring the solar magnetic field. With the equipment available at the time his findings were somewhat inaccurate, although they were not improved upon until the advent of more sophisticated technology in the early 1950s.

Van Maanen's career began at a particularly fortunate time, when technical knowledge was advancing at a tremendous rate, which allowed him to use the latest developments in telescope design for his observations. The Yerkes Observatory had only recently been completed when the young Van Maanen went to work there as a volunteer in 1911. Then, when he joined the staff of the Mount Wilson Observatory, he was able to use the new 60-inch (152 cm) reflector for his determinations of stellar parallaxes. As new technology became available, the Mount Wilson Observatory was gradually equipped with bigger and better mirrors, and Van Maanen was able to exploit the potential of this more sophisticated equipment to study the motion of planetary nebulae and faint stars. His work on the rate of rotation of some novae spirals was also a stimulus

to Harlow Shapley (1885–1972) in his argument against the possibility of "Island Universes".

Vogel, Hermann Carl (*1841–1907*), was a German astronomer who became the first Director of the Potsdam Astrophysical Observatory. He is renowned for his work on the spectral analysis of stars and his discovery of spectroscopic binary stars.

Vogel was born in Leipzig on 3 April 1841, the sixth child of Carl Christoph Vogel, the principal of a Leipzig grammar school. Vogel attended his father's school up to the age of 18 and then continued his education at the Polytechnical School in Dresden. In 1863 he returned to Leipzig to study Natural Science at the University and, shortly after beginning his course, he became second assistant at the University Observatory. He showed remarkable dexterity at manipulating instruments and as a result the Director of the Observatory, Karl Brühns, asked him to take part in the Astronomische Gesellschaft's "zone project". This was part of a much larger programme that aimed to scan the northern skies and to ascertain the co-ordinates of all stars down to the ninth magnitude. Vogel's contribution was to observe all nebulae within a specific zone and this work formed the basis of his inaugural dissertation. In 1870, at the joint recommendation of Karl Brühns and Johann Karl Friedrich Zöllner, Professor of Leipzig Observatory, Vogel was appointed Director of an Observatory at Bothkamp, near Kiel, that belonged to the amateur astronomer, F.G. von Bülow. Vogel's work on the spectra of planets, undertaken while he was at the Bothkamp Observatory, won him a prize from the Royal Danish Academy of Sciences. In 1874 he was asked to become an observer at the proposed Astrophysical Observatory at Potsdam, near Berlin. The Potsdam Observatory was officially opened in 1879 and in 1882 he was appointed the first Director of the Observatory, a position he held until his death on 13 August 1907.

During his time at the Bothkamp Observatory, Vogel was given complete scientific freedom, sole discretion in determining the Observatory's research programme and excellent equipment. He worked intensively on the spectroscopic properties of stars, planets, nebulae, the northern lights, comet III 1871, and the Sun. With the aid of a reversible spectroscope, he attempted to ascertain the rotational period of the Sun and, following attempts made by Huggins in England in 1868, he also attempted spectroscopically to determine the radial velocity of fixed stars.

Having been appointed as an observer to the future Potsdam Observatory in 1874, Vogel became increasingly interested in spectrophotometry. He used this technique to study Nova Cygni in 1876 and his results provided the first evidence that changes occur in the spectrum of a nova during its fading phase. He also began an extensive study of the solar spectrum, but the results of his painstaking measurements were soon superseded by more precise tables compiled by using diffraction gratings. At this point in his career Vogel decided to specialize in spectroscopy, and in response to a proposal made by Angelo Secchi he examined the spectra of some 4,000 stars. His original intention was to classify the stars according to their spectra, a procedure which he believed would reflect their stage of development. However, he became dissatisfied with his findings and abandoned this work to pursue a problem that had intrigued him since his days at Bothkamp Observatory – measuring the Doppler shift in the spectral lines of stars to ascertain their velocity.

Vogel's use of photography to record stellar spectra led to his most sensational discovery – spectroscopic binary stars. His success was based on a study of the periodic displacements of the spectral lines of the stars Algol and Spica, eclipsing binary stars whose components could not, at the time, be detected as separate entities by optical means. From his spectrographs, Vogel derived the dimensions of this double star system, the diameter of both components, the orbital velocity of Algol, the total mass of the system and in 1889, he derived the distance between the two component stars from each other.

Vogel's work ended the controversy over the value of Doppler's theory for investigating motion in the Universe. His discovery of spectroscopic binary stars not only led to the realization that such systems are a relatively common feature of the Universe; it also played an important role in the discovery of interstellar calcium absorption lines.

Vorontsov-Vel'iaminov, Boris Aleksandrovich (*1904–*), is one of the most prominent Soviet astronomers and astrophysicists. He was born on 14 February 1904 and since 1934 has been Professor at the University of Moscow. Besides being the author of several successful textbooks on astronomy, he has compiled astronomical catalogues and published several advanced specialized tests. In 1962 he was honoured by being awarded the Bredikhin Prize.

In 1930, independently of Robert Trumpler (1886–1956), Vorontsov-Vel'iaminov demonstrated the occurrence of the absorption of stellar light by interstellar dust. This fact had not been taken into consideration in 1922 by Jacobus Kapteyn (1851–1922) in his model of the Universe,

one of the most serious flaws in his calculations. The significance of Vorontsov-Vel'iaminov's discovery was that it became possible to determine astronomical distances and, in turn, the size of the Universe more accurately.

Vorontsov-Vel'iaminov has devoted considerable energy to the study of gaseous nebulae, the observations of novae and analysis of the Hertzsprung–Russell diagram, with reference to the evolution of stars. He has made particularly important contributions to the study of the blue-white star sequence, which was the subject of a book he published in 1947.

In 1959 Vorontsov-Vel'iaminov compiled a list and recorded the positions of 350 interacting galaxies which are clustered so closely that they seem to perturb each other slightly in structure. Besides this catalogue, he compiled a more extensive catalogue of galaxies in 1962, in which he listed and described more than 30,000 examples.

Weizsäcker, Carl Friedrich von (*1912–*), is a theoretical physicist who has made fundamental contributions to astronomy by investigating the way in which energy is generated in the cores of stars. He is also known for his theory on the origin of the Solar System.

Weizsäcker was born in Kiel, Germany, on 28 June 1912. He earned his PhD at the University of Leipzig in 1933 and from 1934 to 1936 he was an assistant at the Institute of Theoretical Physics there. He worked at the Kaiser Wilhelm Institute of Physics in Berlin-Dahlem and lectured at the University of Berlin from 1936 to 1942, when he was appointed to a chair at the University of Strasbourg. Weizsäcker returned to the Kaiser Wilhelm Institute in 1944. During World War II, he was a member of the German research team investigating the feasibility of constructing nuclear weapons and harnessing nuclear energy. One of his overriding concerns in this work was that his team should not develop a nuclear weapon which might be placed at the disposal of the Nazi government.

In 1946 Weizsäcker became Director of a department in the Max Planck Institute of Physics in Göttingen, holding an honorary professorship at the University of Göttingen. He became Professor of Philosophy at the University of Hamburg in 1957 and retired in 1969 with an appointment to an honorary chair at the University of Munich. Since 1970 he has been a Director of the Max Planck Institute. He is the author of numerous books on scientific and philosophical subjects and is a member of many scientific academies.

In 1938, Weizsäcker and Hans Bethe independently proposed the same theory of stellar evolution, one which accounted both for the incredibly high temperatures in stellar cores and for the production of ionizing and particulate radiation by stars. They proposed that hydrogen atoms fused to form helium via a proton-proton chain. Bethe and his collaborators went on to outline the complex of reactions which might follow to produce the energy created by a star. Weizsäcker turned to a study of the atomic reactions which take place in the fission of uranium and the problems of constructing an atomic pile.

In 1944 Weizsäcker revived an old cosmogenic theory, the so-called "nebular hypothesis" of Kant and Laplace, which had carried much weight during the nineteenth century, but which by the end of the century had given way to the "collision" theory. The collision theory proposed that planets were produced after another star approached our Sun so closely that a proportion of the solar mass became detached in the form of a whisp of hot gas and dust and then coalesced to form the planets. The chief difficulty with this theory was that, since stellar interactions of that nature must be exceedingly rare, planetary systems must be exceedingly uncommon in the Universe. Furthermore, the stability of the solar material disturbed in such a manner was unlikely to be sufficient to permit the formation of planets.

Weizsäcker suggested that multiple centres, or vortices, formed in the spinning gaseous discoid mass which precede our Solar System and that from them the planets condensed. This model indicated that planetary systems were formed as a natural byproduct of stellar evolution, and that they were therefore not likely to be so rare as would have been predicted by the collision theory.

Weizsäcker's other research has dealt with topics in atomic and nuclear physics and philosophy.

Whipple, Fred Lawrence (*1906-*), is an American astronomer known for his discoveries of comets and his contribution to the understanding of meteorites.

Whipple was born in Red Oak, Iowa, on 5 November 1906. He was educated in California and received his bachelor's degree from the University of California at Los Angeles in 1927; he went on to become a teaching Fellow at the University of California at Berkeley. He spent some time at the Lick Observatory, and received his PhD in 1931. In the same year he was appointed to the staff of the Harvard College Observatory

and a year later he became an Instructor at Harvard. He was gradually promoted to posts of increasing responsibility until, in 1950, he was made Professor, a post he held until 1977. During World War II, Whipple carried out radar research at the Office of Scientific Research and Development, and in 1948 he was awarded the Presidential Certificate of Merit for his work there. He also held a number of advisory posts on scientific bodies such as the Rocket and Satellite Research Panel. In 1955 he became Director of the Smithsonian Institution Astrophysics Observatory, a post he retained until 1973, when he became the Senior Scientist at the Observatory. He was awarded the Donahue Medal six times and in 1971 he received the Kepler Medal of the American Association for the Advancement of Science.

In addition to discovering six new comets, Whipple contributed to the understanding of the constitution and behaviour of comets. In 1949 he produced the "icy comet" model. He proposed that the nucleus of a comet consisted of a frozen mass of water, ammonia, methane and other hydrogen compounds and that, embedded within it was a quantity of silicates, dust and other materials. As the comet's orbit brought it nearer to the Sun, solar radiation would cause the frozen material to evaporate, thus producing a large amount of silicate dust which would form the comet's tail. This explanation has found general acceptance among astronomers.

Whipple has also worked on ascertaining cometary orbits and defining the relationship between comets and meteors. His other interests include the evolution of the Solar System, stellar evolution and planetary nebulae. He actively participated in the organization of the International Geophysical Year in 1957-58 and since the 1950s he had been extremely active in the programme to devise effective means of tracking artificial satellites.

Wilson, Robert Woodrow (*1936-*), is an American radio-astronomer who, with Arno Penzias (1933-), detected the cosmic microwave background radiation, which is thought to represent a residue of the primordial "Big Bang" with which the Universe is believed to have begun.

Wilson was born on 10 January 1936. He studied at Rice University and earned his bachelor's degree in 1957. He began postgraduate research at the California Institute of Technology and was awarded his PhD in 1962. In 1963 he joined the technical staff of the Bell Telephone Laboratories in Holmdel, New Jersey; he was made Head of the Radio-physics Department in 1976. Wilson detected the "three-degree background radiation" in 1965, only two years after he began working at the Bell Telephone Laboratories, and the sensational news of this discovery rapidly earned him international acclaim. He was awarded the Henry Draper Award of the National Academy of Sciences in 1977 and the Herschel Award of the Royal Astronomical Society in the same year. He received the 1978 Nobel Prize in Physics, jointly with Penzias and Pyotr Kapitsa (1894–), for their work on microwave radiation.

Some of the earliest quantitive work on the "Big-Bang" hypothesis, the theory of the origin of the Universe, was proposed and carried out by Ralph Alpher, Hans Bethe and George Gamow in 1948. They predicted the existence of isotropic cosmic background radiation, at a temperature of 25 K. But this estimate, which turned out to be too high, could not be confirmed at the time, because the radio wavelengths in the shorter range of the radio spectrum would have been swamped by other sources and radio astronomy had not been developed sufficiently to be applied to this problem. The theory required a number of modifications and so its prediction of microwave radiation was soon forgotten as other issues assumed more importance in astronomy.

In 1964, Wilson and Penzias tested a radio telescope and receiver system for the Bell Telephone Laboratories with the intention of tracking down all possible sources of static that were causing interference in satellite communications. They found a high level of isotropic background radiation at a wavelength of 7.3 cm, with a temperature of 3.1 ± 1K (their initial result had been a temperature of 3.5K). This radiation was a hundred times more powerful than any that could be accounted for on the basis of any known sources.

As they could not explain this residual signal, Wilson and Penzias contacted Robert Dicke (1916–), at Princeton University, who was also interested in microwave radiation. Independently of Gamow, Dicke had followed a somewhat different line of reasoning to predict that microwave radiation, which was the remnant of the tremendous heat generated by the primordial fireball, was theoretically detectable. At the time his research team was constructing a radio telescope designed specifically to pick up radiation at a wavelength of 3.2 cm. When he heard of Wilson's and Penzias' observations, he immediately realized that their findings confirmed his predictions. The discovery of microwave radiation by Wilson and Penzias was almost a repeat of Karl Jansky's discovery, also at the Bell Telephone Laboratories, of radio-astronomy itself in the 1930s.

Microwave radiation has since become the subject of intense investigation. Its spectrum appears to conform closely with that of black-body tion and its temperature is only three degrees above absolute zero ($-273°C$). It is thought to be the direct consequence of an explosively expanding Universe; the temperature theoretically decreases as the Universe continues to expand. Radio-astronomers continue to scrutinize this radiation for any evidence of anisotropy which may indicate an unsuspected pattern of distribution of matter in the Universe.

Wolf, Maximilian Franz Joseph (*1863–1932*), was a German astronomer particularly noted for his application of photographic methods to observational astronomy.

Wolf was born in Heidelberg on 21 June 1863. He was fascinated by astronomy from an early age and his father, who was fairly wealthy, built a small observatory for him in 1885 which he used for most of his research until 1896. He studied at the University of Heidelberg and was awarded his PhD in 1888 for a thesis on celestial mechanics. He then spent a year in Stockholm, before returning to Heidelberg to join the staff of the University there as a lecturer. In 1893 he travelled to the United States and was then appointed Extraordinary Professor of Astrophysics at Heidelberg. With the assistance of wealthy benefactors, Wolf supervised the construction of a new observatory at Königstuhl, near Heidelberg. He was appointed Director of the Observatory in 1896 and made Professor of Astronomy in 1901. Wolf held both of these posts until his death, on 3 October 1932, in Heidelberg.

Wolf made his first important astronomical discovery in 1883, when he observed a comet which has an orbital period of 7.7 years. In Wolf's honour it now bears his name. He devoted much of his time to developing new photographic methods for application to astronomy. One of his most successful innovations was a technique for discovering large numbers of asteroids. Until this time, asteroids had always been discovered visually, the first, Ceres, being noticed by Giuseppe Piazzi (1747–1826) in 1801; more and more of these bodies had gradually been discovered over subsequent years. Wolf arranged for time-lapse photographs to be taken, using a camera mounted on a telescope whose clock mechanism followed as exactly as possible the proper motions of the "fixed stars". On the developed plate, the stars would appear as discrete spots – the size being a function of the star's magnitude – whereas any asteroids present would appear as short streaks in the foreground.

The first asteroid Wolf discovered using this technique was number 323, afterwards named Brucia. He subsequently discovered more than

200 other asteroids using the same method. In September 1903, he discovered a special asteroid, number 588, later named Achilles.. Its particular significance was that it was the first of the so-called "Trojan satellites" whose orbits are in precise synchrony with that of Jupiter's; they form a gravitationally stable configuration between Jupiter and the Sun. The possibility of the existence of this kind of triangular three-bodied system was first analysed and predicted theoretically by Lagrange in the 1770s and Wolf's discovery of the "Trojan satellites" provided the observational evidence to substantiate Lagrange's theory.

Wolf also detected several new nebulae, both within the Milky Way and outside our Galaxy. Independently of Edward Barnard (1857–1923) he discovered that the dark "voids" in the Milky Way are in fact nebulae which are obscured by vast quantities of dust and he studied their spectral characteristics and distribution. Among the nebulae that Wolf himself discovered is the North America Nebula (NCG 7000), which resembles that continent in shape and is found in the constellation of Cygnus.

Wolf, with Pulfrich, invented the stereo-comparator, which was used for various kinds of observational astronomy. He also carried out research on the sunspot cycle and was the first to observe Halley's Comet when it approached the Earth in 1909. Besides being a keen observational astronomer and a dedicated and inspiring teacher, Wolf is best remembered for his innovative photographic techniques which led to the discovery of many new asteroids.

Woolley, Richard van der Riet (*1906–*   ), is a British astronomer, best known for his work on the dynamics of the Galaxy, observational and theoretical astrophysics, and stellar dynamics.

Woolley was born in Weymouth, Dorset, on 24 April 1906, his father being Rear-Admiral Charles Woolley. He was educated at Allhallows School, Honiton, and at the Universities of Cape Town and Cambridge. He was a Commonwealth Fund Fellow at Mount Wilson Observatory from 1929 to 1931 and an Isaac Newton Student at Cambridge from 1931 to 1933, when he was appointed Chief Assistant at the Royal Observatory, Greenwich. He remained at Greenwich for four years, until he was appointed First Assistant Observer – John Couch Adams Astronomer – at the University Observatory in Cambridge. In 1939 he became the Director of the Commonwealth Observatory at Mount Stromlo, Canberra, Australia. Finally, in 1955, Woolley was appointed as the eleventh Astronomer Royal, succeeding Spencer-Jones at the Royal Observatory; he retained this position until his retirement

in 1970. But even after his retirement, he took up the post of first Director of the South African Astronomical Observatory until he reached the age of 70. He received a knighthood in 1963 and was President of the Royal Astronomical Society from 1963 to 1965, receiving its Gold Medal in 1971.

While Woolley was Chief Assistant at the Royal Observatory, he became well acquainted with the more traditional aspects of astronomy. His duties included meridian astronomy with the Airy Transit Circle, time service control with small reversible transits and pendulum clocks, double star observations, solar spectroscopy and spectrohelioscope observations. The Observatory at Mount Stromlo was devoted mainly to solar physics and so while he was Director there he devoted much of his time to the study of photospheric convection, emission spectra of the chromosphere, and the solar corona. Besides these investigations, he pioneered the observation of monochromatic magnitudes and constructed colour magnitude arrays for globular clusters. Under Woolley's control, the Commonwealth Observatory grew in stature and its equipment was updated to include a 74-inch (188 cm) reflecting telescope.

When Woolley was appointed Astronomer Royal, the Royal Observatory had recently been moved from Greenwich to Herstmonceux in Sussex. At the time of his appointment the establishment seemed to lack purpose and direction; observations were being amassed using obsolete equipment and methods that had been devised by George Airy (1801–1892) many years before. Woolley's first priorities were to press for an agreement on the design of the new Isaac Newton Telescope and to redistribute resources for astrophysical research projects. During the 15 years that he spent as Astronomer Royal he was noted for the balance that he maintained between theoretical studies and observational astronomy. His personal interests during this period were globular clusters, evolution of galactic orbits, on improvements of radial velocities and a re-evaluation of RR Lyrae luminosities. He appointed several physicists to the staff whose studies involved galactic cluster fields, elemental abundance and the evolution of galaxies.

Wright, Thomas (*1711–1786*), was an English philosopher whose interests spread over a wide range of subjects, including astronomy; some of his theoretical work in astronomy anticipated modern discoveries.

Wright was born in Byer's Green, near Durham, on 22 September 1711. He left school at the age of 13 to take up an apprenticeship, which he did not complete, with a clock-maker. Although he was interested in instrument-making, he held a number of jobs outside this field. His most successful work was as a private mathematics teacher and lecturer on popular scientific subjects. In 1742 he was offered the Chair of Mathematics at the Academy of Sciences at St Petersburg (now Leningrad). He refused this position, however, on the grounds that the salary offered was inadequate. He spent the rest of his days in Byer's Green as a writer and a teacher. He died on 25 February 1786.

The main drive behind most of Wright's scientific work was his desire to reconcile his religious beliefs with his telescopic observations and with the knowledge he obtained through his extensive reading. In his early works Wright described the Universe as a series of concentric spheres – hardly an original concept – in which the centre was occupied by some divine power. Then in 1750 he wrote his most influential book, *An Original Theory or New Hypothesis of the Universe*. It did not express his final thoughts on the subject. He wrote another manuscript on the subject, but it was never published. His first essay was, however, a classic work and it created sufficient interest to warrant a new edition to be published in the United States (Philadelphia) in 1937. In it, Wright describes the Milky Way as a flattened disc, in which the Sun does not occupy a central position. Furthermore, he stated that nebulae lay outside the Milky Way. These views were more than 150 years ahead of their time and did not become accepted by the scientific community until they were substantiated by observational evidence in the 1920s.

However, Wright's model does not completely conform with modern views because he persisted in his belief that the centre of the system was occupied by a divine presence. Wright's other work included thoughts on the particulate nature of the rings of Saturn, anticipating the writings of James Clerk Maxwell (1831–1879) by nearly a century, and thoughts on such diverse fields as architecture and reincarnation.

Young, Charles Augustus (*1834–1908*), was an American astronomer who made some of the first spectroscopic investigations of the Sun.

Young was born in Hanover, New Hampshire, on 15 December 1834. From the age of 14 he was educated at Dartmouth College in Hanover, and he graduated in 1852. Initially his ambitions lay

elsewhere and it may only have been family tradition that eventually drew Young towards a career in astronomy. His maternal grandfather, Ebenezer Adams, had held the Chair in Mathematics and Philosophy at Dartmouth College and had been succeeded to the Chair by his son-in-law, Ira Young, in 1833, the year before Charles was born, Young's first appointment was at the Phillips Academy, Massachusetts, teaching classics. In 1855 he enrolled, part-time, at the Andover Theological Seminary to train as a missionary. He abandoned this idea a year later, however, when he became Professor of Mathematics and Natural Philosophy at the Western Reserve College in Hudson, Ohio. Apart from a brief interlude during the American Civil War, Young stayed at the Western Reserve College until 1866, when he accepted the Chair at Dartmouth College that had previously been held by his father and grandfather. Eleven years later Young moved from Hanover to the College of New Jersey, which has since become Princeton University. Three years after retiring from his post at Princeton he died, at Hanover, on 3 January 1908.

Most of Young's serious researches in astronomy were carried out during his years at Dartmouth College. The facilities and modern equipment provided by the College inspired Young's interest in the recently developed field of spectroscopy. He was particularly interested in the Sun and many of his investigations were carried out during solar eclipses. He was the first person to observe the spectrum of the solar corona and he also discovered the reversing layer in the solar atmosphere in which the dark hues of the Sun's spectrum are momentarily reversed, but only at the moment of a total solar eclipse. Young published a series of papers relating his spectroscopic observations of the solar chromosphere, solar prominences and sunspots. He also compiled a catalogue of bright spectral lines in the Sun and used these to measure its rotational velocity.

Besides his solar research, Young wrote several excellent textbooks that introduced astronomy to succeeding generations of astronomers. His first book, *General Astronomy*, was published in 1888 and a more basic text for younger students, *Lessons in Astronomy*, was published in 1891. By 1910, 90,000 copies of these two books had been sold, making them best-sellers of their day. Young's most famous work was his *Manual Astronomy* (1902), which was aimed at a more intermediate level. It was so popular that it underwent numerous reprints and in 1926 was republished in an edition revised by Henry Russell (1877–1957).

Z

Zel'dovich, Yakov Borisovich (*1914–*), is a Soviet astrophysicist who was originally a specialist in nuclear physics, but who became interested in particle physics and cosmology during the 1950s.

Zel'dovich was born in Minsk on 18 March 1914. He studied at the University of Leningrad, and when he graduated in 1931 he began his work at the Soviet Academy of Sciences in the Institute of Chemical Physics. He was made a Corresponding Member of the Academy of Sciences in 1946 and became a full Academician in 1958. During World War II he contributed research towards the war effort and was awarded the Stalin Prize in 1943. He now works at the Institute of Cosmic Research at the Space Research Institute of the Soviet Academy of Sciences in Moscow.

During the 1930s Zel'dovich participated in a research programme that was aimed at discovering the mechanism of oxidation of nitrogen during an explosion, and he and his colleagues reported the results of this work in a book published in 1947. During the 1940s he also maintained an interest in, and wrote about, the chemical reactions of explosions, the subsequent generation of shock-waves and the related subjects of gas dynamics and flame propagation. Zel'dovich, together with Y.B. Khariton, participated in the early work on the mechanism of fission during the radioactive decay of uranium, one of the most significant discoveries of the late 1930s. Their calculations on the chain reaction in uranium fission were published in 1939 and 1940. Besides this, Zel'dovich was also interested in the role played by slow neutrons in the fission process.

It was not until the 1950s that he began to develop an interest in cosmology and since then Zel'dovich's writings have dealt with such diverse subjects as quark annihilation, neutrino detection, and the applicability of relativistic versus Newtonian theories to the study of the expanding and evolving Universe and the earliest stages of the Universe – the quantum, hadron and lepton eras. In 1967, together with C.W. Misher, A.G. Doroshkevich and I.D. Novikov, he proposed that in its initial stages the Universe was highly isotropic, but that as it has expanded, this isotropy has diminished.

Zel'dovich is a prolific writer and has carried out extensive research in the fields of physics and astronomy. His recent cosmological theories have led to more accurate determinations of the abundance of helium in older stars.

Zwicky, Fritz (*1898–1974*), was a Swiss astronomer and astrophysicist who was distinguished for his discoveries of supernovae, dwarf galaxies and clusters of galaxies and also for his theory on the formation of neutron stars.

Zwicky was born in Varna, Bulgaria, but his parents were Swiss and he retained his Swiss nationality throughout his life. He was educated in Switzerland, gaining his BA and his PhD by 1922 from the Federal Institute of Technology at Zurich. He was awarded a Fellowship from the International Education Board in 1925 and left Switzerland for the United States to join the California Institute of Technology. He was appointed Assistant Professor at Caltech in 1927 and continued to work there until his retirement in 1968, by which time he had been promoted to the position of Professor of Astronomy. After his retirement, Zwicky continued to live in the United States. He received the Royal Astronomical Society's Gold Medal in 1973. He died on 8 February 1974.

Zwicky began his research by scouring our neighbouring galaxies for the appearance of a supernova explosion, hoping to discover one that was bright enough for its spectrum to be studied. But since the time when Johannes Kepler and Tycho Brahe observed their rare sightings of such events, no other supernovae have been seen to appear in our Galaxy. Zwicky therefore calculated that only one supernova appears every three or four hundred years in any galaxy. He was among the first to suggest that there is a relationship between supernovae and neutron stars. He suggested that the outer layers of a star that explodes as a supernova leave a core that collapses upon itself as a result of gravitational forces. He put forward this theoretical model in the early 1930s, when there seemed to be no hope of actually observing such a phenomenon.

In 1936 Zwicky began a study of galaxy clusters. He used the 18-inch (46cm) Schmidt telescope at Mount Palomar Observatory to photograph large areas of the sky. This telescope was specially designed to provide a relatively wide field of view, so that a large portion of the sky could be viewed at one glance without sacrificing a high resolution of separate images. Zwicky observed that most galaxies occur in clusters, each of which contains several thousand galaxies. The nearest is the Virgo cluster, which is also the most conspicuous of large clusters. It contains a number of spiral galaxies and Zwicky's spectroscopic studies of the Virgo and the Coma Berenices clusters showed that there is no evidence of any systematic expansion or rotation of clusters. Zwicky also calculated that the distribution of galaxies in the Coma Berenices cluster was similar, at least statistically, to the distribution of molecules in a gas when its temperature is at equilibrium. He compiled a six-volume catalogue of galaxies and galaxy clusters in which he listed 10,000 clusters located north of declination −30 degrees. He completed the catalogue shortly before his death and it is still generally regarded as the classic work in this field.

Zwicky's research interests were not limited to astronomy, but extended to the study of crystal structure, superconductivity, rocket fuels, propulsive systems and the philosophy of science. But his work on galaxies, galaxy clusters, interstellar matter and supernova stars outweighs these other interests in importance and has made a vital contribution to the field of astronomy.

Glossary

aberration Defect in the image formed by a lens, mirror or optical system. Spherical aberration results when different rays of light are brought to more than one focus, producing a blurred image or COMA; chromatic aberration when different wavelengths within a ray of light are brought to more than one focus, producing an image distorted by coloured fringes. Aberration in lenses can be overcome by the use of an ACHROMATIC LENS or a combination of lenses made of glasses of different REFRACTIVE INDICES.

aberration of light from the stars Difference in a star's apparent position in the sky from the apparent position it would have if the Earth were stationary. Such displacement caused by the Earth's SIDEREAL motion results in an optical positioning difference of up to about 20.5 seconds of arc, much greater than any displacement observed by PARALLAX.

ablation In astronomy, progressive burning away of the outer layers (e.g. of a meteor) by friction with the atmosphere.

absolute magnitude The MAGNITUDE of a celestial body as would be apparent from a standard distance of 10 PARSECS. An absolute magnitude of 0.0 represents an actual LUMINOSITY of 95 times that of the Sun.

absorption trough Range of WAVELENGTHS (around 21 cm) at which atomic hydrogen absorbs (or emits) radiation; this is a concept used in the attempt to detect INTERGALACTIC MATTER.

abundance of helium *See* HELIUM ABUNDANCE.

accretion Collection of material together, generally to form a single body.

achromatic lens Lens (or combination of lenses) that brings different WAVELENGTHS within a ray of light to a single focus, thus overcoming chromatic ABERRATION. It was first successfully made by Joseph von Fraunhofer.

aeon (or eon) In astronomical terms, 1,000 million years.

age of the Universe Now reckoned to be about 10,000 million Earth-years.

α-β-γ Theory Explanation of the BIG-BANG THEORY in terms of nuclear physics, proposed by Ralph Alpher, Hans Bethe and George Gamow in 1948; it was later slightly corrected by Chushiro Hayashi.

Alpha Centauri Bright binary star in which both components contribute to a magnitude of −0.27; it is also the nearest of the bright stars (at a distance of 4.3 light years).

alpha (particle) decay Spontaneous emission by a heavier element (such as uranium) of positively charged helium nuclei – alpha particles – comprising 2 PROTONS and 2 NEUTRONS. The result of this radioactive decay is that the original element is very gradually converted into another element, with a decreased atomic number and mass. Alpha particle emission may be simultaneous with BETA PARTICLE DECAY.

Almagest Arabic title for Ptolemy of Alexandria's *Syntaxis*, the writings in which he combined his own astronomical researches with those of others. Although much of the work is inaccurate even in premise, until Nicolaus Copernicus published his results fourteen centuries later the *Almagest* remained the standard reference source in Europe.

alt-azimuth Comprising a means of measuring or precisely locating in co-ordinates the position of objects at any ALTITUDE or AZIMUTH. The term is now used mainly to describe a type of mounting for a telescope.

altitude Angular distance above the horizon.

Andromeda (Spiral) galaxy The largest GALAXY in the LOCAL GROUP, also known as the Great Spiral and M31. It is about one and a half times the size of our own GALAXY, and contains at least 300 GLOBULAR CLUSTERS. Two smaller, elliptical galaxies lie close to it.

antimatter Atomic particles that have the same mass as, but opposite charge and orbital direction to, an ordinary particle. Thus, instead of negatively-charged ELECTRONS, atoms of antimatter have POSITRONS. A quantity of antimatter coming into contact with matter would "cancel out" – annihilate, with total conversion of mass to energy – an exact proportion of matter corresponding to the original quantity of antimatter, provided that the elements in the matter also corresponded with the "elements" in the antimatter, i.e. that the atoms were equivalent but opposite.

aphelion Point representing the greatest distance from the Sun of a body in an elliptical orbit.

Apollo space programme Successful US LUNAR exploration programme, in which *Apollo* spacecraft 1 to 6 were unmanned and reconnoitred potential landing areas; 7 to 10 were manned but did not land; and 11, 12 and 14 to 17 landed and returned safely. (*Apollo* 13 was an aborted mission.) The first men to land on the Moon were Neil Armstrong and Edwin Aldrin, from *Apollo* 11, on 20 July 1969. The final *Apollo* flight (17) lasted from 7 to 19 December 1972, and left a considerable quantity of exploratory devices on the lunar surface.

Arcturus (Alpha Boötis) Major star in Boötes; its (apparent) magnitude is −0.06.

armillary sphere Ancient Greek, Arabic and medieval ALT-AZIMUTH device, comprising a calibrated ring fixed in the MERIDIAN plane, within which a second concentric ring, also calibrated, was mobile around a vertical axis.

asteroids Also called planetoids or minor planets, the asteroids are tiny planets most of which orbit the Sun between Mars and Jupiter. The largest – and the first discovered – is Ceres, with a diameter of 1,003 km. It is estimated that there may altogether be no fewer than 40,000. A few have very elliptical orbits and cross the orbits of several other (major) planets. One or two even have their own satellites (moons).

astrolabe Ancient Arabic and medieval ALT-AZIMUTH device comprising two or more flat, metal, calibrated discs, attached so both or all could rotate independently. For early navigators and astronomers it acted as star-chart, compass, clock and calendar.

astrology Divination using the positions of the planets, the Sun and the Moon as seen against the stars in the constellations of the ZODIAC – a "science" almost as old as *homo sapiens*. Although at one stage in history astrology and astronomy were almost synonymous, the latter has advanced so far during the last three centuries that the two now bear little relation to each other.

astronomical colour index Difference in a star's brightness when measured on two selected WAVELENGTHS, in order to determine the star's temperature. Cooler stars emit more light at longer wavelengths (and so appear redder than hot stars). Modern methods involve PHOTOELECTRIC FILTERING and the UBV SYSTEM.

astronomical unit (a.u.) Mean distance between the Earth and the Sun: 149,598,500 km.

astrophysics Combination of astronomy and various branches of physics.

atmosphere Mantle of gases round a star, planet or moon, sometimes even forming the apparent surface of the body. For a body to retain an atmosphere depends on the body's GRAVITY, and the temperature and composition of the gases. The atmosphere of the Earth is, by volume, 78% nitrogen and 21% oxygen (with 1% of other gases); mean atmospheric pressure at the surface is 10,330 kg/m², and is also referred to as 1 atmosphere.

a.u. *See* ASTRONOMICAL UNIT.

aurora Spectacular array of light in the night sky, caused by charged particles from the Sun hitting the Earth's upper atmosphere. The aurora borealis is seen in the north of the Northern Hemisphere; the aurora australis in the south of the Southern.

autumnal equinox *See* EQUINOXES.

axis Theoretical straight line through a celestial body, around which it rotates.

azimuth Directional bearing around the horizon, measured in degrees from north (0°).

background radiation Or background black-body radiation, is the ISOTROPIC residual MICROWAVE RADIATION in space left from the primordial BIG BANG. At a WAVELENGTH of 7 cm it represents a temperature of about 3K.

Baily's beads Bright "beads" of sunlight showing through the valleys between mountains on the rim of the Moon just before and just after a total ECLIPSE of the Sun, seen from Earth.

Barnard's star Star that had – until 1968 – the greatest known PROPER MOTION of any. Seen from the Earth it moves just over 10 seconds of arc per year, but even this is deceptive because it is approaching Earth at a rate estimated to be more than 100 km/sec. It is also one of the very few stars known (fairly conclusively) to have planets.

beta (particle) decay Spontaneous emission by a heavier element (such as uranium) of negatively charged ELECTRONS – beta particles. The result of this radioactive decay is that the original element is very gradually converted into another element. Beta particle emission may be simultaneous with ALPHA PARTICLE DECAY.

Betelgeux (Alpha Orionis) Brightest genuinely VARIABLE STAR in the sky.

Bethe–Weizsäcker cycle *See* PROTON-PROTON CYCLE.

Big-Bang Theory Theory originally proposed by Georges Lemaître but elaborated by George Gamow and the α-β-γ hypothesis, that the Universe began with the Big Bang, the superexplosion of all the matter now dispersing in the Universe. Since the nuclear physics involved has been explained, and various supporting evidence – notably HELIUM ABUNDANCE and the sources of radio emission – has been discovered, the theory is almost universally accepted (although at one time the STEADY STATE THEORY rivalled it in popularity).

binary star system Two stars that orbit around a common centre of mass; the shapes of such orbits vary enormously.

Black body In astronomy, a body with ideal properties of radiation absorption and emission, against which less perfect actual stars and celestial objects can be measured. Black-body radiation has a continuous spectrum governed solely by the body's temperature: for any particular temperature there is a specific wavelength at which radiation emission is greatest. (This can be depicted – and used – graphically.)

black hole A SINGULARITY in space, surrounded by an EVENT HORIZON, caused by the collapse of a small but massively dense star through the effects of its own increasing GRAVITY. By the time the state of singularity is reached, the remnants of the star may be minimal, but the gravitational force is so strong it prevents even light from escaping. Black holes may form the "power centres" of galaxies, thus explaining INFRARED radiation detected in several galactic centres. The properties of matter entering a black hole are the theme of John Wheeler's NO HAIR THEOREM.

blue dwarf, blue giant High-temperature stars (as opposed to red stars). Blue giants are generally on or near the MAIN SEQUENCE of the HERTZSPRUNG–RUSSELL DIAGRAM; blue dwarfs represent the very dense, but very small, near-final form of what was once a RED GIANT.

Bode's Law Or the Titius-Bode Rule, was first devised in 1772 and comprised the series $0 + 4/10$, $3 + 4/10$, $6 + 4/10$, $12 + 4/10$, $24 + 4/10$ and so on, which was found to describe fairly accurately the distance in ASTRONOMICAL UNITS of the then known planets from the Sun. After the discovery of Neptune (to which the "Law" does not apply at all), the Law was somewhat discredited, although later still, the positioning of Pluto (which corresponds approximately) made it seem possibly more than coincidental.

Bok's globules Small, circular dark spots in NEBULAE, with masses comparable to that of the Sun. They are possibly gas clouds in the process of condensing into stars.

Callisto Fifth (known) moon out from JUPITER, and its second largest.

Cambridge Catalogues The results of five intensive radio-astronomical surveys (1C, 2C, 3C, 4C and 5C) under the direction of Sir Martin Ryle and Anthony Hewish, during the 1950s, 1960s and 1970s, at Cambridge.

canals of Mars Mistranslation – and consequent misunderstanding – of an Italian description of the pattern or channels (*canali*) on the Martian surface. Giovanni Schiaparelli in writing his account was careful to say that terrestrial terms were used only for reference, but in the USA Percival Lowell and in France Nicolas Flammarion took his words literally, and elaborated upon them too, with the result that stories of Martian civilizations became popular. The fact remains, however, that there *are* waterway-like channels on Mars – but not many, and in any case much smaller than any feature that is discernible with terrestrial telescopes.

carbon-nitrogen cycle Use of carbon and nitrogen as intermediates in the NUCLEAR FUSION process of the Sun. Cooler stars undergo the proton-proton cycle.

Cassegrain (reflecting) telescope Telescope devised by Cassegrain in which an auxiliary convex mirror reflects the magnified image, upside down, through a hole in the centre of the main objective mirror – i.e. through the end of the telescope itself. It was, however, no improvement on the GREGORIAN TELESCOPE invented probably slightly earlier.

Cassini Division Gap between SATURN's Rings A and B.

celestial Of the heavens; in the sky; in space.

celestial equator Projection of the Earth's equator as a line across the sky (so that to an observer actually on the equator, such a line would pass through the ZENITH). The directional bearing of a star is given in terms of its RIGHT ASCENSION round the celestial equator.

celestial mechanics Study of the movements and physical interactions of objects in space; astrophysical mathematics.

Cepheid Type of regular VISIBLE STAR, of which the POWER–LUMINOSITY CURVE is particularly valuable in gauging distances in the Universe. On the HERTZSPRUNG–RUSSELL DIAGRAM they are found on what has become known as the Cepheid instability strip. They range, however, from massive young (POPULATION I) stars to old (POPULATION II) stars with comparatively low masses. Delta Cephei was the first of the type to be recognized, although they are now known to be located in many galaxies.

Chandrasekhar limit Mass less than which a star eventually evolves into a stable WHITE DWARF through using all its available energy, and above which it becomes a SUPERNOVA and then, probably, a NEUTRON STAR or, improbably, a white dwarf. The limit is now reckoned as 1.2 solar masses.

Chandrasekhar–Schönberg limit Mass above which the helium core of a star begins to contract (eventually to collapse altogether). The limit is now reckoned as 10 to 15 per cent of the star's total mass.

Cherenkov detector Apparatus through which it is possible to observe the existence and velocity of high-speed particles, important in experimental nuclear physics and in the study of COSMIC RADIATION. It was originally built to investigate the Cherenkov radiation effect, in which charged particles travel through a medium at a speed greater than that of light in that medium.

chromatic aberration See ABERRATION.

chromosphere (of the Sun) The part of the Sun's atmosphere immediately above the surface (the PHOTOSPHERE) and beneath the CORONA.

Clouds of Magellan See MAGELLANIC CLOUDS.

cluster Group of stars or of GALAXIES, usually with some recognizably systematic configuration. It appears that both types of cluster are a structural feature of the Universe, which form over the passage of time.

colour index See ASTRONOMICAL COLOUR INDEX.

coma Inherent optical distortion in REFLECTING TELESCOPES, with the effect of decreasing focal clarity away from the centre of an image. The corrective lens or plate invented by Bernhard Schmidt nullifies coma in Schmidt telescopes.

comet Small planetoid in highly elliptical orbit around the Sun. At its APHELION it is a frozen mass of water and other hydrogen compounds covered in space dust, up to a light-year away from the Sun; at PERIHELION it may be inside the orbit of VENUS and streaming a thawing "tail" of silicate dust behind it. (The tail - or tails - always points away from the Sun, and is made visible by reflected light.) There is now thought to be a "reservoir" of potentially cometary material orbiting the Sun at about 1 light-year's distance; gravitational PERTURBATIONS cause individual comets to leave the reservoir and assume an orbit.

companion star Either one of a BINARY STAR SYSTEM (although usually the less massive), sometimes only detectable by SPECTROSCOPY.

complex number astrophysics The basis of TWISTOR THEORY.

conservation of mass and energy Important physical principle and one of the basic laws of physics, stating that matter is neither created nor destroyed (although mass may become energy, the energy quantitatively represents the mass). One exception to this principle is a SINGULARITY; another follows from the theory of VIRTUAL PARTICLES.

constant of precession See PRECESSION OF THE EQUINOXES.

convection Process in the Sun (and possibly other stars) perphaps caused by SOLAR ROTATION, which produces the immensely powerful electrical and magnetic fields associated with SUNSPOTS.

Copernican model of the Universe HELIOCENTRIC model that replaced the geocentric PTOLEMAIC MODEL, and was thus a considerable improvement. The model, however, still involved EPICYCLES and the SPHERES.

corona of the Sun Upper atmosphere of the Sun, above the CHROMOSPHERE. Normally observable only during a total ECLIPSE, it has no definite shape or limit but merely rarefies into space in all directions. Its temperature in some regions reaches 1 million °C; it rotates synchronously with the PHOTOSPHERE.

coronagraph Device for studying the solar CORONA at any time of the day. It was first invented by Bernard Lyot.

cosmic censorship Theory that the hidden interior within all EVENT HORIZONS is the same and is always, necessarily, hidden.

cosmic radiation, cosmic rays High-speed particles that reach the Earth from outside the Solar System. Heavier cosmic ray particles – such as those sought in X-RAY ASTRONOMY – are ordinarily filtered out by the Earth's upper atmosphere.

cosmic year Time the Sun takes to "orbit" in GALACTIC ROTATION: about 225 million years.

cosmological principle Theory behind most modern interpretations of cosmology, effectively that the Universe is essentially the same everywhere.

Crêpe Ring Rather transparent inner ring (Ring C) of the SATURN ring system. Its diameter measures about 149,300 km.

Cygnus-A Source in the constellation Cygnus of strong radio emissions, possibly caused by the collisions of interstellar dust within two colliding GALAXIES. It was nevertheless identified optically in 1952 as a tiny area of magnitude 17.9.

declination Angular distance above (positive) or below (negative) the CELESTIAL EQUATOR. One of the co-ordinates, with RIGHT ASCENSION, that defines the position of a heavenly body.

deflection of light Gravitational effect that bends a ray of light. Such an effect was predicted within the GENERAL THEORY OF RELATIVITY, although previously considered impossible.

density The mean density of a celestial body is generally reckoned as its MASS divided by its volume, expressed either in comparison with the density of water, in kilograms per cubic metre, or in relation to some other known density. The mean density of the Earth is thus 5.5 times that of water, i.e. 5.5×10^3 kg m^{-3}, and is just less than four times that of the Sun. Yet the mean density of rocks at the surface is about half the overall mean value, and that of the Earth's central core is perhaps $2\frac{1}{2}$ times the overall value.

deuterium A "heavy" isotope of hydrogen; its atomic nucleus (deuteron) comprises one PROTON plus one NEUTRON (as opposed to hydrogen's single proton).

differential rotation Of a stellar cluster or galaxy, the "orbiting" of stars nearer the centre faster than those at the edge. Of a single body (such as the Sun or a gaseous planet), the axial rotation of equatorial latitudes faster than polar latitudes.

diffraction grating Polished metallic surface (usually a metallic mirror on a block of glass or quartz) on which has been ruled a great number (in thousands) of parallel lines, used to split light to produce a SPECTRUM.

Doppler effect, the Doppler shift Effect on the WAVELENGTHS of light (or sound) emitted by a source at a distance that is increasing or decreasing in relation to the observer. If the distance is increasing, the wavelengths shifts towards the "stretched" (the light received shifts towards the red end of the SPECTRUM; sound received goes down in pitch). If the distance is decreasing, the wavelengths are "squeezed" (the light received shifts towards the blue end of the spectrum; sound received goes up in pitch).

double star A "system" of two stars that appear – because of coincidental alignment when viewed from Earth – to be close together; it is, however, an optical effect only, and therefore not the same as a BINARY STAR SYSTEM (although until the twentieth century there were few means of distinguishing double and binary stars).

eccentricity In astronomy, the extent to which an elliptical orbit departs from a circular one. It is usually expressed as a decimal fraction, regarding a circle as having an eccentricity of 0.

eclipse Occultation of one celestial body by another which passes between it and the observer. The solar eclipse is caused by the passing of the Moon between the Sun and the Earth in this way; such an eclipse may be complete (total) or incomplete (partial). ECLIPSING BINARY stars also accord with this pattern. Alternatively – and exceptionally – a lunar eclipse is caused by the passage of the Earth between the Sun and the Moon, so that the Earth's shadow falls across the Moon, again either totally or partially, depending upon the position of the observer.

eclipsing binary A BINARY STAR of which, from the viewpoint of Earth, one of the two bodies regularly passes in front of the other. The resulting variation is perceived LUMINOSITY of some eclipsing binaries has led to their classification as VARIABLE STARS.

ecliptic Apparent linear path through the 12 constellations of the ZODIAC that the Sun seems to take during one Earth year, also representing therefore the "edge" of the plane of Earth's orbit. Because the equator of the Earth is at an angle of more than 22° to the plane of its orbit, the ecliptic is at the identical angle to the CELESTIAL EQUATOR, intersecting it at two points: the vernal and autumnal EQUINOXES.

electromagnetic radiation "Waves" of electrical and magnetic "disturbance", radiated as visible light, radio waves, or any other manifestation of the ELECTROMAGNETIC SPECTRUM. The distance between successive crests of each wave is known as the WAVELENGTH, and varies considerably between electromagnetic forms. The velocity of such radiation in a vacuum is the SPEED OF LIGHT. The units of electromagnetic radiation are quanta or photons ("packets" of energy).

electromagnetic spectrum Complete range of ELECTROMAGNETIC RADIATION, from very short-WAVELENGTH (high-frequency) gamma-rays, through X-rays and ultraviolet light to the small range of visible light, and further to infrared radiation, microwave, and the comparatively long-wavelength low-frequency radio waves.

electron Negatively charged fundamental particle (also called a beta particle) found in the atoms of all elements, where it "orbits" (at different energy levels and with different directions of spin) round the central nucleus. The combined charge of the orbiting electrons is balanced (in a neutral atom) by the charge of an equal number of positively charged PROTONS in the atomic nucleus. An electron is also the fundamental unit of electricity.

ellipticity Of the shape of a planet or GALAXY, the amount of distortion by which it departs from a perfect sphere. The overall ellipticity of the Earth is given as 1/299. One class of galaxy is defined in terms of ellipticity, subdivided E0 to E7, according to degree.

Encke's Division Gap within Saturn's Ring A.

epicycle Circular orbit of a body round a point that is itself in a circular orbit round a parent body. Such a system was formulated to explain some planetary orbits in the Solar System before they were known to be elliptical.

equinox One of two points in the sky that represent where the Sun appears to cross the plane of the Earth's equator. From the Earth's viewpoint, therefore, the Sun reaches one point at a quarter, the other at three-quarters, of the way through the SIDEREAL year: the vernal (spring) equinox is thus on or around 21 March, the autumnal on or around 22 September. The actual points in the sky change slightly every year through a process called PRECESSION.

escape velocity Speed a satellite must attain in order to free itself from returning to the parent body under the effects of GRAVITY.

event horizon The "edge" of a BLACK HOLE; the interface between four-dimensional space and a SINGULARITY.

Explorer **spacecraft** A US series of now well over 50 satellites, many of which remain in orbit round the Earth fulfilling scientific functions. *Explorer* 1 was in fact the first US orbital satellite (launched on 31 January 1958) and was instrumental in discovering the inner VAN ALLEN BELT.

faculae Bright areas on the face of the Sun, commonly in the vicinity of SUNSPOTS. Named by Johannes Hevelius, they are thought to be caused by luminous hydrogen clouds close to the PHOTOSPHERE. They last on average about 15 Earth-days.

fission In nuclear physics, the splitting of the atomic nucleus of a heavy element, resulting in the emission of nuclear energy and possibly causing a chain reaction (with similar results) within a mass of the element.

flare star Dim red dwarf star that suddenly lights up with great – but brief – luminosity, corresponding to an equally powerful but short-lived burst of radio emission. The cause is thought to be a sudden and intense outburst of radiation on or above the star's surface.

fusion In nuclear physics, the combining of the atomic nuclei of lighter elements to form nuclei of a heavier element. Such a process involving the atomic nuclei of elements lighter than iron is accompanied by the emission of energy; for fusion of heavier elements, energy must be supplied. The process is thought to contribute to the condensation of stars from interstellar gas and dust. *See also* NUCLEAR FUSION.

galactic centres Are now thought to comprise BLACK HOLES – which would explain why the centre of our Galaxy appears strangely obscure, and emits only INFRARED radiation.

galactic rotation The revolving of a galaxy round its central nucleus even as it continues its PROPER MOTION. Such rotation, however, is not uniform but DIFFERENTIAL. One revolution of the Sun within our own Galaxy takes about 225 million years, or 1 cosmic year.

galaxy Vast system of celestial objects, typically consisting of between 10^6 and 10^{12} stars, plus interstellar gas and dust. There are three basic types: spiral (further subdivided into normal spirals and spirals with a "bar" at the centre, and yet further subdivided according to the "openness" of the spiral arms), elliptical (subdivided according to ELLIPTICITY) and irregular (subdivided according to whether they are made up of POPULATION I or POPULATION II stars). Another not uncommon type of galaxy is a lenticular form mid-way between the spiral and the elliptical.

Galaxy System of approximately 100,000 million stars, of which our Sun is one. It is a normal spiral GALAXY of class Sb, with a diameter now reckoned to be probably less than 100,000 light-years, and a strong but obscure energy source at the centre (emitting INFRARED radiation). It is undergoing GALACTIC ROTATION. Possibly one tenth of the Galaxy's total MASS – estimated at 1.8×10^{11} solar masses – comprises interstellar gas and dust.

gamma ray Electromagnetic radiation similar to X-radiation, although of shorter wavelength, emitted spontaneously by some radioactive substances from atomic nuclei during radioactive decay.

gegenschein Faint oval patch of light visible from Earth only at certain times of the year, opposite the Sun. Its nature and cause are still not known. It is sometimes known as "counterglow".

General Theory of Relativity Theory formulated by Albert Einstein after his own SPECIAL THEORY OF RELATIVITY, founded upon an understanding of GRAVITATION as a curvature in four-dimensional space–time (rather than as a force existing between two masses). In proposing this new definition, Einstein had also to derive the four-dimensional structure of space–time. The theory is the basis of most modern research, although alternatives – such as TWISTOR THEORY – have been proposed since.

geocentric Having the Earth at the centre.

geodesy Measurement and study of the Earth's size and shape.

globular cluster Spherical, densely populated CLUSTER of older stars. There are a number of such clusters round the edge of our Galaxy.

grating *See* DIFFRACTION GRATING.

gravitational force, gravity As described first by Isaac Newton, gravity is a force that exists between bodies of any MASS whatever (from particles to stars) in proportion to the product of their masses, and in inverse proportion to the square of the distance between them. The weakest of the four natural forces (the other three being the electromagnetic and the two nuclear interactive forces), its real nature is still not fully understood. Einstein's GENERAL THEORY OF RELATIVITY presented another viewpoint.

greenhouse effect Retention and escalation of temperature beneath a mantle of clouds or denser atmosphere.

Greenwich Site now in London of the first ROYAL

GREENWICH OBSERVATORY, designed and built by
Christopher Wren in 1675.

Gregorian calendar Calendar established with
the authority of the Roman Catholic Church by
Pope Gregory XIII in 1582. Correcting at a
stroke the 10-day accumulated margin of error
of the JULIAN CALENDAR, the main difference was
in fact that century years were discounted as
leap years unless they were divisible by 400.

Gregorian (reflecting) telescope Telescope
devised – but never constructed – by James
Gregory, in which an auxiliary concave mirror
reflects the magnified image, the right way up,
through a hole in the centre of the main
objective mirror, i.e. through the end of the
telescope itself. The CASSEGRAIN TELESCOPE is
similar but produces an inverted image.

Halley's Comet Comet whose return in 1758 was
the first to be successfully predicted. With a
period of 76 years, its next return is due in 1986.

halo Nebulous quality round a celestial body
(particularly round a red giant); the galactic
halo, however, describes the spherical collection
of stars forming a surrounding "shell" for our
otherwise compact, discoid Galaxy.

heliocentric Having the Sun at the centre.

heliograph Device for recording the positions of
SUNSPOTS.

heliometer Instrument to measure the apparent
diameter of the Sun at different seasons, also
used to measure angular distances between stars.

helium Element which, after HYDROGEN, is the
second lightest and second most abundant in the
Universe. Its atom comprises two PROTONS, two
NEUTRONS and two ELECTRONS; its nucleus is
sometimes called an alpha particle. Helium is
the product of the NUCLEAR FUSION of hydrogen
in most stars, but this does not explain the
overall HELIUM ABUNDANCE.

helium abundance Presence – and dominance –
of HELIUM atoms in the Universe. The fact that
about 8% of *all* atoms are helium can be traced,
through the α-β-γ THEORY, to the primordial BIG
BANG.

Hertzsprung–Russell diagram (H/R diagram)
Graphic chart plotting the relationship between
the ABSOLUTE MAGNITUDE (implicating the MASS)
and the SPECTRAL CLASS (implicating the
temperature) of thousands of stars. The
majority of stars form a band from top left to
bottom right of the diagram, known as the MAIN
SEQUENCE. Various theories on the evolution of
stars relate to information contained in the
diagram.

high-energy particles Particles of
ELECTROMAGNETIC RADIATION that contain high
energies, measured in terms of electron volts.
The energy in gamma radiation is of the order of
8×10^7 to 8×10^5 electron volts and in X-rays of
8×10^3 to 8×10^1 electron volts.

hot big bang Later, but fundamental, concept
within the BIG-BANG THEORY, that the primordial
explosion occurred in terms of almost
unimaginable heat. The concept, formulated by
George Gamow, led to considerable study of
THERMONUCLEAR REACTIONS and the search for
BACKGROUND RADIATION.

Hubble's constant, Hubble's law States that the
more distant a GALAXY is, the greater is its speed
of RECESSION. The constant applies to the rate of
increase in that speed. It was originally
calculated as 530 km sec^{-1} per 10^6 parsecs, but
has since been estimated at about a tenth of that
value.

hydrogen Element that is the lightest and the
most abundant in the Universe. Its atom
comprises one PROTON and one ELECTRON. The
element occurs both in stars and as interstellar
clouds, in regions where it may be neutral (H I
regions) or ionized (H II regions).

inclination In astronomy, the angle between one
plane and another. The (equatorial) inclination
of a planet is the angle between the plane of its
equator and that of its orbit. The inclination of
the orbit of a planet in the Solar System other
than Earth is the angle between the plane of that
orbit and the ECLIPTIC.

inertia Property of a moving body to continue
moving at the same speed in the same direction
– or of a static body to remain static – unless
and until acted upon by some force for change.
The inertial mass of a body is reckoned as equal
to the body's gravitational mass.

infrared Part of the ELECTROMAGNETIC
SPECTRUM immediately below visible light (but
above microwave and radio waves). It therefore
comprises a range of radiation of longer
WAVELENGTH and lower frequency than those of
visible light, able also to convey greater heat
radiation.

intensity interferometry The use of two
telescopes linked by computer to study the
intensity of light received from a star. Analysis
of the combined results has enabled
measurement of the diameters of stars as
apparently small as 2×10^{-4} seconds of arc.

interferometry Technique for studying sources of
ELECTROMAGNETIC radiation (light or radio
waves) through interference patterns caused
when two waves are combined.

intergalactic matter Hypothetical material
within a CLUSTER of galaxies, whose
gravitational effect is to maintain the
equilibrium of the cluster. Theoretically
comprising 10–30 times the mass of the galaxies
themselves (in order to have the observed effect),

it has yet to be detected in any form – although the most likely form is as HYDROGEN.

interstellar hydrogen The presence of hydrogen gas between the stars of a GALAXY, thus "filling out" the shape of the galaxy in a way that can be detected by SPECTRAL analysis and radio monitoring.

interstellar space Space between the stars of a GALAXY. It is generally not, however, a void vacuum, and is the subject of considerable SPECTRAL research.

ionization Loss or gain by an atom of one or more ELECTRONS, by which process the atom becomes an ion and instead of being neutral, has a charge: positive if it has lost an electron, negative if it has gained one. High temperature is particularly conducive to ionization.

island Universe hypothesis Theory put forward by Edwin Hubble that the Universe is made up of "islands" of galaxies within a gigantic "sea" of void-vacuum space.

isotropic Having equal and uniform properties at all points and in all directions. In astronomy the term describes microwave BACKGROUND RADIATION.

Julian calendar Calendar established by Julius Caesar in 46 BC, which overestimated the duration of the SIDEREAL year by 11 minutes and 14 seconds. It was replaced, from 1582, by the GREGORIAN CALENDAR, by which time it was inaccurate by a total of 10 days.

Jupiter Fifth and largest major planet out from the Sun.

Kepler's Laws of Motion 1. A planet's orbit is elliptical round the Sun, with the Sun at one of the foci. 2. Planets accelerate when nearer the Sun, with the result that a radius vector (imaginary line joining planet and Sun) describes equal areas in equal times. 3. The square of the orbital period of a planet is proportional to the cube of its mean distance from the Sun.

kinematic relativity Theory proposed by Edward Milne as a viable alternative to Einstein's GENERAL THEORY OF RELATIVITY, and based generally on kinematics (the science of pure motion, without reference to matter or force), from which Milne successfully derived new systems of dynamics and electrodynamics.

Kirkwood gaps Several (apparent) zones in the asteroid belt free of ASTEROIDS, probably caused by the gravitational effects of Jupiter.

Kuiper bands Bands in the SPECTRA of Uranus and Neptune at WAVELENGTHS of 7,500 Å, indicating the presence of METHANE.

law of universal attraction Isaac Newton's formulation of the law of GRAVITY.

Leonid meteor shower Shower of meteors emanating from an apparent point in Leo every 33 years; the next is due in about 1999.

libration The "turning" of the Moon so that although the same face is presented to Earth at all times, the overall surface of the Moon visible is 59% of the total. Libration is described as latitudinal, longitudinal and diurnal.

light-year Distance travelled at the SPEED OF LIGHT for one Earth-year: 9.46 million million km.

lithium Lightest of all solid elements, third in the periodic table after HYDROGEN and HELIUM. Its atom comprises one PROTON and three ELECTRONS. One of the electrons is at a higher energy level than the other two.

Local Group of galaxies The CLUSTER of GALAXIES of which our own, the MILKY WAY, is one. Its radius is estimated at 10^6 parsecs. Largest of the Group is the ANDROMEDA SPIRAL GALAXY.

luminosity Brightness of a celestial body, measured in terms of (apparent) MAGNITUDE, ABSOLUTE MAGNITUDE, or using the Sun's brightness as 1 on a solar scale. The luminosity of a star corresponds with its internal RADIATION pressure, which in turn depends on its MASS.

lunar Of the Moon.

Magellanic Clouds Two relatively small, nebulous star CLUSTERS visible only in the Southern Hemisphere; the larger is, however, the brightest "nebular" object in the sky. Both are members of the LOCAL GROUP OF GALAXIES, and in fact seem to be associated, though detached, parts of the MILKY WAY system.

magnetosphere The extent of a planet's magnetic field. The Earth's magnetosphere is shaped roughly like a teardrop, with the point opposite the Sun; this is due to the effect of the SOLAR WIND.

magnitude The measured brightness of a celestial body. Dim objects have magnitudes of high numbers, bright objects have magnitudes of low or even negative numbers. Seen from Earth, stars of (apparent) magnitude 6 or higher cannot be detected with the naked eye. The Full Moon has a magnitude of -11, and the Sun one of -26.8. In order to standardize measurements of the brightness of more distant objects, the system of absolute magnitude is used. A measure of the radiation at *all* wavelengths emitted by a star is known as the bolometric magnitude.

Main Sequence Band that runs from top left to bottom right on the HERTZSPRUNG–RUSSELL DIAGRAM representing the majority of stars. Stars off the Main Sequence are in some way uncharacteristic and include RED GIANTS, BLUE DWARFS, CEPHEIDS and NOVAE.

Mariner **spaceprobes** Series of US spaceprobes launched to explore the planets of the Solar System, particularly Mercury, Venus and Mars.

Mars Fourth major planet out from the Sun.

mascons Abbreviated form of mass concentrations: apparent regions on the lunar surface where gravity is somehow stronger. The effect is presumed to be due to localized areas of denser rock strata.

mass The quantitative property of an object due to the matter it contains. (Weight, in contrast, describes a force with which a body is attracted towards a gravitational focus.) Units of mass are grams and kilograms.

mass of the Galaxy Now reckoned as 180,000 million (1.8×10^{11}) times that of the Sun.

Mercury First major planet out from the Sun.

meridian Theoretical north-south line on the Earth's surface, or an extension of that line onto the night sky, connecting the observer's ZENITH with the celestial pole and the horizon. The meridian is used to state directional bearings. Devices and structures – such as meridian arcs – marking the meridian were once common in observatories.

Messier Catalogue List of the locations in the sky of more than 100 GALAXIES and NEBULAE, compiled by Charles Messier between 1760 and 1784. Some designations he originated are still used in identification; M1 is the Crab Nebula (in Taurus).

meteor Fragment or particle that enters the Earth's atmosphere and is then destroyed through friction, becoming visible as this occurs as a momentary streak of light. At certain times of the year, meteors apparently emanating from a single area of the sky (a RADIANT) form meteor showers. They are thought to originate within the Solar System. *See also* METEORITE.

meteorite Object that enters the Earth's atmosphere and is too large to be totally destroyed by friction before it hits the surface. Meteorites may in some way be connected with ASTEROIDS. *See also* METEOR.

methane Gaseous carbon-hydrogen compound, one of the alkanes, in which every carbon atom is surrounded by four hydrogen atoms.

micrometer Device used in conjunction with a telescope in order to measure extremely small angular distances.

microwave radiation Radiation in the ELECTROMAGNETIC SPECTRUM between INFRARED and radio waves. This range has WAVELENGTHS of between about 20 cm and about 1 mm. Radiation of this type was detected as BACKGROUND RADIATION.

Milky Way Our own GALAXY, the second largest in the LOCAL GROUP.

minor planets *See* ASTEROIDS.

M numbers Refer to the MESSIER CATALOGUE.

Mizar A DOUBLE STAR in Ursa Major.

mural arc Sixteenth- to nineteenth-century astronomical apparatus comprising a carefully oriented wall on which a calibrated device was fixed, by which the altitudes of celestial objects could be measured.

NASA National Aeronautics and Space Administration, US government body set up in 1958, under which the Space Center at Houston, Texas, and the Space Center at Cape Canaveral, Florida, are responsible for manned and unmanned space flights.

nebula Cloud of interstellar gas and/or dust, but containing no actual stars. A spiral nebula, however, is a type of GALAXY, and a PLANETARY NEBULA is a type of star. Nebulae may in fact represent the initial form of a star CLUSTER (that may condense out of it) or the final form of a SUPERNOVA.

nebula variable stars Also called T Tauri variables, a type of VARIABLE STAR of SPECTRAL CLASSIFICATION F, G or K (giants above the MAIN SEQUENCE on the HERTZSPRUNG–RUSSELL DIAGRAM) that loses an appreciable proportion of its mass in its (irregular) more luminous periods, and is thus surrounded by volumes of gas and dust.

Neptune Eighth major planet out from the Sun, discovered in 1846 by Johann Galle and Louis d'Arrest following predictions calculated by Urbain Le Verrier. Similar predictions had been made a year earlier by John Couch Adams but were not followed up.

neutrino Elementary particle with no MASS and no electric charge. Neutrinos are usually detected through their power to change chlorine into argon. The Sun is said to give off great quantities of them, but experiments to trap them as they pass straight through the Earth have failed.

neutron Uncharged particle in the nucleus of all atoms except hydrogen. Through BETA DECAY, a neutron may become a PROTON and an ELECTRON; the process occurs in reverse during the formation of a NEUTRON STAR.

neutron star Remnant of a star after it has exploded as a SUPERNOVA. Usually optically dim, a neutron star sends out regular or irregular radio emissions and is therefore also called a pulsar. The density of such a star may be unimaginably great although the diameter is generally around only 10 km; the gravitational and magnetic forces are correspondingly vast. It is called a neutron star because in such density, PROTONS fuse with ELECTRONS to form NEUTRONS, of which the star is almost entirely composed.

No Hair Theorem Proposed by John Wheeler, it states that the only properties of matter conserved after entering a black hole are its MASS, its angular momentum and its electrical charge; it thus becomes neither matter nor ANTIMATTER.

North Polar sequence Or circumpolar stars, comprises those stars which never set, from the viewpoint of an observer on Earth.

nova Originally faint dwarf star which suddenly experiences a tremendous increase in LUMINOSITY, giving off enormous quantities of gas; the luminosity then fades away. Novae are now thought to be the result of collapsing BINARY SYSTEMS. A SUPERNOVA is thus not at all the same; PULSATING NOVAE, however, may form a link with VARIABLE STARS.

nuclear fusion Process by which the Sun (and other stars) radiates energy. The nucleus of an atom fuses with the nuclei of other atoms to form new, heavier atoms' at the same time releasing large amounts of energy. In the Sun, HYDROGEN atoms are converted into HELIUM by this process, with carbon and nitrogen as intermediates. Cooler stars undergo the PROTON-PROTON CYCLE with a similar result.

nucleosynthesis Cosmic production of all the species of chemical elements by large-scale nuclear reactions, such as those in progress in the Sun or other stars. One element is changed into another by reactions that change the number of protons or neutrons involved.

nutation Slight but recurrent oscillation of the axis of the Earth, caused by the Moon's minutely greater gravitational effect on the Earth's equatorial "bulge".

occultation Eclipse of a star by another celestial body.

Olbers' paradox The fact that the night sky is dark despite the presence of so many "suns". The reason now accepted is that it is caused as a byproduct of the RED SHIFT due to the stars' RECESSION.

opposition of a planet Occurs when the Earth comes directly between that planet and the Sun; it can thus only happen in relation to the SUPERIOR PLANETS and the ASTEROIDS.

parallax Angle subtended by the apparent difference in a star's position when viewed from the Earth either simultaneously from opposite sides of the planet, or half such an angle, measured after a gap of six months from opposite sides of the planet's orbit; the nearer the celestial body, the greater the parallax.

parsec Distance at which a celestial body would subtend an angle of one second of arc from a base line of one astronomical unit (i.e. the mean distance between the Earth and the Sun). One parsec is 3.26 light years.

penumbra Less than full shadow (umbra).

perihelion Point representing the nearest to the Sun that a body approaches in an elliptical orbit.

period–luminosity curve Graph depicting the variation in LUMINOSITY of a CEPHEID VARIABLE STAR with time. In general, the longer the period, the greater the luminosity. By measuring the period it is possible thus to derive an ABSOLUTE MAGNITUDE; comparison of this with the star's observed (apparent) MAGNITUDE gives an indication of the distance.

perturbation Apparent irregularity in an orbit, or occasionally in a star's PROPER MOTION, caused by the gravitational effects of a nearby celestial body.

phases Differences in the appearance of the Moon, in particular, but also of Mercury and Venus, caused by the Earth observer's seeing only a part of the body lit by the Sun.

photoelectric filtering Means of measuring the ASTRONOMICAL COLOUR INDEX of a star, involving colour filters on photoelectric cells to define the colour index between two set wavelengths. The filters correspond to the UBV PHOTOMETRY system.

photometry Measurement of the MAGNITUDES of celestial bodies, originally carried out by expertise of eye alone, but now generally utilizing photographic or photoelectric apparatus.

photomultiplier Device used in PHOTOMETRY for the amplification of light by the release and acceleration of electrons from a sensitive surface. The result is a measurable electric current that is proportional to the intensity of received radiation.

photon A "packet" or quantum of ELECTROMAGNETIC RADIATION.

photosphere of the Sun The solar "surface". Granular in appearance, it comprises spicules of gaseous HELIUM at an average temperature of 6,000°C. Each spicule averages 7,000 km in height, but lasts for less than 8 minutes. The SUNSPOTS are cooler depressions in the photosphere.

***Pioneer* spaceprobes** Series of US spaceprobes the first 9 of which concentrated predominantly on solar exploration and research. From then on, *Pioneer* probes have been sent to the outer planets of the Solar System.

planetary nebula Small, dense, hot star – neither a planet nor a NEBULA – that is surrounded by a spherical cloud of gas which it is shedding in the process of becoming a WHITE DWARF.

planetoids *See* ASTEROIDS.

plasma In astronomy, matter in which the constituent atoms are in a state of IONIZATION; i.e. it comprises positively charged PROTONS or atomic nuclei and negatively charged ELECTRONS moving freely.

Pluto Ninth major planet out from the Sun, discovered by Clyde Tombaugh in 1933.

polarimeter Device that measures the POLARIZATION of any form of ELECTROMAGNETIC RADIATION, particularly light.

Polaris (Alpha Ursa Minoris) Star visible to the naked eye that is at present nearest the North Pole (and therefore also known as the Pole Star). Very slightly variable, its apparent magnitude is 1.99, and its absolute magnitude is −4.6; it is about 680 light-years distant.

polarization of light Reduction of light, considered to travel in three-dimensional transverse waves (vibrating in all directions perpendicular to the direction in which it is travelling), to two dimensions. To achieve this a filter is used. The results may vary from a beam of light in which the waves vibrate in one plane only (plane-polarized light) to one in which the plane rotates but the amplitude is constant (circular polarization). Because light is also polarized by reflection, investigation of polarized light reflected from, for example, the lunar surface enables that surface to be analysed.

Population I stars Younger stars, generally formed towards the edge of a GALAXY, of the dusty material in the spiral arms, including the heavy elements. The brightest of this Population are hot, white stars.

Population II stars Older stars, generally formed towards the centre of a GALAXY, containing few heavier elements. The brightest of this Population are red giants.

positron The equivalent of a negatively charged ELECTRON in an ordinary atom of matter, the positron in an atom of ANTIMATTER is positively charged and spins in an opposite direction.

precession of the equinoxes Apparent movement per year of the two points in the sky representing the EQUINOXES: 50.26″ per year, also called the constant of precession. Precession is caused mainly by the gravitational effect of the Moon on the Earth's equatorial "bulge".

Principia Mathematica Short form of the title of Isaac Newton's great work, published in 1687; title also of the mathematically philosophical work of Bertrand Russell and Alfred North Whitehead, published in 1910-13.

Procyon Major star in Canis Minor; its (apparent) magnitude is 0.37. It has an extremely dim COMPANION, a WHITE DWARF.

proper motion Actual speed and direction in space of a celestial body, measurable only in relation to other celestial bodies.

proton Positively charged particle in the nuclei of all atoms. *See also* ELECTRON, NEUTRON.

proton-proton cycle Process of NUCLEAR FUSION by which relatively cooler stars produce and radiate energy; hotter stars commonly achieve the same result by means of the CARBON-NITROGEN CYCLE.

proto-planets Early stage in the formation of planets according to the theory by which planetary systems evolve through the condensation of gas clouds surrounding a young star. The theory is not, however, generally accepted.

proto-stars Early stage in the formation of stars according to the theory by which GLOBULAR CLUSTERS of stars evolve through the condensation of a vast (predominantly hydrogen) gas cloud, then to disperse and become POPULATION II STARS. The theory, propounded by William McCrea, has gained some acceptance.

Ptolemaic model of the Universe A GEOCENTRIC model in which the Earth remained stationary as the other planets, the Sun, the Moon and the stars orbited it on their SPHERES. It was eventually replaced by the COPERNICAN MODEL.

pulsar Now identified with a NEUTRON STAR.

pulsating (or recurrent) nova A VARIABLE STAR, probably not a true NOVA, in which the change between more and less luminous stages is extreme.

pulsating (or oscillating) Universe Theory that the Universe constantly undergoes a BIG BANG, expands, gradually slows and stops, contracts, and gradually accelerates once more to a Big Bang. Alternative theories include an ever-expanding Universe and the STEADY-STATE Universe.

quadrant Type of early sextant, with which the observer's latitude could be calculated.

quantum A "packet" of energy and a natural unit of electromagnetic radiation.

quark Fundamental particle of which PROTONS, NEUTRONS and ELECTRONS are now thought perhaps to be made up. There are possibly three or four types of quark. It is even possible that quarks themselves may be made up of still more fundamental particles.

quasar Celestial anomaly: a radio source, travelling at immense speed away from the Earth. It may be a type of GALAXY; it may also be "powered" by a BLACK HOLE at its nucleus. Because of its speed and the DOPPLER EFFECT, its ULTRAVIOLET radiation is seen on Earth as faint blue light.

quasi-stellar objects Type of QUASAR without radio radiation.

radial pulsation Periodic expansion and contraction of a star that may be merely an optical effect of RECESSION.

radial velocity Speed of a celestial body away from an observer (written as a minus quantity if the body is actually approaching).

radiant In astronomy, the point in the sky from which a METEOR shower appears to emanate.

radiation Emission of energy. *See also* ELECTROMAGNETIC RADIATION.

radiative equilibrium In a star, represents an even process by which energy (heat) is transferred from the core to the outer surface without affecting the overall stability of the star.

radio interferometer Type of RADIO TELESCOPE that relies on the use of two or more aerials at a distance from each other to provide a combination of signals from one source which can be analysed by computer. Such an analysis results in a RESOLUTION that is considerably better than that of a parabolic dish aerial by itself because of the greater effective diameter.

radio map of the sky Celestial chart depicting sources and intensities of radio emission.

radio scintillation The SCINTILLATION in received radio emission; the equivalent of "twinkling" in visible light from the stars.

radio telescope Non-optical telescope (of various types) which, instead of focusing light received from a distant object, focuses radio signals onto a receiver-amplifier.

radius In astronomy, an old instrument for measuring the angular distance between two celestial objects.

radius vector In astronomy, an imaginary line connecting the centre of an orbiting body with the centre of the body (or point) that it is orbiting.

Raman effect In spectroscopy, the change in the WAVELENGTH of light scattered by molecules.

Ranger **spaceprobes** Series of 9 US spaceprobes, only the final 3 of which were successful. All were meant to photograph the surface of the Moon before crashing onto it. Some good results were obtained.

recession Motion (increasing distance) away.

red giant Large, highly luminous but relatively cool star that has reached a late stage in its "life". It is running out of nuclear "fuel" and has accordingly expanded greatly and become less dense. Many also become VARIABLE STARS of long periodicity. Its next evolutionary stage is to become a WHITE DWARF, in developing into which the star has to cross the MAIN SEQUENCE on the HERTZSPRUNG–RUSSELL DIAGRAM.

red shift The DOPPLER EFFECT on the SPECTRUM of a receding celestial body. Because of the recession there is a shift towards the red end of the spectrum.

Red Spot of Jupiter Huge, generally reddish oval area within the belts and zones of Jupiter's Southern Hemisphere. Apparently a cyclonic swirl of atmospheric gases, it nevertheless seems to be a permanent feature despite continuous latitudinal drift and changes in size (at its largest it has a surface area greater than the Earth's). The reason for its coloration remains a mystery.

reflecting telescope, reflector Telescope that uses mirrors to magnify and focus an image onto an eyepiece.

refracting telescope, refractor Telescope that uses lenses to magnify and focus an image onto an eyepiece.

refraction, refractive index Deflection (or "bending") of light – or any ray as it passes from one medium into another of greater or lesser density, representing a change in overall speed of the ray. REFRACTING TELESCOPES rely on the refraction of light through lenses. The refractive index of a medium (e.g. glass) is a measure of the medium's "bending" power.

relativistic beaming Theory devised by Francis Smith regarding the generation of polarized radiation in NEUTRON STARS (pulsars).

relativity Theory devised by Albert Einstein in two parts, one developed from the other: the SPECIAL THEORY OF RELATIVITY and the GENERAL THEORY OF RELATIVITY.

resolution Of a telescope, the clarity of the final presentation to the observer (in image, radio picture or X-ray read-out).

retrograde In a backwards direction; in astronomy this means in a direction corresponding to east-to-west.

reversing layer Lower CHROMOSPHERE of the Sun, a comparatively cool region in which radiation at certain wavelengths is absorbed from the continuous spectrum emitted from the Sun's PHOTOSPHERE.

right ascension Directional bearing of a celestial body measured eastwards from a point on the CELESTIAL EQUATOR representing the vernal EQUINOX. It is expressed in units of time corresponding to the time taken for the located position to reach the vernal equinox by means of the Earth's rotation.

rotation Of a single body in space: spinning on an AXIS. Of a planetary system, rotation is generally planar in relation to the parent star. GALACTIC ROTATION, however, is usually differential.

Royal Greenwich Observatory Primary national observatory in Great Britain, first sited at GREENWICH in 1675, but in 1958 moved to Herstmonceux, Sussex. From the first, Directorship of the Observatory has entailed appointment as ASTRONOMER ROYAL. In the 1980s the Observatory will lose its primary national status with the completion of the Northern Hemisphere Observatory in Las Palmas, the Canary Islands.

RR Lyrae variables Type of short-period VARIABLE STARS. Spectrally classified as A to F giants, they were once called cluster-CEPHEIDS.

satellite Body orbiting a planet. Since 1957 the term has also been applied to man-made (artificial) satellites; many astronomers make the distinction by calling natural satellites moons (and the Earth's natural satellite the Moon).

Saturn Sixth major planet out from the Sun. The most spectacular of the Solar System, it is circled by a series of concentric rings.

Schmidt camera Telescopic camera incorporating an internal corrective lens or plate that compensates for optical defects and chromatic faults in the main mirror. The system was invented by Bernhard Schmidt.

scintillation In radio-astronomy, a rapid oscillation in the detected intensity of radiation emitted by stellar radio sources, caused by disturbances in ionized gas at some point between the source and the Earth's surface (usually in the Earth's own upper atmosphere).

secular In astronomy, gradual, taking AEONS to accomplish.

secular acceleration of the Moon, of the Sun Apparent acceleration of the Moon and Sun across the sky, caused by extremely gradual reduction in speed of the Earth's rotation (one 50-millionth of a second per day).

Seyfert galaxy Galaxy with a small, bright nucleus, comparatively faint spiral arms, and broad spectral emission lines. Some are strong radio sources; all are subject to violent explosions of gas.

shooting stars *See* METEORS (*or* METEORITES).

sidereal In astronomy, relating to the period of time based on the apparent rotation of the stars, and therefore equivalent to the rotation of the body from which the observation is made. Thus on Earth a sidereal year is 365.256 times the sidereal day of 23 hours, 56 minutes and 4 seconds.

singularity Anomaly in SPACE-TIME at which a state not in accord with the classical laws of physics obtains. An example is a BLACK HOLE; another is the moment of the BIG BANG.

Sirius (Alpha Canis Majoris) The Dog Star, brightest star in the northern sky, with a luminosity of 26 times the Sun's, a MAGNITUDE of −1.42 and an ABSOLUTE MAGNITUDE of −1.45. It is 8.7 light-years away and has a companion star called Sirius B or the Pup.

solar Of the Sun.

solar constant Mean radiation received from the Sun at the top level of Earth's atmosphere: $1.95\,\text{cal cm}^{-2}\,\text{min}^{-1}$.

solar energy Is produced by NUCLEAR FUSION and comprises almost entirely ELECTROMAGNETIC RADIATION (particularly in the form of light and heat); particles are also radiated forming the SOLAR WIND.

solar flare Sudden and dramatic release of a huge burst of SOLAR ENERGY through a break in the Sun's CHROMOSPHERE in the region of a SUNSPOT. Effects on Earth include AURORAE, magnetic storms and radio interference.

solar parallax The PARALLAX of the Sun, now measured as 8.794″.

solar prominence Mass of hot, hydrogen rising from the Sun's CHROMOSPHERE, best observed indirectly during a total ECLIPSE. Eruptive prominences are violent in force and may reach heights of 2 million km; quiescent prominences are relatively pacific but may last for months.

solar rotation Is differential, the equatorial rotation taking less time than the polar by up to 9.4 Earth-days.

Solar System System of bodies that orbit our Sun: the planets and their moons, asteroids, and comets.

solar wind Stream of charged particles flowing from the Sun at a speed of about $600\,\text{km sec}^{-1}$. It is the effects of the solar wind that produce AURORAE in the Earth's upper atmosphere, that cause the tails of comets to stream back from the Sun, and that distort the symmetry of planetary MAGNETOSPHERES.

solstice One of the two points on the ECLIPTIC at which the Sun appears to be farthest away from the CELESTIAL EQUATOR (representing therefore mid-summer or mid-winter).

space-time continuum Einsteinian concept of the Universe in accordance with his theories of RELATIVITY; Four-dimensional actuality, in which any anomaly is known as a SINGULARITY.

Special Theory of Relativity Theory formulated by Albert Einstein comprising two basic yet very original propositions: that a spaceship (or other enclosed vessel) travelling at uniform speed through space contains its own SPACE-TIME CONTINUUM, and that a ray of light passes an observer at the speed of light no matter how (uniformly) fast nor in what direction the observer is travelling. One consequence of this theory was the equation of mass (m) with energy (E), formulated as $E = mc^2$ (where c is the speed of light). Ten years later, Einstein produced his GENERAL THEORY OF RELATIVITY.

spectral Of a SPECTRUM.

spectral classification Commonly, the system devised by Annie Cannon combining the perceived colour of a star with its spectral characteristics. Very generally, of the overall sequence O B A F G K M R N S, stars in the group O B A are white or blue and display increasing characteristics of the presence of hydrogen; in F G are yellow and show increasing calcium; in K are orange and strongly metallic; and in M R N S are red and indicate titanium oxide through carbon to zirconium oxide bands. The groups are numerically subdivided, according to other characteristics, and there are further small classes for very unusual categories of star. Different methods of classification exist but are not in such common use.

spectral lines Dark lines visible in an absorption SPECTRUM, or bright lines that make up an emission spectrum. They are caused by the transference of an ELECTRON in an atom from one energy level to another; strong lines are produced at levels at which such transference occurs easily, weak where it occurs with difficulty. IONIZATION of certain elements can affect such transferences and cause problems in spectral analysis.

spectroheliograph Device with which spectra of the various regions of the Sun are obtained and photographed.

spectroscopy Study of spectra; in astronomy, the investigation of the composition of celestial bodies using information derived from SPECTRAL LINES.

spectrum (plural: spectra) Generally, the range of colours (representing different WAVELENGTHS) that a beam of white light is composed of (a continuous spectrum); particularly, in astronomy, however, the characteristic bright lines (emission spectrum) or dark lines (absorption spectrum) produced by individual elements in the light source. By analysis of such lines, the composition of the light source may be determined.

speed of light (c) 299,792km sec^{-1} (186,180 miles sec^{-1}).

spheres Concept probably older than the ancient Greeks, in which the Sun, Moon, planets and the stars were thought to orbit the Earth travelling on their own crystalline but – except for that of the stars – transparent spheres.

spherical aberration *See* ABERRATION.

spherical collapse Initial stage in the collapse of a star, followed by gravitational collapse and finally SINGULARITY.

spiral nebula A spiral GALAXY – not really a NEBULA at all (although many do appear nebulous).

Sputnik **1** First artificial Earth satellite, launched by the Soviet Union on 4 October 1957.

starlight Energy (seen as light) produced by a star through NUCLEAR FUSION.

Steady State Theory Proposition, now largely discredited, that the mass and density of the Universe is maintained at a constant by continual creation of matter. It was put forward by Fred Hoyle, Thomas Gold and Hermann Bondi as an alternative to the now generally accepted BIG-BANG THEORY. Although the later discovery of radio emissions from stars, BACKGROUND RADIATION and HELIUM ABUNDANCE led to its discrediting, the theory's explanation of the creation of elements within stars is universally accepted.

stellar Of a star, of the stars.

Strömgren spheres Zones of ionized hydrogen gas surrounding hot stars embedded in interstellar gas clouds; they are called additionally H II zones.

sunspot Comparatively dark spot on the Sun's photosphere, commonly one of a (not always obvious) group of two. The centre of a vast electrostatic field and a magnetic field of a single polarity (up to 4,000 gauss), a sunspot represents a comparatively cool depression (at a temperature of approximately 4,500 °C). Sunspots occur in cycles of about 11 Earth-years in period, although their individual duration – a matter of Earth-days only – is affected by the DIFFERENTIAL ROTATION of the Sun; they tend to form at high latitudes and drift towards the solar equator. They are also sources of strong ultra-shortwave radio emissions.

supercluster Unusually large cluster of GALAXIES; many appear to occur in a definite band across the sky.

superior planets Planets farther from the Sun than the Earth is (i.e. Mars to Pluto).

supernova Brilliant explosion of a massive star in a cataclysmic burst of energy, leaving only a dissipating gas cloud round a NEUTRON STAR (pulsar). The Crab Nebula (in Taurus) is considered an example.

supersynthesis A RADIO INTERFEROMETER system in which two SYNTHESIS AERIALS are used; one is static and utilizes the rotation of the Earth to provide a field of scan, the other is mobile.

synchrotron radiation Polarized form of RADIATION produced by high-speed ELECTRONS in a magnetic field; it is this radiation that is emitted by the Crab Nebula (in Taurus).

synodic period Time between one OPPOSITION and the next, of any SUPERIOR PLANET or asteroid.

synthesis aerial A RADIO INTERFEROMETER system utilizing a number of small aerials to achieve the effect of an impossibly large single one.

terrestrial Of the Earth.

three-body problem Eighteenth- and nineteenth-century problem in celestial mechanics to analyse the gravitational effects of three celestial bodies in finding a stable orbital configuration.

tides Effect of the Moon's GRAVITY on Earth's seas, such that an oceanic "bulge" each side of the Earth follows the Moon's progress around the planet.

Titan Seventh (known) moon out from SATURN, and its largest. It is possibly also the largest satellite in the Solar System (although Neptune's TRITON may be proved to be larger). It is 20% larger than the planet Mercury and is known to have an ATMOSPHERE.

Titania Fourth (known) moon out from Uranus, and probably its largest.

transit Crossing of the Sun's face by either MERCURY or VENUS, as seen from Earth. The term is also used to describe the crossing of the MERIDIAN of an observer by a celestial body.

transit circle Large instrument for the accurate observation and measurement of a TRANSIT.

Triton Very large and close moon of NEPTUNE. Probably the largest satellite in the Solar System (although it is not definitely established as larger than Saturn's TITAN), it is likely to be about twice the size of the planet Pluto, and 25% larger than Mercury.

T Tauri variables *See* NEBULAR VARIABLE STARS.

Twistor Theory Model of the Universe proposed by Roger Penrose, based on the application of complex numbers (involving $(-1)^{\frac{1}{2}}$) used in calculations in the microscopic world of atoms and quantum theory to the macroscopic ordinary world of physical laws and relativity. The result is an eight-dimensional concept of reality that although complicated is possibly a more logical understanding of the constitution of the Universe.

UBV photometry Measurement of the ASTRONOMICAL COLOUR INDEX of a star, utilizing the ultraviolet, blue and yellow visual images over two pre-set wavelengths obtained by PHOTOELECTRIC FILTERING. Other standardized filter wavebands are also used.

ultraviolet Part of the ELECTROMAGNETIC SPECTRUM immediately above visible light (but below gamma-rays and X-rays); it therefore comprises a range of radiation of shorter WAVELENGTH and higher frequency than those of visible light.

ultraviolet excess screening Technique devised by Sir Martin Ryle and Allan Sandage to measure the spectral RED SHIFT of suspected QUASARS. It was this process that resulted in the discovery of QUASI-STELLAR OBJECTS.

umbra Full shadow.

universal attraction *See* LAW OF UNIVERSAL ATTRACTION.

Uranus Seventh major planet out from the Sun, the first to be discovered in modern times (by William Herschel in 1781).

Van Allen (radiation) belts Two toroidal zones of high radiation in Earth's upper atmosphere, above the equator, caused by the trapping of charged particles in the MAGNETOSPHERE. The outer zone is composed chiefly of ELECTRONS, the inner of PROTONS.

variable star Star whose LUMINOSITY changes over periods of time; there are many reasons and many types. Periods vary widely in length and even regularity. NOVAE and SUPERNOVAE are classed as variables. The present brightest variable star is Betelgeux (Alpha Orionis).

Vega Major star in Lyra; its (apparent) magnitude is 0.04.

Venus Second major planet out from the Sun; in many ways it is similar to the Earth.

vernal equinox The spring EQUINOX, on or around 21 March.

***Viking* spaceprobes** Series of 2 US spaceprobes that successfully effected landings on Mars and relayed data back to Earth.

Virtual Particle Theory Theory devised by Stephen Hawking to account for apparent thermal radiation from a BLACK HOLE (from which not even light can escape). It supposes that space is full of "virtual particles" in a particle and antiparticle relationship, being created out of "nothing" and instantly destroying each other. At an EVENT HORIZON, however, one particle may be gravitationally drawn into the SINGULARITY, and other appear to radiate as heat.

***Voyager* spaceprobes** Series of US spaceprobes launched to carry out exploration of the outer planets. In 1982 *Voyager* 2 returned some remarkable pictures of Saturn.

wavelength In ELECTROMAGNETIC RADIATION, the distance between successive crests of the "waves" radiated. The number of such crests passing a fixed point in 1 second is known as the frequency (a crest per second = 1 Hertz); a short wavelength thus implies high frequency. Of light, the unit of wavelength is the angstrom (Å), measured as 10^{-10} metres. Visible light is of between 4,000 and 7,500 Å; different wavelengths are perceived by the eye as the different colours of the SPECTRUM. Radio wavelengths, however, may measure from about 50 cm to about 10,000 m.

white dwarf Final stage of a star, at which the nuclear energy is exhausted. Cool, and becoming a dead, black body, it is nevertheless extremely dense.

X-ray astronomy Detection of stellar and

interstellar X-ray emission. Because X-rays are almost entirely filtered out by the Earth's upper atmosphere, the use of balloon- and rocket-borne equipment is essential.

ylem Primordial state of matter – NEUTRONS and their decay products (PROTONS and ELECTRONS) – before the Big Bang. The term was taken from Aristotle and used for the α-β-γ THEORY.

Zeeman effect The splitting of SPECTRAL LINES by a magnetic field.

zenith Exact point in the sky vertically above the observer.

Z_{He} Total mass density (in a star) of elements heavier than HELIUM; values of Z_{He} are small for POPULATION II STARS, large for POPULATION I STARS.

zodiac Twelve constellations originally only representing a calendar of the Sun's apparent progress in the heavens during one Earth-year. The principal planets are to be found along much the same path (the ECLIPTIC) and so, probably early in human history, caused each constellation to become a focus for divination according to the pseudo-science of ASTROLOGY. Since then, however, the millennia that have passed have taken the Sun out of phase with the original calendar. The 12 constellations are: Aries, Taurus, Gemini, Cancer, Leo, Virgo, Libra, Scorpio, Sagittarius, Capricorn, Aquarius and Pisces.

zodiacal light Faint, cone-shaped glow seen briefly in the sky shortly before sunrise or after sunset. Its cause is the reflection of light by particles lying along the plane of the ECLIPTIC.

zone of avoidance Apparent lack of distant GALAXIES in the plane of our own GALAXY, now explained as being caused by optical interference of dust and interstellar debris on the rim of the Galaxy.

Index

The index entry in **bold** type will direct you to the main text entry in which the information you require is given.

179

Tombaugh, Clyde
  Lowell
  Tombaugh
Traité de la Lumière
  Huygens
Traité de Méchanique Célèste
  Laplace
transit circle
  Gill
  Römer
transit timing
  Airy
trigonometrical parallax *see*
    parallax,
    trigonometrical
Triton
  Kuiper
Trojan satellites
  Wolf
Troughton, Edward
  Pond
  South
Trumpler, Robert Julius
  Kapteyn
  Trumpler
  Vorontsov-Vel'iaminov
T-Tauri variables
  Herbig
  Joy
Tusculaneum
  Römer
twenty-one centimetre
    wavelength
  Field
  Oort
Twistor Theory
  Penrose
Two Micron Survey
  Neugebauer
Tycho *see* Brahe, Tycho
Tycho's Star (supernova in
    Cassiopeia)
  Brahe

UBV system
  Pickering
Uhuru
  Giacconi
ultraviolet emission
  absorption
    Stebbins
  quasar
    Arp
  spectrograph
    Huggins
uncertainty principle
  Hawking

unified theory of physics
  Hawking
universal attraction,
  law of
  Laplace
universal meteorgraph
  Secchi
Universal Natural History and
    Theory of the Heavens
  Kant
Universe
  age
    Hubble
    McCrea
    Milne
  background radiation *see*
      background radiation
  Big-Bang Theory *see* Big-
      Bang Theory
  composition
    Bondi
    Kant
  De Sitter model
    De Sitter
  Einstein model
    De Sitter
    Penrose
  electrostatic theory
    Lyttleton
  expansion of
    Bondi
    Dicke
    Eddington
    Hubble
    Lemaître
    Slipher
    Zel'dovich
  General Theory of
    Descartes
  geocentric theory
    Copernicus
  heliocentric model *see*
      heliocentric theory
  hot big bang *see*
      hot big bang
  Hubble radius
    Hubble
  Kapteyn's Universe
    Kapteyn
    Vorontsov-Vel'iaminov
  number of particles
    Eddington
  observable
    Baade
    Hubble
    Kapteyn
  origin of
    Bondi

  Dicke
  Gamow
  Gold
  Herschel, F.W.
  Lemaître
  oscillating
    De Sitter
    Penzias
  Relativity, theories of *see*
    relativity
  scale of
    Baade
    Bessel
    Curtis
    Hubble
    Kapteyn
  Steady State Theory *see*
    Steady State Theory
  Twistor Theory
    Penrose
  unresolved nebulae
    Huggins
Uranographia (Bode)
  Bode
Uranographia (Hevelius)
  Hevelius
Uranometrica Nova
  Argelander
Uranus
  discovery
    Adams, J.C.
    Bessel
    Bode
    Herschel, F.W.
  discovery of methane on
    Kuiper
  orbital deviation and
    discovery of Neptune
    Adams, J.C.
    Bessel
    Challis
    Galle
    Le Verrier
  Pluto's effect on orbit
    Brown
    Lowell
  rotation
    Slipher
  satellites
    Herschel, F.W.
    Kuiper
    Struve, O.W.
  spectra
    Kuiper
Urey, Harold
  Sagan
Ursa Minor
  Thales